anatomy of the
MOTOR CAR

CRESCENT BOOKS
NEW YORK

anatomy of the MOTOR CAR

by L.J.K. Setright
and other contributors

edited by Ian Ward

L. J. K. Setright is the author of all sections of this book except for the
following:

The Motor Car, Decarbonising, Exhaust care, Oil changing, Spark-
plug care, Distributor & timing, Dynamo, Brake repair, Fault finding
and Maintenance by Ian Ward;

Tappets, Carburettor adjustment, Water pump, Oil pump, Universal
joint & Starter by Wordsmiths Ltd;

Fuel pump, Filters, Lighting & Horn by John James;

Alternator and Alignment by Peter Merritt;

Exhaust by Doug Mitchell;

Bodywork repairs by Tom Northey;

Battery by Tony Osman;

Tuning & modification by David Vizard.

Picture acknowledgments
Audi; Automotive Products; BP; L. J. Caddell; Car Mechanics; Ceci;
Champion; Chevrolet; DAF; Ferodo; Fiat; Ford; GKN; G. Goddard; D.
Goodman; T. Hardman; Innocenti; Italfoto; Jaguar; Laurent; London
Art Tech; Mercedes-Benz; Michelin; T. Nesta; Occidental; Papetti;
Pirelli; Popular Motoring; Quattroruote; Quinton Hazell; J. G. Rettie;
P. Revere; Rolls-Royce; Scania; SU; D. Vizard; Weber; Zagari.

First English edition published by Orbis Publishing Ltd. 1976
This edition is published by Crescent Books, a division of
Crown Publishers, Inc.
First U.S. edition published by St. Martin's Press, 1977.

Library of Congress Cataloging in Publication Data
Main entry under title:
Anatomy of the motor car.
1. Automobiles. 2. Automobiles — Maintenance and repair.
I. Setright, L. J. K. II. Ward, Ian, 1949-
TL145.A587   1978   629.22'22   76-26717
ISBN 0-517-26999-6

Printed in Great Britain by Colorgraphic, Leicester

CONTENTS

THE MOTOR CAR

a giant jigsaw puzzle

A CONSIDERABLE NUMBER of independent and yet inter-related systems are required to make a motor car of even the simplest and least sophisticated type: an engine and transmission are required to make it go, brakes have to be incorporated to produce a retarding force, steering and suspension are needed to take the vehicle round corners and over bumps, and lights must be fitted to satisfy the demands of the law as well as to aid night-time driving. These systems are all united within one shell, known as the body, which to many people is the heart and soul of the car.

As the common denominator for just about every part of a roadgoing motor car, the body/chassis unit is certainly very important. In vehicles of the 1970s, the chassis is nearly always incorporated in the body shell, in that this shell is strong enough, without external reinforcement, to support all the components fixed to it and to withstand the stresses resulting from this. Most bodies of this type, usually known as mono-coques, are made of steel panels pressed into shape and welded together. However, aluminium and glass-fibre are also used for body manufacture and, in these cases, a separate chassis is usually added.

The major units within a car which has a separate chassis are usually fixed to that chassis rather than to the body; even with a monocoque, these units, such as the engine and suspension, may be mounted on sub-frames before being joined to the body.

The largest single unit which has to find a home within the car's body is the engine. This can be positioned in several different locations and in several different attitudes. It can be mounted longitudinally or transversely in front of or behind the front or rear wheels and, what is more, it can be arranged so as to drive the front wheels, or the rear wheels, or both.

The location of the engine depends to a large extent on the type of car: it is not very practical to fit an engine in front of the rear axle in a four-seater, nor is it sensible to locate the power unit in front of the front wheels in a rear-wheel-drive car. The cheapest way to build a car is to fit the engine in the front, in a longi-tudinal attitude, and to persuade it to drive the rear wheels; this involves no special problems like gear-boxes in sumps and driveshafts needing constant-velocity joints, as might be the case with transverse engines and front-wheel drive.

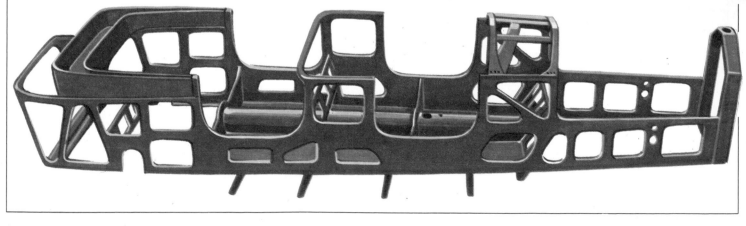

BRUNO BETTI

Above: a cutaway drawing of the Alfa Romeo Giulietta made between 1955 and 1965; this monocoque-construction car had a longitudinal front engine and a rigid rear axle, suspended by coil springs

Left: this is the chassis of the Lancia Lambda of 1922; unlike most girder chassis of the period, this constituted what was almost a monocoque. Nevertheless, all the components had to be mounted on this unit

The reasons for varying engine location are that of gaining as much space inside the car as possible, together with that of making the car handle and hold the road well (by altering weight distribution and changing the choice of driven wheels).

The precise resting place for the power unit may well depend on the type of unit: it may be a piston engine, as is most common, driven either by petroleum spirit or by diesel oil, it may be a rotary engine, again driven by petroleum spirit, or it may be an electric engine, obtaining its power from batteries. Probably the least compact of all these is the reciprocating engine, although its linear dimensions and, to some extent, its volume can be varied by altering the cylinder configuration, *eg* flat, or horizontally opposed, four, straight-four or vee-four. The rotary engine, which makes use of one or more three-lobed rotors in epitrochoidal housings, instead of pistons in cylinders, is far more compact, although it still requires the ancillary units, such as carburettors and a distributor, of its reciprocating equivalent. Electric motors are totally self contained, but the snag is that their fuel cannot directly be stored in liquid form in a tank, and batteries are heavy and bulky.

Both types of petrol engine work on the principle that a mixture of petrol and air, in the correct proportions, when ignited under compression, will convert potential energy into kinetic energy and drive the car's wheels. The mixture is drawn into the cylinder, or chamber, through a carburettor or fuel-injection system, it is then compressed by the piston or rotor before being electronically fired by a high-tension spark. Combustion forces the piston down or the rotor round, which turns the output shaft of the engine and eventually the wheels.

In the diesel unit, air alone is drawn into the cylinder; this is then compressed, a process which raises the temperature considerably, before fuel is injected into it to ignite spontaneously and cause further piston movement.

Electric motors work on the basis that two magnets will attract or repel each other; if this property is harnessed by using several electromagnets mounted radially within a field magnet, continuous movement can be obtained. The power of the motor depends on the current available and the thickness of the wires that make up the electromagnets.

The beauty of electric power is that there is no need

7

for either a clutch or a variable-ratio gearbox, since the torque output of such a motor is fairly high, especially at low speed. Internal-combustion engines have a relatively narrow torque band, so several gear ratios are needed to keep the unit within this band for a range of road speeds. What is more, torque at standstill is zero, so a clutch is necessary if the driver is to start the car rolling.

Although it is possible, with most cars, to start the engine while that unit is connected to the driving wheels, this is inconvenient and inefficient, not to mention unreliable. The clutch makes it possible to start the engine and then engage the drive progressively to give a smooth start.

Most clutches consist of a flat disc, covered on both sides with a material having a high coefficient of friction and sandwiched between two further discs, of metal, one being the engine's flywheel and the other the clutch pressure plate. The flywheel and pressure plate always rotate together and with the engine, while the friction disc is connected to the driven wheels, usually via the gearbox.

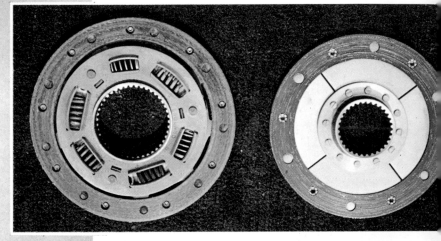

In manual-transmission cars, the clutch is nearly always operated by a pedal, through either a cable or a hydraulic system. When the clutch is engaged, with the pedal released, spring pressure keeps the three discs pressed firmly together, but when the pedal is depressed, the pressure plate is moved away from the other two, thus allowing the two independent parts to rotate separately.

The gearbox is usually situated directly adjacent to the clutch—in fact, in a front-engine, rear-wheel-drive car, the friction plate of the clutch is invariably

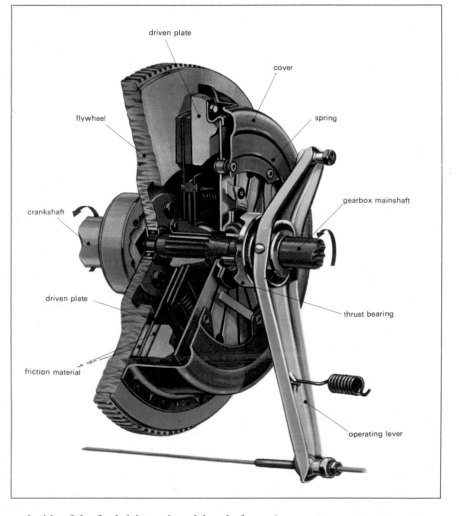

Far left: the layout of the mechanical components of a 1972 Fiat 132; this has a front engine and rear wheel drive, joined together by a two-piece propeller shaft

Near left: the V6 engine used in the Fiat Dino; this was a detuned version of the Ferrari Dino unit. The 'V' layout makes an engine compact and the four overhead camshafts help the fuel in and the exhaust out.
The five-speed gearbox is mounted behind the power unit in the front-engined Fiat

driven plate

cover

flywheel

spring

crankshaft

gearbox mainshaft

driven plate

thrust bearing

friction material

operating lever

mounted on the main shaft of the gearbox. With the gearbox in this position, it is simple, in a car of the layout mentioned, to position the gearchange lever so that it falls easily to hand inside the car. With a front-wheel-drive or rear-engined car, the lever usually has to be linked by cables or rods to the gearbox, a system which sometimes proves less than perfect.

The workings of the manual gearbox are fairly simple: several pairs of gears, with different size relationships within the pairs, are used to give different wheel speeds for a given engine rate. Movement of the gear lever from one position to another disengages one pair of gearwheels from the main shaft and engages another pair. In most cases, the speeds of the shaft and the gears to be engaged are synchronised by friction devices known as synchromesh cones, before engagement takes place; this prevents 'grating'. The clutch aids gearchanging by allowing the main shaft to spin free of the engine while disengagement and engagement take place.

Many cars are fitted with automatic gearboxes, in which the gearchanging is carried out by mechanical units operated either by oil pressure or by electricity. With this type of gearbox, the clutch is replaced by a fluid coupling known as a torque converter. This can multiply the torque output of the engine, as well as allowing the car to be halted in gear while the engine is still running.

In most cars of 'conventional' layout, the gearbox is fitted under a bulge in the front of the passenger-compartment floor. The gear lever is usually found at the rear of the bulge, which continues to the rear of the compartment in order to house the propeller shaft. This shaft, which is universally jointed to allow it to 'bend', carries the drive from the gear of the gearbox to the front of the final-drive unit on the rear axle.

The final drive performs three functions: it turns the direction of rotation through ninety degrees, by means of bevel gears, at the same time providing a reduction gear, and it contains a differential unit, made up of four or more bevel gears, which allows one driven wheel to turn more quickly than the other, something which is necessary when negotiating a bend (the outside wheel has to travel further than that on the inside). From

each side of the final-drive unit, a drive shaft runs to a rear wheel.

In a car with a layout other than the conventional one, the unit functions will be the same, but the construction may be different. The gearbox may be under the engine or alongside it; it may even be driven by a shaft from the clutch and be mounted in unit with the rear axle. The final drive will be driven directly (without a propeller shaft), in the case of an engine which is mounted at the same end of the car as the driven wheels, and it may use spur gears for reduction purposes,

Above: a cutaway view of a conventional diaphragm-spring clutch

Near left: a pair of clutch driven plates (*above*), one with shock absorbing springs, and a flywheel unit from a BLMC Mini

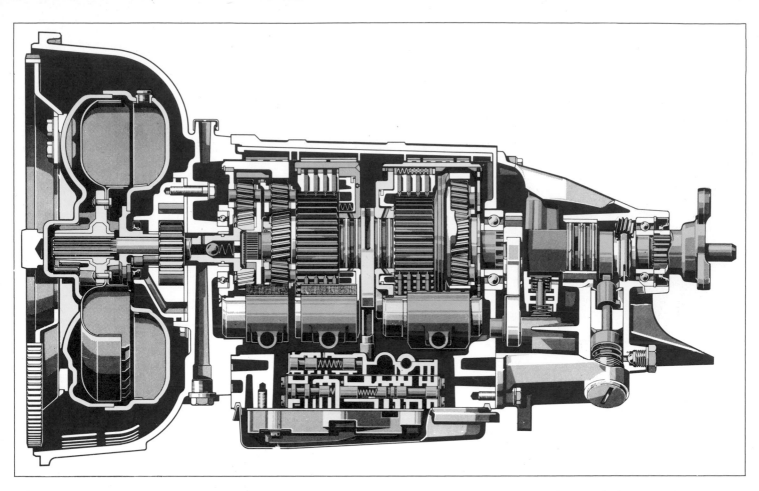

rather than bevels. The gearbox may be chain driven, if it is mounted beneath the engine, and it may be mounted on the far side of the final drive from the engine, as is usually the case with rear or mid-mounted, longitudinal-engined cars.

Suspension is fitted to the wheels of a motor car in order to make the ride as smooth as possible. This means that in order to drive the wheels, the drive shafts have to be universally jointed, or the final-drive unit has to be fixed rigidly to the wheels and allow the movement to be taken up by the propeller shaft. In the case of a front-wheel-drive or rear-engined car, the former is invariably used, because the final drive is in unit with the engine and gearbox and the weight is too much to have 'unsprung'. With the 'conventional' car, either layout can be used, the fixed or 'live' axle being the cheaper.

Several types of spring are used: coil springs, leaf springs, torsion-bar springs and rubber springs. Coil springs consist simply of pieces of thick, springy wire, wound in a spiral. Leaf springs, which are like those found on a cart, consist of several flat blades of metal, placed one on the other and curved slightly. With a semi-elliptical leaf, the ends are fixed flexibly to the car body and rigidly to the axle centre, whereas, with a quarter-elliptical leaf, one end is fixed rigidly to the body and the other end to the axle. The torsion bar is similar to an uncoiled coil spring: it is a straight piece of the same thick, springy wire splined at each end. One end is fixed to the body and the other to a suspension member, in such a way that as the wheel rises the bar twists. Rubber springs consist of substantial blocks of rubber; these are fitted in a similar way to a coil spring, so that they can be compressed by the suspension system movement.

Springs, if fitted on their own, would allow a car to bounce severely after negotiating a bump or dip, the movement dying away only slowly. To prevent this, dampers are fitted; these offer resistance to movement, by the simple expedient of squeezing liquid through a small internal hole.

Above: the automatic gearbox used by Mercedes in several of their models; it has three planetary gear trains, which offer four forward speeds and one reverse

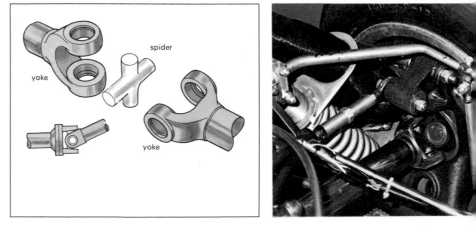

Above: a type of universal joint, commonly known as a Hooke joint; the disadvantage with this type of joint is that the driven shaft accelerates and decelerates as it turns

Above right: a Hooke joint in use at the rear of a Formula One car

Of course, springs and dampers alone are not enough for good location of the wheels, especially with non-fixed-axle or independent layouts. Each wheel has to be free to move up and down, without any significant alteration in transverse or lateral position, and so transverse and lateral arms are used to locate the upright which houses the wheel's bearing.

At the front, the wheel has to be capable of steering the car, so top and bottom pivots must be provided between the upright and its arms, together with an extension arm to join the upright to the steering assembly. With a rear-wheel-drive car, this is straightforward, but front-wheel drive brings further complications. The drive shafts have to be jointed level with the two steering pivots; what is more, they have to be fitted with special constant-velocity joints.

The steering unit is usually mounted on the body or chassis, approximately in line with the projections from the uprights. The unit may incorporate any one of two or three different types of mechanism, the simplest and most popular of modern times being the rack and pinion. Power assistance may be supplied to the steering, this usually taking the form of extra effort

Left: the front suspension and steering gear of a 1969 Fiat 130. The torsion bar springs are indicated by arrows and are activated by lower links from the upright to the body/chassis

Below: a rear view of the 3.5 hp De Dion built in 1899, showing clearly the rear suspension layout of the same name. A rigid bar links the two hubs, so that the wheels always remain parallel, but the final-drive unit is mounted on the chassis and connected to the wheels by two double-jointed drive shafts

transmitted hydraulically from an engine-driven pump specially designed for this purpose.

The wheels themselves may be of several different types and sizes. They may be made of pressed steel, cast light alloy (either aluminium or magnesium), or of steel rims and centres, with spokes, and they may be fixed by several bolts situated in a circle of some five or

six inches diameter, or by one large central nut screwed onto the end of the driveshaft. Large cars usually have wheels of a greater diameter than those of small cars; width, too, varies considerably.

Like wheels, tyres can be of differing types and sizes. They are made of rubber or synthetic rubber braced by cords of steel or textile. It is from the layout of these cords that tyre types take their names—cross ply or radial ply. Sizes have to vary to fit the wheels and most types are available for use with or without an inner

tube, most cars being fitted with tubeless tyres as a standard item.

Radial-ply tyres last longer than the cross-ply variety, but they cost more and are often more sensitive to road surface irregularities.

We have seen now how the basic body is driven, steered and suspended. However, it also has to be stopped. Each wheel has a brake on it, for this purpose, operated, in nearly every case, by hydraulic pressure created by depression of the brake pedal. Some older cars have cable-operated brakes, but these are more difficult to maintain than hydraulic ones.

The brakes themselves can be of two types: disc or drum. Disc brakes are the more modern of the two and work by squeezing a revolving metal disc between two fixed pads of high-friction material (similar to that

Left: a constant-velocity joint of the type used on the rear of a Formula One car to allow the drive shafts to flex. Unlike the Hooke type of universal joint, the constant-velocity unit, as its name implies, revolves at a steady speed and reduces stress on such components as drive shafts and tyres—an important fact in the motor racing of the 1960s and 1970s

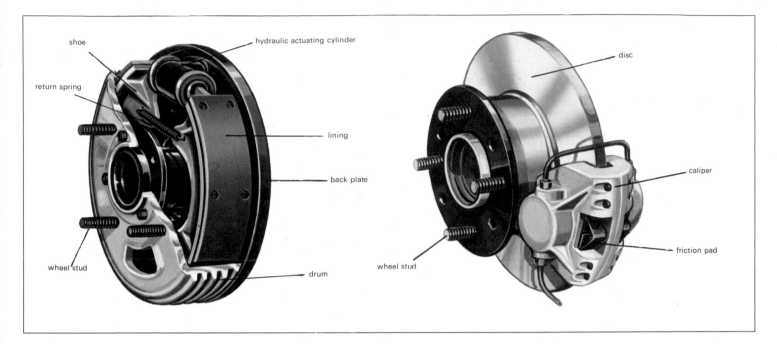

found in the clutch). Drum brakes have a steel drum which revolves with the wheel; inside this drum, two metal shoes are fixed so that they can be moved to touch the circular drum wall. As with the disc pads, the shoes are lined with friction material.

In addition to foot-operated brakes, every car has some kind of parking brake. With only one or two exceptions, this is hand operated, functioning on the back wheels only.

The law requires that cars are fitted with a good selection of lights, in order to see and be seen. In Britain, rear lamps, stop lamps, number-plate lamps and indicators are required, together with headlamps and sidelamps. All these have to be mounted on the body unit so that they show clearly when lit, and they all have to be supplied with electricity.

For this purpose, a battery, usually a lead/acid accumulator of twelve volts, is fitted. This is kept charged by an engine-driven generator, which may take the form of an alternator or a direct-current dynamo. Whichever type of generator is employed, it is likely to be driven by a flexible belt from the engine's crankshaft. The main advantage of an alternator is that it can be driven faster than a dynamo and so it produces enough current to charge the battery even when the engine is at tickover. The main job of the battery is to supply electricity to the auxiliary equipment, such as lights and wipers, when the generator is not being driven fast enough for this purpose. Also, of course, the battery has to be able to produce a very large current to drive the starter motor.

The output of the generator is controlled by a regulator, so that it does not overcharge the battery and so that the voltage does not rise too high. Most of the electrical circuits are protected by fuses, so that, should a short circuit occur, the wiring will not be damaged by the overload.

Windscreen wipers, like lights, are a legal requirement in most countries. In modern cars, they are operated by electric motors, usually having two speeds, but older cars often had vacuum-powered wipers. The vacuum for the latter type of unit was provided by the engine's inlet manifold and stored in a reservoir.

The motor car, then, is made up of a number of vital organs and systems, linked together and supplemented by many auxiliary units. The whole is an ingenious combination of engineering and design.

Above: a drum brake (*left*) and a disc brake, both hydraulically operated

Left: two drum brake units in use on the front wheels of a 1935 Fiat 1500 (*above*) and a Fiat 519S of 1923; The periphery of the drum, in both cases, was ribbed in order to increase the surface area and aid cooling. Since the 1960s, disc brakes have become common, especially at the front, where most of the braking effort is required

ENGINE

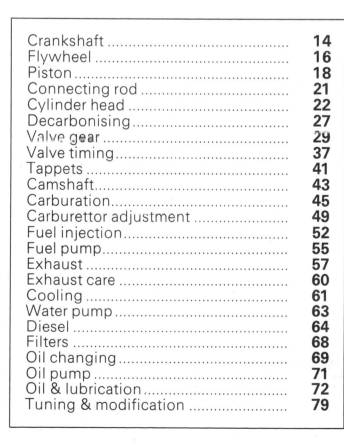

CRANKSHAFT

turning reciprocation into rotation

THE CRANKSHAFT IS THE FINAL COMPONENT in the link mechanism whereby the linear motion of an engine's pistons is converted to rotary motion. It usually constitutes (there are few exceptions) the engine's power output shaft. Its essential feature is a number of eccentrics (otherwise cranks or throws) which are linked to the pistons by connecting rods furnished with suitable bearings at each end to permit the necessary articulation. As the crankshaft rotates in its own main bearings, the eccentrics (the bearing portions of which are called crankpins) rotate in a circle whose mean diameter is equal to the piston stroke.

The number of throws is not necessarily equal to the number of cylinders: in some kinds of engine configuration (eg, V-eight and flat-twelve) two connecting rods may bear on one crankpin. Balancing is an important consideration, and is achieved by fixing counterweights opposite the crank throws, or at some other angle as in some six and twelve-cylinder designs. Their object is not only to eliminate or minimise vibration, but also to relieve the shaft of bending loads. Resistance to bending is also improved by making the shaft of large diameter, so that the main and crankpin bearing portions overlap. This tends to make the shaft very heavy, increasing main bearing loads and the rotational inertia of the shaft; hollow crankpins are an antidote, and when the shaft is cast in a high-grade iron, instead of being forged from a steel billet, it is often possible to make the whole shaft substantially hollow. Lubricating oil is fed to big-end bearings through the interior of the shaft, and the internal cavities must be carefully shaped to avoid oil sludge clogging the oilways under the influence of centrifugal force.

Stiffness of construction is also important in resisting torsional vibration. All crankshafts are subject to this, each shaft having its own natural frequency of torsional vibration which must not be allowed to coincide with the frequency of impulses from the pistons, otherwise the shaft would go into resonance and break. A torsional damper is sometimes fitted to the nose of the crankshaft to prevent such oscillations from developing. The problem is particularly severe in engines with six cylinders in line. A short crankshaft is stiffer in torsion than a long one, hence its natural frequency is higher and may more readily be set beyond the normal working range of the engine. So a six-cylinder design with four main bearings is to be preferred for high-speed work to one with seven main bearings, although the latter will be less affected by bending loads producing a rumble at low speeds.

Crankshaft design is governed by the type of bearings chosen. Plain journal bearings, relying on an hydrodynamic oil film to keep the bearing surfaces apart, are usual. They demand meticulous surface finishing and, according to the nature of the actual bearing material, may require special hardening treatment (such as nitriding) of the shaft, which must then be of a material amenable to this treatment. Ball or roller bearings are sometimes preferred, and although it is possible to split these so as to retain a one-piece crankshaft, it is more common for the shaft to be built up from a number of smaller pieces, the bearings being fitted to the appropriate parts before assembly. A built-up crankshaft is often less robust than a one-piece shaft, but it has a natural ability to

damp out torsional flutter and is often chosen because it allows a much stronger connecting rod to be used: the split big-end eye of the rod appropriate to a one-piece shaft is always a source of weakness.

The means of assembling a built-up shaft vary from simple interference fits (in which a crankpin may be pressed into a hole in a crank web, or chilled and then allowed to expand into it) to complex bolted assemblies relying on radial serrations (as in the Hirth crankshaft) to keep the parts in their proper relationships. In any case, the process relies on skilled fitting, and usually makes the dismantling of the engine more problematic.

Despite the objections to the practice of interposing a main bearing between each pair of adjacent crank throws (greater frictional losses, expense, and susceptibility to torsional flutter) the recent tendency to design engines of relatively large bore and short stroke has encouraged this practice. The length of the shaft is governed by the irreducible length of the cylinder block, and only by having a full complement of main bearings can the shaft be protected from bending loads. It then becomes convenient to feed oil to each crankpin from an adjacent main bearing, although there remain a few engines (eg Ferrari) in which separate oil pumps feed the main bearings and, via an end-to-end oilway drilled through the length of the shaft, to the big-end bearings.

In order that oil can reach the big-end bearings and, indeed, the small ends, which join the connecting rods to the pistons, plain bearings are drilled and have a groove to carry the oil round the whole circumference of the journal. This means that the lubricant will be able to enter the crankshaft drillings regardless of rotational position.

Far left: two different ends, used at the front of the crankshaft to drive the timing gear and the fan belt. The one on the left has a single key, with the gear etc held on by a nut, while the one on the right makes use of splines and a bolt

Left: two crankshafts, the upper one with built-in counterweights and the lower one with separate bolt-on pieces. Both shafts have journals for plain bearings

Below: a drawing showing the parts of the crankshaft and its associated components

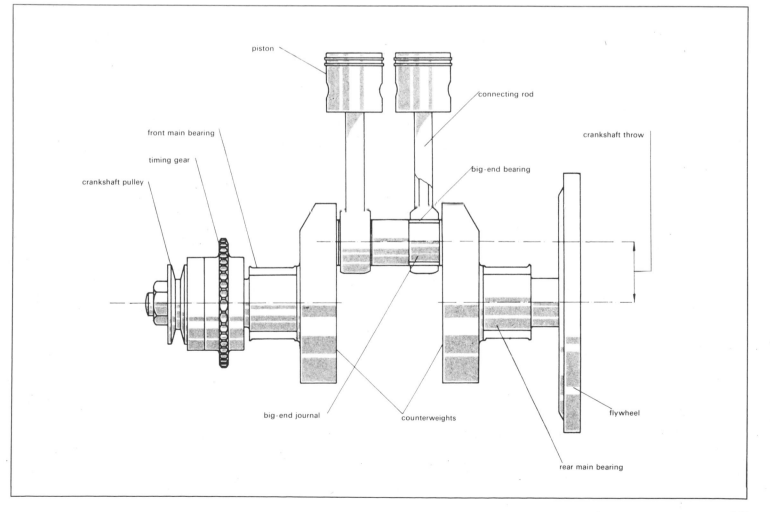

FLYWHEEL

an aid to smooth running

A PISTON WORKING in the cylinder of a four-stroke engine imparts useful positive torque to the crankshaft during only one of its four strokes—the one that occurs during the combustion phase. In other words, the crankshaft is under impulsion for only a quarter of the time it spends in rotation; two-thirds of the remainder, or half the total time taken to complete a four-stroke cycle, is spent by the crankshaft in overcoming the resistances opposed to the piston during the other phases. In a two-stroke engine, the piston does useful work for only part of its downward stroke, so the proportion is not as much higher as is commonly supposed. The effect of these extreme variations in torque during a working cycle is that the crankshaft is strongly tempted to slow down or even come to a complete halt between one combustion phase and the next, and the slower it is running the more likely is it to give up altogether. If the crankshaft were so heavily constructed that its own inertia of rotation were enough to keep it going, the engine could continue to function; but the shaft would have to be very heavy indeed to be effective in this way at starting speeds, in which case its bearings would either suffer inordinately or inhibit performance severely.

A flywheel does the job of maintaining momentum much better. Consisting merely of a large-diameter wheel attached to the crankshaft, and so shaped as to concentrate much of its mass at its periphery, the flywheel exploits the principles of leverage by having a larger radius of gyration than would be convenient for the crankshaft. In fact it need not take the form of a wheel: two spokes with weighted ends would be capable arithmetically of doing the same work, although the arrangement would be impractical. Quite simply, the flywheel acts as an energy accumulator, giving back to the crankshaft during the three idle strokes the surplus energy it took during the power stroke.

The greater the mass of the flywheel rim and the greater its effective diameter, the greater will be the inertia with which it will oppose rotation of the crankshaft under the impulsion of the piston during the power stroke. Instead of accelerating sharply, the heavy flywheel carries on spinning at much the same rate as before—and the greater its inertia, the more surely will it continue to spin at much the same rate, even when the crankshaft is not driving it onward but tending rather to drag it back. The rate of rotation will vary a little, of course—only a flywheel of infinite inertia could resist all acceleration, and who could start an engine thus furnished?—but the torsional variations of output will be considerably diminished.

A single-cylinder engine large enough to propel a car would need so heavy a flywheel that it would be deplorably sluggish in acceleration and rather intimidating on the overrun. By increasing the number of cylinders, the peak torque value attributable to each will be lower, but the fluctuations of torque applied to the crankshaft will be less, so a lighter flywheel will suffice to keep the engine running. When there are four cylinders (we are still dealing with four-stroke engines), the periods of negative torque are eliminated, and the engine would keep running even without a flywheel. It would run roughly, especially at low

Left: flywheels are a feature of all road-going engines, regardless of the number of cylinders, not only to smooth out the power flow but also to provide a location for the starter ring gear and the clutch

Below: in most engines the flywheel is bolted to the end of the crankshaft, but in the BLMC Mini, with its transverse power unit, the component is mounted on a tapered crankshaft end and driven by a peg, fitted to a special washer, in the groove shown

speeds, but it is a simple matter to determine whether to have a heavy flywheel, to make it smooth at the expense of sluggish behaviour, or a lighter one that will make it more responsive at some cost in smoothness. With more than four cylinders, the torque impulses from the several pistons overlap, and the flywheel can be lighter still. A V12 engine, even in a touring car, hardly needs a flywheel at all.

An engine almost certainly will have a flywheel, regardless of the number of cylinders. This unit is a most convenient adjunct to a crankshaft: it can have a ring of gear teeth fitted around its perimeter to be engaged by the small pinion gear of an electric motor for starting the engine. It provides a large-diameter flat face at the end of the crankshaft (where it is almost always fitted), that makes a perfect mating surface for the clutch used to connect the crankshaft to the gearbox. The flywheel may also carry marks that assist mechanics in timing the ignition and valves. In some very early engines, it was even made with airfoil-section spokes to induce a flow of air over the sump!

In those early days, the flywheel was often made of cast iron. A few notable disasters soon persuaded engineers that this material was too likely to burst under the centrifugal stresses imposed by rapid engine operation, and steel became the normal material. It remains so, but aluminium alloys are occasionally used in competition engines; the alternative means of lightening, which is to remove metal by drilling or turning, may be inadequate, impracticable or, sometimes, downright dangerous.

With enough weight in the flywheel, the crankshaft can be dimensioned as meagrely as the designer wishes, or so it would appear from a study of the problems of maintaining rotation. There are, however, other things to consider. The heftier the flywheel and the more exiguous the crankshaft, the more likely is the former to twist and distort the latter. A long crankshaft is even more susceptible to torsional distortion.

When all possible measures to stiffen the shafts have been taken, the next palliative to adopt is a torsional vibration damper: this is merely another smaller flywheel mounted at the opposite end of the shaft, and made with a flexible or slipping connection between its hub and its rim. Some engines carry their dampers outside the crankcase, some inside; a very small number have been made with the flywheel half-way along the shaft, reducing torsional oscillation of the two half-crankshafts so much that dampers may then be omitted.

Another form of crankshaft distortion is in the bending mode, being caused either by the loads imposed by the reciprocating piston and con-rod or by the flapping tendencies of counterweighted crankwebs. Should any bending occur in the section of the shaft adjacent to the flywheel, the flywheel may not enjoy a true planar motion, but will flap as the shaft bends. This could lead to rapid fatigue failure of the metal and is often guarded against by mounting the flywheel flexibly on the end of the crankshaft; its own inertia then tends to keep the flywheel spinning in its proper plane even when the crankshaft is under bending duress.

One of the most popular and durable examples of promotional jargon, the expression 'fluid flywheel' has survived more than four decades to confuse our study of the flywheel proper. The fluid flywheel is not a flywheel at all, either in appearance or in function, but it is fixed to the flywheel, just as a friction clutch is. Also, just as a friction clutch does, it adds its own mass to that of the flywheel to assist it in its task. The fluid flywheel is really a form of hydrokinetic coupling, known as a simple fluid coupling (as distinct from the fluid converter, the converter coupling, and so on) by automatic transmission engineers and those few others who can be bothered to speak their language. Its function is to permit slip between engine and transmission and its construction is simply in the form of two saucer-shaped bodies, arranged rim-to-rim, and furnished on their facing surfaces with radial vanes. One of these 'saucers' is attached to the crankshaft, the other to an output shaft, and the two shafts are all that protrude from a metal casing which is filled with a suitable oil. Rotation of the input shaft by the engine makes the vanes on the input 'saucer' or impeller fling the oil against the vanes of the other (which is known as the turbine) so that it too rotates, imparting the drive to the output shaft. The amount of relative slip between the two elements may be enormous, or it may be as little as 3 per cent—depending on loads and speeds—but whatever the case, the torque input always equals the torque output.

Below: the clutch cover assembly is fixed to the flywheel and thus to the crankshaft, while the clutch driven plate, *centre,* is sandwiched between the two and connected to the gearbox

Bottom: the ring gear is usually shrunk on to the rim of the flywheel. In some cases, as here, the wheel carries marks to show the position of the crankshaft relative to the pistons

PISTON

at the heart of the engine

Right: a cutaway diagram of a piston, showing the various parts

Far right, top: a piston with the combustion chamber built into its crown

Far right, centre: a domed-crown slipper piston; the oil return holes can be seen clearly in the bottom ring groove

Far right, bottom: an old-fashioned piston, with a large number of rings, three of which are below the gudgeon pin, and a split skirt to reduce piston slap further

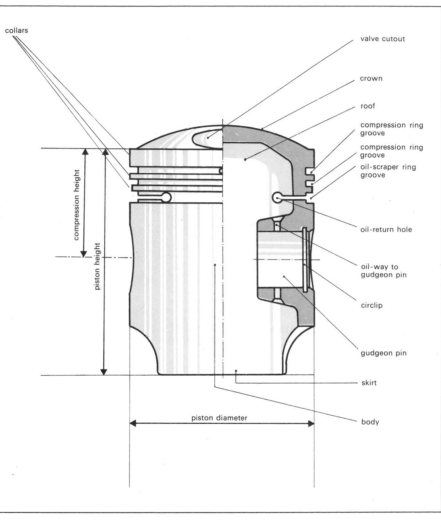

collars

valve cutout

crown

roof

compression ring groove

compression ring groove

oil-scraper ring groove

oil-return hole

oil-way to gudgeon pin

circlip

gudgeon pin

skirt

body

compression height

piston height

piston diameter

PROBABLY NO PART of the car engine has changed less in general configuration since its formative years than the piston. It is still recognisably similar to its counterpart of eighty or ninety years ago. Refinements in detail and in the methods and materials of manufacture have been quite numerous, but its retention of its basic shape and proportions is evidence of an equally basic function.

In its simplest terms, that function is to reciprocate inside a cylinder and seal its bore so as to vary its volume, while offering a means of connection with the rotating crankshaft to which its reciprocations must be related. Every other consideration is subsidiary: such matters as the shape of the crown, the depth of the skirt, the provisions for sealing rings, oil channels, expansion control, internal and external contours, the carriage of the gudgeon pin, and so on, are merely contrivances to improve its efficiency.

In assessing this efficiency, it is important to remember that the piston engine is not merely a mechanical contrivance but is also a heat engine. When the piston rises on its compression stroke, it acquires heat as the air of the fresh charge experiences a rise in temperature,

in accordance with that thermodynamic law which states that work is heat. When the compressed and heated charge is ignited and burns, then the heat liberated by combustion is translated into work done, in return, on the piston: the rapid heat rise is translated into pressure which acts on the piston crown to force it down. As it goes down on its expansion stroke, the piston continues to soak up heat from the burning mixture, for the exchange of heat into work is not very efficient, and if the piston could not accept and shed this heat it would not last long.

Some of its heat is given up to the next fresh charge on the downward induction stroke, but most of it has to find its way to the cylinder wall and thence to the coolant, be it water or air. If the piston were a perfect fit in the bore, the problems of heat transmission would be slight, but the piston would be unable to move. Some clearance is essential, not only to permit the penetration of a lubricating oil film between the mating surfaces but also to allow for the expansion of the piston when it grows hot, and for the contraction of the cylinder when it grows cool. Even if the piston and

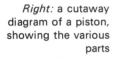

18

Left: a selection of pistons, showing the different types of skirt and the various shapes of crown, some having cutouts to prevent the valves from coming into contact with the pistons at top dead centre

the cylinder were made of the same material (an idea that for good reasons has rarely been tried and even more seldom been successful) they would still expand and contract at different rates and times, and some clearance would still be necessary.

The greater the clearance, the greater the clatter and the poorer the sealing. Pistons of cast iron, once the rule, would expand at much the same rate as the cylinder or its liner (almost always ferrous' allowing clearance to be minimised. Iron pistons, or even the thin-walled steel ones that soon replaced them, were too heavy for high-speed engines: their mass created enormous inertia loads as they accelerated up or down the bore. Maximum piston acceleration is given by $N2S/K (1 + 1/2R)$, where N is revolutions per minute, S the stroke, R the ratio of connecting-rod length to stroke, and K is a constant reconciling the chosen units of measurement: applied to the eight-ounce piston of a touring 1.3-litre car, it reveals that at 6000 rpm the piston momentarily exerts a force of one ton on its gudgeon pin!

Experiments with aluminium-alloy pistons began in 1909 under the engineer S. M. Viale at the Aquila-Italiana factory. Bentley made them work; Hispano-Suiza made them convincing; and by the end of the 1920s they were the rule. At first, they needed lots of clearance, but silicon-aluminium alloys (such as Y alloy) of relatively modest thermal expansion soon proved suitable. Manufacturers learnt to make them elliptical, not circular, in section: expansion was greater along the axis of the gudgeon pin than perpendicular to it, and so clearance could be reduced even more. DAF even built struts of Invar (a nickel alloy of very low thermal expansion) into their Daffodil pistons to control expansion even more strictly.

Sealing rings remained necessary, springy 'piston rings' of cast-alloy iron (nowadays often coated with chromium or molybdenum disulphide for improved bearing characteristics against the cylinder bore) that thus offered the only direct route whereby heat could escape from the piston to the cylinder. The path of heat flow is critical: the metal of the crown must be shaped so as to offer direct paths from the hottest areas (usually beneath the exhaust valves) to all the

Right: a cutaway view of a piston, showing how it is connected to the con-rod and via that to the crankshaft

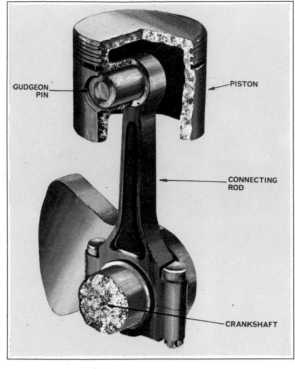

GUDGEON PIN

PISTON

CONNECTING ROD

CRANKSHAFT

Above: a section through a piston ring and its groove, showing that spring pressure seals the ring against the cylinder wall, while the pressure due to piston movement seals it against the top of its groove on the downward stroke

Right: a selection of piston ring types

variation there is in gudgeon-pin sizes. Gudgeon-pin diameter should be judged in relation to the cylinder bore: a ratio of 1:5 shows weakness, 1:3 uncommon sturdiness. With such heavy inertia loads as those already described, alternating at high frequency, the pin is subjected to heavy bending loads: should it bend appreciably, it will distort and weaken or even break the piston—although the bigger the pin, the less room is left for the bosses that support it. Piston design is a fine exercise in stressmanship.

This is particularly true when, as in many modern pistons, the skirt is split by cunningly shaped slots which extend all the way up to the ring belt. The edges and ends of these clots can, if imperfectly designed and finished, act as stress-raisers from which cracks can originate. However, the split skirt is often thought worth the effort of developing it, for it offers the best of

rings, not merely to the overworked top ring as is often the case. This is most difficult to achieve with a steeply domed or deeply dished piston crown: in the latter case (presented by diesels and by Heron-type petrol engines with combustion chambers of the bowl-in-piston kind), it demands that the rings be set well below the top edge of the piston, which is inconsistent with the requirements of certain sleeve-valve or two-strokes with piston-controlled ports.

Some designers rely on copious sprays or squirts of oil to help cool the piston from below, although it causes bad deposits and accelerates deterioration of the oil. Where oil is abundant, special means have to be provided for preventing its accumulation beneath the rings, whence it can be pumped (by the rings' reciprocating action in their grooves) into the upper part of the cylinder to the detriment of consumption and combustion alike. The lowest of the rings may be a multiplex 'oil-control ring' which scrapes excess oil off the bore and passes it through drillings from the ring groove to the inside of the piston wall. Oil-scraper rings used to be fitted low on the piston skirt (they also helped to deaden 'piston slap', a noise made by a cold high-clearance piston rocking in the bore around its gudgeon pin) but a knife-edge bevelling of the skirt edge is simpler and nearly as effective.

The skirt is not always complete. Efforts to lighten the piston and to reduce frictional losses led designers of high-performance engines into all manner of dodges—drilled skirts were popular in the 1920s, and even ball bearings were tried as a substitute for skirts. It was the great (later Sir) Harry Ricardo who found the best solution, the slipper piston, of which most of the skirt is cut away, leaving it intact only in the plane of the connecting rod's swing, where it has to resist side thrust.

Skirts were shortened, too, for the same reasons, but it could be overdone, making the piston wobbly in its bore. As a rough guide, the skirt should extend as far below the gudgeon pin as the rings are above it. Racing and aero engines have relatively short-squat pistons, touring cars have longer ones, and two-stroke or diesel pistons are often very long indeed.

With all these differences, it is surprising how little

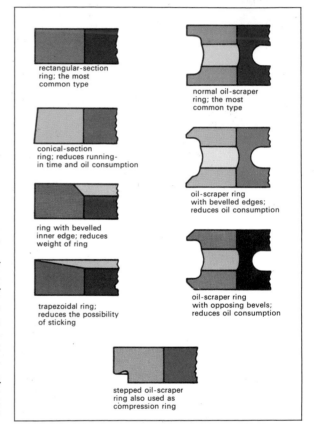

rectangular-section ring; the most common type

conical-section ring; reduces running-in time and oil consumption

ring with bevelled inner edge; reduces weight of ring

trapezoidal ring; reduces the possibility of sticking

normal oil-scraper ring; the most common type

oil-scraper ring with bevelled edges; reduces oil consumption

oil-scraper ring with opposing bevels; reduces oil consumption

stepped oil-scraper ring also used as compression ring

all practical means of reducing clearance and noise. Even an elliptical piston will be problematical at some time, as is clear from the fact that the difference between major and minor diameters may be as much as 0.2 mm—and this characteristic is perforce combined with very large clearances above the lowest piston ring. Below it, the split skirt can adapt itself to the bore in the same way as the split or gapped piston ring, reducing noise appreciably.

What of the piston crown, the bit by which we recognise so much of the character of the engine? Its shape must be governed by external considerations, based on the cylinder-head design, and has little to do with specialised piston technology. It is essentially a controller of gas flows, of combustion, and of compression ratio, but just occasionally we find it doing other odd jobs. One of the oddest was in the 1937 GP Mercedes-Benz, whose designers were fearful of the consequences of valves sticking open—so each piston crown sported four little pimples that, at top dead centre, would just touch any tardy valveheads and give them a nudge so that they could shut again!

CONNECTING ROD

joining piston and crankshaft

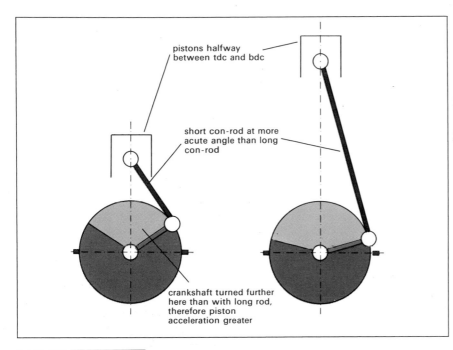

pistons halfway between tdc and bdc

short con-rod at more acute angle than long con-rod

crankshaft turned further here than with long rod, therefore piston acceleration greater

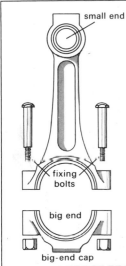

small end

fixing bolts

big end

big-end cap

Top: with the same stroke in each case, con-rod angularity varies in relation to length

Above: a typical con-rod, complete with big-end cap, which can be attached by bolts or nuts

THE MOTION OF AN ENGINE'S PISTON is strictly linear, that of the crankshaft rotational; and so that of the connecting rod (commonly abbreviated as con-rod) which links them is translatory. At the little end, the motion of the rod is virtually in a straight line, but at the big end it is circular—and it is all very unfortunate, for this swinging action of the con-rod is responsible for many of the piston engine's problems. Vibrations, bearing restrictions, difficulties in breathing and burning, even ignition and valve timing, are all sensitive to the proportions of this vital link.

In its construction, the con-rod has few mysteries. The little end (the bearing eye in which the piston's gudgeon pin is a very precise fit) has its dimensions more or less fixed by piston design. The big end (the portion which bears on the crankshaft) is usually split for convenience and cheapness in manufacture and assembly, but idealistic designers, of whom there are very few, insist on the stronger and lighter one-piece rod at the expense of a costly built-up crankshaft. The bearings themselves should be plain; roller bearings are unsuitable for the duty because the angular swing of the con-rod as it moves makes the rollers skid and wear rapidly. Only in the more rudimentary two-stroke engines, lubricated by petroil, is the roller bearing a necessary evil. As for the shank between big and little ends, few designers bother to make it other than in the I-beam section that is easiest to forge, even though it is structurally inefficient.

Most con-rods are machined from steel forgings, although a few astute mass-producers cast them instead. During a long production run, forging dies wear so much that the dimensions and weights of the finished rods vary a lot, making large surplus masses of metal necessary. This means that appropriate amounts may be ground away to reduce all rods to equal weight. A cast rod is naturally more substantial because the metal is less strong, but it is dimensionally more consistent, so the big balancing lugs can be omitted, freeing all the material for useful work. Thus, a cast rod *can* actually be lighter than a forged one—and light weight is of great importance, affecting engine performance and balance. Many motor-cycle engines have aluminium-alloy rods, and racing-car engines, built regardless of cost, may employ titanium. In production cars, however, weight-saving is generally pursued in dimensional design rather than in choice of material.

A short rod is obviously lighter and stiffer than a long one and, by allowing the whole engine to be reduced in height, it encourages further savings in material. On the other hand, a long rod promotes smoother running and allows higher engine speeds to be reached for a given level of mechanical stress. This is because of the different amounts of angular swing of long and short rods in engines of identical piston stroke. If the connecting rod could be infinitely long, the angular movement would be infinitely small, the motion of the piston up and down the cylinder would be perfectly harmonic (i.e. sinusoidal) and there would be no problems of secondary vibration or bearing velocity change to impede the designer. As things are, the con-rod must be of finite and practical length: the conventional distance between the centres of little and big ends is twice the piston stroke.

This gives a fair compromise between conflicting requirements. Were the rod shorter, the whole engine could be shorter and lighter, and the piston would travel faster on its approach to, and recession from, top dead centre—with advantages in better breathing on the exhaust and inlet strokes, and better conservation of combustion heat during the expansion phase. If the rod were longer, the maximum piston acceleration at a given crankshaft speed would be less, inertia loads on the piston, rings, rod and crankpin would be correspondingly less, secondary vibrational forces would be reduced (because there would be less difference between the rates of piston acceleration on upward and downward strokes), and frictional losses between piston and cylinder would be reduced (because of the reduction of con-rod angular swing). The combustion process might also benefit from the more nearly constant volume of the combustion space when the piston was in the region of top dead centre. Note, by the way, that mean piston acceleration is not only irrelevant but also incalculable. The formula for *maximum* acceleration, which is what matters, is:

max piston acceleration (ft per sec per sec)

$$= \frac{N^2 S}{2189}\left(1 + \frac{1}{2R}\right)$$

where N is crankshaft rpm, S is the stroke in inches, and R is the ratio of con-rod length to stroke. This allows some interesting comparisons to be drawn—for example, between the Austin Maxi 1500 (a long-stroke engine with short rods, R = 1.81) and the Fiat 128 (a short-stroke engine with long rods, R = 2.18). Both engines give maximum power at 6000 rpm, when the Fiat's pistons reach peaks of about 44,000 ft per sec per sec and those of the BLMC car about 65,500—or approximately 2030 g—which illustrates the importance of minimising the weight not only of the piston but also of the connecting rod itself.

CYLINDER HEAD

a great part of performance

EFFICIENT BREATHING and efficient burning are the basic requirements of a good engine; mechanical imperturbability is merely a condition of their realisation. Breathing and burning alike are determined largely by the shape and size of the four fundamental holes around which the engine is formed: the inlet passage, the cylinder, the combustion chamber and the exhaust passage. The cylinder is perhaps the least critical of the four; the other three are all contained by the cylinder head, which must accordingly rank as the engine's most important component.

The cylinder head has not always been regarded with such respect. Early engines seldom had separate heads but were integrally constructed; and so long as their performance was limited by such expressions of engineering naivety as the automatic inlet valve, none of the other coronal features was likely to make much impression. It was the designer Henry, working for Peugeot in the years following 1910, who was first really to emphasise the growing conviction among racing-car designers that vast improvements in performance waited on the full development of the cylinder head and all it contained. For the next fifty years, the head and its contents followed a clear line of development (as far as the high-performance engine was concerned), influenced more by Henry and by the Fiat Technical Office of 1920 than by anybody else.

Their emphasis was very much on the mechanical contents of the head rather than on the holes it defined. Valves, springs, tappets, camshafts and all the associated minutiae were brought to an advanced state of design, but the attendant cost and complexity made the exercise seem irrelevant to producers of cheap cars for the masses, to whom the noise and elaboration of an overhead-valve engine (especially one with overhead camshafts) were far more objectionable than the thermal and volumetric inefficiency of the decidedly simple side-valve engine. So long as the quality of petrol, lubricating oils, exhaust valve steels and sundry items remained poor—as was the case until the late 1930s—the side-valve engine remained the ordinary everyday standard, valued for the ease with which tappets could be adjusted or the head lifted for decarbonising. The poor breathing and indifferent burning of its charge were accepted as inevitable.

Before the end of that period, the engineer Ricardo had demonstrated the possibility of improving the combustion of the side-valve engine enormously. By the time that the import of his work had been assimilated by the motor industry, forced developments of materials in the aircraft industry had carried matters to a state where the simpler kinds of overhead-valve engines could be brought into common use. These so raised the performance of the ordinary car, not only in speed but also economy and reliability, that the niceties of breathing and burning could still be generally ignored. Manufacturing economy and convenience dictated that the overhead-valve engine

should have its valves arranged in line and parallel with each other, and that the valves should derive their motion from a camshaft situated (as before) low in the cylinder block. Thus came into fashion an engine style in which the porting and the combustion chamber were corrupted somewhat from the ideals, while the increased mass of the pushrods and rockers, transmitting the dictates of the cams to their respective valves, imposed limitations, sometimes severe, on the high-speed operation of the engine.

Expensive cars that could be expensively maintained might enjoy the benefits of overhead camshafts and all the freedom of valve location and combustion chamber design that they conferred. One or two manufacturers even sought to exploit such design features in the medium price range: Jaguar and Alfa

Below: the Maserati V6 engine used in the Citroën SM. This has twin overhead camshafts on each cylinder bank. The camshaft layout allows a wide angle between the valves of each cylinder, which, with the hemispherical combustion chamber, leads to high efficiency. The spark plugs are placed to one side of the chambers which is not ideal

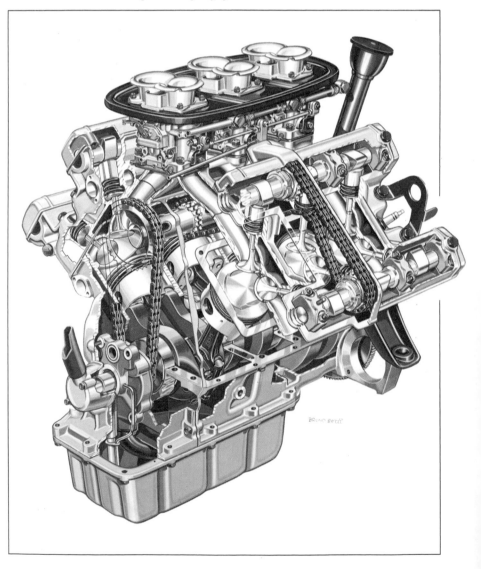

Romeo were the best post-war examples. Despite their success, it was not until the introduction of the toothed rubber belt, coupled with the simple Fiat system of tappet adjustment (used previously in MV Agusta racing motor cycles), that the overhead-camshaft engine became available in all classes of car.

Until that happened, and especially during the early 1960s when it was happening, designers saddled with the pushrod engine sought means of improving its breathing and combustion so as to keep it competitive with the new machines. This was a period of great development, but the emphasis was on power and torque, so when exhaust emissions became a matter for urgent study in the late 1960s, the premises and assumptions underlying all these engineers' studies had to be drastically revised. Then, when fuel economy became the fashionable matter for public outcry and political interference, these were changed again.

Every question of what we want an engine to do may be resolved, or at least strongly influenced, by examination of how a particular cylinder head can contrive to do it. Generally we want an engine to run quietly, economically and cleanly, and to give as much useful power as may reasonably be demanded of it. We want it to run smoothly, to do so for as long as possible, and to be fairly insensitive to uncontrollable variations in fuel quality, ignition timing, temperature, ambient atmospheric conditions, lubricating oil quality, and so on. In short, it all comes back to the twin requirements of breathing and combustion.

It is the shape of the three basic holes in the head that finally fixes what the results will be. The inlet and exhaust passages have an important bearing on breathing, but the combustion chamber also influences it, as well as controlling the processes which take place while both ports are closed by their valves.

It is generally true that more can be lost through inefficient combustion than can be gained by efficient breathing. Let us therefore begin by considering briefly the combustion process. It begins when the spark initiates burning of the compressed and heated mixture in the cylinder, at some time before top dead centre when the piston is still rising to complete its compression stroke. From the spark, the flame travels through the mixture in all available directions, advancing like a wave, a three-dimensional ripple of tremendous speed and furious intensity. How fast it travels depends on how turbulent the mixture is and how hot—and these in turn depend not only on the speed of the piston but also on the design of the cylinder head cavities.

The speed of combustion is vital, for we have now to consider when we wish it to begin and for how long it should continue. Initiation should be as late as possible before top dead centre. On the other hand, the full potential value of the expansion pressure cannot be realised if the work is done on a piston that is already descending again. It should therefore follow that combustion should be started and completed in the instant of top dead centre; yet if it were, the engine would be

Below: a selection of combustion chamber layouts, with side valves and overhead valves. The relative efficiencies of the shapes are shown—side valves are considerably less efficient than the overhead type. The 'hemispherical' chamber can never be truly so, because the poppet valves take up so much of the space, as is shown

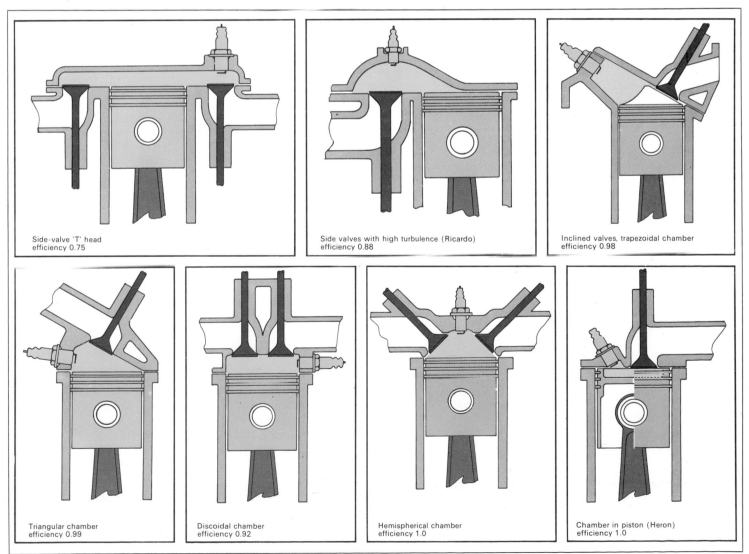

Side-valve 'T' head
efficiency 0.75

Side valves with high turbulence (Ricardo)
efficiency 0.88

Inclined valves, trapezoidal chamber
efficiency 0.98

Triangular chamber
efficiency 0.99

Discoidal chamber
efficiency 0.92

Hemispherical chamber
efficiency 1.0

Chamber in piston (Heron)
efficiency 1.0

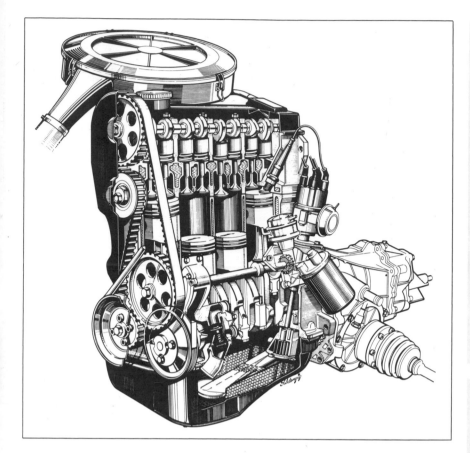

Above: a cutaway view of the Audi 80 engine. A single belt-driven camshaft is mounted in the head and operates the valves directly, which means that the valves have to be parallel, thus limiting the shape of the combustion chamber. Note how the coolant is concentrated around the chambers, where the temperatures are highest

Above right: a longitudinal section of a Fiat 16/20 hp engine of 1904. The cylinders were cast in pairs and the heads formed an integral part of these. The whole was liquid cooled and made use of a side-valve layout

Right: a cross section of the Fiat S57A engine of 1916. This unit was highly advanced for its time, having a single overhead camshaft operating inclined valves via rockers (a similar arrangement to that used in the BMW 2000 series engines of the 1960s and 1970s)

blown to smithereens. We need ignition, not detonation.

Detonation is not entirely the fault of the fuel: a good head design will allow a lower grade of fuel (of lower octane value or knock-resistance) to be employed without running into such problems. It is as much influenced by the shape of the combustion chamber, most of which is a matter of cylinder-head design, and the remainder determined by the piston-crown. Detonation happens when the advancing flame front traps before it a pocket of mixture and, in its advance, simultaneously heats and compresses it to the point where all its particles ignite spontaneously together. It can also happen when a second flame front is despatched from some point of spurious ignition, where part of the compressed mixture is ignited by some incandescent component. This can be particularly damaging, for when two flame fronts move in opposition the rate of pressure rise may be doubled.

Although the elimination of surface deposits is a matter for accurate mixture control by carburation or injection, and for a choice of lubricating oil having a low ash content, the other phenomena may best be eliminated by good design. One of the first requirements of this, is that flame travel should be as nearly as possible equidistant in all directions from the spark. To achieve this, the plug may be located at the centre of the flat face of a hemisphere, or at the apex of a cone.

This last impractical idea is ideally attractive, for it would achieve the next most important of our objects, which is to contrive the highest possible ratio of volume to surface area for our combustion space. The desirability of this is based on grounds of thermal efficiency, which is part of good combustion: the heat built-up in the charge by compression must be conserved for exploitation in combustion, not dissipated through the relatively cool metal walls of the cylinder, piston and head; and, of course, they have to be kept relatively cool if the engine is not to melt, thaw and resolve itself into adieu. Obviously some heat loss

is unavoidable, but too much impairs performance, both directly, through wastage of useful heat, and indirectly through the need for more substantial cooling systems to deal with the greater quantity of heat fed into the coolant. In extreme, but by no means uncommon cases, the ratio of surface to volume is so unfavourable that enough heat is lost to cool the

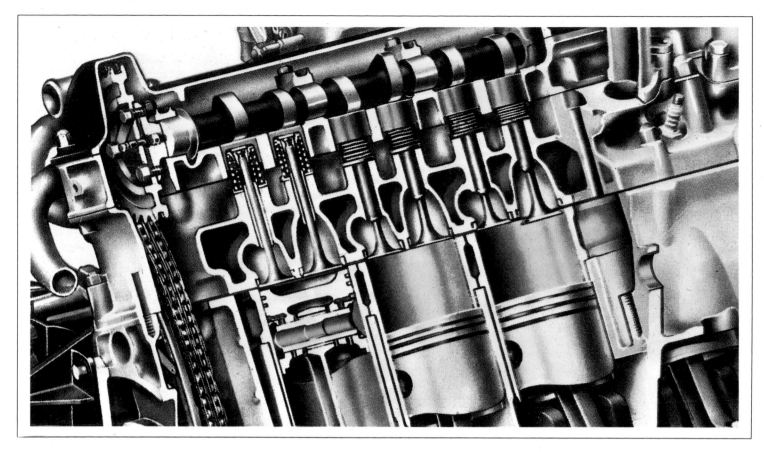

mixture, or some of it, below the level at which it will burn. This is called quenching, and it is a major contributor to exhaust pollution by unburnt fuel.

There is at least one case recorded of an engine being so designed for very high performance, with extensive use of light alloys and generous provision for cooling, that when fed with fuel and sparks on the test bench it failed to develop any power or even to keep itself running: the quenching action of the over-cooled interior surfaces literally put out the fire, and the only output that could be claimed for the engine was a black liquid which oozed from the exhaust pipe. Such an extreme case teaches a useful lesson, which may be seen put to practical use in such modern production examples as the Hillman Avenger engine, in which the distinguished engineer Leo Kuzmicki (formerly playing an important part in the development of the Manx Norton and the Grand Prix Vanwall engines, both of them paragons of power in their times) chose iron for the cylinder head in order to reduce quenching, since that material is a poorer conductor of heat than aluminium. On the other hand, an iron head often imposes a lower limit on the highest usable compression ratio, and high compression is inseparable from thermal efficiency. Of late it has gone out of fashion, because high pressures and temperatures promote the formation of oxides of nitrogen, while high compression ratios also demand high knock resistance of the fuel, which must accordingly be treated with lead compounds (unless expensive alkylates such as triptane are used)—and oxides of nitrogen rival airborne lead in attracting the contumely of environmentalists.

When exhaust pollution made quenching unwelcome, it did the same to squish—a device of design to promote turbulence. A piston crown may be designed to come into very close proximity (as little as I mm) to the inside of the cylinder head over an appreciable area, possibly as much as a third of the piston area. The effect of this sudden constriction of the space occupied by the charge, as the piston rises in its bore for the last part of the compression stroke, is for the mixture to be expelled or squished at high velocity out of that area into the remaining combustion space. This does two things: it increases the agitation or turbulence of the mixture and thus increases the rate of burning (which is good for everything except oxides of nitrogen), and it directs the current predictably so as to ensure more complete combustion and properly oriented flame travel.

This last phenomenon depends on the placing of the spark plug. If it is so located that the flame front travels in opposition to the squished current, all is well and good, and the fuel is fed to the flames. But if the squish current travels away from the plug, the flame front may have to go chasing it and may never quite catch up. Many engines have an end-gas problem caused by this sort of mistake, allowing unburned fuel to escape as an exhaust residuum. Often, the same effect is produced by quenching of the charge in the space remaining in the squish area: quench and squish often go together, offering a convenient, if wasteful, means of controlling pressure rise during the late stages of combustion. The artifice is most commonly employed in engines where the manufacturing economies of in-line parallel overhead valves have dictated the adoption of a somewhat unsatisfactory shape for the combustion chamber, such as the wedge, the heart shape, the very common bathtub, and the bowl-in-piston or Heron head.

The brainchild of Sam D. Heron, a Newcastle man who did most of his great work on engines in the USA, the Heron head entails the sinking of the entire combustion space in the piston crown. The cylinder head casting itself has a flat bottom, which simplifies production enormously. If a fairly low compression ratio is to be used, the combustion chamber may take the form of a hemispherical bowl in the piston, offering ideal flame travel and good surface/volume

Above: a longitudinal section of one bank of cylinders of a Jaguar V12 engine. As in the Audi 80, a single overhead camshaft acts directly on the valves. The main difference between this and the Audi, however, is that the combustion chambers in the V12 are in the pistons, with flat cylinder heads, whereas the Audi has flat-topped pistons with a recessed cylinder head. The inlet ports of the Jaguar engine are between the banks, while the exhausts are on the outside. Note that the camshafts in this case are driven by a duplex chain

ratio. Such a piston would be heavy, though, and temperature gradients in it would create difficulties in conducting heat through the piston rings to the cylinder walls. Anyway, by the time the compression ratio has been raised to realistic levels, the bowl can no longer be shaped purely for good combustion: pockets must be cut in the edges of the piston to make room for the valves to move, and these severely degrade the theoretical excellence of the design. Most current examples have therefore been modified by increasing the squish clearance and making the bowl shallower (as in the Jaguar V12) or by putting part of the chamber in the actual head casting (as in some Fords).

But for these difficulties, the Heron head would have the attraction of a reduced surface area for the combustion space as the compression ratio is increased. This is something that cannot be said for wedges and bathtubs, and most emphatically not of the classical

be better cooled. Decades ago, any self-respecting high-performance engine had four valves per cylinder (unless it were a Bugatti with three) and, since 1960, the arrangement has returned to fashion, inspired by the racing motor-cycle engines of Honda. In cars, Coventry Climax and later Cosworth have led the same fashion (the former in 1964), and the Cosworth embodies an interesting compromise between the Heron head and the pent-roof variant of the hemisphere which most comfortably accommodates four valves. The valve pockets in the piston crowns represent a significant portion of the combustion space, while the pent-roof is flattened until the angle between the banks of inlet and exhaust valves is a mere 30°—just enough to make room for the central spark plug.

Interestingly, Honda have explained in a technical paper that the classical two-valve hemispherical head

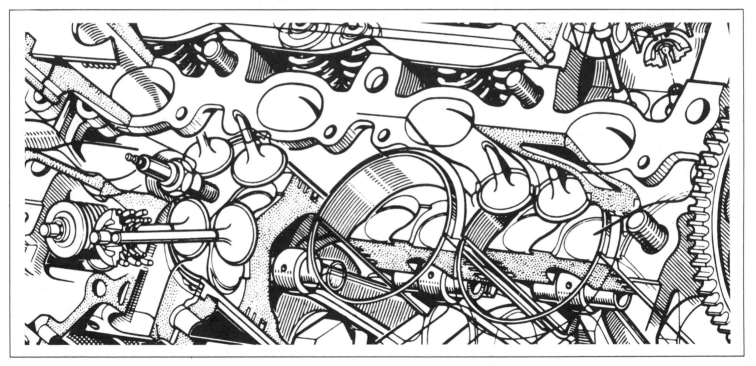

can yield as good a performance as the currently popular four-valve arrangement. It gives higher thermal and volumetric efficiencies, but imposes a lower rev limit, and the two virtually cancel each other. On balance, the small valves of the four-valve arrangement promise greater durability and reliability. For a competition engine this is conclusive enough; for a production car the poorer efficiency of the four-valve engine rules it out of consideration, even though some theories claim that it costs no more to make.

All other aspects of cylinder-head design may be subservient to those discussed above, but they are none the less interesting. The arrangements for the passage of coolant to scour the spaces around the exhaust valve seats and spark plug bosses (the most intense hot spots) can be vital—and when the coolant is air, they can be baffling. The disposition of the the securing studs so that they give equal sealing pressure all round each cylinder, yet keep out of the way of the valve apparatus, may be anything from elegant to hilarious, as in the case of the Weslake Austin Healey with studs passing through the inlet ports. Obviously, it is best to keep the ports free of obstructions in order to aid gas flow, as these will interfere with efficiency.

Above: part of the 3-litre Matra V12 engine, as announced in 1967. In this early version, the inlet ports were between the twin camshafts of each cylinder bank, while the later type, of 1970, which had a smaller included angle between the valves, had its inlets in the centre of the V

hemispherical head. In this last instance, the surface area is increased considerably by the raised dome of the piston crown—and at the same time, the chamber is changed in shape from a hemisphere to something like the rind of half an orange. Thus the surface/volume ratio is raised enormously, which may hold detonation at bay or may increase thermal losses. At least the flame travel remains approximately equal in all directions, even though the distance is not as slight as it might be in other cases.

In general, the hemispherical head promises the best results. It demands inclined valves and expensive valve-gear, which is why it has always been associated with high-grade sporting engines: the wider the angle between the inlet and exhaust valves, the greater the possible valve area and the better the breathing. The only other way of achieving comparable, or even greater, valve area is to put four valves in each head instead of two: it is a matter of simple mensuration to show that four small valves can give more port area within the confines of a given cylinder diameter than can two of the largest possible size. Moreover, the smaller valves can be operated at higher cyclic rates, allowing higher crankshaft speeds—itself an effective way of augmenting the power output, while the smaller valves have a high surface/mass ratio and so can

DECARBONISING

cleaning the combustion spaces

ANY ENGINE WHICH RUNS on a hydrocarbon fuel is likely to suffer from a build-up of carbon deposits. Whether that engine be conventional petrol or diesel, rotary or even gas turbine, the same principle applies, but for the time being we will confine ourselves to discussing reciprocating petrol engines.

There are three main reasons why carbon deposits are unwanted: gas flow is slowed down, combustion chamber size is decreased and 'hot spots' may be formed.

The basic governing factor for the efficiency of this type of engine is the rate at which the fuel/air mixture can enter each cylinder and the rate at which exhaust gases can leave. Smooth-sided passages are better than rough-sided ones, since the latter cause excessive turbulence and restrict the gas flow. Carbon deposits are, by nature, rough and therefore impair this efficiency.

A moderately tuned engine may not suffer by having its compression ratio raised, which is what happens as the combustion chamber size decreases, but others may begin to 'pink' (a tinkling noise caused by pre-ignition).

Pre-ignition is not always due to an over-high compression ratio, it may be caused by a 'hot spot'. The heat-conducting properties of carbon are not nearly so good as those of cast iron or aluminium alloy, so heat built up by combustion can be stored in the layer of carbon, eventually reaching red heat and causing fuel to ignite while the piston is still approaching the top of its stroke.

One of the most common symptoms of excessive carbonisation is 'running on' (the engine continues to run for some seconds after the ignition has been switched off). If either this phenomenon or 'pinking'

are present in a petrol engine, and the recommended grade of fuel is being used, excessive carbon build up must be suspected.

The only really effective way of decarbonising an engine is to take off the cylinder head and scrape the various parts free of this element. There are 'decarbonising agents' on the market which can be introduced to the combustion spaces via the spark-plug holes. Leaving these solvents in for several hours is supposed to free the engine of its deposits but, unfortunately, it is very difficult to remove anything other than a thin surface coating in this manner.

In any engine other than an overhead-camshaft power unit, removal of the cylinder head is a straightforward job requiring only the disconnection of ancillaries, such as the exhaust pipe, coolant pipes, fuel pipe(s), wires and control cables and the disengagement of several fixing bolts or nuts. The carburettor(s) can often be left undisturbed, although, if the decarbonisation process is to be carried out properly, it or they should be removed at some stage to give access to the induction ports.

Of course, should the engine have side valves, it is quite possible that nothing other than the cylinder-head fixings need be undone—the inlet and exhaust will remain on the engine. However, it may still be desirable to take off at least the induction manifold, to avoid foreign bodies entering it and thence the carburettor(s).

Overhead camshafts present a slightly greater problem, in that the drive to the shafts, and sometimes the shafts themselves, have to be removed. In fact, refitting of the shafts involves far more work than does removal, since the valve timing has to be adjusted. Great care should be taken when refitting a camshaft, to make

Left: a rotary wire brush, fitted to an electric drill, is very useful for removing deposits from the valve throats. The valve guides will probably prevent deep penetration, but a very small area will be left untouched if the brush is inserted through the ports, as well as through the throats

Following page, above: the most stubborn deposits may have to be removed from the valves with a scraper, but it is possible to take off most of the carbon by inserting each valve in the chuck of an electric drill

Centre. valve-grinding paste should be smeared round the seating surface of each valve prior to grinding in. If pitting is evident, coarse paste should be used before finishing off with fine

Below: a special valve-grinding tool, with a rubber suction cup, should be used if the valves do not possess screwdriver grooves. Twisting the tool to and fro between the hands will remove any valve-seat imperfections

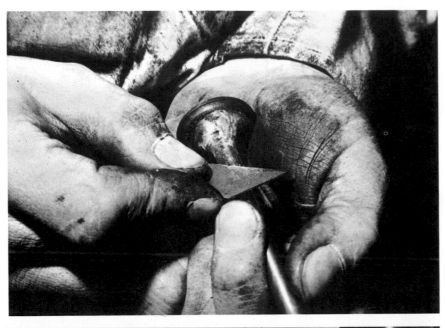

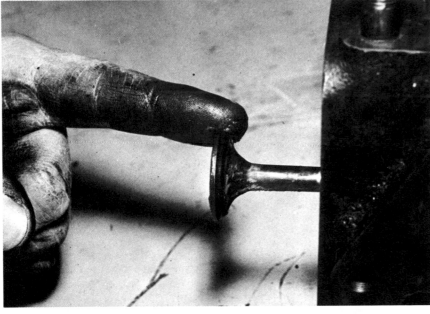

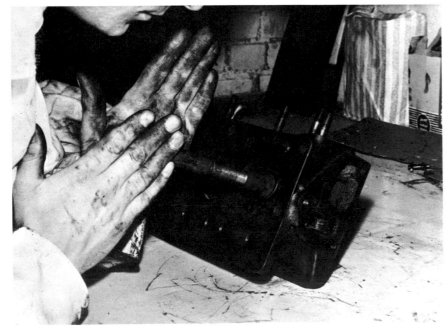

sure that none of the valves hit a piston; the safest avoiding action is to set the crankshaft so that all the pistons are below the top of their strokes.

If the job is to be carried out properly, the valves must all be removed and kept so that they can be replaced in their original seats. Probably the easiest way of remembering the order is to place all the valve stems, in order, through holes in a piece of card, numbering each hole accordingly.

A side-valve engine usually has a plate bolted to the side of the cylinder block, to give access to the valve fixings and valve springs. If the valves are to be removed from an overhead-camshaft engine, the shaft or shafts will have to be removed before the valve-spring compressor is brought into play. With overhead valves and a block-mounted camshaft, the rocker shaft will have to be unbolted in order to clear the way for valve removal.

Once the valves are out and marked, the process of decarbonisation can be started. A rotary wire brush, fitted to an electric drill, is very useful for cleaning the combustion chambers—from which the spark plugs should have been removed—but stubborn particles should be scraped off, using wood if possible, but soft metal if necessary.

The rotary brush can be used to clean out the valve throats and the ports (assuming the manifolds have been removed). The valves themselves can be cleaned by placing them in the chuck of the electric drill and using a scraper to clean the carbon from the head. Care should be exercised here, as it is essential to avoid damaging the valve seat and the stem where it passes through the guide in the cylinder head. Once the major part of the deposit has been removed, the valve can be polished with wet-or-dry paper.

Polishing is not essential for any of the parts, but it will take longer for carbon to build-up on a smooth, shiny surface, with few imperfections, than on a dull surface with many pits and bumps. Unfortunately, this build-up cannot be avoided, but its delay can only increase efficiency, for the reasons mentioned earlier.

The valves should be ground to fit their seats, by resting them in place, with a little grinding paste between the contact surfaces, and twisting them to and fro with either a special suction tool or, in the case of grooved valve heads, a screwdriver. When the seats are an even matt grey, with no pits, the grinding paste should be removed, the stem oiled and the springs and fixing devices replaced. If oil seals are used on the valve stems, new ones should be obtained in order to keep oil consumption to a minimum.

The carbon should be scraped from each piston crown, once again with wood if possible. It is advisable to leave a small ring of carbon around the edge of each piston (about 3/16 in), so that any deposits in the space between the top piston rings and the crowns will not be disturbed and perhaps increase oil consumption.

As each piston is tackled, it should be placed at the top of its stroke and a piece of cloth used to cover the other cylinders and any oil passages. Loose carbon should be wiped away carefully.

Before replacing the cylinder head, its face and that of the block should be wiped and lightly greased to prevent the gasket sticking. A new gasket should always be used as the old one will have been flattened.

It is advisable to measure the tension of the nuts and bolts with a torque wrench, as uneven settings can lead to warping of the head and consequent leakage of compression, coolant or both.

Finally, valve clearances must be adjusted, as grinding the valve seats closes these up and too tight a setting may eventually lead to a burnt valve.

VALVE GEAR

governing the gas flow

UNLESS IT IS VERY UNUSUAL, a four-stroke engine must have at least two valves to each cylinder. One, the inlet valve, must be large enough and open wide enough to admit a fresh charge of as much air and fuel as may be desired at the proper time; the other, the exhaust valve, must be able when opened to allow the egress of all the gases produced by combustion. When they are closed, these valves must seal their ports so as to be gas-tight despite the tremendous pressures reached in the combustion chamber after ignition. They must be able to withstand very high temperatures, attack by corrosive media, violent accelerations and shock loads, and brief spells of operation without lubrication; they must not get in the way of the piston, nor interfere with each other, must not consume much power to operate them, nor be expensive to make. They must not suffer deformation, nor get out of adjustment, nor move in any other way than as the designer intended, even though they may open and close at a cyclic rate of anything from a couple of hundred to several thousand times a minute, and even though the duration of opening may be of the order of one hundredth of a second; and they must be able to keep this up for hours on end, for months without attention and for years without replacement. It is a tall order.

It is amazing that the things work at all, and it is not at all surprising that there have been hundreds of attempts to substitute some other kind of mechanism to perform their tasks. In the context of the motor car, such variants are most unusual, and they appear to have as little chance in the future as in the past of coming into favour, however great their theoretical or practical advantages. In automobile engineering, as in most other kinds, the first successful solution to a problem tends to be adopted so widely that any later ones, however much better, are excluded by the costs of revised tooling, by factory methods, and by deeply ingrained ways of thinking. So, by an accident of history, we still accept today the poppet valve that was the first to be effective when the four-stroke engine was applied to the propulsion of the earliest cars. It is a dreadful device that has been derided as a 'penny on a stick': the disc portion has a conical edge corresponding to that of the orifice it should seal, while the stem passes through and is supported by a cylindrical bearing or guide and is subjected to a never ending conflict of axial loads, from the springs pulling the valve down towards its seat and the operating mechanism that intermittently pushes it in the opposite direction. As with most engine components, the design of the valve is full of compromises: a head shape that is good for mechanical strength may be bad for temperature distribution, one that is good for efficient gas flow at maximum lift may cause unnecessary obstruction of the port when it is only partially open, while the subtleties of seat angling and radiusing (which have a profound effect on gas flow) may be confounded by the proximity of cylinder walls or piston crowns.

Only a few engineers and the best of mechanics worry about these things. Only they concern themselves with such niceties as the relationship between the width of the exhaust-valve seat (which, it used to be thought, had to be fairly wide in order to provide an escape path for the heat of the valve) and the valve-seat pressure, the truth of the matter being that the narrower the seat the greater is the pressure and the better the heat flow; only they accept the importance of really precise contouring of the edges of the valve and of its seat, knowing that these can have so great an influence on the coefficient of discharge of the valve as to be worth a 30% increase in valve lift. Everybody else is much more concerned with the location and size of the valves, and most particularly with the means of opening them.

Without exception among the four-stroke engines in production, the valve is lifted from its seat by a cam —an eccentric device which, as it rotates, displaces the valve either directly or indirectly, and then allows it to be returned to its seat with further rotation, the work of returning the valve being done almost invariably by some kind of springs. The cam appears to be not only eccentric but also brutal, and many have been the efforts to substitute something else: there have been obscure engines in which the work has been done by complicated linkages driven by the crankshaft, all straps and stirrups and sliding pins in sloppy slots; but by a nice philological paradox, all these may now be considered more eccentric than the cam itself.

Even the cam has taken many forms: there have been engines with face cams, conical cams, internal or ring cams and numerous other varieties, but today the cam is always a simple lobed eccentric integral with a shaft driven at half the crankshaft speed by any convenient and positive means. Its shape, which determines the

Top: a very simple valve arrangement used in the Salmson of 1922; in this, one pushrod was used to open the inlet and exhaust valves alternately by means of a centrally pivoted rocker arm; not, of course, the most efficient system

Above: probably the most popular valve mechanism for many years; the valves are mounted in line in the head and are opened by a block-mounted camshaft, via pushrods and rockers, and closed by strong springs; adjustment of the tappet clearance is by means of lock-nutted screws fitted to the rockers

Right: the components of the 'standard' pushrod-and-rocker set-up; the camshaft is mounted in the crank-case or cylinder block, while the valves are mounted in the cylinder head

Below right: the Itala rotary-valve system, introduced in their 25 hp model of 1912 and kept in production until 1922, when it was still fitted to the type 55 six-cylinder engine

timing of opening and closure of the valve and also its rates of ascent and descent, is compounded of many subtleties, but whilst its shape is often the work of very clever men, they are even cleverer who design the valve springs which play a dominant part in the whole proceedings. It is the spring that determines how rapidly the valve may be lifted by the cam, how faithfully it will follow the cam's dictates in descending again and how precisely and positively it will be returned to its seat and kept there until it is next due to open. Not only the mass of the valve, but also that of all the other components in the valve train between valve and cam, must be controlled and shifted by the spring; and this includes an assortment of cotters, rockers, pushrods, tappets, adjusters and oil seals. The most popular kind of spring is helical, concentric with the valve stem and often abetted by another of smaller diameter and different rate fitting fairly closely within it; but it was at one time thought preferable that really high-performance engines should have springs of the so-called hairpin type, which took up a lot of space laterally, but little vertically (so the valve stems could be shorter and therefore lighter) and which could run at very high frequencies without encountering the resonance problems commonly affecting helical springs. In fact, both kinds of spring, helical and hairpin alike, are merely compact and complex versions of the torsion bar, and spring technology has come far

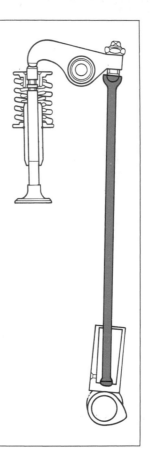

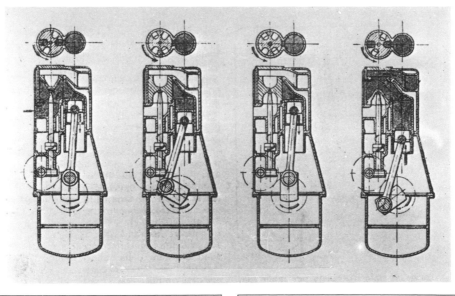

Right: eight different examples of valve arrangements, all of which have been popular at some time for reasons either of high efficiency or low cost

Below: with a rocker it is possible to increase or decrease the lift of the valve relative to that of the camshaft; if a and b are the lengths of the two parts of the rocker, and the camshaft lift is represented by A, then the valve lift is $A \times a/b$; with direct-acting cams, the valve lift is equal to the camshaft lift

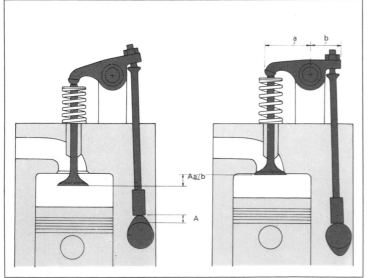

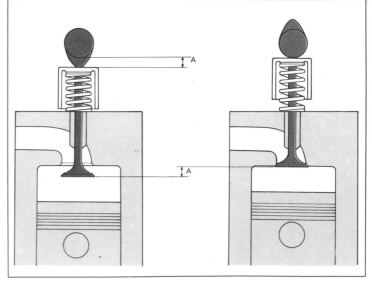

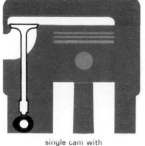

single cam with
side valves

two cams with
side valves

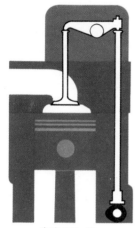

single cam with
pushrod and rocker

single cam with direct
operation of exhaust
valve and indirect
operation of inlet

single cam in head

single cam in head
with valves in V
operated by rockers

with finger rocker

two cams in head
with valves in V

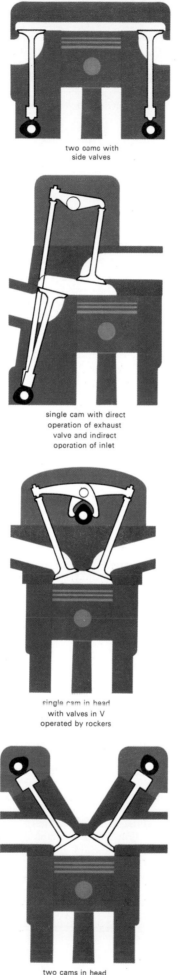

enough now for it to be possible to make helical springs that will not pass through natural resonance frequencies anywhere in the operating range of the engine. The means whereby it is done are numerous. For a start, the number of coils is minimised, although it should never be less than four and a half) so as to reduce the mass and inertia of the spring; and progressive-rate springs are now popular, a progressively decreasing pitch on the coils having the result of varying the number of effective coils throughout the lifting and lowering operation (as they are in turn compressed solid, starting from the closest pitched end), the natural frequency of the spring varying accordingly, and surge being thus avoided, possibly at some cost in noise of operation which can be heard as a hiss. There are still some vehicles around in which the springs are true simple straight torsion bars, although the last cars to employ these were, in production, the Panhard flat twins, and in racing the Formula Two Honda engine used in the Brabham chassis in 1966.

In the primeval days of the petrol engine when speeds were low, when gas inertia was ignored and when big stationary industrial engines provided what little guidance was available, only the exhaust valves would be mechanically opened and subsequently controlled by a rotating cam. The inlet valve was left to its own devices, and was supposed to function automatically. It was made very light and held on its seat by an extremely light spring: when the piston had descended sufficiently on its suction stroke to reduce the pressure within the cylinder below that of the ambient atmosphere, the pressure difference would force the valve open against its feeble spring, which would close it again as soon as parity of pressures was almost achieved. If the spring were too heavy the valve would not open for long enough, but if it were too light the valve might not be properly sealed·when closed, and it could not move sufficiently quickly. When mechanical operation of the inlet valve was popularised by Maybach in the 1901 Mercédès, the stage was set for rapid improvement in engine performance.

From then on, it became common, albeit briefly, for an in-line multi-cylinder engine to have two camshafts. Today, one of the first questions of an enthusiast about a new engine is an enquiry about how many camshafts it has and where they might be; but in those days they were always set in the flanks of the crankcase where they could conveniently be driven by half-speed gearing from the nose of the crankshaft. The camshaft on one side would operate the inlet valves, that on the other the exhaust valves, and the resulting configuration of side valves was popularly described as the T-head. It allowed the manufacture of nice symmetrical castings that did not suffer too much from distortion, and it allowed plenty of room for access to the valves, usually through threaded plugs in the top of the shallow cylinder head; but it made it quite impossible to contrive a compact well shaped combustion chamber, and the studies carried out by Ricardo encouraged most manufacturers to adopt side-by-side valves in what was distinguished as the L-head configuration: it had the added virtue of manufacturing economy, since all the necessary cams could be made integral with a single shaft, reducing the number of bearings and gears in the engine, although making the casting of the cylinder block rather more difficult since inlet ˈand exhaust passages now had to enter and leave it on the same side.

In modest cars for the man in the street, L-head engines survived for decades, especially in the USA and Great Britain. Difficulties of aspiration through the necessarily tortuous passages, of combustion control, and of compression ratio, prevented it from ever being very powerful; but those same breathing difficulties, which became more and more pronounced as the speed rose, gave it a most welcome back-up torque characteristic, so that the 'sidevalver' became renowned for its flexibility. This was an engine characteristic in great demand before the days of the synchromesh gearbox: the Americans tended to have fairly big engines and did not need to change gear much, the English to have fairly small ones, but all too often they could not change gear much, so in either case the side-valve unit was popular until the early 1950s. From the valve-gear point of view, it was attractive in some ways, for the camshaft could

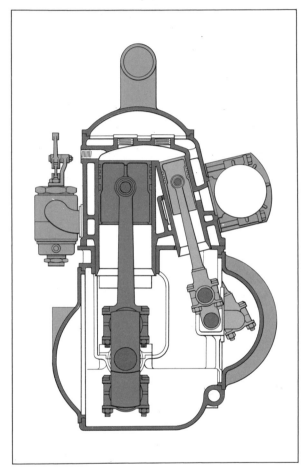

exercise almost direct attack upon the valve stems with no interposition needed except of simple light cylindrical tappets to take the side thrust from the wiping action of the cams, rather than allow the slender and ill-supported valve stems to suffer it. Thus, the valve train weight was as little as it could be; and with the entire apparatus lodged in the crankcase and cylinder block—which were generally integrated—there were very few problems of differential expansion, and so adjustment of the slight clearances necessary between tappets and cams or valve stems was not too often needed. When it had to be done, it could be done easily, for the mechanism was readily accessible—or at least it was until more voluminous bodywork came into vogue, whereupon it began to be very difficult indeed to reach the valve chest.

Long before this unhappy situation came about, particular people had tired of the inefficiency that was the root cause of the 'sidevalver's' flexibility. Studies of the combustion process, in which once again Ricardo was outstanding but by no means the first, and perhaps only by a short head the greatest, had begun to dominate engine-design thinking, as had some aware-

ness of gas flow into and out of it; and no designer conscious of new things can long reconcile himself to a side-valve layout. From that time on, half the developments in valve gear (an unfortunate term, but *valve mechanism* evidently took too long to say for it to become a popular expression) were merely means to a different end, which was securing good combustion-chamber shape and port shapes; the rest have merely been contrivances to allow the valves to be put where they were wanted without vast manufacturing expense or forbidding maintenance difficulties.

Because there is more to engine design than simply making the valves big and moving them easily, the

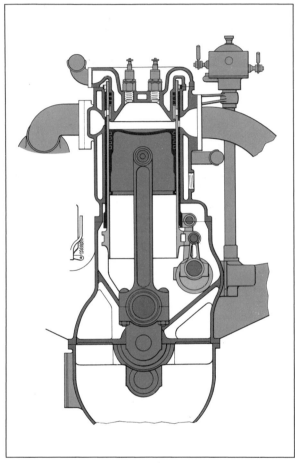

half-way house known as ohiv (overhead inlet valve, the exhaust valve remaining in the original side-valve position) was doomed from the start. It allowed the valves to be very large, admittedly; but the exhaust valve was still badly located for cooling, while the inlet valve (which was large and heavy to start with) had entrained with it a pushrod and rocker to communicate motion from the camshaft—still tucked away in the bowels of the engine—and so the advantages were not very great, while the disadvantages of a singularly clumsy combustion-chamber shape remained to make such engines unsuitable for all but a certain class of Rover and Rolls-Royce customer. The properly efficient overhead-valve engine had both sets of valves overhead—but the production engineers were still wedded to their old crankcases with a place for the camshaft within, where it could be driven by the simplest of means (usually gears or a chain) from the nose of the crankshaft, and where it could conveniently serve also to drive the oil pump and ignition distributor by means of a skew gear conventionally set at or near its middle. With the camshaft down here, and the valves up there, communication promised to be difficult.

Mercedes F1 (1954)

Vagova (1925)

Above, far left: the Hewitt valve arrangement of 1905, with an auxiliary piston to control the flow of inlet charge and exhaust gas

Above left: the Knight double sleeve-valve layout, in which the two sleeves slide up and down under the command of a special crankshaft

Bignan (1922)

Peugeot (1912)

Above: a selection of desmodromic valves employed over the years; different manufacturers have their own ways of causing positive closing of the valves

Right: the Aspin rotary valve is one of the few alternatives to the poppet valve which has been taken seriously as an efficient competitor

A conventional solution was to employ pushrods and rockers. Tappets or cam followers still took the brunt of the cam lobes' attack, transferring the lateral loads through their cylindrical faces to the bores in which they moved piston-like in the crankcase casting. Hemispherical recesses on the upper face of the tappets accepted ball-ended rods, sometimes solid and slender, at other times tubular and stiff, reaching up to higher altitudes than the valves themselves, and prodding rocker beams whose other extremities levered down the valves against the usual springs. It all meant a lot of extra weight, and so the springs had to be stronger, which in turn meant higher seating pressures, and higher loads throughout the valve-actuating mechanism. The fact that engines of this type run to higher speeds than the old 'sidevalvers' commonly did was due to the better breathing and burning that the arrangement made possible, for mechanically the system was basically *less* suited to high-frequency operation. This in itself forced engineers to exercise a good deal more brainpower on the evolution of improved cam shapes, with the result that there have been some pushrod engines capable of running very fast indeed: 10,000 rpm in Formula Three engines a few years ago, and even higher figures in motor cycles earlier still (how about 11,000 rpm in the 'works' 350 Douglas of the early 1950s?) indicate that such systems can be made to work well.

Apart from getting the cam right and the springs reliable, most of the difficulties centred around adjustment and variation of the necessary back-lash in the system. Different expansion rates of all the various components as they grew hot during operation would cause the overall length of the operating train to vary considerably. The back-lash had to be kept as small as possible, not only to reduce the noise, but also to minimise the mechanical shock of impact as clearances were taken up during the valve-lifting phase; but if the clearances were too small, there would be a danger that when everything reached a certain temperature, the clearances would disappear altogether, and the valve might not be free to seat properly, in which case it would quickly be wrecked by flames searing through the gap.

The first and last palliative to be effective was the hydraulic or zero-lash tappet, essentially a small piston inside a larger one, with the intervening space being taken up by high-pressure oil, the pressure being sufficient to ensure that all the usual clearances were taken up at all times, but at the same time not high enough to be capable of lifting the valve off its seat. Ordinary engine oil from the delivery side of the pump was led into the tappets and bled out of them again, and the result was an ohv engine that could be remarkably quiet mechanically. The hydraulic tappet has become almost the norm in the engines of luxury cars and most big Americans, but not without introducing a few snags of its own: the two most notable are, first, a critical tendency to internal corrosion (making hydraulic tappets the most demanding part of a modern engine from the oil technologists' viewpoint) and an inability to operate accurately at very high speeds, which is why zero-lash tappets do not figure in high-performance engines.

Many other refinements were introduced to ohv operation by pushrods. In an effort to reduce the mass of the operating mechanism, camshafts were sometimes set very high in the cylinder block, so that the pushrods could be made correspondingly shorter and stiffer. Some manufacturers, including Riley, Lea-Francis, and Darracq, went one better by having exhaust and inlet camshafts mounted high on opposite flanks of the cylinder block, thus making it possible for the inlet and exhaust valves to be placed opposite each other and inclined into a hemispherical combustion chamber, rather than being condemned to stand in line along the length of the cylinder head, to the detriment of breathing and combustion-chamber shape alike. Other manufacturers tried cheaper ways of achieving the same valve arrangement, sometimes by grotesquely long rockers reaching across the head from one side to the other, sometimes by transverse pushrods transmitting motion from primary rockers at the top of the vertical pushrods to secondary ones in contact with the valves on the far side of the head.

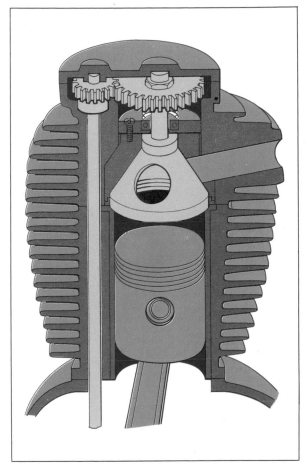

It may seem extraordinary that they should go to such lengths when the logical thing to do, having transposed the valves to their desired positions in the cylinder head, would have been to shift the camshaft or shafts up there too, so as to provide direct attack without all the intermediary burden of pushrods and rockers. In racing, of course, this step was taken early, a sharp Swiss called Ernest Henry stealing the idea from his employer, Marc Birkigt (another Swiss, but cleverer and better behaved) at Hispano-Suiza and taking it to Peugeot for exploitation in their racing cars in the second decade of this century. This arrangement it should be emphasised, was of two overhead camshafts, separately controlling banks of inlet and exhaust valves that could therefore be disposed freely according to the designer's preferences concerning porting and combustion-chamber design; a single overhead camshaft operating in-line valves or, in more developed form, operating inclined opposing valves by means of rockers, had been used by Fiat and Mercédès years earlier.

In racing, and in the best-bred sports cars, overhead camshafts were considered *de rigueur* by the 1920s; in luxury cars, touring cars and especially the cheaper types that were built up in large quantities and down to a price, they were considered untenable by production engineers and salesmen for very much longer. Their objections were wholly practical rather than theoretical, being based mainly on the difficulty of providing a suitable drive from the crankshaft to the camshafts without indulging in expansion joints and expensive gears that were in any case likely to be noisy. Eventually some engineers made tentative experiments with

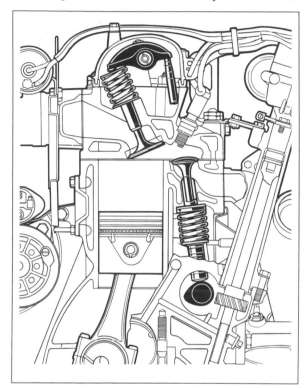

Right: the side-exhaust, overhead-inlet layout of the Vanden Plas 4-litre R's Rolls-Royce engine; this arrangement allows for big valves, but has several disadvantages

Far right, above: a section through the Fiat Topolino engine, showing the side-valve set-up used on nearly every car in the early days of motoring; although simple to operate, the side valve limits combustion-chamber design

Far right, below: the pushrod-and-rocker arrangement is simple, allowing overhead valves and block-mounted cam, but the mass of the linkage tends to limit the speed of operation; this diagram is of a Fiat 124 engine

chains, notably Weller who designed the two-litre AC and invented a spring-bladed chain tensioner that would do a fairly satisfactory job of taking up any slack in the drive. Noise remained a problem because it was more difficult to damp the clatter of valve gear at the top of an engine than in its bottom, and chains were often of parlous durability; moreover, the difficulties of adjusting tappet clearances gave the overhead camshaft a very bad name among mechanics in the trade, who did not take kindly to having to strip most of the mechanism in order to insert shims between the valve stem tips and the conventional piston-type tappets.

Not until the late 1960s were these difficulties overcome, when Fiat and General Motors both made notable contributions to the state of the art and allowed overhead-camshaft engines to be enjoyed by the most ordinary and unambitious of motorists. The problem of providing a satisfactory drive was dealt with by the newly developed internally toothed belt, which was quieter, more positive, more easily tensioned and much more easily installed than the chain. The rest of the noise problem was dealt with at source by refinements of cam profile, designed to take up back-lash gradually, rather than suddenly. As for lash adjustment, the best modern means is probably that which was adapted by Fiat from an earlier design by the engineer Remor for MV Agusta racing motor cycles, and employed first by Fiat in the engine of their 125 car. Here, the adjusting shims fit into a recess on top of the inverted cup tappet so that adjustment is merely a matter of using a special tool to compress the

spring and hold the tappet down, while the appropriate shim can be slipped between tappet and cam. The General Motors method, first seen in the Vauxhall Victor at about the same time, was undoubtedly ingenious: a fine-threaded hole is bored at an angle of $5\frac{1}{2}°$ into the tappet and a taper-faced adjusting screw is wound into it. The taper on the screw corresponds to the angle of the hole, so the face is at right-angles to the axis of the tappet and provides an abutment for the tip of the valve stem. Each turn of the screw alters the

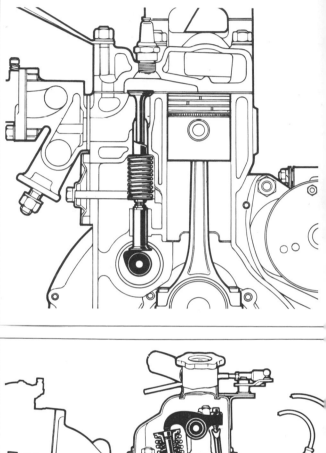

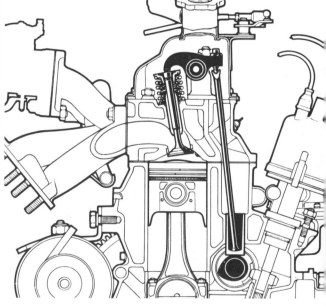

clearance by 0.003 inch. Unfortunately, the Vauxhall system makes the tappet itself rather heavy, putting reciprocating weight where it is not wanted, and thus negating a basic advantage of overhead-camshaft location. Thus, for a valve weighing 3.23 oz, the Vauxhall valve train's sprung mass amounted to 7.734 oz, of which 3.74 were accounted for by the tappet; by contrast, Fiat's corresponding inlet valve, weighing 3.315 oz, was part of a sprung valve-train mass totalling

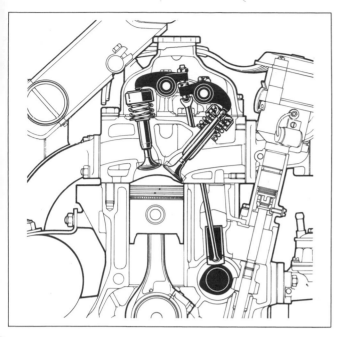

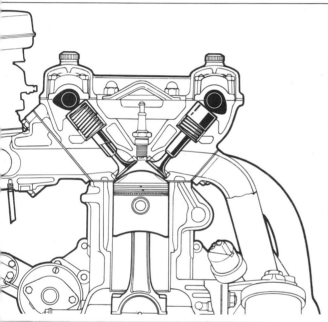

only 6.911 oz, the tappet accounting for 1.834 oz.

Those manufacturers preferring to interpose rockers or finger followers between a cam and the valve stem sometimes provide the necessary adjustment by pivoting the fingers on individual ball studs which can be screwed up or down to vary their height. In the most refined versions of this system, the pillar supporting the rocker or lever pivot is pumped up by engine oil pressure to maintain zero back-lash, on principles exactly similar to those of the hydraulic tappet.

Given all these refinements, the single overhead camshaft is very efficient, and the advantage of shaft duplication are more difficult to justify. The main one is that it leaves the space between the banks of valves clear for the insertion of spark plugs or downdraught inlet ports, or coolant conduits, as well as giving the designer complete freedom to choose whatever included angle he likes between the two banks of valves. This angle is in turn determined by his preferences in combustion-chamber and port design but, in any case, the convention of two inclined valves in a hemispherical combustion chamber, as introduced by Fiat

in 1921 and emulated by all the best racing and sporting engines up to the 1960s, received a rude shock when Honda began to produce racing motor cycles with very small cylinders in which nevertheless they found it worthwhile to set four valves, however tiny. Honda had the advantage of being a young firm unfettered by tradition, so it was mere coincidence that this four-valve layout should constitute a reversion to the Edwardian practice instigated by Birkigt with the Hispano-Suizas.

A multiplicity of small valves is a good thing. It allows an engine to run hotter, for a small valve has a greater ratio of surface area to mass than has one that is larger but geometrically similar; thus, the small valve

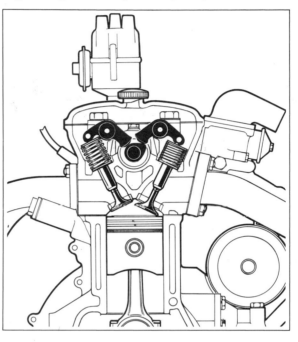

is better able to shed heat. It allows higher rates of revolution, for a small valve has less mass for the cams to accelerate and the springs to control. It allows high volumetric efficiency, for the area of the four biggest valves that can be squeezed into a given head is greater than that of the two biggest valves that can there be placed, and the engine's port areas will be commensurately greater.

The same ends could be achieved by the use of desmodromic valve gear, in which positive mechanical closure of the valves supplants springs and allows longer and higher valve lift. Daimler-Benz did it with complete success in their Grand Prix cars of 1954 and 1955, while Ducati swept their motor-cycling board with it even earlier, and for that matter there were successful four-wheeled exemplars as early as the Grand Prix Delage of 1914. However, it requires a greater degree of engineering skill to make satisfactory desmodromic valve gear than it does to insert half-sized valves in double the numbers into an engine, and so the example of Honda was soon followed by others. In 1962, the V6 GP Ferrari was modified to have 24 valves instead of twelve, a change that allowed the power output and the engine speed both to be raised by about 5%. Three years later, the Coventry Climax V8 GP engine was introduced in 32-valve form, the reduced inertia of the lighter valves making possible an rpm increase of 12%. This was accompanied by improvements in power and torque of 5% and 3% respectively, while the four-valved engine also had a useful power band of 3500 rpm, 1000 more than the range of the two-valve unit. Moreover, the increase in

Left: an ingenious arrangement used by BMW in their 1800 to operate two inclined valves per cylinder with one overhead camshaft; the inclined valves make possible a hemispherical or pent-roofed combustion chamber, either of which is efficient

Far left, above: another way of operating inclined valves with one camshaft; this Fiat 1800 engine has its pushrods in line, driving through opposed pushrods

Far left, below: one of the most popular layouts of the 1960s and 70s is this one, with inclined overhead valves operated directly by a pair of camshafts; this keeps the mass of the mechanism as low as possible; the engine shown is that of the Alfa Romeo Giulia

Above: four types of valve-operating rocker which have been used at various times in the history of motoring

Right: two ways of operating inclined valves; with one cam and rockers, or with two cams

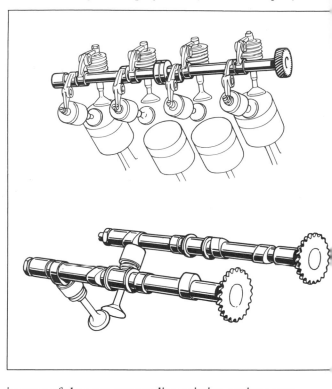

low fuel consumption (not to mention its ability to use very low-grade fuel) due to its automatic charge stratification. At the time of writing, the Aspin and the Cross were both still being earnestly developed and propounded, which was more than could be said for the various kinds of sleeve valve which also attracted engineers in the past. In fact, the sleeve valve is the only type that has rivalled the poppet valve for any significant period in the history of the motor car: the Knight double-sleeve valve was extensively used by Daimler, Minerva, Willys and (especially throughout the best part of the two decades between the World Wars) by Panhard; the Burt single-sleeve valve was employed by Argyll in 1912 and by Vauxhall in 1926, thereafter being taken up by Bristol, and later Napier,

maximum speed being greater than the increase in power, it was possible for gear ratios in a given installation to be lowered, thus multiplying the engine torque so that there was even more surplus tractive effort available at the driving wheels for acceleration from a given speed. Honda having demonstrated in a technical paper some years ago that the pentroof head of the four-valve engine is as good as the hemispherical head of the two-valve type in terms of combustion efficiency (and, incidentally, that the two are appreciably better than any other popular configuration), the speed advantage remains clear, together with the possibility that the smaller valves may be made of a cheaper material because the smaller size means they are inherently cooler running.

Of course, there have been designers and inventors galore to whom the whole idea of the reciprocating poppet valve and all its attendant mechanism was anathema. History records a plethora of rotary valves, piston valves, sleeve valves and numerous others, all apparently intended to substitute nice continuous motions for the nasty accelerations and decelerations to which the poppet is doomed; but they themselves were doomed to failure, simply because the earliest of them came just a few years too late, and because during the critical period of their development, metallurgy was some years ahead of lubrication, which was usually their Achilles heel. Today, poppet valves can be made to function as fast as may be desired, but the best rotary valves have other advantages that may still validly be championed. These include the elimination of hot spots in the combustion chamber, the reduction of operating noise, very fast opening of the ports (important when exploiting gas dynamics for good charging and scavenging), completely clear throughways at maximum port opening, and often a better shape for the combustion chamber. Undoubtedly, the best and most promising are the Cross and the Aspin, the former having been developed to a greater immunity from lubrication problems and the latter showing itself particularly good at combining high power with a very

in some of the most outstanding aviation engines ever to leave planet Earth—or at least ever to make it off the ground with pistons.

The principle of the sleeve valve is that of a loose liner forming the cylinder bore and which is free to move in a required path, its outer surface fitting closely in the fixed bore of the cylinder block, and constituting a bearing, while holes in the sleeve register at appropriate times with fixed ports in the block. With a simple linear motion along the axis of the bore, a single sleeve cannot give satisfactory port timing, but if two concentric reciprocating sleeves are moved out of phase, perfectly satisfactory timing can be attained, and this was the basis of the Knight system. For a single sleeve, the necessary motion is partly axial and partly rotational, the result being a continuous elliptical movement, and this was the outcome of Burt's ideas. It demands very high-quality manufacture, and rather expensive materials, if it is to work satisfactorily, but there are no other objections to it, and it undoubtedly gives exceptional results. It may be worth pointing out that the sleeve-valve Napier Sabre had the highest specific power output of any piston engine in aviation, while the sleeve-valved Bristol Centaurus was, in its final civil form, the most reliable, having an overhaul life of no less than three thousand hours, which is equivalent to about five years driving by the average motor-car user.

WHEN WE ARE FIRST introduced to the four-stroke cycle, we are taught that the four successive motions of the piston, taking place during two consecutive revolutions of the crankshaft, correspond to the induction, compression, combustion and exhaust phases. Like so many other simplifications drilled into us in the elementary stages of our education and upbringing, this is simply inaccurate and untrue. An engine in which the inlet valve opened with the piston at the top of its stroke, and closed again when it reached the bottom to complete the supposed induction phase, followed after an interval of 360° crankshaft rotation by the exhaust valve opening with the piston at the bottom of its stroke, and closing when it had reached the top, would admittedly work—but it would only work very slowly. Its combustion would be dirty, its power slight and its usefulness as an automotive propulsion unit seriously debatable. It takes time to set a column of air in motion, and once this has been done it will keep on keeping on for some time after the inductive encouragement has been suspended, for there is inertia in air as in anything

VALVE TIMING

choosing the right moment

engineering. As the power is increased, so flexibility diminishes: the engine with long valve openings and overlap will not run slowly, just as the engine with elementary timing will not run fast.

The modern petrol engine is essentially a high-speed engine, its maximum cyclic frequency rising steadily with the passage of the years. Touring-car engines

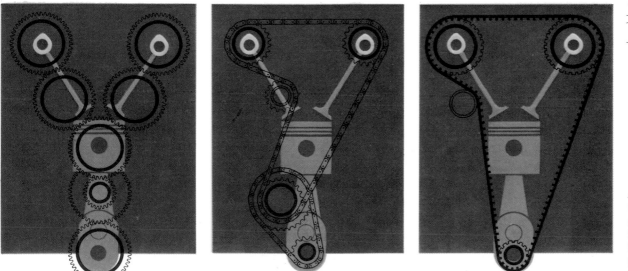

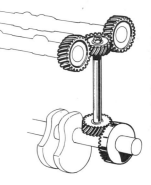

Above and left: four ways of driving overhead camshafts from the crankshaft— from left these are with gears, chain, internally toothed belt and shaft; the toothed belt is a recent innovation and it has two advantages in that it is quiet and it runs outside the engine, needing no lubrication

else having mass. The same applies to the waste gases produced by combustion, and the lesson to be deduced from all this is that if the engine is to be efficient as a pump—which in some senses is what it amounts to— the valves must be opened before basic logic suggests it should be necessary, and their closure should be deferred until some time later than might be thought prudent. In fact, during the 720° of crankshaft rotation involved in a complete four-stroke cycle, the inlet valve of even the most mild-mannered modern touring car will be open for about 230°, the exhaust valve will be open for about the same extent and there will be a brief period of perhaps 25° overlap during which the exhaust valve will not yet have shut, and the inlet valve will already have opened. That leaves only 285° for the compression and expansion phases that theoretically occupy 360°. When one looks at the valve timing of a racing engine, one is faced with the paradox that, despite the reduction of this period (when the useful work might be supposed to be done) to something like 190°, the power output is very much greater. Clearly it is the time (or rather, the proportion of the time) spent in pumping gases in and out of the engine that varies more or less in proportion to the power achieved: in a Grand Prix engine, each valve may be open for about 325°, both open and overlapping for as much as 120°.

Of course, there are attendant disadvantages, compromise raising its ugly head here as elsewhere in

currently turn over at rates of rpm that were considered the giddy limit for sports-car engines twenty years ago, and were the exclusive preserve of racers twenty years before that. About ten years ago, there were racing motor cycles with four-stroke engines reaching 23,000 rpm, and their manufacturer (Honda) subsequently asserted in a technical paper that most of the problems of petrol engine operation disappear beyond 10,000 rpm! Even without going to such extremes—if they are extremes, for research was already being carried out then on engines whose pistons fluttered up and down 50,000 times a minute—the kinetic energy of a moving mass of gas can be exploited in surprising ways.

If the exhaust be opened some time before the piston has completed its expansion stroke, the pressure of combustion gases in the cylinder will be so high that they will rush out precipitately through the exhaust port when it opens, departing with such violence and velocity that they leave a partial vacuum behind them in the cylinder. If the inlet valve is then opened sufficiently early that low pressures will immediately induce a flow of fresh charge air into the cylinder through the inlet port, despite the fact that the piston is still rising towards the top of its stroke, and might be thought to be compressing the cylinder's contents. In fact, during the overlap period, while both valves are open, the rarefaction left in the exhaust ports by the headlong departure of the exhaust gases communicates such a strong suction effect to the inlet port that volumes of fresh air are drawn straight though to the combustion chamber, cooling it and scouring out the last traces of vitiated gases, so that when the exhaust valve closes, with the piston already on its way down the cylinder, the column of air in the inlet tract has been so energetically accelerated that it will keep on piling into the cylinder even after the piston has reached the bottom of its stroke and has started moving upwards again. Clearly the art—or science—lies in knowing when each valve should open and close.

In the case of engines developing very high bhp per unit of capacity, the operating characteristics of the valves themselves become of major importance. In endeavouring to obtain acceleration and opening periods aimed at a certain specific power output, many forms of cam contour have appeared, but since any alteration in this respect must affect the whole of the operating gear in important matters such as power loss, noise, reliability and maintenance of tune, it is obvious that any departure from established practice has to be thoroughly tested. Ideally, each valve should reach its full lift instantaneously, remain fully open for the whole of this period and close in the same manner as it opened. In practice, the limiting factors in obtaining the maximum through-way area for the longest period are three: the rate of acceleration that the valve train can sustain, the rate of deceleration that the valve springs can ensure and the maximum velocity that the valve may be permitted to attain.

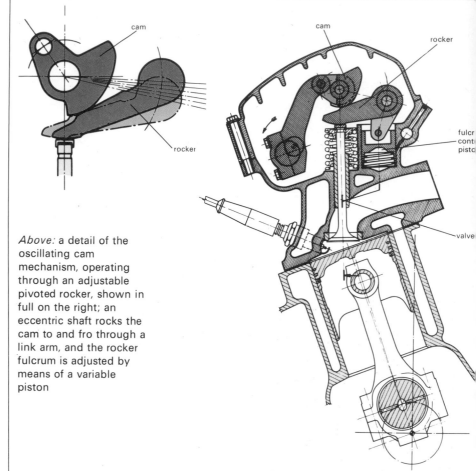

Above: a detail of the oscillating cam mechanism, operating through an adjustable pivoted rocker, shown in full on the right; an eccentric shaft rocks the cam to and fro through a link arm, and the rocker fulcrum is adjusted by means of a variable piston

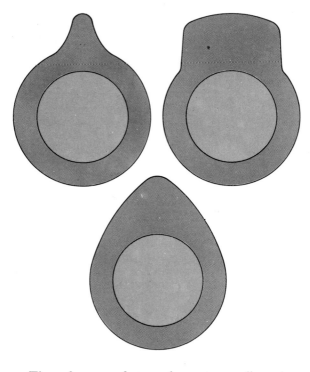

These factors unfortunately turn most discussions of cam profiles into cumbersome and scarcely intelligible displays of advanced mathematics. Essential as it may be to the practitioner, an understanding of such mathematics is not necessary to the discussion of the principles involved. In avoiding the maths, we will instead have to consider a few practical facts—practical because, although the problems they create can be circumvented by elaborate means such as the use of desmodromic valve mechanisms, such means are generally considered too expensive to be justified.

Valve float is the first of these uncomfortable facts. For a valve of given mass and subject to a given spring restraint, there is a critical lift velocity beyond which

Left: three diagrams showing how the camshaft profile has evolved; in the early days, it consisted of a circle with a small bump on it; later this bump was widened to keep the valves open as long as was practical; finally ramps were built in to open and close each valve as smoothly as possible, thus imposing minimal strain on the mechanism

the valve will carry on lifting, even though the cam may be dictating a deceleration towards the intended level of maximum lift. This is one way in which valves can be made to clout pistons. The simplest cure is to make the valve lighter, but then you may run into problems of mechanical strength being inadequate. Next best is to fit stronger springs (assuming, to begin with, that the springs are of such number and design as to obviate surge due to their own harmonic sensitivities), but then you increase the loads on the valve seat and throughout the train of components lying between the seat and the camshaft bearings. If this idea does not appeal, then the only solution (short of admitting defeat and running the engine more slowly) is to reprofile the cam so that the valve does not exceed its critical or 'escape' velocity.

Next, we have to consider another factor which can increase the loads on the valve gear. This is the rate of acceleration of the valve (and attendant bits) from its seat. It is obviously desirable that the valve be accelerated as quickly as possible to its limiting velocity: the more urgent its elevation, the more effective is its opening—not only because a sudden opening has a beneficial effect on the generation of pressure and shock waves upon whose exploitation volumetric efficiency so much depends. Nevertheless, there remains the fact that inertia loads on the valve-operating mechanism are another expression of valve acceleration; and clearly there must be mechanical limits to what any particular set of valve gear can stand. Sometimes designers err on the side of caution: in no less celebrated a case than the V16 supercharged BRM, it proved that severe breathing restrictions and consequent failure to realise the anticipated power were due to a pessimistic figure (actually 52,000 ft per sec^2) adopted for maximum valve acceleration, this limit in turn imposing a deleterious reduction in the valve lift possible.

Limited though they must be, the accelerations to which the valve may be subjected by the cam and paraphernalia lifting it off its seat are considerably more violent than those that can be produced in the opposite direction by any valve springs of tolerable strength.

Below: the cylinder head of the Alfa Romeo 6C 1750 Sport, showing the shaft and gear drive to the twin camshafts

Bottom left: the cam block and belt-drive pulley of the Fiat 128

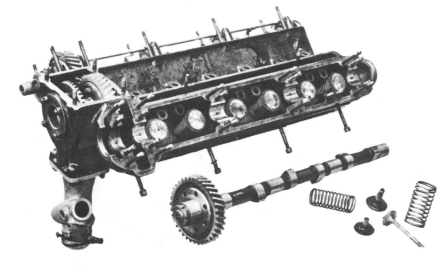

punishing smack as the essential clearance is taken up —a process bad for ear and engine alike.

These opening and closing ramps are of no little importance to the timing of the valve sequence. The more shallow their gradients, the longer does it take for valve opening to be really effective, and the sooner does the effective closure of the valve occur—in other words, they can shorten the timing, reducing a theoretical duration of opening by as much as 20°. They also make critical the correct adjustment of the tappet clearances: it is not uncommon for an extra 0.01 in of clearance to delay opening and precipitate closure by as much as 20° each, and so reduce total duration of opening from, say, 280° to 240°—a reduction which could be of great relevance to exhaust-system design in a six-cylinder engine.

Already we have said enough to make it clear that the conventional summary of camshaft timing, by reference to the degrees of crankshaft rotation corresponding to the opening and closure of each valve, is inadequate. Taking the DB4 Aston Martin cam as an example, we find that the inlet opens 28° before top dead centre and the exhaust closes 22° after tdc, the exhaust opening 62° before bottom dead centre and the inlet closing 68° after bdc. In the jargon of engineers, this is shorthanded as 28–68–62–22; and you can go further and add up the total duration of opening of each valve, arriving at figures of 276° and 264° for inlet and exhaust valves, respectively. As a first approxi-

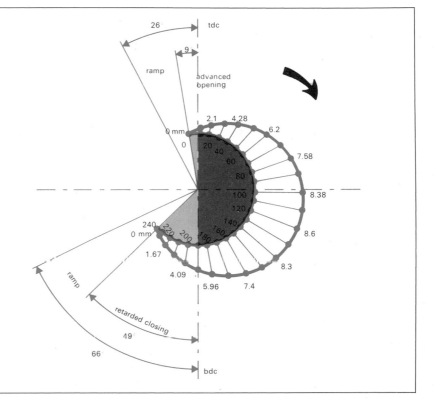

Proportionally longer, then, is the time that must be spent in decelerating the valve; and deceleration, remember, involves not only slowing it down as it comes to the top of its lift but also returning it to its seat. Perhaps it is easier to think of this second or closing phase as positive acceleration downwards, rather than as negative acceleration upwards—if only because we shall then be less confused by the need to abate this acceleration in the final stages of closure, so as to lower the valve as gently as possible onto its seat. If this is not done, then valve and seat will suffer damage, as also will the intervening components of the valve train as the system collapses to produce the clearances normally necessary to allow for differential thermal expansion.

The gradual deceleration is produced by what is commonly called a ramp, a portion of the cam profile that gets gradually nearer to being tangential to the base circle of the cam. It has its counterpart on the opening flank of the cam, which slowly establishes contact with the valve before the full opening acceleration is applied to the system. Without such a ramp, the valve train would have to endure a most almighty and

Above: a diagram showing valve lift as a function of crankshaft angle (Abarth Formula Italia); in theory the valve should be open only for 80°, but in practice this has to be enlarged for maximum efficiency

mation, it tells us something, although not much, for we know that, as a general rule, a duration of more than 250° is rather sporting and 300 or more is definitely racy. Likewise, overlap (the interval between inlet opening and exhaust closing) is mild at 30° and very sporting at 80, while 120 puts the engine right into the Formula One class.

Nevertheless, the shorthand 30–70–70–30 business can be very misleading. Properly to see what a cam does, you must look at a graph of lift plotted against crankshaft rotation. From this, you can see and measure the area underneath the curve, the height of

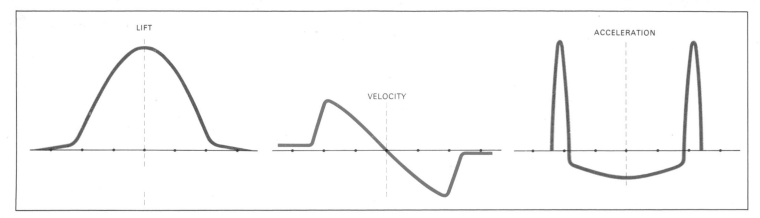

LIFT

VELOCITY

ACCELERATION

Above: graphical representations of the lift, velocity and acceleration of the valve as a function of time; the lift of the valve is dependent not only on cam lift, but on rocker arrangement; the velocity curve should be continuous, because any break indicates that the tappet clearance is too large and is causing knock; it is important that the negative acceleration is not too great, otherwise the valve may cease to follow the profile of the cam

Right: a diagram (top) showing the opening periods of inlet and exhaust valves relative to crankshaft angle; the lower diagrams show how a gauge can be used to check the exact timing of the camshaft by measuring the crankshaft position at which the valves begin to open and reach full closure (in turn measured on a dial gauge)

Bottom right: the 'rubber-band' drive to the primitive camshaft of the 1899 3.5 hp Fiat

which is a measure of the area of valve opening at any chosen instant, and the total area under which is a measure of how much flow can take place during the operation of the cam. By plotting the curves for exhaust and intake cams on the same chart, a clear idea of the value of the overlap can be gathered.

Even these curves can be misleading if they are calculated from the shape of the cam itself. What the valve does, may be, and usually is, rather different from what the cam orders, for the mechanism interposed between these two principal elements is—for all its apparent rigidity—elastic and springy. Rockers flex, pushrods bend, slight compressive tremors occur during heavy accelerations, and the upshot of it all is that at certain points in the cycle the valve may be lagging behind the cam, while at others it may be ahead of it. This has been known for a very long time: the Lorraine Dietrich which did so well at Le Mans in the mid 1920s had very long and very thin pushrods which could be seen flexing, but fortuitously the flexure was such as to improve the valve action at high speeds! Today, it is not unusual for cam profiles to be corrected to take the elasticity of the valve train into account; but the process is fraught with problems, for such corrections cannot be equally effective at all speeds, nor equally effective at all points in the valve train. For instance, if the calculations allow for the flexure of everything, including the rods and rockers, then the tappet itself will be forced to undergo some very rapid and distressing reversals of acceleration, moving the area of accelerated wear and possible damage from the valve to the cam and tappet assembly, where it is usually more difficult to reach and often more expensive to repair.

Now that we know the main problems governing valve motion we can consider how the cam profile is generated so as to produce them. Inaccuracies apart, valve motion is harmonic and may be graphically represented either by a sine wave, in the case of the simplest or harmonic cam (the circular eccentric), or by a combination of parts of different sine waves, as is more common. The main trouble with the simple harmonic cam, whose flanks are compounded from a quartet of circular arcs, is that it makes no provision for the gradual take-up of clearances; although such cams served us well for many years, they are now considered obsolete. The multi-sine-wave cam embodies the necessary opening and closing ramps, and naturally calls for more care in calculation and in manufacture, since there are more curves to be blended into each other. The addition of further corrective curves to deal with discrepancies in valve-train motion complicate the issue still more—although not as much as the seemingly arbitrary decision of certain cam specialists such as Iskenderian to substitute polynomial theorems for the trigonometrical ones from which the harmonic series derive. When this is done, only the prodigious capabilities of the electronic computer make the exercise feasible, thus limiting the availability of such devices.

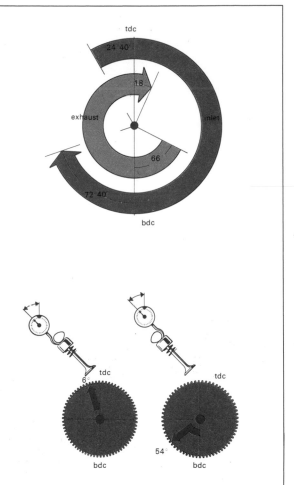

TAPPETS

an important part of the valve train

THE TAPPET, known also as the cam follower or valve lifter, is a small member interposed between each camshaft lobe and the valve lifting mechanism, or the valve itself, depending on engine design.

'Valve lifting' means raising the valve off its seat. Only on side valve engines is the valve actually lifted upwards; overhead valves are actually depressed in order to 'lift' or open them.

As a camshaft rotates, each lobe produces both a vertical and a side thrust. The side thrust does no useful work and the purpose of the tappet is to eliminate it so that only vertical motion is transmitted to the push rod or valve.

The centre of the tappet is usually offset in relation to the cam—this is done so that the tappet is rotated slightly on each contact with the lobe, thus spreading tappet wear over a large area.

Tappets for conventional-camshaft engines are usually of cylindrical or mushroom shape, about one inch long, and are located in guides machined in the engine block. Sometimes, the inside of the tappet is partially hollowed out so that the push rod fits down inside it; in others, an adjustment screw and locknut is fitted to one end, the pushrod resting in a depression in the screw head. Lubrication is sometimes provided by spiral oil-retaining grooves, machined on the cylindrical face, but more often by oil mist or splashes, or by oil running down the push rod.

The automatically adjusting hydraulic tappet incorporates a spring-loaded plunger inside the main body. A cavity in the plunger is charged with oil through a ball valve. Initially, the spring expands the tappet to take up all the clearance in the valve train. As the cam lifts the valve, the ball valve closes, retaining the oil in the plunger. When the tip of the lobe has passed the tappet, the spring expands slightly, so that oil is drawn into the plunger cavity from that collected at the base of the push rod, the cavity thus being constantly replenished. When the valve stem lengthens with normal heat expansion, the cavity is compressed slightly and surplus oil leaks out through the slight clearance around the circumference of the plunger.

Tappets for overhead camshafts take other forms: some are caps resting directly over the tops of the valve stems (with direct-acting camshafts), while others are levers or 'fingers' (with indirect-acting camshafts), hinged either at the centre or at one end, sometimes with a roller to actuate the valve.

All tappets are 'case hardened'; that is to say, a very hard surface layer is produced on them by heating in a carbonaceous medium. Case hardening enables the tappet to withstand the constant battering it receives, without risk of shattering.

When the engine is running, the valves become heated and the valve stems expand. A certain gap, or clearance, must therefore be provided in the valve-operating train to accommodate this expansion, otherwise the valve will not close properly. On the other

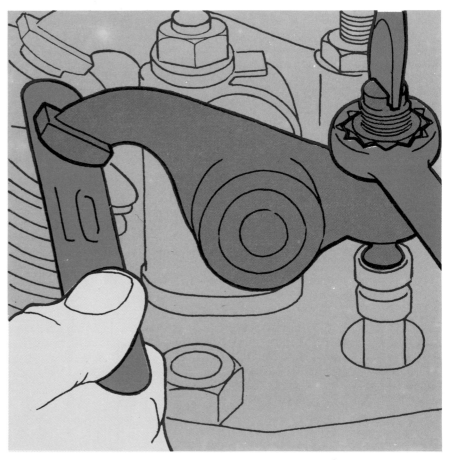

Above: in an engine with valves operated through pushrods and rockers, it is usual to adjust the tappets by means of spanner, screwdriver and feeler gauge

hand, excessive clearance reduces the valve lift and hence the period during which it is fully open. On older vehicles, valve clearances were generally less than today, being about 0.003 in (0.1 mm) for the inlet valves and 0.005 in (0.15 mm) for the exhaust. Frequent adjustment was necessary.

Today, intervals of 6000 or even 10,000 miles between checks and adjustment are commonplace. Clearances are generally between 0.010 and 0.015 in (0.25 and 0.40 mm) for inlet valves and 0.012 and 0.018 in (0.30 and 0.45 mm) for the exhaust, although some manufacturers specify the same clearance for both inlet and exhaust valve mechanisms. The correct clearance for each valve can be set only when the relative cam is turned directly away from the tappet affected. If the camshaft is not visible, the correct cam positions can be found by taking note of the opening and closing of the valves; appropriate information will be found in the manufacturer's handbook.

Measurement of the clearance is made with a feeler gauge, inserted between the cam and tappet or the valve stem and its operating member. The clearance is correct when it is just possible to enter a gauge blade of the designated thickness between the gap. Some manufac-

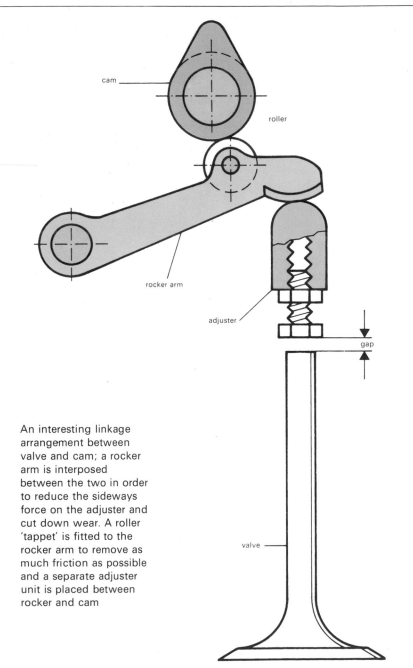

An interesting linkage
arrangement between
valve and cam; a rocker
arm is interposed
between the two in order
to reduce the sideways
force on the adjuster and
cut down wear. A roller
'tappet' is fitted to the
rocker arm to remove as
much friction as possible
and a separate adjuster
unit is placed between
rocker and cam

Top: two types of tappet,
both with adjusters built
in; that on the right has
a roller to reduce friction
between itself and the
cam

tappets or adjustable push rods. Always re-check the
clearance after tightening the locknut, in case the set
screw has moved. Another method is by a self-locking
nut holding down the rocker arm at its centre against a
spring; some manufacturers require the engine to be
running when this type of operating mechanism is
adjusted.

Sometimes shims or pads (known also as capsules)
of varying thicknesses are incorporated into the valve
operating train. The Jaguar, for example, uses a series
of pads, lettered A to Z, rising in steps of 0.001 in from
0.85 in to 0.110 in. If, for instance, an inlet valve
clearance measures 0.007 in, the correct clearance being
0.004 in, and the pad in place is lettered D, the clearance
must be reduced by 0.003 in, therefore a 0.003 in
thicker pad is required, lettered G. With this system,
the pad is usually located in a shallow recess in the
tappet and it may be necessary to compress the valve
spring in order to remove and replace it.

Similar pad or shim systems are used by other
manufacturers. On some overhead camshaft engines,
the camshaft has to be removed before the pads can be
changed. This necessitates the measuring and noting
down of all of the clearances and the correct replacement pads before the camshaft is removed. On some
Vauxhall overhead-camshaft engines, the clearance is
adjusted by a small socket head screw set in the side of
the tappet—one complete turn varies the clearance by
0.003 in (0.08 mm).

When the engine is dismantled, the cam lobes and
the cam face of each tappet should be carefully checked
for wear. These parts, ideally, should be smooth and
free from scores; the circumference of the tappets and
the bore of their guides or housings should be perfectly
round and an easy fit without sideplay. The cam face of
each tappet will show whether the normal rotating or
non-rotating wear pattern is present. The tappet may
be excessively worn, but still in the case-hardened
layer; or it may be 'soft worn', when this layer has been
eroded away. If this softer metal is exposed, wear
increases at a much faster rate and will already have
become apparent by the necessity for frequent adjustment of the valve clearance.

With hydraulic tappets, the walls as well as the ends
should be checked for wear and blowholes (which will
result in oil leakage).

If more than 0.003 in (0.08 mm) side play in the
tappet guides is present, the guide should be reamed
out and an oversize tappet fitted.

Remember that if any part of the engine that affects
the valve clearance is removed and subsequently
replaced, 'bedding down' usually occurs necessitating a
further tightening of securing nuts or screws. Such
items include the cylinder head, rocker arm supports
and overhead camshafts. It is essential to check, and
adjust if necessary, the valve-operating-mechanism
clearances, after this second tightening of these major
components.

turers provide a simple go/no-go gauge in the tool
kit—the 'go' gauge should pass easily between the
gap, but the 'no-go' gauge must not enter.

A common method of adjustment is by set screw and
locknut; with a conventional camshaft and overhead
valves, the screw is usually located in one end of each
rocker arm. Side-valve engines have either adjustable

CAMSHAFT

controlling the valve mechanism

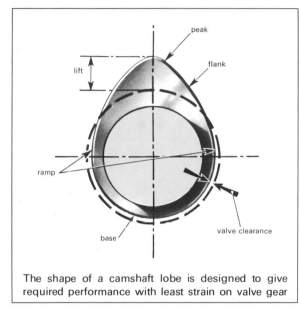

The shape of a camshaft lobe is designed to give required performance with least strain on valve gear

THE CAMSHAFT is a shaft which rotates about its longitudinal axis and carries cams, or eccentric protuberances, intended to impart a linear or angular movement of a cyclic nature to some other component of a machine. Although cams (and hence camshafts) occur in a variety of places in some cars—in steering boxes, ignition distributors, fuel pumps, fuel injection devices, door locks, etc—the term camshaft is, if unqualified, always taken to refer to the shaft which controls the operation of the inlet and/or exhaust valves in a normal four-stroke internal combustion engine.

The camshaft is today invariably (and was in the past generally) located parallel to the crankshaft, from which it is driven by spur gears, chain, toothed belt, or some combination of two such media (never yet by all three) at a rate of revolution half that of the crankshaft. In the earliest side-valve engines, it was natural that the camshaft should lie below the tappets upon which the cams acted to raise the valves, and the conventional location of the camshaft in the crankcase remained the normal practice long after the overhead-valve engine became the rule, for the drive to the camshaft from the crankcase could thus be kept simple and therefore cheap. The drawback of this layout was that the mass of operating linkage between the cams and the valves themselves was increased by the inevitable length of the pushrods. A few designers sought the palliative of locating the camshaft high up in the cylinder block, so as to reduce the mass of the reciprocating valve mechanism.

For really high-performance engines, location of the camshaft above the cylinder head was established as the normal practice as early as 1911. In this application, two camshafts were employed—one controlling the

inlet valves, the other the exhaust valves—and could control the valves much more directly, thanks to the elimination of the pushrods. The advantage of reducing the mass to be reciprocated was that valve springs need be less powerful and power-consuming, since they would have less work to do in returning the valves to their seats. Alternatively, by keeping strong

Top: this cutaway of the Fiat 125 engine shows clearly one of its two overhead camshafts

Above: a typical four-cylinder camshaft

43

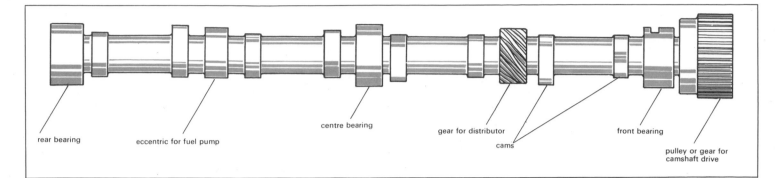

rear bearing   eccentric for fuel pump   centre bearing   gear for distributor   cams   front bearing   pulley or gear for camshaft drive

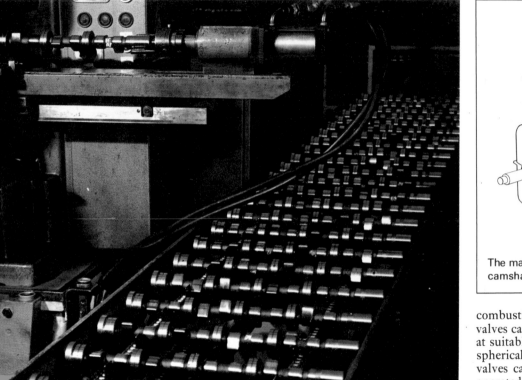

The majority of engines have a single block-mounted camshaft opening the valves via pushrods and rockers

Above: at the Fiat factory camshafts are produced on a production line. The rough castings are machined to tiny tolerances and then passed along a conveyor belt, ready to be fitted to a new engine

springs it was possible to increase the rate and extent of valve lift, and so to increase the effective opening of the valves and thus the volumetric efficiency of the engine —or to retain the normal rates of lift while running the engine at higher rotational rates, so as to develop more power.

Overhead camshafts were for a long time considered unsuitable for any but the most powerful or expensive car engines. The cost of providing a suitable drive, the difficulty of ensuring that it was not too noisy, and the complications of valve lash or clearance adjustment, remained an objection until the development of toothed rubber belts (internally reinforced to render them inextensible) in the 1960s allowed overhead camshafts to feature in mass-produced engines. The difficulties of clearance adjustment were sometimes illusory—an overhead-camshaft engine often retains its settings for much longer than any other, but, in most cases, clearance adjustment involves the laborious job of removing the camshaft(s) and fitting new shims (spacers) before replacing the cam and rechecking the gap—but were in any case overcome by ingenious and simple measures developed most notably by Fiat, but also by General Motors and others. These involve the use of shims or adjustable wedges which regulate the gap between tappet and valve without the need for dismantling.

The overhead camshaft allows a very free choice in combustion chamber design. With a single shaft, the valves can be arrayed in a line, or splayed, or arranged at suitable angles of opposition in a pentroof or hemispherical combustion chamber. With two shafts, the valves can be disposed at any desired angles and be operated directly without any rockers or lever tappets. The fact that lever tappets are often used anyway is due to other advantages they offer. However, cylindrical or piston tappets are more popular.

As specific performance and rates of revolution have steadily increased with the passing years, the design of the cams themselves has assumed much greater importance than hitherto. In order to minimise stresses, the aim has always been to make valve motion harmonic: this might be graphically represented by a sine wave, in the case of the simplest harmonic cam (the circular eccentric), or by a combustion of parts of different sine waves, as is more common. Such multi-sine cams, formed from four circular arcs, served well for many years; but they made no provision for gradual take-up of clearances and were very noisy. Modern cams incorporate additional arcs serving as ramps, to quieten the attack of the tappet on the valve and, in some cases, further corrective curves are added to deal with discrepancies in valve motion, caused by elasticity of the various components in the train between cam and valve. In extreme cases, the usual trigonometrical equations from which the harmonic series derive, have been supplanted by polynomial equations requiring electronic computer services to complete the necessary calculations.

Camshafts are often made of case-hardened steel, but high-duty cast iron alloys are increasingly popular, especially for mass production. A typical iron contains nickel, chromium, and molybdenum.

CARBURATION

feeding mixture to the engine

THE PURPOSE OF A CARBURETTOR is to provide means whereby the engine can draw the mixture of fuel and air that it requires for combustion, and whereby the driver can control that supply so as to control the performance of the engine. Indeed, that simple statement contains the essential difference between carburettors and fuel injection systems: the latter are designed to give the engine what it should have, the carburettor allows it to take what it needs. Whether the carburettor succeeds in supplying those wants will depend on its design, its adjustment, the conditions in which it works and the treatment it is given.

Consider the basic chemical nature of the mixture it must supply. It is possible to define a 'chemically correct' mixture as one which will burn completely inside the engine, producing an exhaust composed almost entirely of nitrogen and carbon dioxide: this mixture contains one part of petrol to some 15 parts of air (by weight). It will not do for all circumstances, however. If economy be desired, the mixture may be weakened (that is, the proportion of petrol reduced) by about 12%, at a cost in power of about 7%. Enrich it by 25% and the power will be increased by 4% or thereabouts, the exact figures depending on the aromatic properties of the petrol (which will vary according to the manufacturer and, in most brands, according to the season of the year) and the detonative propensities of the engine. These variations of mixture strength represent the feasible limits for all but the most extraordinary experimental engines; any further weakening or enrichment can only do harm.

It is clear from this that the carburettor must be capable of supplying an appropriately adjusted and accurate mixture according to the driver's demand for more power or frugality. Its task is made more difficult by the complexities of providing for good combustion, variable engine speed and correspondingly variable volumetric efficiency, changes in atmospheric density and temperature, variations in engine temperature, disturbances to the car's equilibrium caused by braking or cornering and the like, and the need for reliable starting and idling. All these factors affect the engine's fuel requirements, in addition to those which remain constant in any given example—such as the effect of air filters, inlet and exhaust manifold design, silencers, and sundry emission control devices.

None of these things presents any insuperable difficulties, but until fairly recently there was no single carburettor that coped satisfactorily with them all. The carburettor was still viewed as it had been at the dawn of motoring: an essentially simple device that worked well enough for the cost of improving it to be more than most customers would pay. Only when strict legislation was introduced to control exhaust emissions did the carburettor blossom in all the complexity and comprehensive competence that had so long been latent in it. The fact that the cars to which these new and sophisticated instruments are fitted behave so badly is the fault of the regulations: if the new carburettors were used on the old engines they would be found capable of yielding refined performance.

In its earliest forms, such refinement would have been impossible because of the crudity of early engines. There were, in those days, carburettors working on principles that have long been abandoned: the surface carburettor relying on evaporation of petrol from a wick or from a number of soaked wooden balls was one such, capable of working with the very light petrols available at the turn of the century but not now. The basis of the modern carburettor was nevertheless to be found in the earliest petrol-engined vehicles, nearly ninety years ago. This was the spray

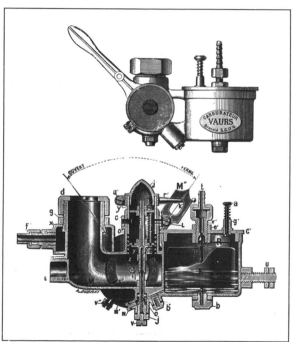

Right: two very early carburettor designs by the French company, Vaurs. The lower one is an improved version of the top one

Below right: the 'automatic' carburettor of the 1924 Fiat 501, with a float chamber to control the fuel level

Below: an extremely primitive carburettor used on a Ford model T in 1922

carburettor, working on the scent-spray principle.

Like all modern instruments, the primitive carburettor made use of a venturi or choke—a constriction, more or less streamlined in shape, in the pipe whereby air is admitted to the engine's inlet port or ports. This venturi displays a phenomenon noted in the study of elementary thermodynamics: when a gas flows through a duct, its velocity is highest and pressure lowest at the point of minimum cross-sectional area. It is the engine's business to induce the flow of air; what the venturi does is to create an artificially strengthened suction which can draw a flow of petrol into the airstream at the point of minimum pressure. It would not do to pour the petrol into the duct, for it would flow without relation to the passage of air, and

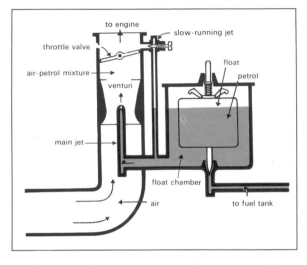

flooding would ensue; instead, a float chamber (like a miniature domestic water cistern) holds a supply of petrol at a level just below that of the orifice through which the petrol emerges into the airstream, and the suction suffices to draw it up and through the hole.

In this way, the flow of petrol obviously increases as the velocity of airflow and hence the suction increase. Unfortunately, the laws governing the flow of liquids are different from those for gases: thus the two flow rates do not increase in direct proportion. This is the basic shortcoming of the simple spray carburettor: it can only work properly at one speed. Increase the engine speed and the flow of air through the venturi will increase in proportion (both in quantity and velocity), but the flow of petrol will increase more. The discrepancy is great enough to be serious: doubling the engine speed would enrich the mixture by about 25%. Correspondingly, reducing the engine speed would weaken the mixture. Not only does this variability ruin all hopes of consistently accurate carburation, it also makes starting the engine virtually impossible without some additional means of enriching what would be an impossibly weak starting mixture—for no normal engine is capable of burning a petrol/air mixture weaker than about 1:21.

Additional complications had already been introduced at a very early stage: a throttle (a valve in the form of a hinged flap, a sliding plate, a revolving barrel, or more rarely some other device) was placed in the air duct to control the amount of air admitted and thus regulate the performance of the engine, after early attempts to control it by altering the spark timing had been found inadequate. Thereafter the complications proliferated as more and more anomalies were found in the behaviour of the basic carburettor. Spluttering when the throttle was suddenly opened proved to be due to the inertia of the petrol resisting prompt

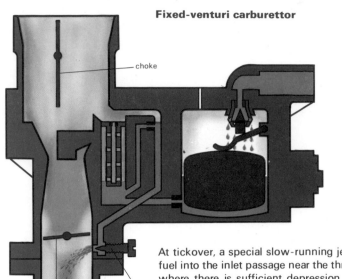

Fixed-venturi carburettor

At tickover, a special slow-running jet feeds the fuel into the inlet passage near the throttle valve, where there is sufficient depression to atomise the liquid (the yellow area indicates the air-flow)

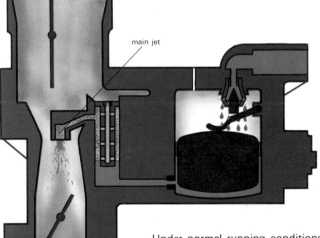

Under normal running conditions, the main jet takes over, this being situated in the narrowest part of the venturi where the air-flow is greatest and the fuel atomisation most complete

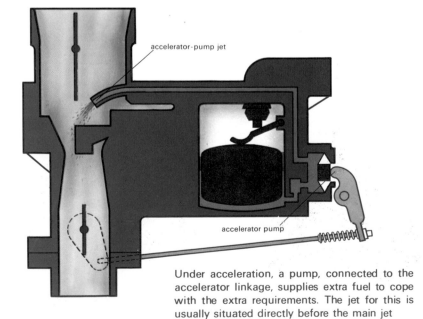

Under acceleration, a pump, connected to the accelerator linkage, supplies extra fuel to cope with the extra requirements. The jet for this is usually situated directly before the main jet

increase in flow rate, causing a temporary weakening of the mixture. Starting a cold engine was found to demand a mixture as rich as 1:2, and warming-up thereafter needed about 1:5, despite the theoretical impossibility of burning such a rich mix. In fact not all the petrol was burned: the surplus was turned into carbon, and the exhaust was rich in carbon monoxide.

A related problem was found to be that of properly atomising the petrol in the air: large droplets have too much inertia and do not follow the path of the airflow into the cylinder. A well atomised supply consists of the most minute droplets, each surrounded by a sphere of vapour much bigger than the droplet itself. Good vaporisation ensures ready inflammation and good combustion, but it also has a pronounced cooling

which the Weber is a good example. Commerical considerations had more to do with the extent of their respective domains than did the efficacy of these types as carburettors, and their manufacturers preserved a singular obstinacy in refusing to recognise the virtues of the rival kind. Only in the early 1960s was a carburettor combining the characteristics of both put into production by Keihin of Japan for Honda, to be followed in the early 1970s by Solex in a special instrument for Mercedes-Benz. The constant-vacuum type is a simple instrument that is difficult to adjust, the fixed-venturi type is complex in construction but easy to adjust. Put the two together and you have a complex carburettor that is hard to get right.

The constant-vacuum carburettor has, like all

Far left: a simple carburettor, showing the basic important parts. Depending on their application, these instruments can be downdraught, updraught (shown) or sidedraught, the direction of fuel/air flow deciding the title

Constant-vacuum carburettor

damper

vacuum chamber

piston

variable venturi

tapered needle

throttle valve

'choke' operating lever

movable jet

Above: the constant-vacuum carburettor has only one jet, the mixture being controlled by a tapered needle connected to a piston which rises due to the increased suction as the throttle is opened. At tickover (*left*), the piston is almost completely down, while under running conditions (*centre*) piston/needle height varies with throttle opening. There is no accelerator pump, but an oil damper delays piston movement thereby increasing air velocity and richening the mixture. The 'choke' lowers the jet (*right*)

effect which can lead to the carburettor becoming choked with ice when the atmosphere is cool and humid. Other problems were created more by the carburettor's working conditions than by its inherent failings. Unskilled or uneducated drivers might not make proper use of mixture-enriching devices for starting, being particularly likely to leave them in operation too long. Lateral or longitudinal accelerations induced by cornering fast or braking hard would disturb the fuel level in the float chamber so much that the carburettor jet might be starved of petrol, causing the engine to cut out in mid-corner or stall during braking. Climbing steep hills or parking on steeply cambered roads produced the same displacement of the petrol level, and might make starting impossible.

In time, the development of the carburettor for the motor car continued along two diverging paths, though other kinds of carburettors evolved for other vehicles—notably motor cycles, which often had and have instruments which are masterly combinations of efficiency and simplicity. In cars, the two principal types were the constant-vacuum carburettor exemplified by the SU and the fixed-venturi carburettor of

others, a throttle valve, a venturi, and a constant-level supply of petrol. Its special feature is a venturi or constriction created by the obstruction of a slide (usually in the form of a piston) that is caused to rise and fall by the variations in partial vacuum caused by throttle position and engine load. As it moves to obstruct the inlet passage more or less, it thus maintains a constant pressure-drop across the petrol jet orifice. This, as we have seen, would not be enough to ensure the correct flow in all circumstances; but by attaching to this slide a needle of varying cross-section which moves in and out of the petrol discharge orifice and thus alters the cross-sectional area of fuel flow, the necessary adjustments are made. Over its working range, the constant-vacuum carburettor thus gives a sensibly constant mixture strength under all conditions.

Moving the petrol jet downwards towards the tip of the tapered needle allows more petrol to flow, and after the engine has been started with this aid the jet can be moved progressively up again until the engine is warm and can run on a normal mixture. The slight enrichment needed for idling is arranged by modifying the

47

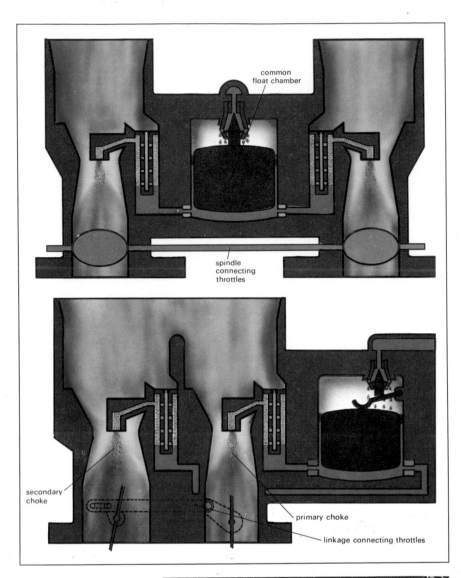

common float chamber

spindle connecting throttles

secondary choke

primary choke

linkage connecting throttles

Above: there are two types of multiple-choke carburettor. In the one shown at the top, the instrument is the equivalent of two single-choke units sharing a common float chamber. The lower diagram shows the compound carburettor, in which the secondary choke comes into operation only when the throttle is opened past a predetermined point. This type of carburettor is designed to improve fuel economy

Far right: an underbonnet view of the Aston Martin Speed Model of 1934, showing the twin SU carburettors

Near right: the three twin-choke Weber carburettors of the Fiat Dino V6 engine

contours of the needle. For acceleration, the inertia of the slide is relied on (it may be further slowed by a simple oil damper) to delay its opening, so increasing the pressure drop at the venturi and stimulating a stronger flow of petrol.

Ostensibly simple, the adjustment of this type of instrument demands subtle understanding of its working. Varying the weight of the slide, the rigour of its damping, the strength of the spring which tends to close the venturi, and the thickness and contours of the needle, all produce changes which interact.

The fixed-venturi carburettor makes up in multi-

plicity of air and petrol passages what it lacks in variable geometry. The details vary enormously in the different makes and models in production all over the world, but in principle the idea is to bring various supplementary petrol jets and air bleeds into operation at various conjunctions of engine speed and load, each one serving to enrich or impoverish the mixture as necessary. Apart from spring-loaded accelerator pumps which are used in some types to squirt extra petrol into the inlet tract when the accelerator is pressed for more power, most of the changes in air and fluid circuitry are effected by purely pneumatic means: when a particular jet is subjected to suction, fuel will flow from it until the suction is relieved by a change in throttle position or airflow velocity.

One of the most popular methods of improving the flexibility of response of a fixed-venturi carburettor is to give it two air passages, each with its own throttle and its own particular set of jets. The throttles do not open simultaneously but progressively in succession, so that for gentle driving only the primary throttle will be used together with the variety of starting, pilot (slow-running) and normal jets serving it. At full load both throttles will be open, the secondary passage having probably only a main jet feeding it. Such an instrument is called a compound carburettor, and is to be distinguished from the multiple-barrel or choke carburettor in which all throttles are synchronised and similarly furnished with jets etc: instruments of this type are simply multiples of the basic carburettor built into a common casting.

Multiple-choke carburettors usually have two passages or 'barrels' but sometimes three. Compound carburettors invariably have two, which may or may not be of different sizes. In the USA large complex carburettors are made with four or even six barrels, comprising two or three compound carburettors.

Modern refinements continue to complicate this fundamentally simple apparatus. Mixture-enriching devices for starting (commonly called 'chokes' even though they are often supplementary fuel supplies rather than air stranglers) are automatic, responding by thermostatic control to the temperature of the engine. Vaporisation of fuel from the float chamber is no longer allowed to escape into the atmosphere in countries where strict laws against the emission of unburned hydrocarbons are in force, but has to be piped to some form of condenser and returned to the fuel tank. Other automatic devices such as spring-loaded flaps in the throttle plate admit extra air when the engine is running at high speed with closed throttle, weakening what would otherwise be too rich a mixture.

One way and another, the modern carburettor is almost as complex as the petrol-injection apparatus which is its only rival.

THE MAJORITY OF CARBURETTORS will be one of two basic types: the fixed-venturi carburettor or the constant-vacuum carburettor. The fixed-venturi type may also be termed fixed-jet or constant-choke, and includes products of Solex, Zenith, Ford and Weber. Constant-vacuum types may be described as variable-jet or controlled-jet, and include those of SU and Stromberg manufacture.

Although the purpose of both types is the same, the construction and operation of each is entirely different, and the adjustment of the two types must be considered independently.

However, before carrying out any carburettor adjustments, check the ignition timing and examine the sparking plugs and points; reset or renew them as necessary. Having done this, inability to obtain a satisfactorily smooth running engine may be due to burnt or badly seating valves. Equally likely is the possibility that an air leak is present in the inlet manifold or in the carburettor itself, thus weakening the mixture. Such an air leak could be caused by a faulty gasket or a worn throttle spindle.

Fixed-venturi carburettors

Fixed-venturi carburettors maintain a constant fuel/air ratio by means of three or more jets. Each of these jets contributes to the fuel/air ratio over part of the engine speed range.

A slow-running jet supplies fuel at small throttle openings, whereas at medium throttle openings, fuel is drawn in through a compensating jet. At large throttle openings and higher engine speeds, a main jet comes into operation.

A number of effects are utilised to control the time at which the various jets come into operation: the vacuum generated in the carburettor, the degree of throttle opening, and the tendency for the fuel level to decrease in certain parts of the carburettor as fuel consumption increases with engine speed.

Although the compensating and main jets are inoperative at low engine speeds, the slow-running jet is operative at all speeds. However, because of the relatively small quantity of fuel supplied by the slow running jet, adjustment of it will not appreciably affect the fuel/air ratio at medium and high engine speeds. Normally the slow running jet is the only jet which can be adjusted.

To set the slow-running adjustment, the engine must be at its normal operating temperature. Screw the throttle-stop screw in (clockwise) until the ignition warning light goes out completely. This will prevent the engine stalling when the mixture is being adjusted. Screw out (anti-clockwise) the slow-running adjustment until the engine 'hunts' in a rhythmic manner. Screw in the slow-running adjustment until the hunting disappears and the engine runs smoothly.

Note that on some makes of fixed-venturi carburettors, the slow running adjustment screw determines the mixture by regulating the air flow, and on others it regulates the fuel flow. Therefore, to achieve the same (say, weakening) effect, the screw may have to be unscrewed, or screwed in.

Reduce the engine speed to the normal tick-over speed, with the ignition warning light flickering. If necessary, reset the slow running adjustment as before.

Accelerator pumps on fixed-venturi carburettors are usually operated by a spring-loaded linkage from the throttle. Two settings may be provided on the linkage. The setting giving the shorter stroke is the summer setting, for warmer temperatures. The longer stroke is the winter setting, when the air temperature

CARBURETTOR ADJUSTMENT

regulating the air/fuel ratio

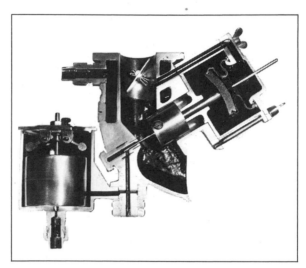

A section through one of the earliest SU carburettors, which embodied the same basic principles of operation as do the modern versions. Probably the major difference is that this old model used a rubber diaphragm to provide an air seal (along the lines of the Stromberg of today), whereas present-day instruments use a precision machined piston

is lower and a richer mixture is required. In practice, many people do not pay any attention to this adjustment and the carburettor functions reasonably well with the accelerator pump linkage on the short stroke (summer setting), throughout the year.

The choke usually takes the form of a butterfly in the upper part of the carburettor barrel, which restricts the air flow to the engine.

The choke butterfly is connected to the throttle butterfly by an adjustable linkage, so as to provide a higher slow-running speed in cold conditions, to prevent stalling. The degree of throttle opening necessary will differ from one type of engine to another. To set this adjustment correctly, it will be necessary to resort to the car manufacturer's maintenance literature, or to set it by trial and error. To ensure accurate reassembly, if the carburettor is stripped for cleaning, this linkage should be marked in such a way that it may be reassembled to its original setting.

Fixed-venturi carburettors are quite simple to strip and clean, provided that a note is made of the correct position of each component as it is removed; additionally, ensure that the necessary renewable items are available, such as fibre washers and gaskets, which can often be bought in service-kit form. Jets should be cleaned by blowing, or by using a jet of compressed air, in the opposite direction to the fuel flow (particularly with internally tapered jets, from the smaller aperture towards the larger aperture). Any attempt to clear jets with wire may result in the hole becoming enlarged, thus giving incorrect metering of the fuel supply when the carburettor is operating.

Wash any sediment from the passageways in the body of the carburettor, and from the float chamber, with petrol, and blow them dry with compressed air. When reassembling the carburettor, use new gaskets and seals, but do not use any gasket sealing compound. Ensure that screws are tightened firmly and evenly, but without any undue force, as it is easy to strip threads, or distort parts of the carburettor body.

Constant-vacuum carburettors

Constant-vacuum carburettors, such as the SU or Stromberg, maintain a constant fuel/air ratio by means of a single jet, within which a tapered needle is moved as the throttle is opened, in conjunction with a piston which controls the area of the venturi throat.

The needle and the piston are not linked to the throttle mechanically, but are lifted by the vacuum created in the carburettor when the throttle is opened. The diameter and position of the needle, and the position of the piston, ensure that the correct fuel/air ratio is obtained under all operating conditions.

On accelerating, the throttle is opened and the vacuum will raise both the needle and the piston; an oil controlled damping device causes the piston movement to be slowed down, so temporarily enriching the mixture.

Adjustment of the slow-running mixture on a constant-vacuum carburettor will affect the mixture supplied at high engine speeds and it is therefore important that the slow-running mixture is set correctly.

Before adjusting the slow-running mixture, check that the piston operates freely by lifting it and allowing it to fall. It should drop with a metallic click. Be very careful not to damage the sliding surface of the piston. If the piston sticks, loosen and reseat the dashpot cover; ensure that the dashpot cover screws are

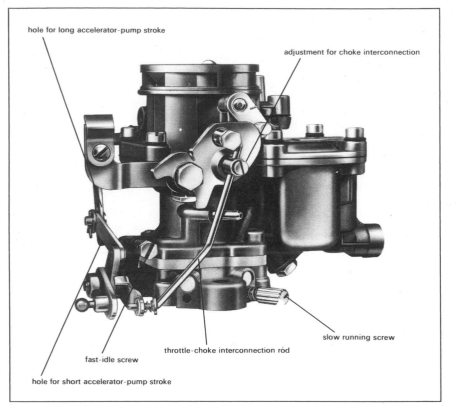

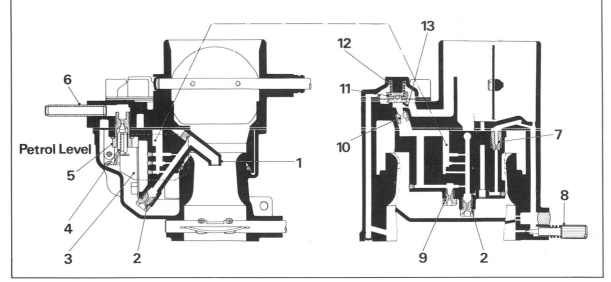

Above: the Zenith W-series single-fixed-venturi downdraught carburettor. Note how the interconnection between throttle and choke is adjustable, to give the optimum fast-idle speed. The throttle body is insulated by a thick gasket from the main carburettor body in an effort to reduce the transfer of heat

Left: sections through the Zenith series IV instrument, showing all the major components that may need to be removed or adjusted for maximum efficiency. **1** petrol outlet; **2** main jet; **3** float; **4** needle; **5** needle seating; **6** petrol inlet; **7** slow running jet; **8** slow running screw; **9** compensating jet; **10** ventilation screw; **11** economy diaphragm valve; **12** compression spring; **13** full throttle air-bleed hole

tightened evenly and replenish the dashpot oil to the correct level.

Run the engine until it reaches its normal operating temperature and screw in the throttle-stop screw, until the ignition warning light goes out. Turn the adjusting nut on the jet to obtain maximum engine speed. Turn it upwards until the engine speed begins to fall, then turn it downwards just enough to regain maximum idling speed.

Check the adjustment by lifting the piston slightly; the engine speed should increase then fall again to the original speed. If the engine speed falls below the original speed, the mixture is too weak, and the adjusting nut must be turned downwards. If the engine speed does not fall to the original speed, the mixture is too rich, and the adjusting nut must be turned upwards. If necessary repeat the test, turning the adjusting nut, one flat at a time, until the adjustment is correct.

Constant-vacuum carburettors may be dismantled for cleaning, but care must be taken not to damage the piston or the needle. Before dismantling, mark the dashpot cover so that it may be refitted in the same position. Disorientation of the dashpot cover may cause the piston to jam.

If a rubber diaphragm is fitted, examine it for any damage or deterioration. If there is any sign of cracking or perishing, it must be renewed. If the needle is suspected of being bent, this may be confirmed by rolling it along a flat surface. Unfortunately this check will only confirm that it is bent, not that it is straight, and it may be necessary to check it by the substitution of a known good one.

Clean the piston, and the dashpot interior, using petrol and a soft, clean cloth. Ensure that the cloth leaves no fluff because this may cause the piston to stick. The piston and the dashpot interior must never be cleaned with abrasive, neither should any attempt be made to remove any metal to prevent the piston sticking. If sticking occurs, it may be caused by damage to the piston or dashpot, incorrect orientation or bad seating of the dashpot.

Multiple carburettor installations

Multiple carburettor installations are adjusted for mixture strength and idling speed in much the same way as individual carburettors. However, it is essential that the throttles of individual carburettors on a multiple carburettor installation are synchronised.

Both types of carburettor may be synchronised by listening to the hiss, generated in each one, with a stethoscope or a piece of rubber tubing, and adjusting the throttle openings to obtain an equal 'hiss' from each one.

Fixed-venturi carburettors may also be synchronised by blanking off each one in turn, at tick over speed, and adjusting the throttles so that the reduction in engine speed is the same for each carburettor.

Oddly enough, the apparently simple operation of synchronisation very often proves to be a job for the specialist.

Floats and float chambers

The function of the float chamber is to maintain the correct level of fuel in the carburettor, so that there is sufficient for the engine requirements yet not so much that there is a risk of flooding.

The level of the fuel in the float chamber is maintained by a float and a needle valve. As fuel is used, the

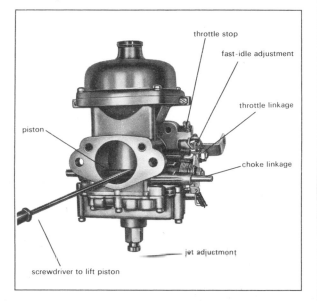

throttle stop
fast-idle adjustment
throttle linkage
choke linkage
piston
jet adjustment
screwdriver to lift piston

float falls and allows the needle valve to open, admitting more fuel. As the float chamber fills, the float rises and progressively closes the needle valve, maintaining the fuel at the required level.

Remove the float chamber cover and the float, and wash out any sediment with petrol; dry the components with a compressed air jet. Check that the float is not punctured by immersing it in a bowl or bucket of heated water; air bubbles from the float will indicate a puncture. Determine the effectiveness of the needle valve by blowing in the fuel inlet and gently closing the needle valve with the finger. Reassemble the float chamber, fitting a new gasket.

The correct adjustment of the carburettor will ensure that the engine can develop maximum power with minimum cost and pollution. More apparent, however, will be the pleasant operation of the engine, and the smooth and quick acceleration under all operating conditions.

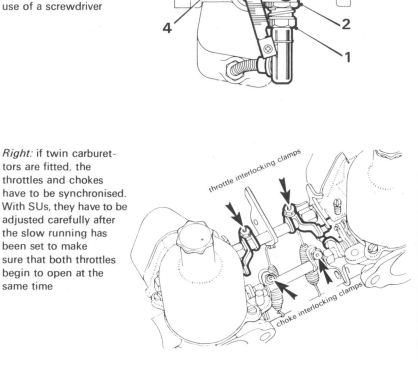

Right: a diagram of an SU HS carburettor showing the important external components.
1 jet adjusting nut; **2** jet locking nut; **3** dashpot; **4** fast-idle screw; **5** throttle stop screw; **6** fast-idle cam lever. One of the best ways to check the accuracy of the mixture setting is to lift the piston slightly. SU instruments usually have a special lifting pin, situated on the main carburettor body, while Stromberg units (*below left*) require the use of a screwdriver

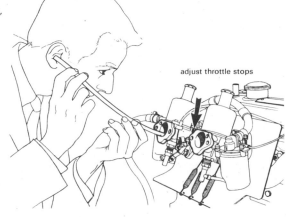

throttle interlocking clamps
choke interlocking clamps

Right: if twin carburettors are fitted, the throttles and chokes have to be synchronised. With SUs, they have to be adjusted carefully after the slow running has been set to make sure that both throttles begin to open at the same time

adjust throttle stops

Right: the cheapest way, and one of the most effective, of matching the 'sucking' of two carburettors is to adjust the throttle stops while listening to the intake hiss through a piece of rubber tube or even a stethoscope. Special equipment is available for this job, but it is far more expensive than a piece of rubber tube

FUEL INJECTION

an alternative to the carburettor

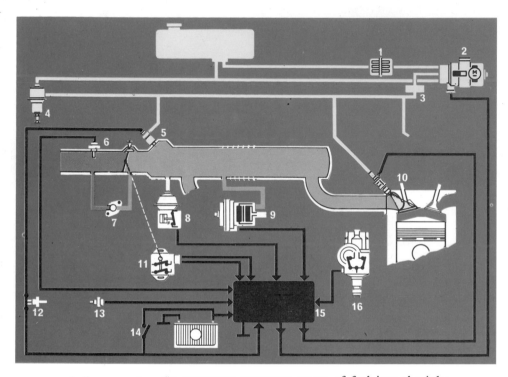

A diagrammatic representation of an electronic indirect fuel-injection system, showing the layout of the components:
1 fuel filter
2 electric pump
3 damper
4 pressure regulator
5 cold-starting injector
6 air-intake-temperature sensor
7 supplementary-air valve
8 pressure switch
9 pressure sensor
10 injector
11 throttle switch
12 thermal switch
13 temperature sensor
14 ignition switch
15 electronic control centre
16 breakerless distributor

BY SQUIRTING MEASURED DOSES of fuel into the inlet manifold, inlet ports, or even into the cylinders themselves, fuel injection apparatus gives an engine what it should have; a carburettor, from which fuel is sucked by the flow of intake air, allows it to take what it wants. Since neither system has yet been made perfect, neither achieves these ideals, but social pressures on technology have, in recent years, been responsible for a considerable improvement in both, and in particular for a readier acceptance of the idea that injection might supplant the carburettor in ordinary cars as it long ago did in racing cars.

It would be a mistake to suppose that the success of injection in racing proved that it gave more power. It does not necessarily do so: the only reason for the superior power of most injected engines is that the venturi, or restricted throat, of most carburettors (necessary to promote the pressure drop that sucks fuel from the jet) imposes a limit on the air-breathing ability of the engine, and it is the rate of air intake that determines the power output. There are, however, carburettors that allow as free an airflow as the best injection systems—the Amal GP, long used on racing motor cycles, is a good example—and when one of these is used for each cylinder, the power realised need be no less than when injection is applied to individual inlet tracts as in current racing engines. Racing engines tend to have a large number of cylinders, however, and the weight and complexity of a corresponding number of carburettors (each of which must be adjusted individually to some extent, even in the most ingenious

multiple mountings) then constitute severe disadvantages; the centralised control and delivery systems of injection apparatus are by comparison lighter, more compact and easier to adjust. More severe still in racing is the carburettor's sensitivity to surge of fuel in the float chamber as the car corners hard or brakes heavily: the best Grand Prix cars corner at as much as $1.7\,g$, when the fuel inside a carburettor would be flung to one side so forcefully that its surface would adopt an angle 59 degrees away from the horizontal—with what ensuing difficulties in starving or flooding the jets may be imagined.

The ordinary roadgoing car does not have a lot of cylinders and does not corner with such ferocity. What advantages then remain to justify the adoption of injection? In theory, there are at least ten:

1 because of the absence of venturi restrictions which ordinary carburettors cannot avoid, volumetric (or breathing) efficiency is higher, and so therefore should be the power output;
2 mixture distribution is better, each cylinder being given the same dosage;
3 mixture strength is uniform for each cylinder;
4 fuel economy is better because of 2 and 3;

The Ferrari 1512 Formula One car of 1965. Its flat-twelve, 1489 cc engine used fuel injection, as do all Formula One cars. Racing is the most popular application for fuel injection, other than diesel engines, although many manufacturers have at least experimented with injection for road cars

5 there is mechanically induced reduction of the liquid fuel to fine droplets, hence no need to heat the inlet air to ensure adequate vaporisation, and therefore no loss of volumetric efficiency due to the lower density of heated air;

6 acceleration response is better, the extra fuel needed being injected forthwith instead of flowing only after air flow has changed and depression has drawn it from the jets;

7 cold starting is better because of 5 and 6;

8 idling is more uniform because of 2 and 3;

9 inlet-valve cooling is improved, because latent heat of evaporation need not be taken out of the fuel earlier in its passage (this is not valid in the case of direct injection into the cylinder);

10 icing in very cold weather is absent, because of the same reason as in 9.

It is an impressive list, but it is a theoretical one. In practice, the first four items may be invalidated by the requirements or even the mere habits of production engineers, who cannot discount cost and complexity with the freedom of the idealist. Thus, the production touring or sporting car with fuel injection will have an injector nozzle for each inlet port of its engine, but all those ports will draw their air from a manifold controlled by a single upstream throttle assembly and drawing from a single air cleaner and silencer. All the aerodynamic solecisms of the carburettor manifold are thus inherited, and volumetric efficiency may accordingly be no higher, for it is often the case that manifold design handicaps airflow more severely than the carburettor venturi.

Because different quantities of air may reach different cylinders through such a manifold, the mere fact of equal doses of fuel being delivered to each does not ensure equal mixture distribution nor uniform mixture strength. It is consequently unlikely that economy (or freedom from certain noxious exhaust emissions) will be as good as might be expected.

On the other hand, if each intake port be furnished not only with its own injector but also with its own inlet pipe, throttle and air filter, results may be achieved that should be superior to any but the very best multi-carburettor arrangements, with advantages in cost, weight, accessibility, and ease of maintenance.

All this presupposes the ability to determine how much fuel should be injected, and when. Until very recently indeed, the history of fuel injection has been a confusion of blind alleys and wild geese that made this supposedly straightforward determination more like an exercise in roundabout assumptions; and the history is a long one, dating back at least to 1903 when the Wright brothers' first sustained powered flight was propelled by an engine with petrol injection—if not to the nineteenth-century origins of the diesel engine. For a long time it was oil-engine practice that was followed in experiments with petrol injection, most successfully by Bosch and Daimler-Benz in the development of fully aerobatic aero engines for the Luftwaffe; and a Bosch jerk-pump system was evolved for the BMW 328 sports cars specially built

Chevrolet's Cosworth Vega engine. The main differences between this and the ordinary Vega unit are that this has twin overhead cams and fuel injection. The injection tubes can be seen, one on each induction pipe. The intakes are linked at their open ends so that only one throttle is necessary (*top*)

for the 1940 Mille Miglia race, though it was not in fact used.

The jerk pump contains a number of plungers moved by a camshaft geared to the engine speed, each plunger displacing fuel from its cylinder through small-bore piping to an injector nozzle feeding an inlet port or engine cylinder. A rotating rack and quadrant mechanism turns the plungers in their bores so as to vary the unmasking of plunger-controlled ports which, in turn, govern the quantity of fuel transmitted on each stroke; this mechanism is linked to the throttle pedal and to a pneumatic sensor of inlet manifold vacuum, so as to cater for variations in engine demand. It was an imperfect system when applied to the petrol engine, but for racing machines exploiting alcohol-based fuels that were not sensitive to mixture strength, it worked well enough, and the 1954/55 Mercedes-Benz Grand Prix cars introduced it most effectively to racing. Already, there had been other attempts, also reliant on the forgiving nature of alcohol fuels: the Hilborn continuous injection system, in which the only variation in supply was by varying the pressure of fuel pumped to the injector nozzles in the ports, was much favoured at Indianapolis and was tried successfully in England by Connaught in their 1953 Formula Two car. Vanwall went to Bosch for help with their Grand Prix car, and in 1958 were probably the first to run a racing car with petrol injection when other fuels were proscribed.

Nevertheless, it was the perfection by Lucas of an ingenious shuttle metering system that made possible the more popular modern approach to the problem, in which an electrically driven pump pressurises the delivery of fuel to an engine-driven distributor that puts each injector in communication with this pressure in its appropriate turn. A cam or lever moved by the accelerator pedal adjusts the abutments that stop the metering shuttle at the end of each stroke, and thus varies the quantity of fuel displaced by each movement. For racing this is sufficient, but for a road car there is once again a need for finer control, provided by a

pneumatic transducer sensitive to intake manifold pressure. A similar sensor can adjust the mixture according to ambient atmospheric pressure. This Lucas system provides timed doses of fuel to each cylinder, but it was demonstrated by BRM (who were the first to employ it) that the timing was not critical. Other manufacturers of injection apparatus took advantage of this insensitivity to simplify their systems by adopting a continuous spray, the quantity of fuel delivered being varied by alterations in delivery pressure. The Tecalemit-Jackson system, capable of giving an engine as much power potential as any form of injection or carburation, was one such. In general, however, it was found that the means of sensing all the different parameters that affected the engine's need for mixture, in terms of quantity and richness, were the aspect of design that needed most development, and numerous injection systems that appeared in the 1950s and 1960s (particularly in the USA but also in Europe and Japan) left something to be desired.

The difficulties of translating things such as throttle position and manifold depression into measures of engine load, and relating the answer to engine speed and atmospheric pressure and ambient and engine temperatures (the needs of cold starting and fast idling during warm-up had to be remembered), promoted great variety in experiments. Bosch, Bendix, Lucas and others tried electronic control, arguing that it enabled any number of factors to be measured and corresponding adjustments to be made: a miniature transistorised computer sorted all these transducer signals and issued a pulse of current of a certain duration to solenoid-controlled injector nozzles supplied with fuel at constant pressure. The longer the pulse, the more petrol would be squirted into each port during each operating cycle of the engine. Other firms, such as Kügelfischer, relied on mechanical refinements, such as a three-dimensional cam controlling the fuel-distributor output.

It was perhaps unfortunate that for a long time nobody tried to make the injection apparatus measure what the carburettor measures automatically, which is the mass flow of air into the engine. In 1970, the Tecalemit engineer Jackson produced an electro-pneumatic system that actually measured what was required (instead of inferring it from other measurements), and the idea of mass-flow measurement was enthusiastically taken up thereafter by Bosch, who modified their existing electronic system accordingly. Unlike Bosch, the Tecalemit subsidiary Petrol Injection Ltd did not get their system into production; but more recently they have announced a modified version (reverting to timed injection) that is likely to find takers. As in so many of the latest developments involving injection and carburation alike, the object is now mainly to ensure the reduction of anti-social exhaust emissions in conformity with existing and anticipated legislation; a particular feature of the PI systems is the very fine atomisation of the fuel.

The requirements of emission-control regulations have affected the carburettor quite severely, making it much more complex in its most recent forms. This complexity is such as to put the carburettor and injection systems on a more even footing in terms of cost and difficulties of maintenance, matters which hitherto had been by far the most compelling of all reasons why injection should not supplant carburation. The operational simplicity of electronics now appear as positive attractions, and the usually low fuel consumption of an injected engine supports the view that the age of the glorified scent-spray may be over and the day of the little squirt about to dawn.

FUEL PUMP

supplying the carburettor

An SU electric fuel pump of the type used on many popular British cars, especially from the British Leyland stable (SU is owned by BLMC). The inlet and outlet pipes are shown here—underneath them are valves and, in the case of the inlet, a filter. At the other end is a set of contact points which operate in a similar fashion to a buzzer

TO AVOID FIRE HAZARDS, the petrol tank is usually sited at the opposite end of the car from the engine. Because the tank is positioned low down under the floor on most cars, gravity feed is not a practical possibility and fuel has to be pumped from tank to carburettor. The pump used is one of two basic types—mechanically or electrically operated.

Mechanical pumps

These are always driven by means of an eccentric lobe on the camshaft. This operates the pump lever which is connected, by means of a rod, to the pump diaphragm. When the cam operates the lever, the diaphragm flexes and draws petrol into the lower chamber past a one-way valve. At the same time, more fuel is drawn into the upper chamber from the inlet pipe, passing via the sediment filter in the top of the pump housing.

As the operating lever passes onto the back of the cam, a spring reasserts the diaphragm. The petrol just drawn into the lower chamber is then pushed, via another one-way valve, through the outlet pipe to the carburettor's float chamber.

Each revolution of the camshaft repeats the process. The interesting part of the operation is that the fuel is pushed on its way by spring pressure only. Thus when the needle valve in the carburettor float chamber closes and no more fuel can flow, the diaphragm stays down, although the operating lever is still being pushed to and fro.

Because of the very simple component parts and uncomplicated action of the pump, it needs very little attention and not a great deal goes wrong with it. The main service procedure is a very simple one. It merely involves moving the top clip, lifting off the dome, taking out the small sediment filter inside, cleaning it with petrol and replacing it. If the filter becomes damaged it is possible for specks of dirt to lodge in the valves and stop them closing, so it is important to keep it clean and sound.

Air leaks are another possibility and these usually occur because of damage to the sealing gasket under the rim of the dome cover. This is usually made of cork and it is as well to check it and fit a new one from time to time. The top dome, incidentally, is either made of glass or metal and may be secured with a single screw instead of a wire clip.

The makers of the AC pump—one of the most common—market an overhaul kit, comprising a new diaphragm, two new one-way valves, a new top gasket and assorted other gaskets. It is not an expensive item to buy and, once installed, will completely refurbish your pump.

You will need to take the pump off the engine to overhaul it and this is usually a matter of two nuts (if the pump is mounted on studs), or perhaps two bolts. The inlet and outlet pipes must be disconnected, too.

An AC-Delco mechanically operated fuel pump with the glass bowl and filter removed. The actuating lever *(right)* moves the diaphragm (pink edge can be seen) up and down; this, with the help of two valves feeds the carburettors

Before dismantling, mark the two flanges of the pump, so they can be put back in the same place. Note the position of the two one-way valves before taking them out as this will help to get the new ones assembled correctly. Fitting the new diaphragm has its complications. With the mounting flange of the pump in a 12 o'clock position, fit the diaphragm with its locating tab at 11 o'clock, engage the notch in the pull rod and turn around to 8 o'clock. Finally, when reassembling the two halves, finger tighten all the screws, then pull the operating arm towards the pump and hold it there while tightening.

Electric pumps

This type works in much the same basic way as the mechanical type. Movement of a diaphragm sucks in petrol in one direction and pushes it towards the carburettor when flexed the other way. The difference is that the operating rod is moved by a solenoid which is controlled by a set of contact-breaker points.

What happens is that spring pressure on the diaphragm pushes fuel out through the outlet pipe towards the carburettor. The diaphragm is connected to the rocker mechanism attached to the points and the movement closes the points. Current flows and energises the solenoid attracting the armature which is attached to the diaphragm. This is pulled towards the solenoid, drawing in fuel as it moves. Movement continues in this direction until the rocker mechanism throws over again and the points are opened. Then the spring behind the diaphragm takes over again and reverses the direction of the movement, pumping the fuel out.

Somewhat more complicated than the mechanical type, the electric pump is nevertheless still remarkably trouble free. A filter protects the pump against dirt in the petrol. This needs taking out and cleaning every 6000 miles. It is reached by undoing a hexagon plug in the base of the body—the filter is a gauze tube behind it. Some of the other types of electric pump will have to be taken off the car and the filter reached by dismantling from the bottom end. The service technique is a simple one of washing the filter in petrol and then replacing it.

If the pump stops operating altogether, disconnect the electric feed wire from its terminal. With the ignition switched on and the terminal well away from the pump, attempt to create a spark by gently brushing the wire against the car chassis. If there is no spark you will have to track the wire further back, looking for damage or disconnection.

If there is a spark, you can be reasonably sure that current is reaching the pump. The next check is to take off the plastic top cover and look at the points. They should be closed. If they are not, look for stiffness in the contact-breaker mechanism.

If the points are touching and there are still no signs of life from the pump, it is possible that the points are worn or corroded. A temporary cure can be effected by cleaning the points surfaces with fine emery cloth.

Complete overhaul of the pump is possible as a do-it-yourself exercise, but make sure, before you start, that you can get the necessary parts. They are not easy to buy, as some makers believe that the pump should be completely replaced. A good local auto-electrician could probably help.

EXHAUST

removing the waste products

WHEN A MUSICIAN BLOWS into a wind instrument, the sound which comes out at the other end depends upon what happens to the air inside the instrument. The player can modify the pressure of air by his lungs and cheeks, and the way in which it flows by the keys. However, there is something else which gives an instrument its distinctive sound—think of the difference, for example, between the tone of the trumpet and the euphonium—and that is the design and size of the tubes. The euphonium, with its deep-throated 'oomp-ah', has rather big-bore tubes, while the trumpet's clarion note comes from a slimmer conformation, and it is this difference in design which gives them their characteristic sounds. In some ways, the exhaust system of a car follows similar rules. It is extremely important that the tubes which make up the car's exhaust system are properly 'tuned' to enable them to do their job efficiently.

The prime objective of an exhaust system is to get rid of the burnt gases which form when combustion of the petrol and air mixture takes place in the combustion chambers. This can be done quite effectively by the use of open tubes—as with a racing car—but the resultant crackling roar is quite unacceptable for a road-going car, so methods have to be introduced to quieten things down.

Ideally, the exhaust gases should be allowed to escape as smoothly, completely and quickly as possible, but these gases come in pulses as the sequence of exhaust strokes take place, and poor tubes and silencer design can result in too much 'back pressure' building up, having a strangling effect. Taken to an extreme, such as when a driver reverses into an earth bank and blocks the tail pipe with mud, the engine will not run at all.

As said earlier, the noise emitted by an exhaust system depends upon the way in which the exhaust gases are allowed to expand. Try a simple experiment. Clap your hands smartly with the palms held flat and you will hear a sharp 'smacking' sound; using the same degree of force, do the same with the palms cupped, and you will hear a much deeper and, apparently, softer sound. Both noises derive from the escape of air from between your palms, the difference being that in the first case the air has suddenly to erupt from between mating surfaces, and in the second the cup allows expansion before the air is expelled. This is the principle which governs the silencing systems for road-going cars.

Hot gases have to expand, so, to avoid the accompanying noise which would follow if this were allowed to happen uninhibitedly, expansion chambers and silencers have to be employed in an exhaust system.

An expansion chamber is just what it is called, a box in which the initial 'puff' of exhaust gas from the combustion chamber can expand to reduce the effects of back pressure. Depending upon engine design, there may be more than one expansion chamber, but

in most cases the first is usually mounted quite close to the manifold. However, this is only the first step. The burnt gas is still hot and needs to expand further if the noise of its escape from the tail pipe is to be reduced to acceptable levels, hence the silencer. Silencers are usually fitted towards the rear of the car, but here again the position can vary according to design and the rev/torque band of the engine.

The most widely used silencer on production cars is the 'baffle' type. In this, a series of perforated plates separates the interior of the silencer box into compartments. The thinking behind this is that the exhaust gases can be slowed to some extent and can expand further if they are led through a sort of labyrinth. If the design is right, no excess of back pressure will be set up, and the flow from the combustion chambers will be relatively smooth, although still coming in a series of puffs. To prove this point, place your hand behind the tail pipe of a car with the engine idling and you will feel the pulses of each 'shot' of gas as it emerges. The pulses should be regular if the exhaust system as a whole is doing its job well, but it does not necessarily follow that irregularity means a poor exhaust system—the ignition or induction system may be at fault.

Another approach to the silencing problem is the 'straight-through' design. Here the arrangement is that the exhaust pipe continues straight through the silencer box and out to the tail pipe. Inside the box, the pipe is perforated and the surrounding area inside the

Above: the intricate 'plumbing' of the early 1968 Matra V12 of Jean-Pierre Beltoise. The car has four tailpipes from the twelve cylinders. Earlier cars had an elaborate system of six tail pipes that not only made the engine much more efficient, but gave the car a tremendous high-pitched shriek. However, the six-tailpipe system made the Matra too temperamental, with several flat spots in the torque curve; this was cured by the later system, although top-end power did deteriorate slightly

Near right above: an exhaust manifold as used on many standard saloon cars. There are three ports, the middle one taking the burnt gases from both number two and three cylinders. This system is inefficient, but quite acceptable on low-powered cars

Near right below: the smoothly styled piping of the 1968 Ferrari FI car

Right: an exhaust used on a high-performance car should have curved pipes, all of approximately the same length, for good efficiency

Opposite page Top: the gargantuan tubing of a 1968 Can-Am car. Note how much wider the bore of the pipes for this 7-litre machine than for 3-litre Formula One machinery due to the larger amount of gases to be expelled

Centre left: a 'baffle' silencer with its separate compartments which purposely hinder the flow of the exhaust gases to cut down the noise

Centre right: the straight-through silencer with its glass-fibre wool encasing the centre chamber

Bottom: the exhaust system at the rear of Alan Mann's sports-racing prototype, which was fitted with a Cosworth DFV engine

silencer is packed with glassfibre 'wool'. Some gas expansion takes place within the box, but at the same time the sonic properties of gas expansion are damped by the deadening effects of the fibre wool, rather in the manner that felt or some similar material is used to quieten the noise transmitted to the interior of a car during normal motoring.

In practice, the baffle system is more effective in the total reduction of exhaust noise than the straight-through type, but the difference is often not dramatic. On the other hand, the straight-through silencer interferes less with the gas flow in the system, which results in better power output.

It might appear from the foregoing that the bigger the bore of the pipes constituting an exhaust system the better, but this is not necessarily so. Wave effects may be set up which will work against the potentially greater acceptance of the pure bulk of expanding gas, and even the acknowledged experts cannot agree on an exact formula. What is called 'harmonic tuning' is a

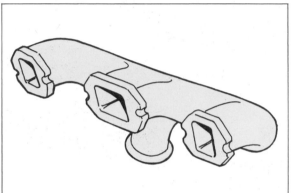

complicated subject and not precisely defined.

Basically, the harmonic effect is caused by the puff of gas discharged from the cylinder during the exhaust stroke, which travels down the pipes setting up a pressure wave, until it reaches the open end of the tail pipe. At this point, the wave is reflected back up the pipe. To illustrate this, if you make ripples on the surface of water by, say, dropping a stone, the ripples will be regular in wave pattern and when they meet an obstruction, such as the edge of a pond, they will be bounced back in the same frequency. When exhaust gas initially leaves the port, it is under high pressure, but the wave reflected from the tail pipe is a low-pressure wave which can produce a negative pressure situation at the valve—a highly desirable effect, since it helps to scavenge residual burnt gas from inside of the cylinder.

Although in some ways the exhaust system can be said to begin with the manifold, this, with its allied parts such as valves and ports, is only the start of the exhalation cycle. As with human beings, the engine has to breathe in before it can breathe out, so the two actions are closely inter-related. Unlike a human, an engine cannot hold its breath: the process is continuous. As the outlet valve starts to close, the inlet valve begins to open and one has the difficult and undesirable situation of exhaust gases remaining in the cylinder while a fresh charge of mixture is trying to get in. This condition, when both inlet and exhaust valves are open at the same time, is called the 'overlap'. The exhaust valve closes after the piston has reached its

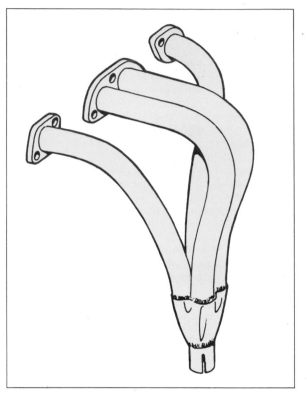

'top-dead-centre' position—when it has commenced going down on the induction stroke—and it is just at this point that the negative pressure, caused by the reverse exhaust pressure wave, is wanted, since it not only scavenges the remnants of burnt gas, but also encourages induction by helping to overcome the inertia of the mixture lurking inside of the inlet manifold and port.

Most four-cylinder family saloons have three-branch exhaust manifolds: one branch serves number one cylinder, another number four cylinder, and the third which is 'siamesed' (two pipes joined as one) takes the exhaust gases from both two and three cylinders. Depending on the firing order, this can cause problems in preserving a smooth flow, but for a car which is not tuned for brisk performance it does very well and, of course, is cheap to produce. With a modified version of the same basic engine, such as a 'GT' model, usually sporting twin carburettors, a more sophisticated exhaust manifold is required and most versions have four-branched manifolds with one pipe serving each cylinder. In this type of set-up, each pipe should be of the same length so that the 'puffs' of exhaust gas are evenly spaced out when the manifold discharges them, one after the other, into the single pipe which usually conducts the gases rearwards. This is why you see such complicated 'bunch-of-bananas' arrangements on racing cars and on some

highly-tuned production models.

Now, since the object of the exhaust exercise is to obtain a smooth and regular gas flow through the system, it is also necessary to utilise the wave reflection, so that it arrives at the exhaust port at the right time. This is why the length of the pipe is important: too long and the negative pressure will arrive too late; too short and it will arrive too soon. There is a certain model, made by a British manufacturer, which offers two different engines in the same body, both using basically the same exhaust system. On the bigger-engined version, the exhaust tail pipe has been extended by about ten inches, with a sort of after-thought piece of tail pipe. Presumably, the original system did not suit the larger capacity engine because the harmonics (wave motions) were out of phase.

From a purely practical angle, however well a manufacturer may design his exhaust system, if it is damaged it cannot perform properly. For example, if a silencer has become corroded to the extent that it is

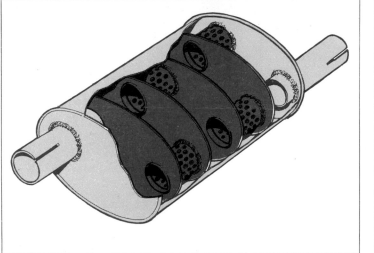

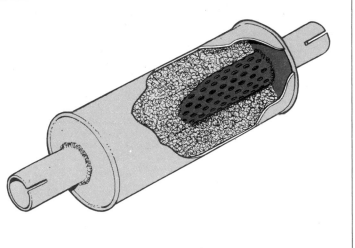

holed, this will radically affect the engine's breathing and, in consequence, its performance. Acceleration, fuel consumption and flexibility will all suffer to some extent, and there is the added danger that carbon monoxide fumes may be drawn into the car.

One failing with the ordinary steel original equipment exhaust system is that it is so short lived. In as little as eighteen months, corrosion can eat away the metal so that holes appear, causing the problems and dangers mentioned, especially if a car is used mainly for short runs. Doing short trips, the engine never has a chance to warm up properly and, instead of the acids which form during combustion becoming vaporised and blown out with the exhaust gases, they gather in such places as the silencer or expansion box and eat away at the steel from the inside.

One way of extending the life of an exhaust system is to aluminise the steel, which costs very little on top of the plain metal type. Probably the best way is to use stainless steel which lasts four or five times as long as mild steel and costs only twice as much.

If you are thinking of changing from the original system to a straight-through type, stainless steel, or any other non-standard layout, make quite sure that the new part has been designed for your car, otherwise you are likely to experience trouble due to tuning problems. If there are any doubts about the suitability of any system it is wise to consult a specialist. Apart from the fact that he should know what he is doing, there is always a come-back if things do happen to go wrong.

UNFORTUNATELY, no matter how well a standard exhaust system is painted, it will eventually corrode through. The reason for this is that it is not possible to paint the inside thoroughly and the exhaust gases contain extremely corrosive compounds.

One answer to this is to fit a stainless-steel system (these are commercially available), and the other is to use a metal coating, such as galvanising, on the surfaces of the parts. However, for the time being, the majority of car manufacturers use ordinary mild steel as the material for their exhaust pipes and silencers and this usually means at least a silencer-change every year or two and often a system-change at the same time.

There are several compounds on the market which can be used to seal small leaks in pipes and silencers. These take the form of pastes which set rock-hard upon the application of heat. Larger holes require the use of patches and these can be either metal plates, made from pieces of scrap sheet, or special bandage. The paste is most useful for sealing leaks in the joints between two pieces of pipe—it tends to be blown out of anything other than pinholes in silencers.

Should a large hole develop in a silencer, the area around the hole must be cleaned before any repair can take place. This repair work is made easier if the silencer is removed from the car, but this procedure is usually not a necessity. Assuming the puncture is larger than a pinprick, paste should be applied around the edges of the hole before a metal plate, cut from something like a discarded oil can, is placed over it.

The plate can be fixed in place either with wire wrapped round the whole of the silencer body, or with self-tapping screws.

If bandage is being used, the paste will be unnecessary. If the hole is a large one, a piece of tin foil, placed between the breakage and the bandage, will prevent the latter from being burned by the hot exhaust gases.

The bandage itself should be cut into strips large enough to cover the hole, and these should be overlapped to give a firm repair. The patch should be held in place with wire, which is usually supplied with the bandage.

Repairs to exhaust pipes should be carried out in the same way. Some cars use flexible pipe sections to allow for engine movement; these can be treated in the same way as ordinary pipe, but it will be a help to force paste into the grooves between the pipes. Because of the flexibility expected of these pipes, repairs to them are likely to be shorter-lived than those to the standard item.

Exhaust systems are usually suspended by flexible hangers and/or rubber mountings. These often break, but they should be easily replaced simply by undoing the mounting bolts.

If new parts are required for the exhaust system, these cannot be fitted until the old ones have been removed. This job is often more difficult than it looks. If two exhaust parts are rusted together and cannot be freed by means of a hammer or any amount of pipe wobbling, then heat should be applied, by means of a blowlamp, taking great care not to damage any paintwork, brake or fuel lines etc, or to heat the petrol tank.

The usual way to hold two pieces of pipe together is to fit one inside the other, providing the outer piece with slots to facilitate clamping. The heat should expand the outer pipe more than the inner, thus breaking the rust bond.

A new pipe may not have slots cut in it; if this is to be the outer part, these will have to be provided by sawing about two inches down from the end of the pipe, making at least two opposite cuts about 3/32 of an inch wide.

EXHAUST CARE

silencer repair and replacement

When the two parts are placed together, paste should be used to ensure a good seal round the joint. It is preferable to use a new clamp, tightening it until the slots close up enough to prevent the joint moving. In this way, the connections should last indefinitely.

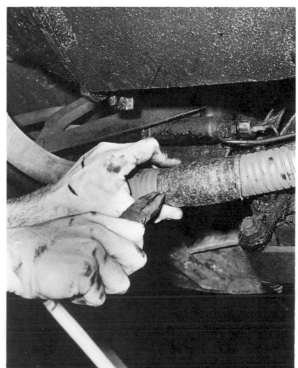

Above: the exhaust-pipe securing clamp is in a very exposed position underneath the car, and is inclined to get damaged and rusty. Checks must be made, therefore, in case it has fallen away and left the exhaust unsupported

Left: on repairing an exhaust pipe after it is holed, one must wire the foil and bandage; this will hold everything together while the bandage dries and ensure no leakage of exhaust gases

COOLING

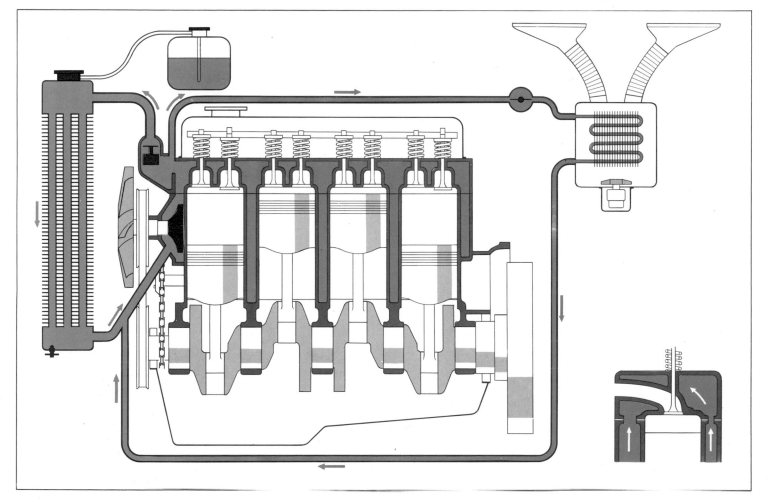

SINCE THE WASTE HEAT generated by a motor car has ultimately to be shed into the air, all motor cars are ultimately air-cooled, but air is not always the most effective medium for removing heat from some critical region deep within an engine, so water or oil may act as intermediary. The amount of heat to be shed is considerable: of all the calorific value of the fuel consumed by the engine, only about one third is converted into useful work, the remainder being lost, in roughly equal proportions, through the exhaust and cooling systems.

The cooling system of a motor car includes the exposed surfaces of the engine, from which waste heat is radiated. However, most of the necessary work is done by more efficient heat-exchangers: the cylinders and cylinder heads may be surrounded by water which is then circulated through a radiator where it gives up its heat to the air, or by metal fins which present a large surface area from which heat may escape.

The choice of air or liquid cooling has always been controversial. Air is cheaper, lighter and more readily obtainable than water—though to remove a given

quantity of heat demands four times the weight and 4000 times the volume of air as of water. But air can be collected and rejected, whereas water must be carried on the car; and the jacketing, conduits, pump and radiator of a water-cooled engine will probably weigh more than the substantial fins of an air-cooled one. However, the fins force the cylinders of an air-air-cooled engine to be more widely separated than those that occupy slender water-jackets, so the crank-shaft and crankcase must be longer and therefore heavier—or longer and yet equally stiff, even in torsion, and therefore *much* heavier. For an engine of many cylinders, this is the most persuasive objection to air cooling; for a simple horizontally-opposed twin it constitutes no objection whatever.

In either case, appreciable power is expended by any cooling system in pumping the cooling medium around the engine: whether the pump impels water or air hardly matters. Much more critical is the ease with which the coolant can be brought into contact with the heat; it is a matter of the designer's competence in arranging for water to be guided as near as

A typical water-cooled, four-cylinder engine, showing the circulation of the coolant. The pump is situated to the right of the fan (yellow). At the top right of the picture is the car's heater, which is a small version of the radiator *(left)*. Inset is a cross section of the cylinder head

possible to the exhaust valve seats and spark plug bosses, to name two of the most important zones, or for their heat to be guided through properly shaped fins to where the air can flow over their surfaces.

The choice of materials is quite important. Early air-cooled engines had cast-iron cylinders and heads, and suffered so gravely from overheating that it was probably necessity that mothered the invention of the aluminium-alloy cylinder head, cylinder, and piston—though the chronological order of these developments is slightly uncertain. It was, at any rate, a long time before air-cooled engines could be run as economically as liquid-cooled ones: they had to be run on a rich mixture, so that they were partly fuel-cooled.

The earliest water-cooled engines had no radiators and no circulatory systems: they relied on the evaporation of the coolant. When a closed circuit utilising a radiator was evolved, natural convection currents were trusted to keep the water circulating. The introduction of an engine-driven water pump improved the efficiency of the water-cooled system considerably, as well as giving the car designer more freedom in the location of the radiator, which has variously been above, behind, beside or before the engine.

In either kind of system, heat transfer is most efficient when the surface giving up heat to the air is very much hotter than the air—in other words, when the temperature gradient is steep. Because of this, small, closely-pitched fins may be better than large coarse ones on an air-cooled cylinder, and in very hot climates air-cooling may be better than water.

The effectiveness of a water-cooling system may be improved by raising the temperature of the coolant: the introduction of ethylene glycol was originally based on its boiling point being very much higher than that of water. It was a troublesome fluid, however, and experimental work showed that, by pressurising the cooling system to about 40 lb per sq in, water could be kept liquid at the same temperature (about 130°C) without boiling. Some glycol could be retained as an anti-freeze agent, but more than 30 per cent is undesirable: water is a better coolant than any other liquid at the same temperature, so superior is its heat transfer ability. Indeed, the higher the boiling point, the better does water compare with any other liquid coolant in this respect, so that adding even a small amount of water to glycol makes it a lot better. By the time the proportions reach 70 per cent water/ 30 per cent glycol, heat transfer is virtually as good as with plain water.

Many modern cars have their water systems pressurised to 14 lb per sq in, many more to 7, which suffices to raise the boiling point of water to 112°C. The greater efficiency of these high-pressure systems allows the radiator to be made smaller, lighter and cheaper. There is a slight incidental danger: at pressures above 4 lb per sq in, the old-fashioned, fail-safe, bellows-type thermostat valve may be forced to close, whereas the modern wax-filled type is not so affected.

The presence of the thermostat valve is explained by the need for a vehicle's engine to be brought up to its normal working temperature as quickly as possible, for it is most inefficient when running cooler than necessary. The bulk of the cooling water is therefore isolated from the engine by this valve, allowing the relatively small amount in the engine's water jackets to be heated quickly. When working temperature is reached, the valve opens and normal circulation begins.

The reason for having a large mass of water in the total system is that it constitutes a valuable safety barrier against overheating when the engine is subjected to brief spells of very arduous duty. The water

can accept a lot of surplus heat that can thereafter be shed steadily over a fairly long period. The air-cooled engine has no such heat-buffer in reserve: in such conditions it puts more heat into its lubricating oil (which is in any case the immediate transfer medium for removing heat from pistons, piston rings, and bearings), so it is usual for an air-cooled engine to require a heat-exchanger (oil cooler) for its oil—and this, although smaller and lighter than a water radiator, is unlikely to be any cheaper.

These radiators always used to be made of copper, a material having exceptionally good thermal conductivity. Aluminium has recently come into limited use instead, for although its conductivity is slightly inferior, it is much lighter. Either metal may suffer or cause galvanic corrosion, according to the other materials present in the cooling system, and it is common nowadays for carefully formulated corrosion inhibitors to be added to the water (or to the anti-freeze), according to the metals involved. Thus, an aluminium and iron engine may need a different additive from one with an all-aluminium construction.

Top: the air-cooled vertical-twin of a Fiat 500 saloon. The trunking, on the left, carries air into ducts, where a fan, mounted on the front of the dynamo, induces circulation. Air does not conduct heat as well as water, so the cylinders are finned to increase their external surface area

Above: the flat-four of the Citroën GS. This unit is front mounted, so ducting is not necessary

THOUGH A FEW MAKES of cars (the Volkswagen Beetle and the Chevrolet Corvair, for example) have air-cooled engines, the engines of most modern automobiles are cooled by water.

The water, heated by close contact with the engine, is cooled by its passage through the radiator matrix. The differing densities of the hot and cold water alone are sufficient to set up a circulation, known as the thermosyphon effect, and for many years this was adequate for engine cooling. Higher speeds and hotter engines, however, meant that the rate of circulation had to be boosted to increase efficiency, and so the water pump was added.

On the conventional engine, the pump housing is mounted on the end of the engine block nearest to No 1 cylinder. An impeller (a disc-like casting with curved, radial blades on one side), mounted on a shaft, rotates inside the housing. The shaft terminates at its outer end in a pulley, which may also support the

WATER PUMP

circulating the coolant

fan, and is belt-driven from the crankshaft pulley.

The pump shaft has to be sealed against water, as well as supported by bearings. A common type of seal is a thick rubber disc kept permanently under compression by a stiff coil spring. Carbon discs, felt washers, glands and sealing plates are all found in various forms of seal. The shaft bearings are often twin ball races; some need no lubrication, others require a lithium-base grease applied at 12,000-mile intervals.

An inlet to this centrifugal pump is connected to the bottom tank of the radiator; the outlet often discharges from the outside of the pump through a port in the front of the engine block. The cooled water circulates from the bottom tank of the radiator through the pump, into the engine cooling chambers and out through the cylinder head; then, through the thermostat chamber to the radiator header tank. When the engine is cold and the thermostat is closed the water is bypassed back from the thermostat chamber to the inlet side of the pump. This centrifugal type of pump and circulatory system is found, with small variations, in the majority of modern water-cooled automobile engines; but a few vehicles, such as the rear-engined Chrysler Hillman Imp, have a self-contained water pump, separate from the engine.

The only parts of a water pump likely to fail are the seal and bearings. If a leak around the shaft is detected, or if an unusual noise, indicating a bearing failure, is heard, repairs should be put in hand immediately. As special tools are frequently required to draw the impeller and bearings from the shaft, a factory-reconditioned unit may well turn out to be cheaper and more satisfactory than repairs to the existing unit.

Removal and replacement entails draining the system, removing hoses and the fan (and possibly the radiator), then unbolting and carefully separating the old pump from the cylinder block. New gaskets should be fitted with the replacement. Copper washers should be used under any fixing bolts that extend into the water jacket.

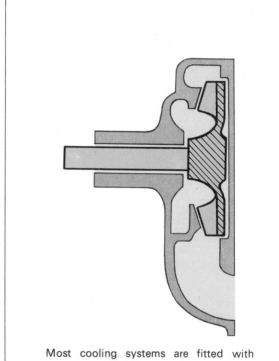

Most cooling systems are fitted with water pumps of the centrifugal type, as shown above in section. Water enters through the central blue section and is spun outwards by the yellow rotor so that it is forced into the outer channel and down the outlet pipe

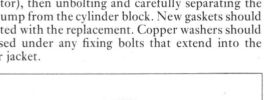

Left and below: the workings and outside views of centrifugal pumps, as used on the vast majority of motor cars

DIESEL

combustion by compression

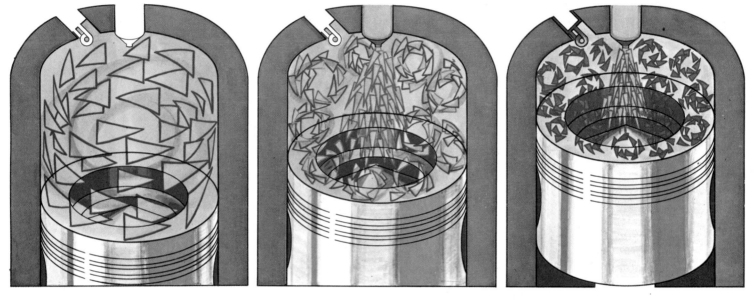

RUDOLF CHRISTIAN KARL DIESEL, born in 1858, the son of an expatriate Augsburg craftsman, and brought up in poverty, passed out of the Technical University in Munich with the most brilliant examination results in the Institution's history. One of his teachers was the founder of modern refrigeration engineering, Carl von Linde, and, from him, Diesel learned a lot of the theory of heat engines. Contemplating this, Diesel saw that he could make an engine four times as efficient as the abysmal steamers of the time, by generating the heat of combustion actually inside the working cylinder, and subjecting the working fluid (air) to as wide a temperature range as possible by utmost compression and expansion. According to his theory, extremely high pressures would be necessary since the temperature reached would partly depend on the pressure—and so the air would have to be compressed before any fuel was introduced, lest combustion be premature.

It was this feature that distinguished the diesel engine from the conventional, spark-ignited, internal-combustion engine that was enjoying contemporaneous development. In the spark-ignition engine, the fuel was mixed with the air before admission to the cylinder, wherein it was compressed as much as was safe before ignition; in the diesel engine, only air was admitted to the cylinder, where it was compressed as much as was necessary to raise it to the temperature at which fuel, then injected into it, would ignite spontaneously.

The first diesel patent was taken out in 1892 in Berlin. His first engine ran on coal dust, but it was when he converted to partially refined oil that it became a success. Unfortunately, Diesel had no business talent, although he might ultimately have profited greatly from the enormous commercial

exploitation of his type of engine. He died in 1913 in the North Sea after falling from a ship in which he was travelling for consultations with the British Admiralty. Today, half the world's registered tonnage of ships, a large proportion of its railway locomotives and most commercial vehicles, are diesel driven. There have been, and are, a number of cars similarly powered, but for a variety of good reasons the practice has never been popular with the majority of manufacturers.

In constant heavy-duty jobs such as those of the locomotive, the earthmover, or the ship, the diesel makes fair sense. In lorries and 'buses its virtues are debatable. In cars they are scarcely detectable. The essentially heavyweight diesel engine is also essentially

Above: compression and combustion in the diesel cycle. Note the glow plug which assists the ignition process when the engine is cold. In the first stages of compression (*left*), the air takes up a swirling motion, forming a vortex. This is brought about partially by the shape of the inlet tract, partially by the piston-crown shape and partially by the combustion-chamber design. As compression progresses, the vortex is broken up into smaller turbulent areas (*centre*). As the fuel is injected, it mixes with the air and begins to ignite. The build-up of compression (*right*) speeds up the combustion process, which continues until injection ceases

Left: the first four-cylinder diesel engine, which was announced by Benz in 1923

feeble, and with safety regulations forcing cars to get heavier anyway, there is little attraction in the idea of making them even heavier and, at the same time, denying them the power necessary to move their increased weight at a reasonable rate.

A comparison of diesel and petrol engines built for automotive duty in Europe shows that the average diesel weighs about nine pounds per horsepower. To assess a fair average for petrol engines is more difficult, since so many of them are humble little affairs of a litre or so, intended for cheap, light cars and, because of nature's inexorable square/cube law, such engines must be relatively heavy. However, if we confine ourselves to the larger petrol engines that afford a more direct comparison with the diesels already considered, their power-to-weight ratio works out at about three pounds per horsepower.

This difference is largely due to different marketing requirements. Lightness of a spark-ignition engine does not necessarily imply flimsiness and want of durability, but such engines are built for a market where cost must be low and depreciation can be ridiculously high—in which circumstances it does not pay the manufacturer to make his engines particularly durable. Even so, a lot depends on the pattern of usage: on the rare occasions when a petrol-engined car is used virtually continuously and not subjected to many cold starts and short trips, the engine proves to be capable of covering a very high mileage without overhaul. This is typical of the usage of most diesels, which are commercially operated with maximum utilisation very much in mind. Nevertheless, those rare engine manufacturers, who make both kinds of engines to equally high standards, find very little difference in their durabilities: the general superiority of the diesel from this point of view is simply due to the fact that the diesel *has* to be well and robustly made for, if it is not, it will break under the enormous strain.

Mechanically, the massive construction of the diesel engine is more of a liability than an asset. The thick-crowned pistons are very heavy; so are the connecting rods with their generous big-ends and unusually large gudgeon pins and bosses, and these reciprocating parts impose tremendous loads on the bearings. Consider not only these inertia loads, but also the tremendous compression loads of the diesel, which are likewise ultimately transmitted to the crankcase which has in turn to be inordinately robust. Bear in mind too that the components of a diesel engine are subjected to these heavy mechanical stresses all the time. This is simply because there is no throttle in the air intake of the diesel. When a spark-ignition engine is working at less than full load, the intake is partially closed by the throttle valve linked to the accelerator pedal, and this has the effect of reducing the effective compression ratio: a petrol engine with a ten-to-one compression ratio is only working at five-to-one when running at half throttle. By contrast, the diesel is running at its full compression ratio under all circumstances, the output being varied by metering the dosage of fuel injected. The compression ratio varies from about sixteen to one in large engines to over twenty to one in the smaller varieties used in private cars, and the high consequent loads make life hard for pistons, gudgeon pins and crankshaft bearings. Even worse for them is the shockingly rapid rise in pressure in the cylinders when the fuel is injected, spontaneously bursting into flame. The rigours of the diesel cycle are reflected in the stringent specifications required for bearings and lubricating oils in diesel-engine service.

From the same fact of running constantly at maximum compression comes the first of the diesel

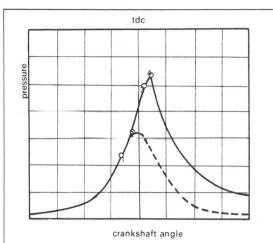

This graph shows the variation of pressure, within a diesel cylinder, as the crankshaft turns and moves the piston up on the compression stroke. The solid curve indicates the situation under normal circumstances (where fuel is injected and combustion takes place), while the dotted line represents the lower pressures found if air alone is compressed. Point 1 is the start of injection; 2 is the start of combustion; 3 is the finish of injection; 4 is the finish of combustion

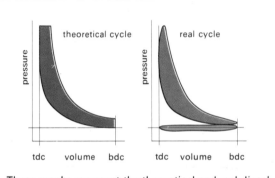

These graphs represent the theoretical and real diesel cycles. The orange area shows the work done on the power stroke, while the blue section is induction and exhaust

The four-stroke diesel cycle is exactly the same as that of the petrol engine (the Otto cycle). However, the pressures within the cylinders are far greater in the case of the diesel unit. Because of these enormous pressures, the engine has to be built very sturdily and is therefore extremely heavy for its size

engine's advantages, its good part-load fuel economy. Thermal efficiency is intimately related to compression ratio and, in part-load operation, the diesel is greatly superior to the petrol engine. At full load, there is much less difference and what there is may largely be accounted for by the fact that the diesel gives off less waste heat.

The average specific fuel consumption of automotive diesel engines running on full load is about 0.38 lb per horsepower per hour. In the case of petrol engines, the figure is more like 0.48, but this is an average taken from a range that covers wide extremes, and there are plenty of petrol engines that do a good deal better. It is undeniable that the best that petrol engines can do merely equals the average of what diesels manage; but there are in fact not many diesels that get appreciably lower, and the distinguished handful that achieve as little as 0.33 or thereabouts mostly display a somewhat impoverished performance, even by diesel standards.

One of the unfortunate things about the diesel engine is that it has to be run on lean fuel/air mixtures since anything richer would make it smoke intolerably. In the circumstances, it is inevitable that the diesel

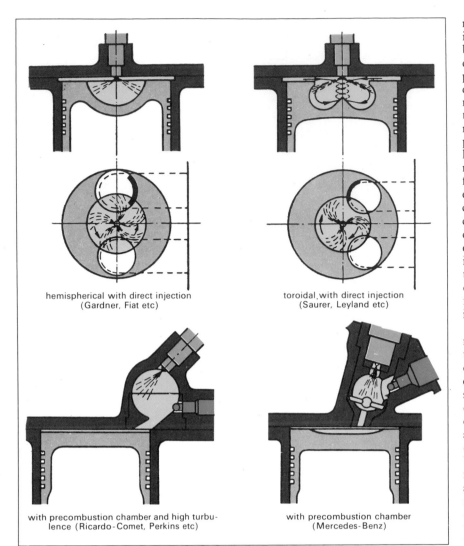

hemispherical with direct injection
(Gardner, Fiat etc)

toroidal with direct injection
(Saurer, Leyland etc)

with precombustion chamber and high turbulence (Ricardo-Comet, Perkins etc)

with precombustion chamber
(Mercedes-Benz)

A selection of diesel-engine combustion chambers. Those with precombustion chambers and glow plugs are typical of small, car-size diesels and have higher compression ratios than the others. There are many variations on the toroidal cavity (which is a sort of sphere turned halfway inside-out) and of spray patterns. They all influence the rates of turbulence of the air and of mixture of the fuel therewith. These in turn affect the rates of combustion and pressure-rise

cannot compare with the petrol engine for torque or power. It is worth remembering too that if the diesel is particularly good at fuel economy in part-load operation, this capability is relatively little exploited because the engine has so little power (and the vehicle it propels is so heavy) that it becomes necessary to drive at, or near, full load for a much larger proportion of running time. Precisely the same reasons are responsible for the curve of specific fuel consumption of the diesel being flatter than that of the petrol engine: since the diesel has to run on a relatively weak mixture even at peak bmep (brake mean effective pressure), it is not only less powerful, but also less thirsty. This is the reason, and a poor reason, for relatively low cooling losses at full load.

Likewise, the idea that diesels are strong on torque is a fallacy. Torque curves are usually mirror images of those for specific fuel consumption; and here again, because of the diesel's combustion limitations, the torque curve is particularly flat, giving the illusion of ample torque over a wide range of operating speeds whereas the truth is that the peak of the curve is lopped rather than the lower portions being raised.

The difficulties of burning the charge cleanly and completely, and most of the other limitations of performance of the diesel engine, are attributable to the means by which the fuel is introduced to the air compressed in the cylinder. This makes the processes of injection and combustion matters for serious study, and research on them goes on earnestly and continuously, as it has throughout the history of the type. The

nature of the fuel is the first consideration: heavy industrial engines can run on all kinds of turgid filth, but automotive diesels require a light petroleum distillate, having about the same calorific content as the petrol used in cars but otherwise exhibiting rather different characteristics. Its anti-knock or octane rating is irrelevant, the corresponding feature being the cetane rating, which is a measure of the fuel's readiness to ignite at a certain temperature and pressure. The two ratings are not related, although a high-cetane fuel will have a low octane value. This is not to say that knock is not a diesel problem: it is, in fact, one of the most notorious, being caused by an exceptionally rapid pressure rise during the course of combustion. Unfortunately, the requirements of good compression/ignition make it impossible to spread the combustion over a longer period, so the entire process of injection of the fuel, volatilisation of the droplets, ignition and combustion, must take place in about thirty degrees of crankshaft rotation. This in turn demands very precise timing of the injection of the fuel, and equally precise metering of the amount injected.

To achieve this, expensive and extremely accurate mechanical pumps jerk the requisite quantities of fuel to spring-loaded nozzles feeding into the combustion chamber. When the pressure at the nozzle is high enough to raise the needle valve off its seat against the spring pressure, it is automatically high enough to ensure that the fuel is sprayed into the combustion chamber in the most minute droplets, and in the most appropriate directions; the amount of fuel delivered is determined by the time during which this pressure can be maintained, governed in turn by the pump in response to the engine speed and the position of the accelerator pedal. The mechanical arrangement of this system is inevitably complex, and these injection components must be viewed as among the most remarkable examples of high-precision, mass-production engineering in the world.

Nevertheless, they suffer severe limitations. As already explained, it is impossible to seek more power from a diesel engine by giving it a richer mixture than normal: excess fuel simply cannot be properly burned, and the residue emerges as grey, or even black, smoke—soot, deriving from the 86 per cent carbon content of the fuel. Smoke is also produced when starting, because the cold engine reduces the temperature of the air compressed in the cylinders and thus impairs the efficiency of combustion. Self-starter motors therefore have to be very powerful to achieve high cranking speeds and, in fact, the majority of small diesels, such as those used in cars rely on electrical preheating of the combustion chamber, a procedure that may occupy as much as a minute before starting the engine. Thereafter, no electrical services are required, although in a vehicular application, the engine must be furnished with the usual generator, starter-motor and ancillary equipment. Because of this independence of ignition, the engine cannot be switched off, and is usually stopped by interrupting its fuel supply: the driver pulls a knob which overrides the other injection pump controls and cuts off the fuel.

The smoke given off by a badly adjusted diesel engine is only one of the many pollutants it emits. Its exhaust is also very rich in oxides of nitrogen (on average 1.7 times as much as from the average petrol engine before the introduction of clean air laws), sulphur dioxide (3.8 times as much) and particulate matter, including not only soot but also lead compounds (7.8 times). If the exhaust has an acrid smell, this is caused by aldehydes compounded during the combustion process which also liberates large quantities of carbon dioxide. On the other hand, the diesel exhaust is notably superior to that of the petrol engine in hydrocarbon and carbon monoxide pollution.

In fairness to the memory of Diesel, it must be pointed out that most of these difficulties would be overcome if current engines retained the fuel injection system that was an important feature of his designs. The way he arranged things, the fuel was heated to the point where it was ready to burn if there were any air in which to do so, and was then forced by compressed air into the combustion chamber, entering as an already burning emulsion. The less satisfactory airless injection system universal today was proposed by a British engineer, Ackroyd-Stuart, who had taken out some oil-engine patents between 1885 and 1890 following-on the work of Priestman of Hull. Another British engineer, McKechnie, vandalised Diesel's design in 1910 by substituting cold airless injection of the fuel for the original and correct hot compressed-air injection.

Another environmentally obnoxious feature of the diesel engine is the noise it makes, a noise that has been found expensive and difficult to cure. If the engine be enclosed by acoustic shielding, most of the noise can be kept from the car's occupants and from outsiders in the vicinity. This is seldom practical because the space for such shielding is seldom available, and if there is room to enclose the engine in a sound-proof box, that box has to be airtight—which means that the normal cooling system will have to be extended and modified in a way that is bound to be costly. Another method, practised to some extent in naval vessels, is to fit a contoured shield of a suitable (and usually heavy) acoustic cladding closely around the engine carcass: in this case, accessibility for maintenance is very difficult, and incorrect fitting of the shield could damage the engine, while cooling is still a problem. The long-term solution is to re-design the engine so as to dampen, stiffen or isolate all surfaces that radiate noise. In many cases this is inconsistent with the other mechanical requirements of the components involved, most notably the cylinder block and various timing chests. The noise actually comes from the combustion space, and there is a limit to what can be achieved by modifying it, and the combustion process itself, so as to reduce the noise at source.

Literally, the most burdensome problem of all is the sheer mass of metal necessary to withstand the gross stresses imposed by the ultra-fast pressure rise during combustion. A four-cylinder, 1½-litre diesel engine frequently used in cars develops about 45 bhp and weighs 425 lb; a common 3-litre petrol engine for ordinary saloon cars weighs the same and develops 140 bhp. The same relationship applies to higher power ratings: if 200 bhp were required, it could be obtained from a notably hefty and durable high-grade petrol engine weighing 600 lb, while the equivalent diesel would turn the scale at 1800. The burden of all that extra weight is likely to offset any fuel economies attributable to the diesel. In fact, the penalty is even greater: because the petrol engine is so much smaller and very much faster-revving than a diesel of similar power, most of the transmission line associated with it need only have about one-third the torque capacity of what would be necessary for the compression ignition engine. Only in the final drive, downstream from the reduction gears, need the transmission components be as massive as in diesel-vehicle practice. This means a tremendous saving in weight and an equally tremendous saving in first cost.

As for fuel costs, the differences are largely illusory. At present, diesel fuel is considerably cheaper than petrol—not at roadside filling stations, but to the big operators who use it in bulk and can buy it a lot more cheaply. Nevertheless, these differences are largely artificial situations brought about by the taxation system, though petrol being the more refined distillate is basically more costly anyway. If there were to be a marked change in the use of these fuels, there would undoubtedly be corresponding changes in the pattern of taxation. In countries where petrol is cheap, very few people bother with diesels, preferring the lower cost and higher efficiency of petrol units.

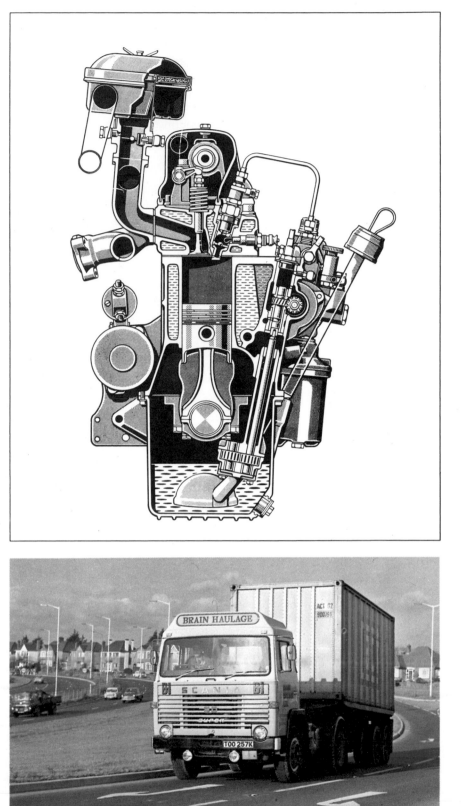

Top: a transverse section through a Mercedes 190D engine of 1958. It is a four-cylinder unit, producing 60 bhp from its 1988 cc

Above: a Scania articulated truck with a turbocharged diesel engine

CUTTING DOWN ENGINE WEAR is the primary function of the various filters fitted to the car engine, but they also play an important part in the car's performance and economy. Five main types of filter do five separate jobs, and most cars will have at least two types fitted.

Oil filters

The engine oil filtration system may be one of two types—either 'full flow' or 'partial flow'. The former is the type most commonly used in modern engines and is situated between the oil pump and the engine's moving parts. All the oil passes through it and the design is such that there is no restriction of the flow yet, at the same time, contaminant particles of harmful size are strained out.

The partial flow system, which is sometimes called a 'bypass system' is not fitted in the main oil line. Instead, part of the oil flow is diverted through it. The amount is about ten per cent and it means that the whole of the oil in the sump is filtered about ten times every running hour.

Both the oil and the filters must be changed at regular intervals recommended by the car manufacturer, the usual interval for this being five or six thousand miles. Just in case servicing is neglected, however, in order to safeguard the engine, a by pass circuit is installed. Even if the filter is completely blocked, oil can still get to the engine's moving parts.

The actual filter used can be one of two types. One can be dismantled with a replaceable element; the other is a sealed canister from which the element cannot be removed. This type is replaced as a complete unit. The filtration medium used in both types is usually a pleated resin-impregnated paper.

Air filters

These come in all shapes and sizes. The casing may be made of metal or plastic and access to the filter element inside may be by means of clips, screws, nuts and bolts or a push-fit cover, but the filter element is likely to be one of three types.

Pleated resin-impregnated paper is by far the most common. Oil-wetted wire mesh is another alternative and there is also the oil-bath type. All of them are designed to do the same job: to separate the air from all the dust and dirt contamination it may be carrying. With both the pleated paper and the oil-wetted mesh, air can pass through freely but the dust particles get trapped. With the oil-bath type, incoming air is drawn across the surface of the oil, and dust, etc is trapped in it. Usually, a second wire-mesh filter is incorporated.

Eventually, any type of air filter will become choked with dirt and if this happens the ingress of air is restricted. If there is less air to mix with the fuel in the carburettor, the air-fuel balance is altered and made rich. Petrol consumption increases as a result.

Regular servicing will prevent this happening. Manufacturers' recommendations are usually that a pleated-paper-type element should be changed every 12,000 miles. At interim stages, it is usual to take out the element, tap out the loose dirt and then rotate it to present a clean area to the air intake.

With the wire-mesh types, the mesh has to be washed in petrol, dried and re-oiled. Oil-bath types need dismantling, cleaning and the oil replenishing.

Crankcase breathers

These do two jobs. There is one to allow air to be drawn into the engine and another to allow fumes to escape. Both will probably have some sort of filter incorporated, and both will require some sort of servicing. If the air-inlet type becomes clogged,

FILTERS

taking out the dirt

Filters are used in motor vehicles to clean just about every fluid used in the engine. The well known filters are those for the lubricating oil and the air supply to the cylinders. Less well known is the fact that filters are used to clean the fuel, either being built into the fuel pump or housed in a separate container under the engine-compartment lid, as shown here

sludging of the oil can result. If the outward-breathing one stops working, crankcase pressurisation and high oil consumption can occur.

Servicing requirements depend entirely on the particular device fitted. Some have paper elements which need renewing, others have wire-mesh filters which need washing in petrol, others are sealed units which have to be replaced completely. The car's service manual will tell you which type you have and how to service them. Usually, servicing is required every 12,000 miles.

Petrol filters

At some point between the fuel tank and carburettor, a filter of some sort will be fitted. Normally it will be found inside the petrol pump. Mechanical pumps have a round filter gauze under the dome at the top. SU electric pumps have a thimble-shaped filter fitted in the base of the pump. Both types can be withdrawn quite simply for cleaning and this is usually recommended at every 6000-mile service.

Servo air filters

Changing these is not a frequent job. It is recommended that it is carried out at 40,000 miles, except in extremely dusty conditions. The operation varies according to the type of servo unit. Normally, it involves a simple rubber dust-cover and a retainer. Sometimes, the disc-shaped filter has to be cut to allow it to be fitted over the operating rod. Another type uses an open-ended cylinder-shaped filter.

OIL CHANGING

an essential part of motoring

LUBRICATING OILS are becoming more sophisticated all the time. It is not all that many years ago that engine oil was single grade only and contained no additives at all. In those days, it was recommended that different grades of oil be used for summer and winter. The lack of detergents in the oils meant that sludge formed within the engine and frequent oil changes were necessary.

Today, engine oil contains many additives to make it more effective and to improve its high-temperature stability. It is no longer necessary to use summer and winter grades, since the advent of multigrade oils means that the two grades can be combined in one oil.

However, no matter how efficient the oil, it will eventually deteriorate and will have to be changed. The interval between oil changes varies, nowadays, between 3000 and 6000 miles, depending on the make of car and the state of tune of the engine (it is usual for highly stressed power units to require more frequent oil changes than the lazy ones).

As wear takes place in the engine, metal particles find their way into the oil. These particles could do devastating damage if allowed to stay in the oil, so they are filtered out. After several thousand miles the filter will begin to block; this is when it should be changed. In many types of car, the filter is changed with the same frequency as the oil, while in others the requirement is one filter change to every other oil change.

There are two types of oil filter: the throwaway type and the replaceable-element type. Throwaway oil filters are complete units which screw direct into the engine; they cannot be taken apart and so they have to be replaced as a whole. Replaceable-element types consist of a canister, into which the filter element is placed. Instead of changing the whole assembly, the element can be replaced.

The procedure for changing engine oil is fairly standard for most cars, the differences being in the positioning of the important parts such as the drain plug and the oil filter.

The first job is to start the engine and run it until it is warm. This thins the oil so that it will run out of the drain hole more readily than if cold. Having done this, the drain plug should be unscrewed. This plug is situated somewhere near the lowest point on the sump (at the bottom of the engine) and is usually recognisable as a plug. Most cars have a standard hexagonal head on the drain plug, allowing the plug to be undone with a normal spanner. Several makes, however, use an

Above left: a pit or lift is a great advantage for oil changing, but the job is quite easy if the front of the car is raised on a jack or ramps; here, the engine oil is draining

Above: this is the replaceable-element type of oil filter; oil is likely to pour out when it is removed. The sealing ring can be seen in its groove

Oil changing/ENGINE

Allen screw which cannot be removed without an Allen key.

Before the plug is removed completely, a container, large enough to contain a sump-full of oil, should be placed in the best position to catch all that oil. While the sump is draining, the filter should be removed (if the job is due). The throwaway type is removed by turning the whole body of the canister in an anti-clockwise direction. Some filters have a hexagonal knob pressed into the end of the canister, so that a spanner can be employed to assist with this removal. Should the filter refuse to move and be the type without a hexagon, it may be possible to turn the canister by tapping it in the correct direction with a cold chisel and hammer. Once this type of filter has been removed, it is only necessary to clean any spilled oil from around the seating before fitting the new unit. A new sealing ring should always be used, but this is usually already affixed to the filter casing. Even if the canister does have a hexagon, a spanner should not be used during the refitting process, since it is possible to overtighten the unit and damage the seal, the thread or both. Hand pressure is enough to prevent leaks.

The replaceable-element oil filter is removed by unscrewing the bolt which passes either through the filter casing into the engine or through something like the oil-pump body into the filter casing. Once the bolt has been fully unscrewed, the canister may need tapping to free the bond between it, the sealing ring and the seating. Preparation should be made to catch anything up to a pint of oil contained in the filter canister. With the filter off, the element should be tipped out of its casing, making sure that any plates, springs or washers are retained for use with the new element.

After washing out the canister, using paraffin or petrol, the new element should be fitted with the various bits and pieces in the correct places. The sealing ring is most commonly fitted to a groove in the oil-filter seating and this ring should be replaced.

The filter casing should be refitted to its mounting carefully, so that it is seating evenly on the sealing ring. Ideally, the fixing bolt should be tightened to the torque shown in the maker's literature.

By the time the filter has been replaced, the oil should have drained out. The plug should be cleaned, especially if it is of the magnetic type, and replaced. The correct amount of oil can now be poured in through the filler hole, usually situated on the cam or rocker cover.

Finally, the engine should be run and the joint between the filter and the engine checked for leaks. If there is a leak, the filter should be reseated. When the oil has run back down to the sump, the level should be checked on the dipstick to confirm that the correct amount of lubricant has been added.

It is recommended that the lubrication system be flushed with special flushing oil. This becomes really worthwhile if the old oil is heavily contaminated with metal particles and sludge. The procedure should be carried out before the filter is changed. After draining the old oil, the plug should be replaced and the sump half filled with flushing oil. The engine should be run at fast idle until it is warm again and then the flushing oil should be drained. The filter can now be changed and the procedure continued as before.

It is unusual, in modern cars, for gearbox or rear-axle, oil-draining facilities to be provided. All that is necessary is an occasional top-up. As with engine oils, transmission oils have improved a great deal and several manufacturers consider that the oil will last as long as the gearbox or rear axle.

In order to check the level of the oil, the level plug/

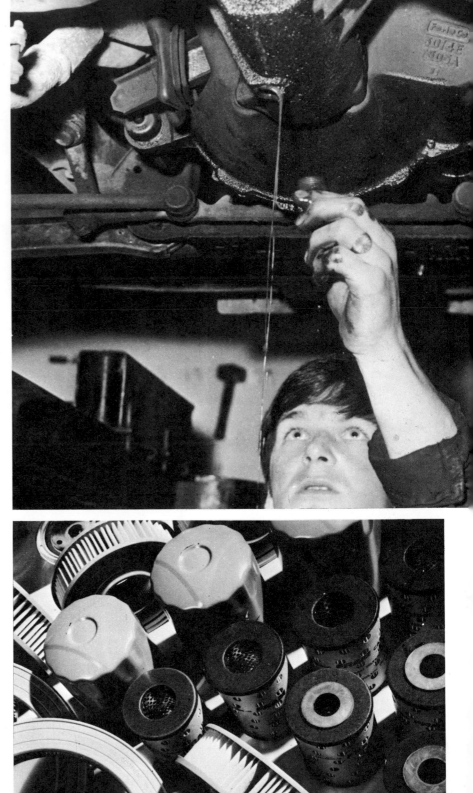

filler should be removed. This is usually situated on the side of the gearbox or on the rear of the differential housing and involves some contortions on the part of the mechanic. If topping-up is required, a flexible tube is usually the best weapon with which to attack the problem. Some cars, especially those with automatic transmission, have a gearbox filler tube under the bonnet; this simplifies matters considerably.

If the gearbox or rear axle do need to be drained, then the plug, if fitted, is usually situated at the lowest point, in the same way as on the sump.

Top: gearbox and back axle oils usually need only be topped up in modern cars, as oils have improved a great deal; filler/level plugs are usually on the gearbox side

Above: a selection of filters

70

MANY HIGHLY STRESSED, rapidly moving components in a modern internal-combustion engine need constant lubrication if seizure or excessive wear are to be avoided. The function of an oil pump is to supply oil, under pressure, to those parts of the engine which require this positive lubrication.

The most common form of oil pump used to be the gear type. It consists of two meshing gears, which rotate inside a close-fitted housing. As the gears rotate they carry oil around, against the housing. The meshing of the gear teeth forces the oil out, into the pump discharge tube.

This gear-type oil pump produces a positive flow of oil to the various parts of the engine to which it is directed. If the flow is blocked, the oil pressure can increase sufficiently to damage the pump. Alternatively, if the engine oil is particularly thick, the pressure required to force the cold oil through the small bearing clearances can cause a similar pressure build-up, damaging the pump. To eliminate these possibilities an oil-pressure relief valve is fitted. This returns oil to the sump, or to the oil tank if a dry-sump system is used, when the pressure created exceeds a predetermined value.

Another form of oil pump, more common than the gear type, is the rotor variety. This consists of a rotor, with four or five external lobes, which rotates inside an outer ring (termed a stator) having five or six internal lobes. The axis of the inner rotor is offset from the axis of the outer ring. The effect is that, although the outer ring is driven by the inner rotor, the volume between the lobes varies as the two rotate. Oil is thus caught between the lobes and forced out into the pump discharge tube.

The action of this type of oil pump can be likened in some ways to the operation of the Wankel or rotary engine. The rotor-type oil pump also requires a pressure relief valve. A less common type of oil pump is the rotary-plunger type of pump. This has only one moving part: a worm gear rotates a rotary plunger. A peg engages a profiled groove in the rotary plunger to provide the reciprocating movement, so producing the pumping action. A non-return valve is also necessary. The oil flow from this type of pump is intermittent and the pressure produced is generally lower than that produced by the gear or rotor-type oil pumps. It is therefore inherently unsuitable for many engines, but is used in some engines which utilise roller or ball-races as big-end or main bearings, and as such require only minimal lubrication.

In rare instances a plunger oil pump is reciprocated by an eccentric peg on the end of a shaft, which engages a slot in the plunger. A particular disadvantage of both the gear and rotor-type oil pumps is that after the engine has been stopped, oil can drain back through the system to the sump. Neither of these is therefore entirely suitable for a dry-sump lubrication system which might as an alternative employ a form of plunger pump.

The final type of pump is known as the sliding-vane oil pump. This consists of a four-vaned rotor, the vanes of which form a seal against the walls of an ovalised chamber by being free to slide in and out of the rotor to take up the ovality. As with the rotor-type pump, the volume between the vanes varies as the rotor spins; oil is drawn in as the volume increases and is squeezed out as it decreases. This type tends to wear more quickly than the others.

Most modern internal-combustion engines use a wet-sump lubrication system and the engine bearings are usually of the plain white-metal type. These bearings require only a comparatively low-pressure

OIL PUMP

keeping the lubricant on the move

oil supply, of the order of a few pounds per square inch, to provide adequate lubrication. Oil supplied to a bearing at one point is drawn around between the two bearing surfaces by rotation. In this way a wedge of oil is formed which is of sufficient strength to take the full load of the bearings.

The high oil pressure produced by a gear, rotor, or vane pump is used to provide a sufficiently fast flow of oil to absorb and carry away heat from the bearing surfaces and other parts of the engine such as the pistons, which would otherwise overheat.

Those engines which use a dry-sump system normally have dual oil pumps. One of these is used to provide oil pressure for lubrication. The second (the 'scavenge' pump) is used to remove the oil from the sump to the oil tank. To prevent a surplus of oil accumulating in the sump, the second pump usually has a larger capacity than the lubricating pump.

Oil pumps require no routine maintenance, although if they incorporate a strainer this should be cleaned periodically. The job need only be done infrequently, when the sump is removed, and only when removing sludge from the sump.

Oil pumps are usually driven from the camshaft or crankshaft through suitable gearing. It is this gearing which is likely to be damaged if the oil-pump outlet has been blocked and the pump has suffered from over-pressure.

It might be thought that constantly being immersed in oil, oil pumps would have an almost indefinite working life. In fact they have a long working life, but they do eventually wear. As a result the oil pump output will in time become insufficient for the requirements of the engine.

Most service manuals specify maximum limits for wear between the components of the oil pump. If these wear limits are exceeded, it is normal practice to change the oil pump as an assembly. Such renewal is generally only undertaken as part of a major engine overhaul or reconditioning.

Above left: a partially dismantled vane-type pump, in which the rotor, which has sliding vanes, spins inside an ovalised chamber; the pressure relief valve is seen with its spring

Above: a complete pump, with a perspex cover to show off the 'works' which are of the rotor type

OIL & LUBRICATION

reducing friction to a minimum

COMMERCIALLY AVAILABLE motor oils are so good that it is almost unheard of that an engine's failure should be attributed to some deficiency in its lubricant. The oil may deteriorate in use, the engine's performance may deteriorate correspondingly, but unless there be a catastrophic failure the average car owner remains unaware that his chosen oil may not be doing all it should. And yet there are many cases where loss of performance, engine wear, or worse, can only be due to inadequate lubrication: steady uprating of engine performance was a problem until a couple of years ago, and the oil industry was troubled by the knowledge that the engines of some of the latest cars (especially from mainland Europe) were simply too much for the oils put on the market only three years earlier. Today, the industry reckons that a new oil will only have a marketing life of two years.

In the earliest days of motoring, when things seemed so stable, there were simply good oils and bad ones, and we knew which was which according to whence it came. The best mineral oil came from Pennsylvania (which incidentally produced some of the worst fuel, the best gasoline coming from California and the East Indies), and if even that was not good enough—and for aero and racing engines it often was not—then the only answer was a high-smelling vegetable oil derived from castor or rape seeds.

Only in the last decade has castor oil ceased to be the basis of most racing oils. It was abandoned by aviators much earlier, new synthetic oils taking over the task—first in Germany, and then everywhere jet engines were under development. These synthetic oils have been developed to the point where they are just becoming cheap enough to offer the ordinary motorist; the racing driver has occasionally used them (sometimes without knowing it) since the early 1960s.

The secret of vegetable and synthetic oils alike was

Right: an aerial view of Occidental Petroleum's oil refinery in Antwerp

Below: a small Leyland motor tanker used by Shell of Canada for delivering petrol and oil during the 1920s; it is shown parked outside the company's premises

their behaviour when very hot. Ordinary mineral oil becomes very thin and runny when hot, and then offers too little resistance to being squeezed out of bearings, allowing metal-to-metal contact. Castor oil retained its film strength at high temperatures, but was impossibly stiff at low ones; synthetic oils are designed to remain stable over a very wide temperature range, their most daunting requirement being to withstand the heat soak in the centre bearings of a jet engine after shut-down. The chemical differences between the three classes of oils are far-reaching, but in this physical respect they differ only in degree: all oils flow more easily when hot than when cold.

To put it another way, oil viscosity decreases as its temperature increases. This viscosity, or resistance to flow, may be measured in various ways: if you are a physicist or an oilman you may work in Centistokes or in Saybolt Universal Seconds, but if by their standards you are a layman you will accept the conventional

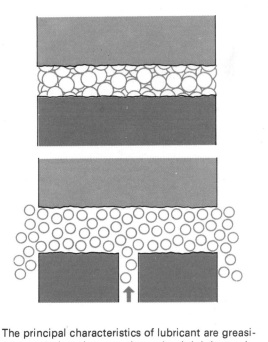

The principal characteristics of lubricant are greasiness and viscosity; greasiness (*top*) lubricates by the molecules adhering to the metal, while viscosity lubricates by resisting the pump pressure and keeping the surfaces apart

ratings prescribed by the American Society of Automotive Engineers. These SAE ratings are little more than broad classifications allowing quite wide margins of error, and originally they were expressed in a single figure: an SAE 50 oil was thicker than SAE 40, for example. In those days one would use a thinner or numerically lower grade in winter than in summer but then the chemists discovered how to make multigrade oils that were as fluid as a 30-grade at low temperatures and as viscid as a 40-grade when hot. So we had an SAE 30W-40 oil: the higher figure showed how thick the oil remained when it was hot (at 98.9°C), while the lower figure indicated how fluid it was when starting at 0°C.

However, the W (winter) viscosity was not actually measured at this lower temperature, but was theoretically inferred from measurement at 38°C. The theory was not always valid, alas, and when the SAE finally declared that after 1968 the viscosity at zero would have to be measured actually at zero, several of the so-called 20W-50 oils that had by then been developed turned out not to earn their 20W rating at all, which is why the W disappeared from some cans. Others made the grade, and it was a matter for congratulation that an oil with such a wide range could be produced. Today there are 10W-50 oils on the market, not to mention a synthetic which would qualify as a 7W-60 had it ever occurred to the SAE to create such a classification.

There is a paradox here. The more widely spaced the figures appear, the less widely does the viscosity of the oil vary. It is too easy to fall into the layman's trap of thinking that a multigrade oil grows thicker as it gets hotter, whereas what really happens is that it does not get as much thinner as would a monograde subjected to the same temperature rise. A measure of this stability is the viscosity index, which oilmen shorten as VI: the smaller the drop in viscosity at high temperature, the higher is the VI.

Improving the viscosity index is one of the most important tasks of the oil chemist today, and the chemical additives with which he achieves it are in fact

Right: for a high-performance engine, it is sometimes advisable to fit a small radiator in the oil system in order to keep the oil temperature down and the viscosity up; it can also be useful to fit a thermostatically controlled bypass, to avoid overcooling the oil

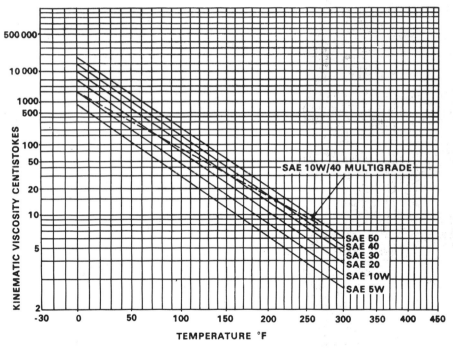

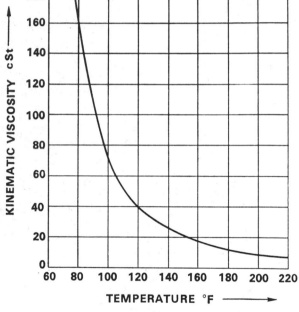

Above: two graphs showing the variation of oil viscosity with temperature; the one on the left is drawn on logarithmic graph paper and shows an impressive straight line, while the other gives a more accurate indication, being drawn on linear paper

called VI improvers. They are one of the most important (but nevertheless only one) of the many classes of additives that go into a modern multigrade oil, and the amount of these additives is increasing steadily. Buy yourself a pint of reputable oil, and what you get is three quarters of a pint of mineral base oil and a quarter of a pint of additives—not just VI improver but also anti-oxidants, corrosion inhibitors, detergents, dispersants, and several others. They are not necessarily made by the oil company whose name is on the can: a few big firms provide 'additive packages' for others to add to their own base stocks. They are not generally capable of lubricating: the additive package without the base stock would not be a super-oil. The additives are there because an oil has to do more than provide lubrication by reducing friction: it must also assist in cooling the engine, must keep it clean, protect it against corrosion and wear of various kinds, and act as a sealant to keep the combustion gases where they belong.

The oil must even provide some sort of lubrication when it is not present! That is a *reductio ad absurdum*, of course, but near enough the truth to draw attention

to something known as boundary lubrication. It is a kind of residual lubrication when the oil film breaks down or has drained away—as when starting from cold, which is when most severe engine wear takes place. An electrochemical bonding of certain oil particles to the metal surfaces can take place, preserving a last-ditch film of protection that is again particularly effective in the case of castor oil. Modern engines sometimes have synthetic dry lubricants 'plated' on to critical areas, such as molybdenum disulphide on the edges of piston rings.

Lubrication problems in cold starting explain the need for the fluidity of the W end of the multigrade spectrum. It ensures a quicker and more copious flow throughout the engine in starting at any temperature. There is a critical range where cold starting is affected by low-temperature viscosity, a range that extends from −10° to −25°C, when thick oil makes the engine stiff and reluctant to reach the cranking speed necessary for combustion. Until fairly recently, a 10W oil could only manage an SAE 40 rating at high temperature, so cold starting ability involved a certain sacrifice; yet the 50 rating is thought essential to minimise con-

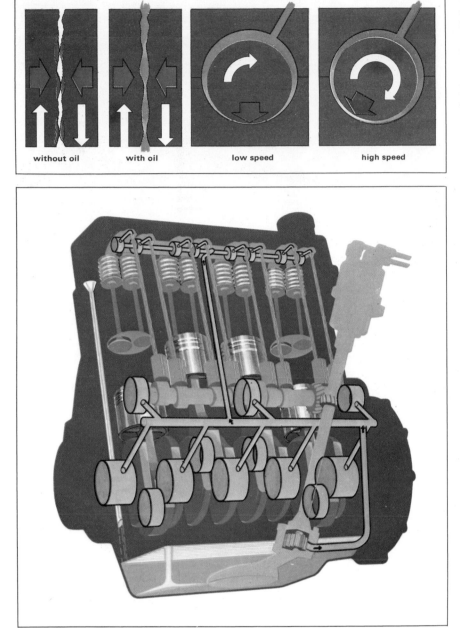

without oil   with oil   low speed   high speed

sludge. Modern clean-air laws demanding positive crankcase ventilation aggravate sludging quite alarmingly, and have also led to a new phenomenon, the so-called 'mayonnaise' emulsion of condensed water and oil that forms inside rocker boxes and similar places.

High-temperature problems are quite different. Diluents of the oil (not only condensates but also unburnt fuel) may be boiled away above about 80°C, but so may some of the oil itself: the volatility of the base stock is most important, for the more volatile oils tend to vaporise from the hotter engine parts. These vapours are lost through the engine breather system, resulting in excess consumption and thickening of the remainder. The ring belt round the piston is the most critical area: the film of oil preventing metal-to-metal contact here may only be a tenth of a thousandth of an inch thick, and if it were too volatile it would too readily be boiled up and blown away—just as, if it were too fluid, it would be squeezed out by mechanical pressure.

The loss of volatile fractions is not the only cause of viscosity increase in heavy-duty service. Another is oxidation, resulting from exposure of the hot oil to air in the crankcase. The thickening effect is sometimes obscured by fuel dilution (a particularly nasty problem in diesel engines, for diesel fuel is not volatile) which does nothing to restore the oil's lubricity. Anti-oxidant additives resist this degradation, but after long use even the best of them cannot cope, and the higher the temperature the less their effect: oxidation actually doubles with every 18 degrees C rise in temperature.

In some cases, the opposite condition causes trouble: a loss of viscosity can occur where there is not a trace of dilution. The most severe cases are in engines with built-in gearboxes sharing a common oil supply. In 1500 miles of typical European urban service, a 20W-50 oil may suffer an 18% loss of viscosity at 99°C in a conventional engine, while in a combined engine-and-transmission unit the loss is as high as 42%. What happens is that the long chains of the VI improver are literally chopped up into short strands so that they are no longer effective. Sheer heavy duty in conventional engines will do the same: at the end of a 1000 km sports-car race, engine oil that was rated at 20W-50 on the starting grid will be more like 20W-40. The engine's mechanical threshing reduces the plastics spaghetti to mostaccioli.

sumption and wear. Consumption is of increasing importance because of the greater freedom for sustained high-speed running on motorways: if the oil thins out too much, it will too easily find its way out of the engine.

Hence the importance of the VI improvers. These additives are polymeric, meaning that their molecules are large and complex, as are the molecules of most modern plastics. In fact it is not too fanciful to think of them as a kind of liquid plastic spaghetti: when added to a base oil they increase its viscosity at high temperature more than when cool, because as they grow hot these long chainlike molecules grow larger and more resistant to displacement. Thus a fairly thin oil can be used as a foundation to ensure easy starting and rapid circulation, while the VI improvers preserve its viscosity in hard high-temperature driving.

Other additives are vital to low-temperature operation. This is when oil suffers most contamination, when most corrosive wear takes place. Water, acids and other combustion products condense on relatively cool cylinder walls, drop, or are scraped off, into the crankcase and are emulsified with the oil to form

Top: the two drawings (*left*) show how oil separates supposedly smooth surfaces (this is highly magnified); the other drawings show how a wedge of oil builds up round the crankshaft as speed increases and separates the surface

Above: a diagram showing the circulation of oil (yellow) from the pump to the various bearings

Right: oil is passed through the crankshaft to the big-end bearings and is squeezed out to fall back into the sump

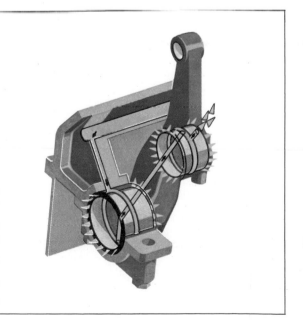

Obviously viscosity cannot be expected to do everything. Gears bring tremendous pressures to bear on the oil film interposed between them, and for this there are certain so-called extreme pressure additives that play an important part in oils meant specifically for gearboxes, axles and the like. Unfortunately these additives are unsuitable for use in heat engines, because the conditions of duty make them increase corrosive wear. The alternative used to be to rely on high film strength, but the odd nature of valvegear wear problems has brought about something of a revolution in lubricating techniques that rely on yet another class of additives. In the modern engine the greatest wear problem is presented by the valve-operating mechanism, with tremendous tearing, scuffing and pitting occurring at rocker tips, cam noses, tappet surfaces and similar critical areas.

Scuffing, which affects cam lobes and tappets in particular but cylinder bores as well, is what happens when the oil film breaks down to allow metal-to-metal contact; and to keep it at bay demands high chemical

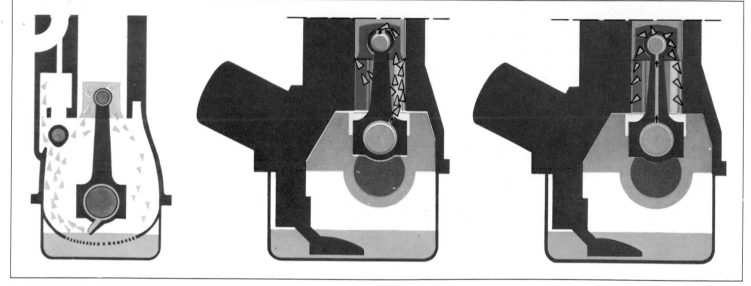

reactivity in the oil to prevent local welding and tearing of the metals. Pitting, which particularly affects valve lifters, is a different process, a fatigue phenomenon that is believed to result from deformation of the surface of the tappet, causing it to break away in small flakes. Many car manufacturers specify some kind of protection from pitting and scuffing, which the oil companies achieve by use of very specific additives that create when under pressure a kind of metallic soap or 'intermediate metallic compound' on the critical metal surfaces. This is formed by reaction with constituents of the additive package, usually organic phosphate compounds: the popular one for preventing scuffing is known as ZDDP for short, zinc dialkyl dithiophosphate.

Unfortunately the use of these phosphates tends to debase the oil's anti-wear properties in thin-film or boundary conditions, and is detrimental to corrosive wear too. Protection from corrosive wear is seldom specified by car manufacturers; yet it probably accounts for the majority of wear in cylinder bores and on piston rings as the result of lead deposits, fuel, combustion condensates, and other contaminants settling on the bores near the top of the piston stroke. However, the most crucial place for rust and corrosive wear inside the engine is in hydraulic tappets: oilmen reckon that there is no bigger headache, and if a car manufacturer makes a special issue of corrosion

protection it is sure to have something to do with these hydraulic lifters!

Manufacturers' stipulations for anti-wear properties are usually well defined, but again the anti-scuff treatments create problems elsewhere. It could for example be a matter of having to choose between having cam lobes worn by scuffing or having the oil-pump gears worn because of the reduction in thin-film strength. This is typical of the compatibility problems that arise in formulating an oil: it must not fight with metals, seals, gaskets, fibre gears, nor any of the other constituent materials of the engine, even including the paints and resins used for closing the pores of castings. It must moreover keep them all clean, and do it manifestly since this is something that the customer can see for himself, however much he may be in the dark about the oil's other functions.

Maintaining cleanliness involves two processes. One is the inhibition of any tendency to form deposits, the other is the maintenance of these deposits in suspension. Inhibition is the preferred action, so as to catch what are called deposit precursors—half-burnt stuff blown past the piston rings into the sump, especially during the compression stroke, and all the acids, water and other foreign matter drawn in from the atmosphere or produced from combustion, which tend to form sludge in low-temperature operation (stop-go traffic, short local journeys, etc) or varnish in

Top: low-temperature operation of an engine places a great deal of stress on the oil, causing contamination by water and combustion products; this leads to the formation of 'sludge' as shown here inside a rocker cover

Above: there are three ways of lubricating the small ends and piston rings. In a low-pressure system (*left*), a scoop on the big end lubricates that bearing directly and splash lubricates the small end and rings; in high-pressure systems, the small end and rings can be splash lubricated by oil squirted out of the big end (*centre*), or directly lubricated through a drilling in the con-rod (*right*)

Right: even the best oils will only reduce wear to a minimum; small particles will still be deposited in the oil by various rubbing surfaces; a magnetic sump drain plug will at least collect some of the particles

Below: additives can reduce the formation of deposits; two oil-pressure relief valves are shown, the one on the left having been used in detergent-free oil and the other in oil with detergent products added to it

high-temperature, high-load work. Keeping particles of all these alien substances separate and in suspension in the oil is the job of the dispersant additives. The detergent additives keep the metal surfaces clean by a process of preferential adherence, but like practically all the others they are gradually consumed or worn out by their work, constituting as they do a sort of sacrificial safety barrier. It therefore pays the motorist, as well as the oil companies, to change his car's oils much more frequently than the car manufacturer pretends is necessary.

Like anti-scuff reagents, detergents can degrade the anti-wear properties of the base stock, so once again a lot of care and skill is needed in order that a given blend of base stock and additives be successful. Deposits and organic phosphates clash with other additives in another very important area, in which engine performance may be impaired or even suddenly and drastically curtailed: combustion-chamber deposits are very dependent on the composition of the oil.

As ever, that additive package is a mixed blessing. Its most effective antirust ingredients are based on metals, notably compounds of calcium (though there are many other metallic compounds present, based on barium, molybdenum, tungsten and—as already noted —zinc), and these leave deposits in the combustion chamber that can damage the engine if a lengthy spell of stop-go traffic work be followed by a burst of high power output. These deposits then become incandescent; and even if they do not cause gross pre-ignition (which distorts valves and burns holes in pistons) they will cause enough to reduce power, induce overheating, and accelerate wear.

Some recent work on this problem led to the substitution of magnesium sulphonates for the traditional calcium compounds. They leave less weight of deposits, which in any case tend to soften rather than to glow and are therefore less likely to cause pre-ignition. In fact the likelihood of destructive effects, which increases with what is called the ash content of the oil, has been shown to be no greater with a magnesium-based ash content of 1.4% than with calcium-based ash of 0.5%. Most high-grade engine oils on the market have ash contents of about 1%, though some have as little as 0.65%. In oils developed specifically for racing, the ash content may be brought as low as 0.36%.

Racing oils of the vegetable type are simply not suitable for street use, however. Oxidation is the main bugbear, creating dreadful deposits under piston crowns and around valves. Rust-inhibitors have adverse effects that rule them out, and in the end only the high film strength of castor oil remains to its credit. The synthetic oils developed for racing are a different matter: their constituents are chosen rather than determined by nature, and certain varieties may be highly recommended for use in road cars. There have been snags in the past, though: a French company put a synthetic oil on the market a few years ago and ran into terrible trouble because it reacted disastrously with the slightest trace of conventional mineral oil in the engine. More recent synthetics are completely and safely miscible with conventional lubricants, and are merely very expensive.

Racing has a few problems of its own. One is that ZDDP forms new chemical structures in the presence of alcohol fuel, leaving nasty deposits and causing drastic wear on certain surfaces. Another is that the very high rates of flow in a racing engine cause frothing and foaming of the oil, aggravated by the fact that the scavenge pumps of a dry-sump racing engine have a much higher capacity than the pressure pump, so that

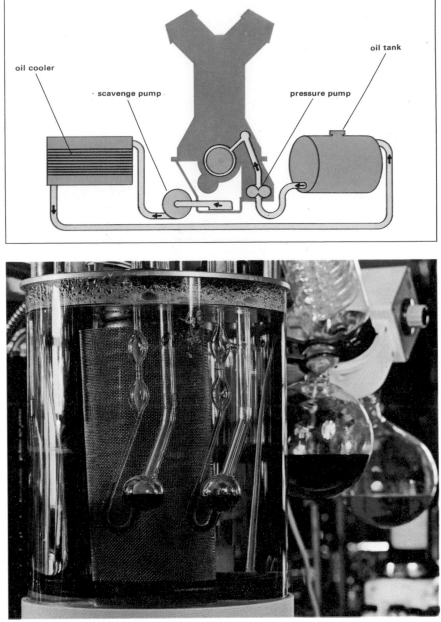

air is entrained with the oil. The antidote is a tiny admixture of a short-molecular-chain silicone oil, such as is commonly added to suspension damper fluids to check aeration; and this is generally present in commercially available oils, though in smaller dosages. On the whole, oils for touring cars have a much harder life than anything in racing.

To deal with all these problems the chemists formulating a new oil may spend as much as two years on screening and testing its ingredients. A suitable base stock has to be chosen from what is available—itself a knotty problem now that the choice of petroleum stocks is influenced by political and economic considerations —to have the appropriate qualities of lubricity, volatility range, and so on. The VI improvers and all the other additives have to match it and be compatible with themselves and everything else, and even the nature of fuels likely to be used has to be taken into account. For example the presence of tetraethyl lead and related anti-knock compounds has a marked effect on combustion chamber deposits on the one hand, and on valve lubrication on the other. The lead acts as a lubricant for the valve faces and seats (and stems, though this is less critical) by coating the critical areas with lead salts formed during combustion. In their absence, particles of iron and iron oxides emerge from the material of the valve seats and, being harder than the surrounding metal, are hammered in to form craters around each nodule: the valve gradually sinks into its seat, at a rate that can reach a tenth of a milli-metre an hour in a cheaply produced cast iron head with no separate valve seats. The lead compounds which form a solid solution covering the valve face and seat (they are different ones in each case, so specialised are the reactions taking place in different parts of the head) prevent the adhesion, the welding and tearing that forms these nodules, and reduces the abrasion caused by any rotation of the valve whether deliberately induced or otherwise.

Of course there are more kinds of lubrication in a car than are to be found in the engine, but the others are less beset by problems. High-melting-point greases may be necessary for hub bearings, to avoid the danger of liquefied grease flowing out of the hubs into the brakes. Solid lubricants such as molybdenum di-sulphide or graphite may be added in large doses to greases for suspension or steering bearings so that

Top: many competition cars have a 'dry-sump' lubrication system, in which the oil is stored in a tank, to which it is pumped by a scavenge pump

Top left: the oil tank and part of the oil cooler, associated with a dry-sump system in a racing car

Above: as oil improves, so the stress placed on it becomes greater, and it is necessary to carry out stringent laboratory tests to make the product better; here, an Ostwald viscometer is in use, to check the oil's density

friction is kept low even when bearing pressures force the bulk of the grease away from the mating surfaces. Many bearings for suspension elements, steering joints, and body hinges are nowadays made of plastics that have very low coefficients of friction on dry metal and therefore need no lubrication at all—or they may be loaded or impregnated with molybdenum di-sulphide to improve their performance. Plastics often have peculiar frictional properties: nylon is lubricated by water, for instance. So is rubber, and the design of water pump seals may have to take this into account. Waxy additives in coolant antifreeze may ensure the lubrication of water pump glands, while other seals for the retention of oils in the engine must be made of appropriate synthetic rubbers that are not attacked by hydrocarbons as natural rubber is. In fact tribology the science of mutually rubbing surfaces—is developing at a great pace, and the art of lubrication is undergoing a profound metamorphosis that makes the detail of a modern car very different from that of one built ten years ago. Engine lubrication will remain the most difficult for the foreseeable future, however, and is the aspect in which neglect will prove most costly to the present car owner.

TUNING & MODIFICATION

the quest for power

TUNING AND MODIFICATION of a vehicle's power plant means increased performance and, very often, more economy. In the old days, a tuning wizard was portrayed as a man with a screwdriver, an oily rag, and a few spanners. After a bit of tinkering under the bonnet, adjusting the mixture and playing with the ignition the car would be 10 mph faster as if by some undefined magic. Unfortunately, the character was more imaginary than real. Even then, it required no little skill, and understanding to perform such a motoring miracle, and now, with engines far more complicated, equipment and technology of a much more complex nature are demanded of the aspiring mechanical wizard.

To the average man, tuning, or tune-up as it is called takes the form of checking points and plugs, replacing and gapping them as necessary. The service is complete for many when the carburettor is adjusted for a proper idle mixture. But, of course, this just scratches the surface of the art. If the engine components needed attention then the car will obviously go better, but what ignition and carburation settings are required? The service manual will give the settings for the *average* car off any production line, but this cannot take into account the great variation that exists among similar production cars. They differ because manufacturers employ broad production tolerances in the various parts in order to keep costs down to a realistic level. The objective is to produce parts only just accurately enough to do the job and yet still fit. A particular engine may have all the tolerances cumulatively combined to render the standard carburettor jetting less than ideal. Thus, it is often that re-jetting the carburettor could, and very often does, result in better performance. It is in an instance like this that modern technology proves itself. The device best suited to identify the ideal settings and generally trouble-shoot an engine is a rolling road dynamometer. It is an expensive piece of equipment but one which pays dividends in getting the best from an engine which to all intents and purposes is standard.

A rolling road dynamometer measures horsepower at the rear wheels, usually in conjunction with an electronic engine analyser which busily detects many common faults that would otherwise go unnoticed.

It becomes apparent that the modern day tuning wizard has, apart from his screwdriver, rag and spanners, a dynamometer and associated equipment to the value of many thousands of pounds. With this, all the ancillary equipment on the engine including carburettor, ignition, and so on can be set individually to suit the particular engine. Each item he changes may only make a very small difference to the power output of the machine, but the dynamometer is able instantly to indicate the direction (negative or positive) and degree to which each change influences performance.

Assuming that we start with a car which is exactly to factory specification, then just how much difference can a really good tune-up make? Take a simple thing like spark plugs; changing these spark plugs to a more suitable heat range can very often net the odd 1 or 2 hp. Breaker points are another area which can often stand improvement. Curing point bounce may give another couple of extra hp at the top end of the rpm range. Setting the ignition timing for maximum power very often sees 3 or 4 hp, and re-calibrating the carburettor by swopping jets, emulsion tubes, air correctors or even needles in the case of constant depression type carburettors, can see a likewise increase. By the time you have found each individual increase, you have quite a big performance bonus, and usually better economy as well. A 10 per cent increase in hp is a commonplace gain, but with a good operator on the dynamometer, gains of twice that amount are not infrequent.

Above: a beautiful example of a 1000cc Mini engine built by the author; equipped with gas-flowed head, special camshaft and twin-choke Dell' Orto carburettor it produced 85 bhp at 6800 rpm

Left: the correct distributor-points gap is important for maximum power, as any alteration of this gap leads automatically to an adjustment of the ignition-timing setting

Modifications are slightly different. Basically this is a case of altering the specification of an engine in an effort to get more hp. Naturally, after this has been done, it should be accompanied by a session on a rolling road dynamometer to make sure that everything that has been changed is being used to its best advantage by having the carburetter and ignition settings suitably matched.

Assuming that we are burning our mixture properly and that our mixture is, in fact, correct for the application, then all engine modifications are fundamentally aimed at achieving one particular thing, and that is to allow the engine a greater rate of air consumption. The amount of air an engine can consume is obviously directly related to its hp output, for the more air that goes in, the more fuel that can be burnt. When more air is packed into a cylinder, the increased explosive force of combustion is readily converted to extra power with each stroke of the piston. Another way to increase the power is to alter the number of power strokes in a given time. If two power strokes occur in the space of time allotted for only one previously, power will naturally increase. In fact it will have doubled in this case. Making an engine produce more power is really a case of trying to achieve both these ends. Increasing the breathing efficiency of each stroke of the engine, and trying to fit more power strokes into the cycle of the engine means higher revs with more performance.

One of the most common things to concern oneself with in the search for power is the cylinder head. Modified cylinder heads are often termed 'gas-flowed' to indicate that they have been specially adapted to allow a greater flow of internal gases in and out of their relevant ports than in the head's standard form. Such modifications allow the engine to breath better—to consume more air.

Another common modification to cylinder heads

Right: a beautifully prepared works BMW 3.0 CSL, used with great success in the European Touring Car Championship of 1973

Below left: tracing engine deficiencies is made easier by the use of an electronic performance analyser such as this one

Below: two Lancia cylinder heads, the nearer one having big valves and skimmed face

The fitting of a bigger carb or carbs, is equally popular in the pursuit of extra power. The idea is not necessarily to introduce more fuel to the engine, but once again, to force more air to the engine. Obviously, one carburettor supplying four cylinders presents a greater restriction to the air intake than four carburettors supplying four cylinders. The restrictive effect of a one carb system becomes more noticeable as revs rise. Accordingly, the fitting of a multi-carb system makes only a minor difference to power at low rpm, but a major improvement in the mid and upper rev ranges where a single carburettor may have been stifling the engine.

The carburettors used on an engine can be the most obvious sign of whether or not an engine has been modified for increased performance, hence the fact that insurance companies tend to load cars with multi-carburettor installations. For this reason, and the fact that carburettors are expensive, it's always best to see if you can achieve the hp you want without resorting to a carburettor change. In many cases this is possible, but some cars come equipped with such ridiculously small carburettors, that any increased hp without a carburettor change becomes impractical.

If gas-flowed big-valve heads and sophisticated carburettor installations successfully allow the incoming charge easy access to the engine, then the next step is expelling the burnt charge from the engine. Most present-day exhaust manifolds are primarily designed

Below: a Renault 5, surrounded by the parts used to prepare it for the Italian Renault 5 championship

Right: two cylinder heads; the top one polished, the lower one with enlarged valves

involves raising the compression ratio. This has the effect of raising the thermal efficiency of the engine—the efficiency with which the heat energy liberated by the fuel is utilised. Though often believed by the layman to be the be-all and end-all of cylinder head modifications, increasing CR usually only contributes a few per cent to the power output. The main increase comes from the better flow characteristics of the head, and better flow is achieved only through careful design. It has nothing to do with the shiny surfaces so reverently prepared by manufacturers to enhance sales potential—and profit margins. The only thing that really counts in a gas-flowed cylinder head is the shape of the ports and chambers.

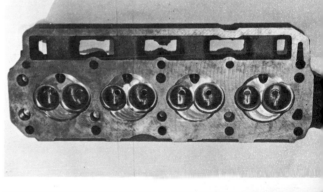

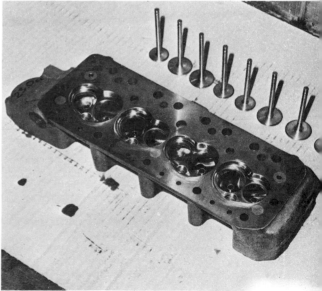

with cost in mind. As a result, they are usually simple cast-iron pipes connecting the cylinders. At low rpm this may be of no terrific disadvantage, but as soon as revs rise and with a concurrent increase in exhaust quantities, then the standard manifold can become the factor limiting decisive power output. The science involved in exhaust system design is quite complex, and although formulas have been devised which predict what dimensions should be used, we find that in practice, what goes on in the exhaust system is so complicated that the final design has to be done by a kind of trial and error on the engine test bed.

For a road-going system where silencers must be used, the biggest task to carry out is to reduce exhaust back pressure to a minimum. The silencer, as well as damping out the noise produced by the engine, tends also to damp out the pressure fluctuations in the exhaust, which can often be used to aid exhaust extraction. On a racing system where no silencer is used, the situation is slightly different. Here these pressure pulses not only cause the scavenging of the combustion chamber when the piston is up around TDC, but also pull the incoming charge in, such that a fresh charge may start to come out of the exhaust valve even before the piston has started coming down on its induction stroke. It is the combination of shock-wave tuning and of the inlet and exhaust system on competition engines which can give volumetric efficiencies (that is the efficiency with which an engine will induce its fresh charge) of over 100 per cent.

Another item which comes in for some close attention when a lot more hp is required is the camshaft. The standard camshaft fitted to an engine is, of necessity, a compromise. It must be capable of giving a good spread of power and yet be quiet in operation. For a high performance engine, a cam with a longer opening period is often used. These sorts of camshaft my well add power to the top end of the rev range, but do nothing for the bottom end of the rev range—the end most important for town driving.

With racing cams it really is a question of robbing Peter to pay Paul. The period of opening becomes so long that these cams give virtually no power under 4 or 5000 rpm. In other words, they start working where most road cams finish! A virtually intolerable situation for a road car, even a high performance road car.

Given the choice of methods of increasing hp output, the factory engineers will often go for increasing the capacity of an engine for numerous reasons. First of all, increased capacity gives you more power throughout the rev range and secondly, increasing the capacity of an engine at the factory is a pretty cheap way of getting more power. If you think about it, it must cost very little more to make a piston a bit larger and a crankshaft with a little longer stroke, especially if the original engine design allowed for such modification. Increasing the capacity, however, is not solely the prerogative of the factory engineers and many performance engine specialists follow this route as one of the items on their agenda for more hp. Unfortunately engine specialists cannot increase the capacity as cheaply as the factory because for them it may involve the use of special pistons to do the job, and in some cases, special crankshafts. These, which are made in small numbers, are expensive.

Another method, which used to be popular in the pre-war days and is now well on the road to recovery from a post-war slump, is supercharging, both the conventional supercharger and the exhaust driven turbo-charger. Of all the forms of engine modification, supercharging sounds more potent, glamorous and exciting than the rest, due, no doubt, to some of the

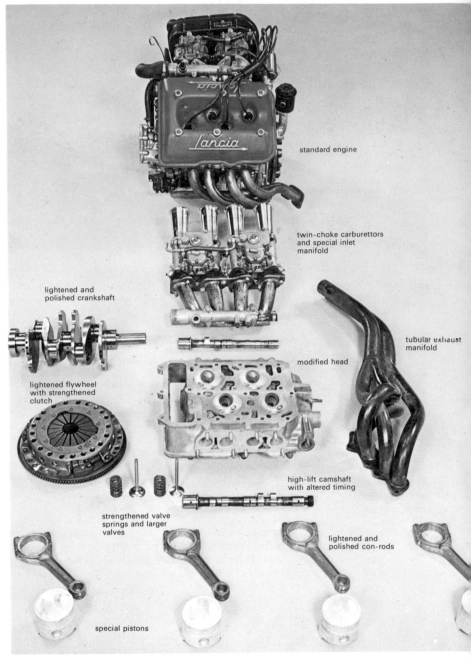

standard engine

twin-choke carburettors and special inlet manifold

lightened and polished crankshaft

tubular exhaust manifold

modified head

lightened flywheel with strengthened clutch

high-lift camshaft with altered timing

strengthened valve springs and larger valves

lightened and polished con-rods

special pistons

Above: the parts used by the Milan tuning firm of Baggioli to raise the power output of the 1600 cc Lancia V4 engine from 114 to 135 bhp

Left: a special camshaft can alter the power output of an engine considerably; here a high-lift shaft is shown alongside a standard item

tremendous power outputs achieved by supercharged engines. When one considers that the average family saloon car engine puts out 40 or 50 hp, then outputs in excess of 1000 hp are bound to be somewhat awe-inspiring! Like most other forms of tuning though, supercharging does one thing, it allows the engine to have a higher air consumption, principally because it forces the air into the engine. The supercharger itself is nothing but a glorified pump but can easily account for an hp increase of between 50 and 200 per cent, depending on the application. You may well ask at this point if it's that effective, why car manufacturers don't use it as original equipment. It's quite simple—if a car manufacturer needs a 150 hp engine, it is easier to produce a 3-litre unsupercharged engine than a 2-litre supercharged one. In the first case he has only to make an engine; in the second he has to make an engine plus a supercharger. As pointed out before, capacity increase at the factory comes cheaply; the cost of a supercharger may be 25 times greater than the cost of increasing the capacity of an engine. Apart from that, living with a supercharger is not necessarily sweetness itself. A

conventional engine-driven supercharger usually means increased fuel consumption simply from the fact that the engine is having to drive the supercharger all the time, whether or not the extra power is needed.

The exhaust driven turbocharger though is another kettle of fish. Correctly designed, the effect of a turbocharger on fuel consumption can be a lot less than a Roots or vane type, belt-driven supercharger. Apart from that, the exhaust driven supercharger has certain qualities which tend to keep the exhaust emissions down and this point in itself may find it favour amongst manufacturers, as present trends indicate. As well as this, the turbocharger is far more efficient as an air pump than a vane type supercharger, and in spite of requiring a more involved technology to produce it, it is usually more reliable. But even the turbocharger is not without its problems. Because of the fact that the intake turbine is driven via a shaft from an exhaust turbine, propelled by the exhaust, the supercharger has little effect at low rpm. It also suffers from what is popularly known as throttle lag, but should be more correctly termed boost lag. When the throttle is opened suddenly

Top left: a standard crankshaft alongside a lightened and polished version

Top centre: a comparison between standard polished pistons

Top right: standard and polished con-rods

Above left: a three-branch exhaust manifold to speed the gas flow from a Mini cylinder head

Above: supercharging can be a dramatically effective way of increasing output without 'tuning'

Confronted with such a wide variety of methods of increasing power, even quite a well informed enthusiast can be forgiven for wondering which route to take for extra performance. It is difficult to give a hard and fast rule. Probably the first thing to do when considering how to gain extra performance is to divide all the tuning equipment into two categories; that which falls into the 'bolt-on' category, and that which requires the engine to be removed in order to be implemented.

The bolt-on category is, as would be expected, generally cheaper, but this equipment is also more limited. However, this need not be considered a great disadvantage, for in many cases, bolt-on tuning equipment can still supply the extra performance that the driver requires. If bolt-on performance equipment supplies the answer, then so well and good. If not, then the 'engine out' job must be considered so that more extensive engine surgery can be performed, such as a camshaft change or increasing the capacity by boring or stroking.

Once the route to increased performance has been chosen then the question is what to buy—not on a price per item basis, but on a price per hp gained basis. There are many modified cylinder heads on the market. One item might cost £25 and another £40. It could well be that the £40 one provides better value for money. If it produces a 10 hp increase, the extra performance is costing £4 per hp. The £25 modified head, on the other hand, may only produce a 5 hp increase, in which case it has cost £1 more per hp. But it doesn't end there. Just buying a cylinder head is only the beginning; numerous other factors must be included in the costing, such as gaskets and parts involved, time and labour charges, and lastly, and probably one of the most important steps, the cost of a run on a dynamometer must be considered to see that you are getting your money's worth of extra hp. Compare one firm's prices with another. Ask what sort of hp you can expect as a result of using certain items of a firm's equipment. All reputable firms will be only too glad fully to inform a genuine potential customer. Finally, remember you get what you pay for—quality always costs money.

Top left: a much-lightened clutch

Top right: special valves and springs and camshafts are very useful

Above: a BLMC Special Tuning modified Midget

it takes a little time for the exhaust to speed up the turbine and thus give supercharge pressure. The turbocharged car as having a slightly elastic throttle and is best described to those who have never driven a turbocharged car, as having a slightly elastic throttle cable. In spite of its disadvantages, what it does for the hp of an engine is quite amazing and it almost boils down to how much hp is required, not how much hp is available. If the engine is strong enough to take the hp increase, the turbocharger will deliver.

TRANSMISSION

CLUTCH

a progressive coupling between engine and wheels

ANY DEVICE, usually mechanical, for coupling two components of a transmission system together so that they rotate as one, can be known as a clutch. In fact, the word is used to describe many such devices, including the face-dogs and/or synchromesh cones of constant-mesh gearboxes, the friction disc assemblies in certain types of limited-slip differentials, and the viscous couplings sometimes interposed in the drives to cooling fans. The most general use of it refers to the fluid or (most particularly of all) friction clutch whereby engine torque is transmitted to the gearbox input shaft.

With very few exceptions, the clutch is mounted on the face of the flywheel at the output end of the engine crankshaft. Early examples made use of a conical recess machined in the flywheel, into which a leather-faced male cone was pressed by a large helical spring, coaxial with the output shaft. These cone clutches were often very fierce in action, but there was good reason in their design: it enabled the utmost friction area to be disposed at the greatest possible radius from the centre, with very little difference between maximum and minimum radii. All these are important factors in clutch design: a large area allows better dissipation of frictional heat, large area and radius allow greater torque capacity, and minimal difference between outer and inner radii of the friction material

ensures even wear by minimising differences in rubbing velocity.

Another important factor is rate of rotation: the capacity of the clutch to transmit torque is reduced if its rate of rotation is reduced by, for example, gearing between the crankshaft and the clutch input shaft.

Contrary influences include the greater weight of a large-diameter clutch, the much greater centrifugal loadings upon its components, and their greater inertia of rotation. The last of these causes the driven portion to keep spinning at little less than engine speed after disengagement and therefore hampers gear-changing. Until about 1930, it was common to find a clutch stop fitted to sporting cars. This was a friction brake that made contact with the driven portion when the latter was fully disengaged, and slowed it rapidly. The advent of the synchromesh gearbox rendered the clutch stop otiose.

Most later development concentrated on refining the single-plate clutch, in which the driven member is a disc, faced with friction material on both sides and clamped, by spring pressure, between two surfaces (the faces of the flywheel and of a concentric 'pressure plate') that revolve as one. Until about 1950, many such clutches were faced with cork and immersed in oil, but thereafter the dry type, relying on a friction lining of coiled asbestos yarn, became the general rule.

Above left: two types of modern-day clutch, used by Ford. The top one has a single friction plate (*left*), which is squeezed on to the flywheel by the cover assembly (*right*), containing a pressure plate and, in this case, a diaphragm spring. The lower clutch is a twin-friction-plate unit used mainly in racing. A second pressure plate is fitted between these plates (*centre*) and splined to the edge of the cover assembly (*left*). This can handle extra torque

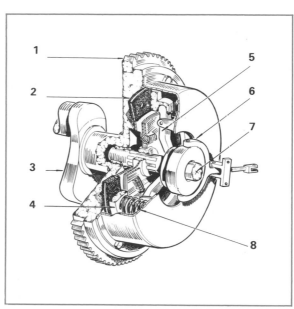

Left: a cutaway view of a coil-spring clutch. Diaphragm springs have replaced the coils in most cases; they produce more even tension and lighter pedal pressure. The main parts are:
1 flywheel
2 driven plate
3 crankshaft
4 pressure plate
5 release lever
6 withdrawal fork
7 gearbox mainshaft
8 coiled pressure spring

Above left: a selection of the clutches made by the GKN group. The cover assembly, of which only half is shown, is the modern diaphragm type, whereas the top one is a coil-spring unit. The dark clutch in the centre is a special part made for a tractor. This operates in an oil bath and has a long life

Above: the two sections of a diaphragm clutch. Note that the driven plate or friction disc has six coil springs built into it. These act as shock absorbers by allowing a small amount of movement between the lining section, on the outer edge, and the splined centre section

Greater refinement came in the 1960s with the diaphragm-spring clutch, in which an annular spring (conical when extended) replaced the numerous helical springs set about the periphery of the older type. The diaphragm spring creates a more uniform pressure and requires less force to disengage or control it, than does the helical spring.

Clutches with a multiplicity of small-diameter plates are no longer used except in racing and similar applications. Their virtues are greater torque capacity, greater resistance to bursting loads at high rates of rotation, and less rotational inertia; their vice was a tendency for the plates to stick to each other even when under no pressure.

In all these cases, disengagement of the clutch was, and is, by means of a pedal for the driver's left foot, this pedal being linked mechanically or, more recently, hydraulically to a forked lever which bears on a thrust race or carbon block, in turn pressing the pressure plate away from the driven plate, against the load imposed by the spring or springs. The leverage given by the pedal allows sensitive control over the rate of re-engagement, thus permitting the drive from the engine to be taken up progressively.

Some other types of clutch have been tried, usually in an attempt to reduce pedal effort or to eliminate the pedal altogether. One is the centrifugal clutch, in which the pressure is applied not by springs, but by levers loaded by bob-weights forced radially outwards by centrifugal force: as the engine is accelerated, the force grows stronger, until at a certain chosen rate of rotation the clutch is fully engaged. Another device was the electromagnetic clutch, in which the driven member was encased in a drum containing small iron particles. Energising electromagnetic coils around the drum created a magnetic field which locked these particles together and prevented any relative movement of the components within the casing. External-contracting band brakes have also been used around the annulus of an epicyclic gear train (one where an internally toothed ring surrounds 'planet' gears which orbit a single 'sun' gear), arresting its motion and thus making the remaining gears transmit the torque to which they are subjected. This was a feature of the Wilson preselector gearbox, and is still to be found in some automatic transmissions, although most rely on plate clutches to engage the gear trains.

GEARBOX

a necessary torque multiplier

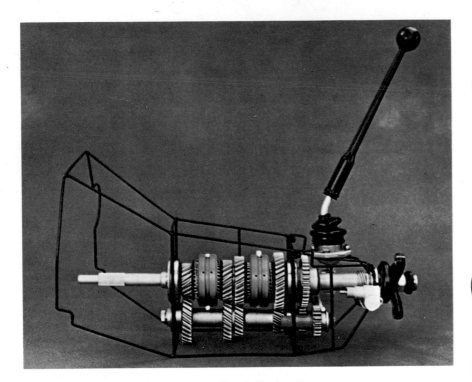

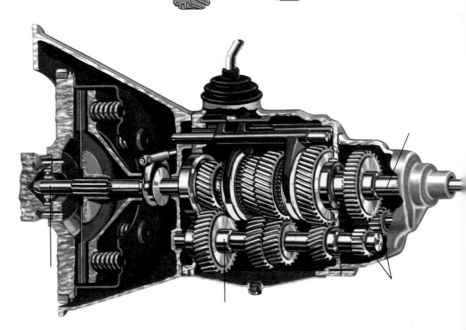

IT IS BRUTAL, BUT IT WORKS was René Panhard's properly scathing comment about the gearbox of his new car, eighty-odd years ago. Some of today's gearboxes are not as advanced as we might reasonably expect, but the majority are designed to suffer brutality rather than to display it. It has been estimated that if as many as sixty per cent of current drivers know why to change gear, only twenty per cent know how and barely five per cent know when. In Panhard's pioneering days, most cars had extremely inflexible engines and changing gear was the only way to vary the speed of the car; that is how the expression 'change speed' became current, so that we still speak of, say, a 'four-*speed* gearbox' when a 'four-*ratio* gearbox' would be more accurate.

What altered the gearchanging habits of the motorist in the vintage era was the evolution of engines whose principle merit was that they breathed well at high revolutions. This was the work of Henry and his associates in the Peugeot design office: his widely emulated overhead-camshaft engines, with four valves per cylinder and fairly mellifluous porting to the pent-roof heads, were alarmingly gutless at low speeds by the standards of the time. In cars designed according to his tenets, the performance at which the peak-power figures hinted could only be realised by keeping the revolutions well up, and this dictated a gearbox with very close ratios. An entirely new style of driving had to be cultivated. In 1908, the internal ratios of a Grand Prix Fiat's four-speed box were typical of those in the gearbox of any large gentlemanly

88

tourer, almost perfectly evenly spaced in increments of about 1.53:1 so that the ratios were 1:1, 1.53:1, 2.38:1 and 3.68:1—but in 1912, the ratios of the GP Peugeot were 1:1, 1.13:1, 1.52:1 and 2.04:1. The Peugeot might not be very electrifying in its acceleration from standstill, but once it was well under way in its 50 mph bottom gear it could be kept pressed up to the bit.

This was the new way to secure really high performance, and the makers of sporting cars duly followed Henry's lead. The early 3-litre Bentley, before it was detuned and castrated for the carriage trade, could be had with gearbox ratios of 1:1, 1.3:1, 1.6:1 and 2.6:1, and the salesmen used to astonish

were communicated by rods or cranks to selector forks which engaged collars on the flanks of the gears: first the dog coupling input to output shafts was moved out of mesh, and then the appropriate spur gear on the output shaft was slid along until its teeth engaged those of the corresponding layshaft gear. Speeding up the engine with the clutch momentarily engaged while the gearlever was in the neutral position would accelerate the rotation of the layshaft (because of the permanently meshed pair of gears) until the speeds of fixed and sliding gears were the same, whereupon they would slide into engagement easily enough. The drive path would then be from input shaft to layshaft and thence

Far left: the bare bones of a four-speed all-synchromesh gearbox. First and reverse gears are straight cut, while all others are helical

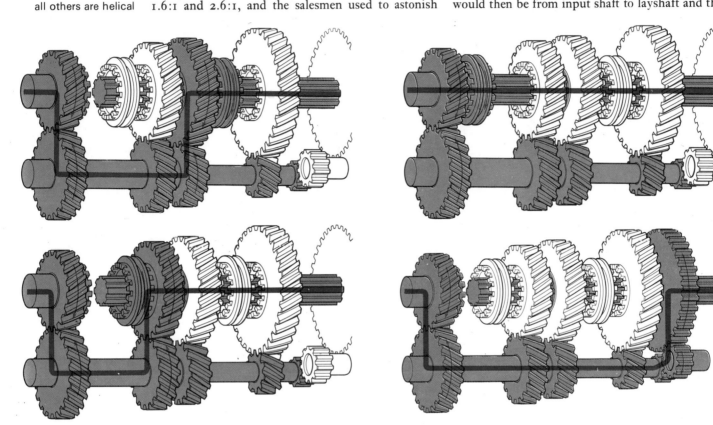

Above: six diagrams showing the power-flow through a four-speed gearbox in neutral *(top left)*, first *(above left)*, second *(top)*, third *(above)*, fourth *(top right)* and reverse *(above right)*

Left: a sectional drawing of the same gearbox, showing how it connects to the clutch

potential customers by driving at a steady 60 mph while slipping freely from one gear to another of the uppermost three. Most customers had never done 60 at all, let alone in second gear!

What made the gearchanging so tricky was the need for the rotational rates of two spur gears to be synchronised before one could be slid axially along its shaft to move sideways into mesh with the other, fixed to another parallel shaft. Then, as now, the majority of manually operated gearboxes were of the two-shaft layout, the input and output shafts being coaxial and treated as one (the mainshaft) while the parallel shaft (emulating the 'back gear' of lathes and certain other machine tools with which the designers would be familiar) was called the layshaft. This arrangement provided direct drive in top gear, the two portions of the mainshaft being coupled together by a dog clutch—a kind of gearwheel with teeth on its face rather than on its rim—so that the input and output shafts rotated as one. A spur gear on the input shaft was permanently meshed with another fixed to the layshaft (all the layshaft's gears were fixed) but the gearwheels on the output shaft were splined so that, although they must always rotate with it, they were permitted axial movement: in top gear, or in neutral, they were all slid away from the layshaft gears. When a change down from top gear was undertaken, the motions of the gearlever

to the output shaft, and the reduction in gear ratio—or the increase in engine revolutions, which would inversely express the same thing—was the product of the ratio of the first pair of meshing gears multiplied by that of the second pair.

It was often found that the change into top gear was easier than the others, for the facial serrations of the dog clutch did not have to be as precisely formed as the involute teeth of the spur gears, and could be made with a measure of deliberate backlash or sloppiness which greatly eased its engagement. This led to the development of the constant-mesh gearbox, albeit by easy stages which began with the advertisement of a 'silent third' and progressed down through the gears until they were all similar—though it was decades before the sliding-pinion bottom gear was finally ousted, and it is with us still in the reverse gear of most manual boxes. In the constant-mesh box, the gears carried by the output shaft are permanently enmeshed with those of the layshaft, but are carried on bearings which leave them free to rotate idly. The appropriate gearwheel may then be locked to the output shaft and made to revolve with it by a dog clutch splined to the shaft and slid along it by the same sort of selector fork and collar as previously moved the sliding pinions.

This was a great improvement. Not only was the gearchange much sweeter, and the need for synchro-

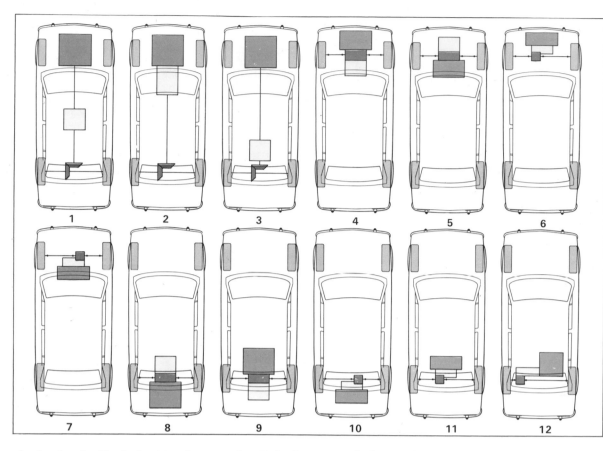

Left: twelve variations
of how the gearbox is
situated in relation to
the engine, differential
and axles of a road car.
1 A centrally mounted
gearbox, used mainly on
veteran and vintage
machinery, but also seen
on the Morgan Plus
Four
2 The most common
layout for rear-wheel-
drive cars, with the box
mated directly to the
engine
3 For better weight
distribution, the gearbox
is mounted in unit with
the differential. This
layout is used on the
Alfetta and Ferrari
Daytona
4 The Citroën GS
layout, with the engine
at the extreme front,
allows ample passenger
space
5 The rather unusual
layout of the Renault 4
and 16 series
6 The famous Issigonis
layout, used on the
Mini, also gives plenty
of passenger room
7 Yet another variation
for the front-wheel-
drive car, this time on
the Peugeot 104
8 This rear-engined
layout is of the type
used on the various
Volkswagen air-cooled
models
9 This mid-engined
layout is used on all
current Formula One
cars and also on the De
Tomaso Pantera
10 No cars are now
built with a transverse
rear-mounted engine
11 The layout that is
used on the Ferrari Dino
and the Ferrari Boxer
12 A somewhat unusual
mid-engine layout,
which is employed on
the eight-cylinder
Lamborghini Urraco

nisation by double-declutching less exacting (indeed it was possible to snatch the lever from one position to the next without any pause at all), but also it was now possible to employ helical-gear teeth which ran far less noisily than the old straight-cut spurs. A gearbox of this kind can be sheer bliss to operate, especially if the ratios are close in the old Henry fashion. Most racing cars and all motor cycles are still thus equipped, and their drivers seldom ask for better.

If the dog clutches could be replaced by some kind of friction clutch, perfect synchronisation of the output shaft and the selected gearwheel could be achieved rapidly and smoothly. A friction clutch strong enough to transmit full torque would be far too big and heavy, but a small clutch that had to do no more than over-come the inertia of a freely rotating gear and layshaft assembly could be quite small. From this reasoning sprang the invention of synchromesh, introduced by General Motors in the 1928 Cadillac: a small all-metal friction clutch is built onto the face of the selector collar, surrounding the dog clutch. When the selector moves the collar towards the chosen gearwheel, the friction clutch engages a conical surface on the face of the gear, and the friction accelerates or decelerates the gear wheel until it matches the rate of rotation of the output shaft. Further movement of the selector collar then pushes the dog clutch through the bore of the friction clutch to engage the corresponding dogs on the face of the gear wheel. This relative movement of the collar and the friction clutch is made possible by spring loading of the sleeve which allows concentric assembly of the two.

Synchromesh rapidly assumed widespread and deserved popularity. Early versions were soon im-proved, one of the first amendments being to reverse the positions of the dogs and the cones so that the former were outside the latter and endured less severe stresses when subjected to full torque. Various baulk-ing systems, which made it impossible for the dogs to

engage before perfect synchronism had been achieved by the clutch cones, followed; the best known are the Warner and the Porsche systems but, although different systems give different feel or feedback through the gearlever when the baulking mechanism is at work, the effect is similar in all cases.

Even with all these refinements, gearchanging still called for some modest skill and co-ordination on the part of the driver. At the same time, many engineers felt that the crudeness of the conventional gearbox (in which the forces involved tend to bend the shafts, distort the bearings, and tear the casing apart) was an affront to mechanical propriety. While the infinitely or steplessly variable transmission remained an un-attainable ideal for decades, it was known that a discrete number of suitable ratios could be obtained from trains of epicyclic gears: the teeth of these are always enmeshed, and their disposition leaves ample room for friction clutches of generous size to control the locking and unlocking of the armatures and rings carrying the gears. First and simplest of these epicyclic transmis-sions was the two-speed (and reverse) gearbox of the Ford T, which went into production twenty years before the appearance of synchromesh. Many drivers knew no other way of changing gear but the curious pedalling tricks by which the Model T was controlled; however, the wider performance range of later and more sophisticated cars demanded more speeds.

By the time that synchromesh was well established, an elegant epicyclic alternative was available in a few cars. This was the four-speed Wilson preselective self-changing gearbox, the precursor of nearly all the automatic transmissions in use today. In it was a series of four coaxial epicyclic gear trains, the annulus of each presenting a smooth cylindrical exterior upon which a band brake could operate to clamp the annulus (or ring gear) and stop it moving. According to the brake selected, any one of the lowest three speeds or reverse would be secured; and the progres-

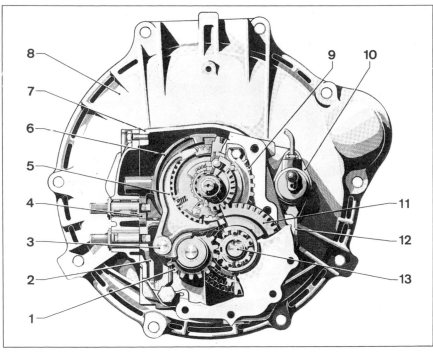

The driver could change his mind at any time and move the lever to another position, except when actually releasing the pedal. In the Talbot car, designer Roesch arranged that gearchanges would take place in an automatic sequence leading up to and down from top gear unless the driver interfered but, in the 1930s, there was no demand for such refinements: drivers were happy enough that they could enjoy anything from a leisurely change to a racing snap without any skill or doubt. Touring cars such as the Daimler and Armstrong Siddeley had a fluid coupling interposed between engine and gearbox, to give ineffable smoothness of take-off and to cushion each change, although this impaired the high mechanical efficiency of the Wilson box. Sporting saloons such as the Riley sometimes had instead a centrifugally operated friction clutch, sometimes called the traffic clutch, which allowed the engine to idle in gear. Racing cars such as the ERA did without a separate clutch and relied on the brake band controlling bottom gear to provide the necessary progression of grip when starting.

The Wilson gearbox was almost entirely confined to British cars, and remained in production until the demise of the Armstrong Siddeley. Shorter lived but more refined was the French Cotal gearbox: it had fewer trains and hence a less attractive progression of

Above and right: two cutaway drawings of the five-speed manual gearbox used on the Mercedes 230, 250, 280 and 300 series.
1 = 1st, 2 = 2nd, 3 = 3rd, 4 = 4th, 5 = 5th and R = reverse

1 Reverse Gear
2 Shift ring 5 & R
3 Shift rod 5 & R
4 Shift detent 1 & 2
5 Shift fork 5 & R
6 Shift fork 1 & 2
7 Transmission case
8 Clutch housing
9 Reverse mainshaft
10 Slave cylinder
11 Helical gear 5
12 Oil filter plug
13 Countershaft
14 Clutch pressure plate
15 Drive shaft
16 Clutch plate
17 Flywheel
18 Starter ring gear
19 Release bearing
20 Synchroniser ring 4
21 Sliding sleeve 3 & 4
22 Helical gear 3
23 Helical gear 2
24 Helical gear 1
25 Main shaft
26 Sliding sleeve 5
27 Helical gear 5
28 Speedometer drive
29 Three-arm flange
30 Transmission cover
31 R gear countershaft
32 Sliding sleeve 1 & 2
33 Oil drain plug
34 Countershaft gear
35 Release member
36 Diaphragm spring

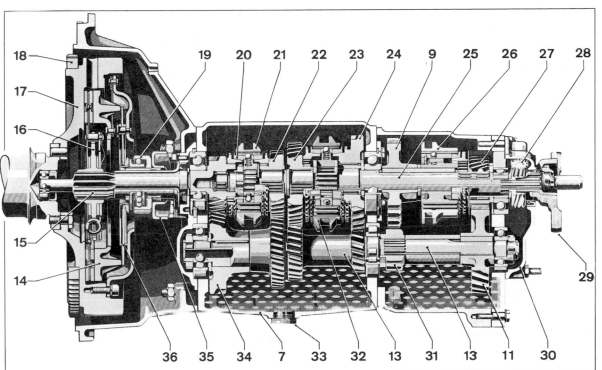

sive operation of the brake, by spring-loaded toggles, ensured positive and shock-free take-up of the drive, quietly and as quickly or slowly as the driver wished. Each band brake constituted a clutch and could be used as such, but the clutch pedal also operated the selector linkages to engage whichever speed the driver had determined in advance to use by moving a lever to the appropriate notch of a quadrant. When he 'preselected' top gear, the corresponding toggle would be cocked, and when next he fully depressed and released the clutch pedal the selector mechanism would be triggered as for the other speeds; but in the case of top gear, all the band brakes would be freed, while a cone clutch at one end of the series of gear trains locked the whole lot together so that they rotated as one unit to give direct drive from the input shaft to the output shaft.

ratios, but instead of the gruesome mechanical linkages characteristic of the British design it rejoiced in electro-magnetic control of the gears, under the fingertip direction of a tiny gearlever (looking like a cherry on a cocktail stick) moving in a miniature gate.

It was General Motors in America that gave the epicyclic gearbox mass appeal. In 1937, the Buick and Oldsmobile were marketed with a semi-automatic transmission in which all gearchanges were arranged to occur whenever the prevailing combination of vehicle speed and engine speed and load dictated. The system was semi-automatic only inasmuch as a conventional clutch still had to be worked by the driver when starting and stopping; two years later they had productionised the fluid coupling and the fully automatic Hydra-Matic transmission was born. Although the hydrokinetic couplings associated with conventional automatic transmissions have been the subject of endless experiment and change in the ensuing years, practically all automatic gearboxes have been essentially similar to this GM design, making use of two or three epicyclic trains to give three or four speeds forward and the usual one in reverse.

The notable change from the early Wilson and Cotal boxes has been in the means used to control the gear trains. Not only the annuli but also the planet carriers may be held fast, enabling a greater number of speeds to be offered by an epicyclic train and thus saving the cost of manufacturing gears. The old contracting band brakes are supplemented by multiplate clutches coaxial with the gearshaft, and the operation of these is usually by high-pressure oil from a pump built into the gearbox. In the bottom of the gearbox casing is an elaborate hydraulic circuit embodying valves which direct the oil pressure in varying ways, according to the demands conveyed by connections with the engine throttle and inlet manifold vacuum and the driver's control lever. Such hydraulic systems are not an essential feature of the automatic gearbox; in the Renault version, for instance, the brakes and clutches are applied by solenoids controlled by electronic circuitry.

Even the epicyclic gear train is not inviolate. The Automotive Products transmission, employed by British Leyland in some of their front-wheel-drive cars such as the Mini, substitutes bevel-gear differentials for some of the usual spur-gear sets, and incorporates a sprag-clutch or freewheel in bottom gear, as do some others.

One of the most commendably neat automatic gearboxes was the now defunct Hobbs Mechamatic, which saw effective service in everything from delivery vans to a special racing Lotus Elite. In this, one single epicyclic-gear train of compound construction (three coaxial sun gears, one planet carrier and no annulus) gave four forward speeds and one reverse under the control of two plate clutches and three disc brakes, all operated by hydraulic pressure behind diaphragms.

While on the subject of exceptions to generality, some variations in the layout of manually operated gearboxes should be noted. Not all such boxes offer direct drive in top gear, for instance, although it is often held desirable that they should: this is because mechanical losses are negligible in direct drive, whereas in the other speeds (supposedly less used) there is a penalty of about 4%. Other engineers insist that it is better to have an all-indirect gearbox in which the drive passes from the mainshaft to the layshaft through one pair of spur gears in each speed, so that power losses are about 2% in each case. In practice, all-indirect boxes are popular for rear-engined and front-wheel-drive cars, since the layout enables the output to emerge from the same end of the gearbox housing as the input entered. In the past there have been cars (particularly in Edwardian times) of conventional layout but with direct drive in third gear, top being then an 'overdrive' in the sense that the output rpm will be higher than the input rpm. This is not a good definition of overdrive, which should be related to the car's matching of tractive effort against resistance in the gear concerned, but the usage is prevalent and should be noted.

The balance of tractive effort and resistance is what should determine the ratios of each gear and the number to be made available. In brief, it may be said that the lowest gear ratio offered need be no lower than is necessary for a start to be made on the steepest gradient envisaged, nor any lower than would multiply the torque to the point where tractive effort would

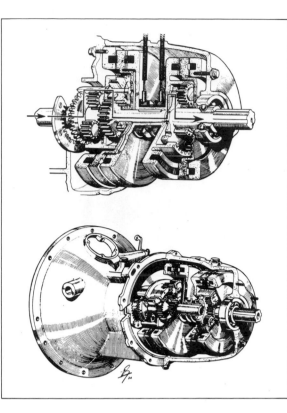

Left: two cutaway drawings of the French Cotal electro-magnetic pre-selector gearbox. This French design was similar to the British Wilson box but, instead of having cumbersome mechanical linkages, the Cotal box was operated electro-magnetically by a delicate gear lever. This gearbox was used in the nineteen thirties, but never saw great success

appreciably exceed the tractive capacity of the tyres; and, of course, it must be no lower than the maximum permissible stresses that the transmission can allow.

Top gear may be chosen according to any of a number of design considerations; but how many others should be offered between top and bottom, and what their spacing should be, will depend on the shape of the engine's full-throttle torque curve and the size of the production budget. An engine that is big and flexible, with lots of back-up torque and high-speed asthma, may call for no more than three speeds. A small engine, or one with a torque curve rising to a peak at or near the peak-power speed (they rarely coincide) may need five or six.

Geographical influences are evident in gearboxes, too. Italy, a country of many hills and some long flat roads, used to go in for three quite closely-spaced low gears and a remote high top gear. Germany, with everything from Alps to Autobahns, also favoured a high top and a low bottom, but with the intermediate ratios evenly spaced. The English used to be congenital top-gear staggerers, but had no mountains worthy of the name, so their top gear was rather low; the next was close to it because that was the only other gear in frequent use and an easy change was demanded, and any others were calculated to serve the unlikely eventuality that the driver would dare to attempt one of the more famous hills such as Porlock, Sutton Bank or Wrynose. As for the Americans, they always had such big engines that they could go everywhere in top anyway, and they soon forgot how to change gear. The automatic transmission certainly helped them to forget; but nowadays, when the pressures of international marketing have constrained all cars to be more alike than in the past, the very processes of memory and oblivion are obscured. The Grand Prix racer and the heavy truck perpetuate Panhard's *fin du siècle* brutalities (although most heavy trucks now have synchromesh and some have semi-automatic gearboxes), while everything else apes General Motors. Whether this is something to be remembered or forgotten should perhaps be left to the reader.

OVERDRIVE

making light work of cruising

MOTORING JARGON is a dreadful jumble of popular and ill-chosen usage, and of all the morass of misleading expressions and half-understood connotations it embraces, the terminology of the drive line contains more than its fair share of vagueness and confusion. Consider the word *overdrive*: it means a gear ratio (within a gearbox) such that the speed of the output shaft in relation to that of the input shaft is in a ratio higher than unity—or lower, if you refuse to subscribe to the jargon; *and* it means a supplementary gearbox, usually but not necessarily epicyclic, downstream from the main gearbox and likewise offering a multiplication rather than a demultiplication of the latter's output shaft speed; *and* it means any overall gear ratio so high that the engine cannot reach the peak of its power curve. The facts that an overdrive gear speed need not have an overdrive effect, and that an overdrive effect can be achieved without recourse to overdrive gearing, suggest that the word is overworked.

To avoid unnecessary confusion, let us first ratify one piece of established jargon. The higher the numerical ratio of a reduction gear—that is, the slower the output shaft revolves for a given rate of input shaft revolution—the lower we consider the gear. Engineers outside the automotive world consider it higher; that is their problem, not ours. In our car's gearbox, bottom gear is the lowest, top gear the highest. If the overall ratio of top gear (taking into account the final drive or axle gearing and the rolling radius of the tyres) allows the engine speed, at which maximum power is developed, to correspond to the road speed at which the tractive effort at the driving wheels is the same as the sum of wind and mechanical resistance to motion, then the car is correctly geared to reach the highest speed of which it is capable. However, any trifling increase in resistance, be it of wind or gradient, will prevent the car from reaching its true maximum speed.

Car manufacturers long ago learnt that the reluctance of the average driver to explore the maximum-speed capability of his car was matched only by his reluctance to change down from top gear once he had engaged it. What people wanted was lively top-gear acceleration: the easy way to provide it was to lower the gearing (usually in the final drive) and so increase the torque multiplication. This produced two unwanted side-effects: the car was fussier at all speeds, because the engine would be working at a higher crankshaft rate for a given road speed, and there was some risk of the engine being overspeeded and perhaps endangered by the ease with which it would run beyond the speed at which it developed maximum power. Inevitably it would wear out more quickly if subjected to sustained high-speed cruising, for which top gear ought really to be higher, not lower: a top gear that was theoretically too high would prevent the car from reaching its proper maximum speed unless aided by a downhill gradient or a following wind. In that event, it would still be running within its normal safe working range, while at cruising speeds only slightly lower it would seem more at ease and consume less fuel.

For many years, these opposing requirements were compromised by making the third and fourth ratios of the conventional four-speed gearbox very 'close' or numerically similar. The car might be very nearly as fast in third as in fourth; it might even be faster, as in the case of certain Frazer Nash models of about 1930 and certain Citroën models thirty years later. The snag was that it was a four-speed car with virtually three-speed performance, as it were: a car with two top gears and two others. Restoration of acceleration and hill-climbing prowess called for another gear, and when the need was crucial and money was no object, a

five-speed gearbox could be made—as, to the consternation of their Grand Prix rivals, in the case of Delage whose high-revving 1926/7 straight-eight 1½-litre could peak at about 8000 rpm in fourth gear and then relax for the rest of any long straight (and straights, like races, were longer in those days) at 6500 in fifth.

In those days, as still today in many front-engined rear-drive cars, top gear was direct, a 1:1 ratio in which the output and input shafts of the gearbox were coupled together. This eliminated the frictional losses involved in the meshing gears of the lower ratios, and thus made top gear (which was most used) mechanically the most efficient. In a case such as that of the Delage, fifth gear would not be used much: it would be better to make the 'other top' gear, fourth, direct drive, and provide a geared-up fifth—an overdrive gear. The same solution had been found in other, earlier cases such as the Rolls-Royce Silver Ghost which, for a time, had a four-speed gearbox in which third was direct and fourth was geared up. Alas, Royce found that customers insisted on going everywhere in overdrive, which could be neither as quiet nor as lively as direct third, and he could not educate them to think of third as top when there was another higher ratio available!

By the 1930s, the American manufacturers were occasionally running into the same problems. A three-speed gearbox was the norm there, but some of the fastest cars needed more. The answer was to make two top gears available where they really counted—in the back axle—so that both were direct drive as far as the gearbox was concerned. The fact that the gear-change mechanism was clumsy and the extra unsprung

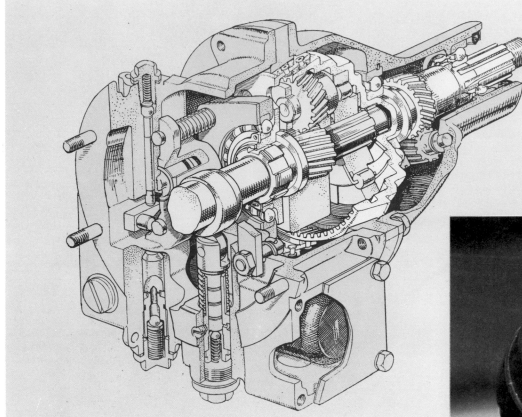

Below: the neat overdrive switch of the Triumph Dolomite Sprint, which is also used on the Triumph 2000/2500 series. Most overdrive switches in the past have been placed on stalks on the steering column, but this type has proved more popular as it can be used directly in conjunction with the gear lever

weight in the axle undesirable did not matter much to the average American, whose driving habits were such that he proved just as incorrigible as the average Rolls-Royce owner.

In another twenty years, the problems recurred, because new motorways, fuels, oils, bearings and tyres encouraged people to drive for long distances at or near maximum speed. To enable this to be done on the rising, rather than the drooping, portion of the power curve, a new apparatus became available. It was a two-speed epicyclic gearbox attached to the rear of a car's normal gearbox, providing a continuation of the direct drive line when all three elements of the gearset (sun gear, planetary pinions, and annulus or ring gear) were locked together by the hydraulically operated cone clutch, or a higher ratio when the clutch moved to lock the sun to the casing. The apparatus was known as the de Normanville (Captain de Normanville was the patentee) or more fully as the Laycock-de Normanville overdrive. It was little less than sensational at the time, featuring in the then new Austin-Healey 100, the Jensen and optionally in the popular Standard Vanguard; many other British cars, mainly of the high-performance type, soon acquired it as an option or even as standard equipment.

By the end of the decade, it had even reached foreign manufacturers. Ferrari used it in the 250 GT 2+2 model that appeared in 1960—but as was too often the case with Ferrari engineering at that time, the installation was botched. It was a feature of the Laycock mechanism that the hydraulic operation of its clutch employed oil from a supply shared with the gearbox and pressurised by an integral pump worked by an eccentric on the overdrive input shaft. In the Ferrari, the gearbox had to be filled with an oil that was suitable for the overdrive; alternatively, the latter had to suffer an unsuitable oil to preserve the gearbox. No good could come of such an arrangement.

Above: most overdrive units consist of an epicyclic gear train, operated either hydraulically or mechanically; this cutaway shows a Laycock-de Normanville overdrive, which is characterised by its hydraulic clutch operation. The shaft from the gearbox is shown in red, while the output shaft to the wheels is in blue. In overdrive, movement is transmitted through the gear train, while in direct drive, the clutch (in green), which is splined to the input shaft, presses against the gear housing and locks input against output

In Britain, the Laycock-de Normanville overdrive went from strength to strength. It was soon realised that the overdrive could be made operable while one of the indirect ratios of the gearbox was engaged, thus acting as a ratio-splitter: with careful juggling of cog sizes in the gearbox, a fairly regular progression might be contrived in which overdrive third nicely bridged the gap between direct third and top, overdrive second doing the same between direct second and third. Thus a four-speed gearbox might be made part of a seven-speed transmission. It was never thought safe to apply the overdrive to first gear, for the ratio of first was invariably so low as to multiply the torque of the engine three or more times, the resulting output torque from the gearbox being too much for the overdrive to stand. When allied to large engines, the overdrive might not be able to take the torque in second gear either, and in really lusty machines, it was thought more prudent to limit its operation to top gear only. All this could be arranged with the aid of simple electrical switches tripped by the gearbox selector rods, for the driver's control over the overdrive was by means of an electrical two-position switch whose circuit could be interrupted by the gearbox switches if the wrong gear were engaged. In the appropriate gear, all the driver had to do was flick his control switch (which might be on the facia or the steering column, and later found favour in the knob on the gearlever) and the job was done. There was no need to touch the clutch, although in some installations the change up into overdrive would not be made unless the overdrive were temporarily relieved of full-throttle torque. The simple treatment was briefly to release the accelerator—just as a brief blip of the throttle would smooth a downward change from overdrive to direct top, without any of the clutch-dipping practised by so many drivers.

Bearing in mind the simplicity of the electrical circuit, which had to do no more than operate a solenoid controlling the valve which admitted high-pressure oil to shift the cone clutch to the overdrive position, it is amazing how little thought went into most installations. It was too easy for a driver to slow down in overdrive top gear, select perhaps first or second gear, and then when accelerating hard again

substitute for it. Two exceptions to this generality that spring to mind were the MG and Triumph sports cars, in which the overdrive compensated for the shortcomings of gearboxes that were never designed for anything but placid family saloons, with ratios much too wide to suit sporting driving.

Here lies a hint to the gradual disappearance of the epicyclic overdrive unit. While gearboxes were in production that needed its help, it enjoyed a steady demand but, although the cost of retooling to make a five-speed gearbox might be greater than the cost of buying and fitting a heavy and complex (and therefore expensive) Laycock overdrive, sooner or later every gearbox has to make way for a new design. When that happens, the obvious course is to make a five-speed

Left: motoring journalist Roger Bell, with his Group One Triumph Dolomite Sprint, at Britain's Thruxton circuit. These cars dominate their class not only because their 'standard' 2-litre engines produce almost 200 bhp, but because as the cars have overdrive systems, they virtually have six-speed gearboxes. Overdrive-third is particularly useful; this gear is higher than direct third and lower than direct fourth, and 'bridges' the gap

and passing from third to the top gear he expected, to find instead that overdrive was back in use and the engine revs had slumped. If overdrive were effective in third gear as well as fourth, then the sudden abatement of acceleration would be felt when changing up from second. Such oversights were still thus rewarded in many cars made years later.

Perhaps the reason was a revulsion from the elaborate and ill-reasoned (not to mention frequently maladjusted) system of kick-downs, drop-outs and inhibitors that made the use of overdrive in the original Austin-Healey unnecessarily complicated and the use of the later Borg-Warner overdrive (an unsuccessful attempt to rival Laycock) impossibly unpredictable. In fact, very little complexity was involved in providing a solution to the problem of the recurrent overdrive: as apparently only Bristol had the wit to demonstrate, in their 405 model first shown late in 1954, all that was needed was a simple relay. When overdrive top was engaged and the driver changed down (or even merely moved the gearlever into the neutral position) the gearbox switch isolated the driver's relay switch, which snapped back into the normal position; next time top gear was engaged, it would be direct top. Obviously such a system could only work when overdrive was limited to top gear, as in the Bristol, but the objection was more imaginary than real, for in most other installations overdrive third is so similar to direct top as to constitute a somewhat useless (and mechanically less efficient)

gearbox replace the old four-speeder, and by the middle 1960s there were many European manufacturers who had done just that. Fifth gear might be, and usually was, an overdrive ratio in the sense of being geared higher than 1:1. Occasionally, as in the Getrag gearbox adopted for the Jensen-Healey and optional in the BMW 2002, fifth is direct and the final-drive gearing (or the tyre size) may be altered to give an overdrive effect if desired.

In fact, it is really immaterial whether the highest gear is direct or not, save in the sense that a direct drive is more efficient than an indirect one. If a gearbox has a direct-drive ratio, all the others it offers must lose some power transmission efficiency through at least two pairs of meshing gears; whereas if all the gears are indirect, with the output shaft not coaxial with the input, each ratio involves only one pair of meshing gears, so all are of roughly equal efficiency. All-indirect gearboxes are not uncommon in front-wheel-drive cars, and are the rule in rear-engined cars —and when a gearbox is all-indirect it matters not at all whether any given ratio is higher or lower than unity. All that matters is the overall transmission ratio, from engine to wheels: in such a car, a gear can only be described as an overdrive if it is (however deliberately) too high. There is hope for the language yet— but if early pioneers of overdrive had been less obsessed by mechanics and had called the thing a cruising gear, it and the customers would have given far less trouble.

AUTOMATIC TRANSMISSION

taking the effort out of driving

Above: the 'automatic'
automatic—the DAF
Variomatic transmission

Far right: the Automotive
Products transmission, as
fitted to automatic minis;
it uses bevel-differential
gears. The diagrams
show how the various
gear ratios are obtained,
the arrows indicating the
directions of rotation of
the components. Purple
components transmit
drive, blue components
are idling, grey com-
ponents are stationary,
yellow brakebands and
clutches are disengaged
and orange brakebands
and clutches are
engaged

ACCORDING to the degree of automaticity offered, an
automatic transmission is one that relieves the driver of
the skills and obligations of gear changing and/or clutch
operation. Ideally it will ensure that for any given
combination of vehicle speed and engine load it will
automatically provide a suitable gear ratio for the
transmission and multiplication of engine torque to the
driving wheels. This ideal is seldom achieved, though
efforts have been made since the earliest day of the
motor car. Spaulding in 1897, Fouillaron in 1900, and
several later designers and manufacturers, conceived a
steplessly-variable-ratio belt transmission, while in the
1930s the epicyclic gearbox enjoyed some limited
popularity either in the Wilson form as a pre-selective
mechanism combined with a fluid coupling, or as a
Cotal gearbox in which gears were electro-magnetically
held under the control of a simple electric switch.
Nevertheless, the simple friction clutch and manually
operated gearbox, perfectly summarised by the pioneer
Panhard with the words *C'est brutal, mais ça marche,*
has in successively refined forms held sway from the
dawn of motoring to the present day, being still pre-
dominant in all major countries outside the USA.

It is not to be supposed that four generations of
designers have all had the same blind spot. In retaining
the old cogbox so long they have been justified by its
reasonable reliability and high efficiency. At least it is
high in mechanical efficiency, absorbing and wasting
very little of the precious power it is meant to transmit:
but as an agent of transmission it is by no means
efficient overall.

The trouble is that the variation of transmission ratio
in such a gearbox can only be made in a limited series of
finite steps, each constituting a fixed gear ratio and
therefore inconsistent with the characteristic power
delivery of a piston engine. In each gear there is only
one road speed at which the engine can deliver full
effort, so that with a five-speed box there are only five
speeds at which the car can be getting the utmost from
its power unit. The rest of the time the engine will be
struggling up through its working range or wheezing
away beyond it; and although the cogs may faithfully
transmit, say, 96% of the effort to final drive, it will still
be only 96% of something that may be a lot less than
maximum torque. This is why the mechanical efficiency argument is somewhat specious. To put it in

simple terms, 86% of maximum effort all the time may be better than 96% occasionally.

Once people accept this idea they are well on the way to accepting the idea of automatic transmissions. Ultimately we can look forward to a transmission offering stepless variation of gear ratio from as low as may be needed to as high as could be managed in the most favourable conditions.

Hydrostatics, which can provide this, are on their way but at present are severely limited by problems of noise, vibration, and mechanical inefficiency. Variable belt and pulley drives can also do it and are on the market already. In Germany ZF and Reimers do a steplessly variable belt drive for buses and the like, but the belt squeezed between hydraulically powered pulleys is really a sort of steel chain and 65 bhp is the most that it can be called upon to transmit.

Better known and proving increasingly successful is the DAF Variomatic transmission, which handles the same power in production cars and has dealt with more than 200 bhp in competition cars. It relies upon a set of flexible belts squeezed between the faces of adjustable pulleys that are expanded or contracted automatically so as to provide the most appropriate transmission ratio for prevailing conditions. A system of spring loading and a centrifugally operated servo mechanism ensure that the ratio automatically selected is appropriate to the speed, while a pneumatic mechanism, energised by engine inlet manifold depression, provides for matching the gear ratio to the load.

Full throttle cancels this vacuum secondary control of ratio and ensures maximum possible acceleration by keeping the engine at peak output and letting the car catch up with it; so long as the throttle pedal is kicked right down the transmission will continually adjust the ratio so as to give the highest possible road speed. Releasing the accelerator pedal just a fraction allows vacuum control to be resumed, giving a change up to what may very well be an overdrive ratio.

The supplementary virtue of the Variomatic is that there is no need for the designer to compromise the final drive ratio in order to achieve the best performance: he just picks one that is sure to be somewhat too high, and leaves the pulleys to choose whatever lower overall ratio is appropriate to prevailing circumstances. It is this feature which explains the ability of DAF cars to reach unexpectedly high speeds in favourable conditions (for example, down steep hills) despite their modest power and correspondingly modest true maximum speed in neutral conditions.

However, although the highest Variomatic ratio can be really long-striding, the lowest cannot conveniently be much lower than 4:1. Simple mechanical considerations dictate this, rather than any basic conceptual limitation; but the effect is that the ratios, while being steplessly variable, are not truly infinitely variable. This applies to all automatic transmissions, and necessarily so. If it were otherwise there is not a halfshaft in existence that would not be snapped by the infinitely multiplied torque of the bottom ratio.

In practice, the lowest ratio of an automatic transmission is chosen to give the car as much hillclimbing ability as customers are likely to need. The result is invariably low enough to produce another limiting feature: the coupling between engine and gearbox, whether of the fluid type as in most automatic transmissions or a centrifugal friction clutch as in the DAF (where it is not a necessary part of the Variomatic drive but is included so as to eliminate the clutch pedal and the skills needed to operate it) makes it difficult to get the car off the mark with as much verve as might be expected. Certainly it is seldom that an automatic

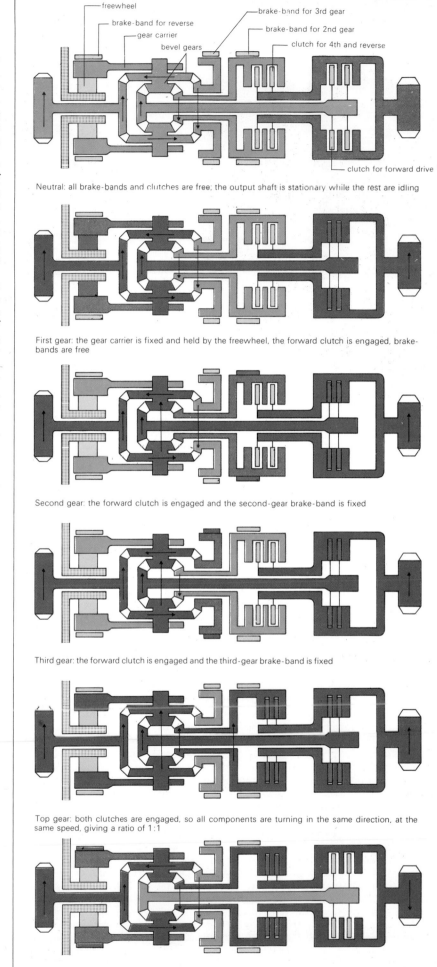

Neutral: all brake-bands and clutches are free; the output shaft is stationary while the rest are idling

First gear: the gear carrier is fixed and held by the freewheel, the forward clutch is engaged, brake-bands are free

Second gear: the forward clutch is engaged and the second-gear brake-band is fixed

Third gear: the forward clutch is engaged and the third-gear brake-band is fixed

Top gear: both clutches are engaged, so all components are turning in the same direction, at the same speed, giving a ratio of 1:1

Reverse: the reverse clutch is engaged, and the forward clutch disengaged, while the reverse brake-band is fixed

Far left: the forward clutch of the AP transmission. It comprises two friction discs, two pressure discs and one thrust plate. At the end of the shaft a hole is visible, through which high-pressure oil flows to operate the clutch

Near left, above: a bevel-differential unit as used by Automotive Products. As shown in the cross-section opposite, this unit is made up of one bevel-gear set within another, with brake facilities built into the various parts. This is more compact than the epicyclic alternative

Near left, below: epicyclic gears are used in most automatic gearboxes. The three 'planet' gears revolve around the central 'sun' gear and within the outer 'annulus'. The planets are fixed to a carrier, as shown on the right, and by braking one of the set, the ratio between the other two can be altered (if the planet carrier is stopped, and the sun is driven, the annulus will turn backwards, but if the annulus is stopped, the planet carrier will turn forwards)

transmission will produce wheelspin in normal driving away from stand-still. In the case of the DAF such initial sluggishness can be offset against surprisingly good acceleration once the car is on the move with the clutch fully engaged and the engine into its stride, when the transmission efficiency never drops below 90% and at mid-range may climb to 94%.

Given a low enough gear ratio, anything can spin its wheels from standstill. Indeed, with high-powered engines it is the limit of tyre adhesion and hence the onset of uncontrollable wheelspin, rather than the demands of gradients, that determine the starting gear ratio. When the 1937 Grand Prix Auto Union set a world record for the standing kilometre in 18.4 seconds, it was limited by wheelspin in 1st and 2nd gears up to about 100 mph; calculations at the time showed that steplessly variable gearing would only have improved the figure to 18.31 seconds.

Electrical transmissions, which might be supposed the best, can make maximum torque available at all times and provide a quite inimitable degree of control. Electrically driven rail cars can spin their wheels and check the spin again in less than a revolution, but suitable systems have yet to be devised for cars.

At present the most common kind of automatic transmission comprises a constant-mesh planetary or epicyclic gearbox connected to the engine by some kind of hydrokinetic coupling. It usually permits power-sustained or 'hot' shifts—transitions from one gear ratio to the next are in any case very much quicker than any combination of conventional clutch pedal and hand lever can match—and it commonly allows the engine to work at its best speed when under load. The gear-change itself is most commonly worked by oil pressure from a special pump. The pressure operates braking bands and plate-type clutches in order to alter the ratios of epicyclic or bevel gear sets. For a three-speed gearbox, there will usually be two sets, top gear being obtained by locking the input and output shafts together, by means of a plate clutch.

Usually, the change points are governed by engine speed and throttle opening, although a manual override is fitted in most cases. Throttle opening will only have an effect up to certain speeds, where the engine speed will over-rule this. Such a transmission is usually bulky and heavy, it is usually consumptive of power, it often makes towing or push starting impossible, and it

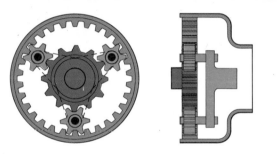

can only be made economically by being manufactured in large numbers. The result of this last and most important detraction is that car manufacturers can seldom buy an automatic precisely suited to their needs and they are not always prepared to match their engines to the transmissions.

Part of the difficulty usually encountered in marrying some ill-suited engine and transmission is the difficulty of ensuring that gear changes take place smoothly, and at exactly the right time, automatically. The timing could just as well be left to the driver, who has in his head a far better and cheaper computer than any of the manufacturers could provide, and might be prepared to move a lever or press a button. The transmission engineers would then be left with the need to devise some way of compensating for a generally rather haphazard treatment of the accelerator pedal by drivers relying on automatic transmissions.

Yet changes can go through with perfect timing and with perfect smoothness, and when the transmission is perfectly matched to the engine the resultant performance can be of a high standard. This can only be achieved when torque converter characteristics, gear ratios and engine performance are all properly reconciled. There is a limit to what can be achieved in the way of choosing gear ratios when using conventional epicyclic gear trains (or their bevel-differential equivalents as found in the Automotive Products gearbox), but the limitations are not onerous in practice. That leaves the engines and the converter to be matched, and this is a business whose subtlety can only be appreciated after some study of the whole range of hydrokinetic couplings of which there are many different kinds.

Of those that are most familiar to motorists, there

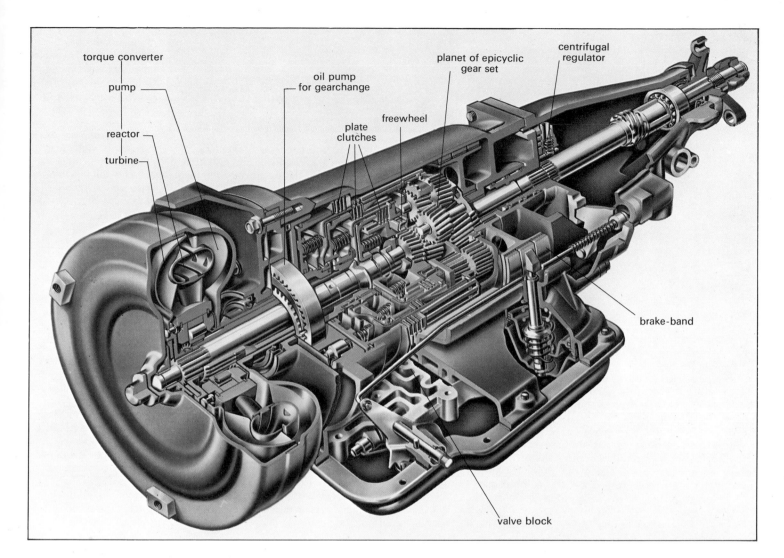

torque converter

pump

reactor

turbine

oil pump
for gearchange

plate
clutches

freewheel

planet of epicyclic
gear set

centrifugal
regulator

brake-band

valve block

A cutaway view of the General Motors Hydramatic transmission, detailing the components. There have been many versions of this gearbox, some with more than one torque converter and some with a lock-up clutch to override the torque converter in top gear

is some difference between the torque converter and the simple fluid flywheel. The latter is much the less complex, and since it is still used in some Mercedes–Benz cars it gives us a suitable starting point.

To be strict we should call it a fluid coupling. It is simple in construction, comprising two radially vaned saucers face to face. Oil flung centrifugally by one is caught by the other, the force of impingement appearing as a torque (turning force) at the output or turbine shaft (get used to the idea of the input rotor being called the pump and the other the turbine, for this is common parlance applied to all hydrokinetic devices). Thus we have a transmission of torque without any mechanical connection between the driving and the driven members. They can therefore slip relative to each other, but this does not affect the most important feature of the fluid coupling: the input torque is always equal to the output torque.

The efficiency of the coupling is measured by the amount of slip that exists at any given time, in other words by the difference between input and output speeds in a particular set of conditions. Most of the time, fluid couplings operate at about 97% efficiency once they have reached coupling point (that is, there is a minimal 3% slip), but they are very inefficient while running up to coupling speed. So the designer has to consider very carefully what sort of behaviour he wants when matching a fluid coupling to an engine: if it is to carry engine torque at high efficiency and low slip, the coupling may have to have a torque capacity very much greater than what the engine can deliver. Otherwise slip will be severe and excessive heat will

accumulate in the coupling. Because of the straight design of the blades and the symmetry of the pump and turbine, engine braking is possible.

Now, let us move on to the fluid converter. In this a third element is added between the pump and the turbine, and the blades of all three are curved instead of straight. The third element is called the reactor, and it is fixed so that fluid flow from the pump is diverted: the fluid impinges on the turbine at a more favourable angle, thus amplifying the torque applied to the turbine. Actually the torque on the turbine equals the sum of the torques on pump and reactor, and the resultant output torque may be much higher than the input.

This is the principle of hydrokinetic torque multiplication or conversion, and it is used in construction machinery; but it is not suitable for cars. This sort of fluid converter is usually at its most efficient at about 40% slip, but the higher the efficiency the lower is the torque conversion possible and—more important—the lower is the efficiency at the extreme ends of the slip range where all the engine power is dissipated in heat.

The answer to this problem is to mount the reactor on a freewheel or overrunning clutch; then, the reactor is free to move in the same direction as the turbine, but it is always locked against rotation in the opposite direction. At coupling point, therefore, the reactor automatically removes itself from the circuit in which it can no longer play an effective part, and the mechanism acts purely as a fluid coupling with no torque multiplication. We therefore call it a converter coupling, but the motor industry evidently cannot be bothered. Nevertheless this is what you get in your

Far left: the Automotive Products torque converter; on the left are the turbine and stator, while on the right the pump carries the ring gear for the starter

Near left: in order to obtain the right gear at the right time, the gearbox oil has to be channelled through these complex passages

car's automatic transmission when the salesman assures you that it contains a torque converter.

In effect the best characteristics of fluid coupling and fluid converter are combined in the converter coupling. The transition from one function to the other, from converter to coupling after reaching coupling point, is a rather protracted business, for the curved blading necessary for converter operation is not altogether suitable for coupling operation. Furthermore, the coupling point is normally reached when input and output torques are equal, but at that point the output speed will still be about 10% less than the input speed. On the overrun some engine braking is possible in the coupling range, but not reliably below.

The full-load efficiency of a converter coupling is usually below 90% in the converter range, rising to about 95% or 96% in the coupling range. This efficiency is directly related to the product of the torque multiplication ratio and the slip ratio, from which it follows that when driven gently at low speed the efficiency is poor—which is why automatic gearboxes usually change up very early when the driver is dawdling, and why most of them tend to give poor fuel consumption. On the other hand, when input speed is high but the load moderate, efficiency takes a turn for the better and in these conditions can reach as much as 98%.

In industrial applications and for sporting driving, stall speed (when output speed is zero and torque multiplication is at its maximum) and the engine's maximum torque speed should be the same, and coupling point should be just a little below maximum power; but this would call for a heat exchanger to cool the fluid, so to save money in cars it is usual for the compromise to be biased in favour of restraint, as you can tell by watching the rev-counter during acceleration. Often an automated car is set to show a mere 2000 rpm during a stalled take-off (one where the brakes are held while the throttle is opened), despite the peak torque being developed at well over 3000 rpm. Change-up points are often premature, while it is objectionable to have to kick hard down on the accelerator to effect an early downchange, and indeed this kick-down facility is erratic, it produces jerky results, and it may be positively dangerous.

Below: this neatly sectioned automatic gearbox clearly shows the main components, including the two epicyclic gear trains and the freewheel in the torque converter. This box has three forward speeds and reverse, obtained by fixing the various components of the gear sets. The gears on the far left of the picture drive the speedometer

It is much better to hold or change down to low gear by means of an inhibitor facility such as the modern automatic box always provides. By means of a lever or buttons the driver is able to prevent the gearbox from changing up, or to force it to change down, the control mechanism ultimately modifying the action of the high-pressure hydraulics or (in rarer cases) the electromagnetic devices controlling the clutches and brakes which hold or release appropriate components of the epicyclic gear train. These hydraulic or electrical systems usually monitor engine speed and load and vehicle speed in order to determine the appropriate selection of gear ratio. The number of gears is commonly three, though two-speed epicyclic trains were once fashionable and an increasing number of four-speed gearboxes are coming into use.

In any case there is no need to combine the converter coupling, nor even the simple fluid coupling, with an automatic epicyclic gearbox. An ordinary synchromesh gearbox will do, but there must be a conventional clutch between it and the fluid coupling if gear changing is to be feasible. This has been a popular combination in Germany (*vide* the NSU Ro80 and the Volkswagen 1500). The clutch pedal is generally made superfluous by a pressure-sensitive micro-switch built into the gear lever and linked, by an electrical servo system, to the clutch release, so that the friction clutch is disengaged whenever the gear lever is touched.

Note that this supplementary clutch does not have a lock-up effect on the fluid coupling. A lock-up clutch used to be a common addition to automatic transmissions: Borg-Warner incorporated one in their old DG series transmission, and General Motors did the same in an old Hydramatic transmission. Yet you can look for one in a Hydramatic and never find it: just as the original Hydra was many-headed, so have there been many versions of this transmission. Some had two fluid couplings, one always being full and operational, the other being drained or filled with fluid as and when required—which was in 2nd and 4th gears.

A later version was even more curious—if less disturbingly leisurely in its operation—for its single coupling had a free-running stator built into it; anchored to the gearbox output shaft rather than to the casing, this odd intruder gave a little torque multiplication (only about 30%) but kept drag torque very low.

It is also possible to vary the angle of the stator blades as is done in gas turbines. General Motors tried this in their Super Turbine 300 transmission peculiar to Buick—along with a five-element twin-turbine converter arrangement. As mentioned earlier, hydrokinetic converters and/or couplings can be combined in various ways. The multi-stage fluid converter, for example, is one in which the circulating oil impinges successively on two or more turbine members which are separated by fixed reactors. Its output characteristics are generally similar to those of a simple three-element converter, but maximum efficiency is always lower and overheating hazards are correspondingly greater. Maximum torque conversion is greater too, because of the extra stages, but maximum efficiency occurs at a lower slip ratio. In effect the thing is fine for conditions where part throttle cruising is punctuated by strong acceleration, as in the USA. A lock-up clutch is almost essential to provide direct drive and prevent runaway overheating in the higher speed range.

Another cunning trick is to divide one or more of the elements of a converter coupling into a number of smaller elements which can rotate at different speeds on their freewheels. In this way the characteristics of two or more converters can be combined into one called a polyphase converter, the advantage being higher efficiency over a wide slip range and the disadvantage the sheer expense of making the thing. Split-drive devices can give better results more cheaply. For instance, by the mechanical shunt converter combination where the power flow from the engine is divided into two parts by differential gearing, one part going to a direct mechanical drive and the other through a fluid converter, both being collected on the output shaft by an over-running clutch. Again we find General Motors active along these lines with the Buick Dual Path affair, in which all torque was routed through the converter in low gear, but only two-thirds went through it in high gear, the remainder being transmitted mechanically through a planetary gear train. Buick claimed a high conversion speed for this, suitable for sporting or European style engines which developed peak torque at relatively high speeds.

This kind of facility, together with high mechanical efficiency in the crucial range, where the ordinary converter coupling is making the transition from torque multiplication to so-called lock-up, is also a feature of the latest type 4-element coupling. Not yet in production, it is called the Variable Kinetic Transmission and is the brain child of the same H. F. Hobbs who was earlier responsible for an efficient but commercially unsuccessful 4-speed automatic gearbox. We have seen 4-element converters before, notably from General Motors, but the extra element has always been a second reactor, to all intents and purposes akin to the first one which is located between the pump and the turbine. In the new Hobbs device the fourth element is a circulatory turbine that also goes between the pump and turbine, but at the periphery of the assembly rather than near the hub. As usual, the reactor is coupled to the output shaft through a freewheel; but the new circulatory turbine is connected to the planet carrier of an epicyclic gear train whose annulus is driven by the input shaft, while the sun wheel is coupled by differential gearing to both the output shaft and the turbine rotor. This gearing allows the circulatory turbine to run with the pump—faster when the ratio of input to output speeds is lower than 2:1, slower when it is higher.

So what? So the rate of fluid circulation can be increased to give greater torque multiplication when, for example, the car is being accelerated from rest. Not only is there more torque multiplication, but also it becomes possible for the stall speed of the coupling to be higher, which means that instead of labouring at a miserable 2000 rpm at full throttle with the car held stationary by the brakes (the usual technique for a full-bore getaway with an automatic), the engine can run at 4000 rpm or more and is able to deliver its maximum torque right from the word go. It gives a maximum torque multiplication of no less than 4:1, which means that a supplementary stepped-ratio gearbox should not be necessary.

Whether or not this latest manifestation of the art should prove commercially successful, it is clear that automatic transmissions are in continuous development and are becoming increasingly popular in one form or another. There remains the remote possibility that gas turbines or differential diesels might ultimately take the place of the conventional piston engine, or some other power unit that like them can do without a gearbox and all the other ancillaries and superfluities, clutch pedals included. The gas turbine is virtually an engine with its own automatic transmission built in; the differential diesel could almost be described as a transmission system with an engine built in. The long term promise of either may be debated, but the short-term success of the conventional automatic transmission is beyond a doubt.

UNIVERSAL JOINT

drive at an angle

ENGINE TORQUE HAS TO BE SMOOTHLY TRANSMITTED to roadwheel axles that are continually but irregularly tilting due to road unevenness, twisting due to drive and brake torque reaction and, in some vehicles, turning to and fro as the wheels are steered.

As the result of this varied motion both the angle of drive to the axle and its distance relative to the gearbox or final drive unit are constantly changing. To meet these circumstances a universal joint or joints combined with either a telescopic propeller shaft (prop shaft) or short solid drive shafts are normally employed. The complete assembly is referred to as a drive line.

The principle of transmitting rotary motion from one shaft placed at an angle to another by means of a universal joint was solved very many years ago by Hooke and Cardan. Their joint used two yokes on planes perpendicular to each other and pivotally connected by a control block (spider) fitted with cross pins.

Early types of universal joints for cars included the globe joint, in which forks on two shafts fitted into two grooves cut at right angles in a steel ball, and discs, made up of leather or, more lately, rubberised fabric. These discs formed a flexible joint between two shafts, being attached to each shaft by three bolts spaced alternately around the disc.

A modern Hooke's joint consists of two yokes, a spider journal (also known as a cross pin or cross piece), four needle bearings which support the journal within the lugs (or ears) of the yokes, and four circlips or snap rings which retain the needle bearings in place; although sometimes the yoke is peened over to retain the bearings (*staked type*). Some older models had bronze bushes instead of needle roller bearings.

The output velocity of a Hooke's type joint fluctuates twice per revolution, the extent of the fluctuation depending on the angle between the driving and driven shafts. This is because, as the joint rotates, one pair of cross pins follows the plane of rotation of the driven yoke so that the attitude of this intermediate member is continually changing. At a joint angle of 28 degrees the speed variation may be as high as 25 per cent, so that in practice the maximum joint angle is limited to 18 degrees to 20 degrees on either side of the zero (or in-line) position.

This irregularity in velocity transmission is overcome by using a double joint or two separate joints connected by a shaft. At the second joint there is a similar variation in velocity, but providing the planes of the two joints are exactly aligned, and the angle of the driving shaft and the driven shaft to the connecting shaft are equal, the variation at the second joint is equal and opposite to that which occurs at the first, and consequently cancels it out to give a uniform speed at the final drive.

Thus a double Hooke's joint is perfectly satisfactory for in-line front-engine, rear-wheel-drive vehicles and it is widely used today. Difficulties arose, however, as other engine and drive layouts were developed, particularly with front or rear-engined units driving directly on to the front or rear wheels respectively. It was found that there was insufficient space and the drive angle was too great for Hooke's joints.

One of the first practical solutions to the problem, the constant velocity joint, was evolved by A. H. Rzeppa in 1926. He applied the fundamental principle that, for an output velocity faithfully to reproduce the input velocity, an intermediate member must be maintained at all times in a plane (the *median plane*) which bisects the angle between the driving and the driven shafts. Rzeppa's solution was to employ a 'ball and socket' joint with an intermediate member, for transmitting the torque, made up of six steel balls. The 'ball' and 'socket' were each grooved to accommodate the separate balls, which were retained in a special cage forming the median plane.

The modern continuous velocity joint is based on the Rzeppa principle, but some improvements have been

Below: gearbox output shafts, with rubber joints built-in between the shaft and the connecting flange

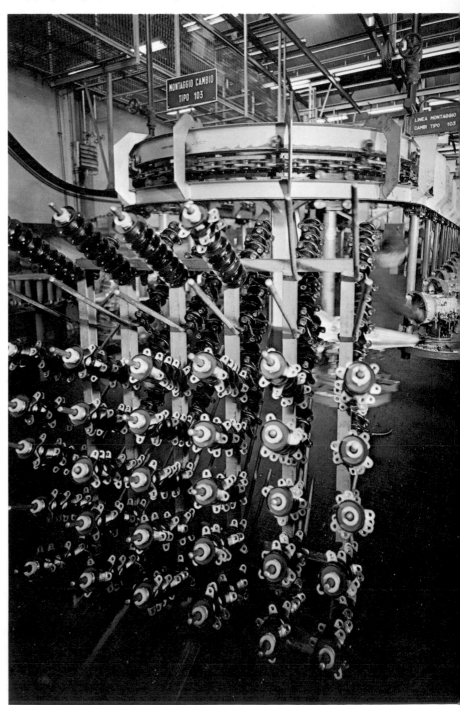

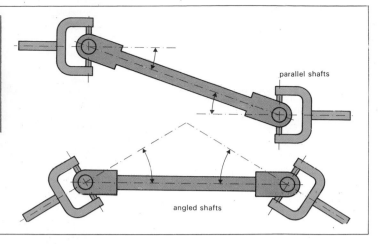

Hooke's joints are used on most propeller shafts, although they are not so popular in drive shafts, because the speed of the driven shaft is not constant and the variation has to be cancelled out by a second joint; as long as the angles of the shafts (α) are equal and the shafts parallel, the variations are equal and opposite; otherwise they become greater

parallel shafts

angled shafts

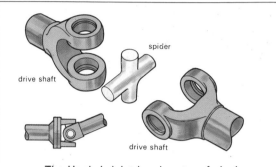

spider

drive shaft

drive shaft

The Hooke's joint involves two forked ends on the drive shafts, with a cross shaped piece (spider) linking the two

made, chiefly that of having an elliptical, instead of circular, section for the ball tracks, thereby improving the 'conformity ratio'; this means that the contact points of the balls are always located to the best advantage. The joint transmits constant speed over a wide angle, so that only one joint per drive line is normally required. A variation of the constant velocity joint incorporates a limited 'plunge', giving lateral movement up to 2½ inches (75 mm). This type of joint is particularly useful with independent wheel suspensions. Its efficiency, 100 per cent at zero drive angle, drops only to 96 per cent at an angle of 40 degrees, although the vehicle design does not normally require it to exceed 30 degrees.

There are a great many combinations of universal joints, single and split propeller shafts, drive shafts and rubber couplings to be found in modern drive lines. Some joints—so-called 'pot joints' (grease packed and sealed in rubber covers)—and other covered joints may

not at first even be recognised for what they are. Typical drive line layouts include the following.

With a front, in-line engine driving the rear wheels the usual arrangement is for a Hooke's type universal joint located immediately behind the gearbox to be connected by the propeller shaft to a second Hooke's joint mounted in front of the differential casing. One variation of this arrangement is the divided, or split, propeller shaft. The front section, supported towards its rear end by a rubber-mounted bearing attached to the underside of the body, is driven from the gearbox by a rubber coupling. The rear section has the usual Hooke's type joint at each end. This split shaft overcomes the tendency to whip that might become apparent on a long shaft, and allows the floor of the car to be lowered. The purpose of the rubber coupling and bearing support is to dampen out vibrations and to absorb the initial drive take-up shock.

The propeller shaft is usually a steel tube, between 2 in and 3 in (50 and 75 mm) in diameter. The varying distance between the rear axle and the gearbox is accommodated by manufacturing the shaft in two parts with splined ends, one part sliding in the other.

With a front engine and rear-wheel drive, the rear axle half shafts are sometimes replaced by drive shafts with a Hooke's type universal joint at each end. This system gives the wheels complete freedom to rise and fall independently while the drive is maintained.

With front engine, front-wheel drive and rear engine, rear-wheel drive, the usual arrangement is for a constant velocity joint to be fitted on the outboard (road wheel end) of a short drive shaft. Between the inboard end of the drive shaft and the final drive unit a rubber coupling is fitted. This may take the form of a rubber 'doughnut' or a rubber encased spider secured by four U-bolts. This coupling is sufficiently flexible to absorb suspension movements and drive take-up shock.

When drive line defect occur they make themselves known by vibration and unusual noises when the vehicle is in motion, particularly when slackness in the drive line is taken up on acceleration. With worn outboard constant velocity joints, knocking noises will be apparent when driving on or near full lock.
Points to check are:
a) Worn propeller shaft splines at the sliding joint—check by grasping each side of the joint and trying to twist in alternate, opposite directions. Any movement is indicative of wear, and a new shaft is necessary.
b) Bent propeller shaft—this will cause excessive vibration and throw a great strain on the universal joints.
c) Worn universal joint needle bearings—check by grasping the shafts on each side of the joint as for spline wear. Alternatively, a screwdriver can be inserted between the spider and the yoke and levered to detect movement.
d) On rubber couplings and disc type joints—check for

Below left: the spider elements used in Hooke's joints; roller bearings placed in caps on each of the four ends allow the drive shaft forks to pivot freely

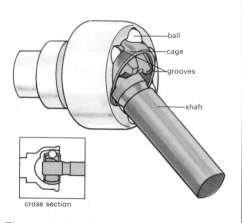

ball
cage
grooves
shaft

cross section

The constant-velocity joint, based on the Rzeppa principle, eliminates the problem, encountered in the Hooke's joint, of varying output velocity

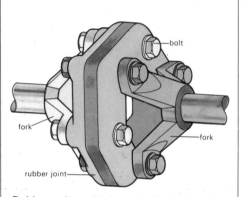

bolt
fork
fork
rubber joint

Rubber universal joints give limited angle change, but keep the shaft velocity constant; as can be seen, the three flanges of each shaft are bolted to the rubber 'doughnut' at equal intervals. The metal band round the outside is removed after the joint has been fitted

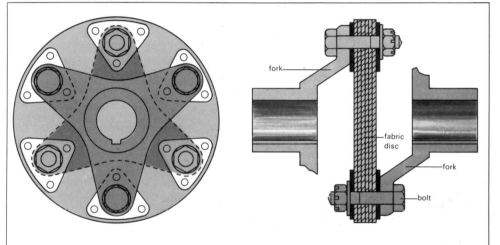

fork
fabric disc
fork
bolt

A cross-section through an older type of flexible universal joint, using fabric instead of rubber. The arrangement of the forked drive-shaft ends is the same as for the 'doughnut' type, but the maximum possible angle difference is even smaller (3–5° instead of 5–6°)

splits, loose nuts and bolts, oval wear of the bolt holes, and deterioration due to contact with oil.

e) Lack of lubrication—on both the telescopic shaft joints and needle bearings or bushes—which will be evidenced by vibration coupled with squeaks.

f) Propeller shaft centre bearing—check for play and for soundness of any rubber anti-vibration support.

If no lubrication points are fitted to the joints it may be assumed that the bearings are packed with lubricant and 'sealed for life'. Otherwise, a lithium based grease is best used for needle bearings. Splined shafts require lubrication as well which is specified in the manufacturer's handbook.

Propeller and drive shafts are very carefully balanced and it is essential, if replacement becomes necessary, that they are replaced in the same position relative to the gearbox and final drive flanges, and that the two sections of a split shaft are similarly treated. Marks are normally provided on the shafts and flanges and these must always coincide (or be positioned as stated in the manufacturer's handbook) on replacement. If there are no marks, they should be scribed on the components before dismantling commences.

If the joints are of the Hooke's staked type, they can be replaced only as complete units. If, however, the bearing ends have circlips or snap rings, replacement parts are available as kits consisting of the spider journal, needle bearings and securing rings. If grease nipples are fitted on the old joint they should be

transferred to the new. Replacement of 'pot joints' may involve dismantling the final drive and the manufacturer's handbook should be consulted.

If no pit is available, the rear of the car should be jacked up and lowered onto stout support blocks. After top gear is engaged and the handbrake applied so that the propeller shaft does not turn. Loosen the four bolts uniting the propeller shaft and final drive flanges. Remove these bolts and push the propeller shaft forward to seperate the flanges. Then, lower the end of the shaft and pull it rearwards to disengage the splines.

Where a centre bearing is fitted, separate the centre universal joint flanges and remove the rear section of the shaft. Now separate the front flanges, dismantle the centre bearing and remove the front section of the shaft.

To dismantle the joint itself, remove the securing rings then, with a leather mallet, gently tap the yokes in turn; it will be found that the needle bearing races will eventually emerge.

To fit a new joint, place the spider journal in the yoke holes, grease the bearings and lightly tap them in from outside. Fit new securing rings.

If wear is apparent on a constant velocity joint, the whole joint must be replaced. Removal procedure varies from one vehicle to another, but usually a castellated nut locks the joint in place and a hub puller is required to remove it. On replacement the nut must be tightened with a torque wrench to the recommended figure.

Top: a Rzeppa type constant velocity joint, employed in the drive line of a single-seat racing car

DIFFERENTIAL

distributing torque to the wheels

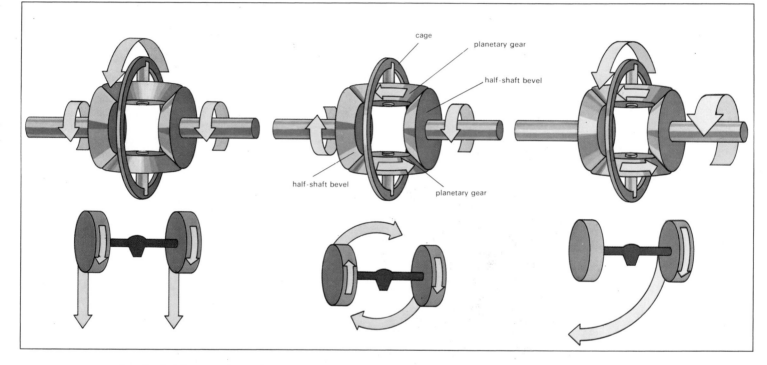

cage

planetary gear

half-shaft bevel

half-shaft bevel

planetary gear

HOUSED WITHIN the final-drive gearing of a car's transmission is a set of gears whose purpose is to allow each driving wheel to receive its share of the torque transmitted from the engine, and yet still enjoy some measure of independence from the other driving wheel, so that the two can revolve at different speeds. It is this set of gears (but not the crown wheel within which they are housed) that is called the differential; and it is needed because when the car is driven round a curve its outer driving wheel must travel a greater distance than the inner one, and therefore complete a greater number of revolutions in the same time. For similar reasons, a car with four-wheel drive needs three differentials: one between the front wheels, one between the rear wheels and another between the front and rear axles.

The important thing to remember about a differential is not that it allows the wheels to rotate at different rates, but that it balances the torque equally between them. At the inner end of each of the half-axle shafts, which drive the wheels, is a bevel gear; these two bevels, facing each other, are linked by two or more mating bevels which are carried in a cage bolted to the final-drive crown-wheel gear. Their path is accordingly an orbit around the axis of the half-shafts, so they are often called star or planetary gears. When the car is being driven in a straight line on a flat road, each tyre will offer the same resistance to engine torque as the other: the loads on the planetary-gear teeth mating with one half-shaft bevel will be the same as those on the teeth mating with the other, so the whole assembly rotates as one. When the car is steered into a curve, the

inner tyre offers more resistance to torque than the outer (because it is being required to do the same amount of work in a shorter distance), and the tooth loads become unequal: the planetary gears then begin to turn, urging the bevel on the outer half-shaft to accelerate until equilibrium is restored.

The mechanism is simple and seldom gives trouble, for the relative speeds of movement of the gear teeth are low, and the operation is only intermittent. However, if the operation should be continuous there could be a danger of overheating: it is therefore important that both driving tyres should have the same effective circumference. Two different brands of tyre that are nominally the same size could easily differ by as much as five per cent in the number of revolutions per mile; the use of a well worn spare tyre on one driving wheel and a new, deep-treaded tyre on the other could produce similar discrepancies (in this context, it is the rolling *circumference*, not *radius*, that matters: in radial-ply tyres especially, the two are not related).

Because the differential balances the torque shared between the two wheels by reacting to differences in the resistance they offer, it cannot allocate to one more than the other is capable of handling. If one tyre should be bogged down in a patch of mud so that it spins freely and cannot develop any grip, it will offer no reactive torque—the tractive torque it can transmit will be nil. Since the torque to each wheel must balance, the other also gets nil: one spins madly, the other stays still and neither does any work; the car does not move.

Faced with such a situation, the skilled driver

Above: diagrammatic representations of the essential working parts of a differential and their relationship to the wheels of a car. In each diagram, the stationary parts are shown in green and the moving ones in blue. Drive is fed to the unit via the cage. If the planetary gears are still (*left*), both half-shafts will rotate at the same speed as the cage. Should the cage be fixed (*centre*), and one wheel turned, the other wheel will turn at an equal speed in the opposite direction. With one wheel held (*right*), the other half-shaft and wheel will turn in the same direction as the cage, but at twice its speed

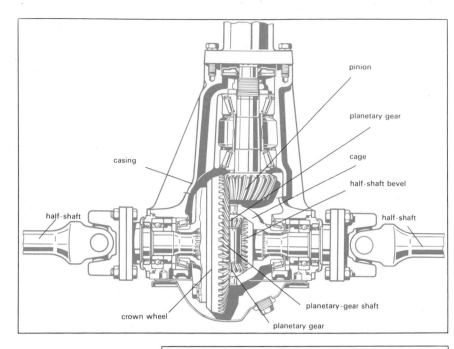

pinion

planetary gear

casing

cage

half-shaft bevel

half-shaft

half-shaft

half-shaft

planetary-gear shaft

crown wheel

planetary gear

Above: the internal components of a hypoid-bevel final-drive unit, showing the differential components. The set-up shown would be used with either independent or de Dion suspension, since the half-shafts are connected to the unit by universal joints. The casing is filled with oil through the plug shown

Right: a photograph of a differential, showing how the crown wheel is bolted to the cage containing the bevel gears

attempts to get out of it by rocking the car backwards and forwards, alternately engaging reverse and forward gears (which is particularly easy with automatic transmission). The secret of this procedure lies in the inertia of the spinning wheel: it is reluctant to change its rate of rotation, let alone its direction, so for a moment, as the clutch is engaged, it will offer some resistance to the torque transmitted to it. For that moment, brief though it may be, the same amount of resistance is translated by the differential into tractive torque for the gripping wheel.

Better still, if the spinning wheel can be held in some way (such as by jamming it with sackcloth or even wedging the parking brake on that side so as to offer some drag), sufficient torque should be available at the other wheel for the car to be moved. This is the principle of the limited-slip differential: by offering some frictional resistance to the runaway spin of the half-shaft driving a tyre bereft of grip, it ensures that some torque may still be delivered to the other. The differential incorporates a locking mechanism that is, in effect, a friction damper making the differential itself more and more inefficient as the disparity between the left and right tyres' reactions grow more and more extreme. These 'diff-lock' contrivances are usually friction clutches which provide a partial lock (or

briefly, in some circumstances, a complete lock) between the differential cage and the half-shafts, by-passing the bevel gears that are within the cage.

The means of achieving this vary somewhat. In the Borg-Warner LSD (limited-slip differential as commonly abbreviated), cone clutches clamp the half-shaft bevel gears to the inside of the cage; in the Thornton Powr-Lok LSD (made by Dana in the USA, Salisbury in Britain and ZF in Germany, among others), there are plate clutches. Both kinds depend on the very slight movement of the bevels as the planetary gears tend to force them apart in ordinary operation: when runaway wheelspin is incipient, the loss of reaction torque alters this separating force, and the displacement of the gears causes the appropriate clutch to clamp more firmly.

An older type of self-locking differential made by ZF dispenses completely with the gear mechanism inside the cage. Instead, there is a device that resembles a roller bearing gone wrong: the inner and outer tracks or races are not circular, but have a sinusoidal profile, the rollers are not cylindrical but flattened, and the cage carrying them is bolted to the crown wheel. It is, in essence, a sprag clutch or freewheel that is very inefficient: the disparity between power input and output rises sharply with change of relative speed of the half shafts (each of which is connected to one of the annular tracks), so, once again, it is friction that deals with the excess of tractive effort over resistance.

Another gearless LSD, this time from the USA, is the No-Spin. In this, two dog-clutches lock the half-shafts to the flanks of the crown wheel, being lightly spring-loaded into engagement. The angle of the dog faces is such that, if one wheel turns faster than the other, its dogs ride out of engagement. Thus, torque is always transmitted to whichever wheel is offering more resistance and is therefore turning more slowly. The interruption of drive to the faster wheel allows it to slow down and, as soon as the two wheel speeds are rebalanced, the drive to the freed one is again engaged.

It is not because of the need for traction on slippery surfaces that the LSD has become popular for high-powered cars, but because of the need for greater traction and directional stability when accelerating hard or cornering under power. Cars with live rear axles tend to lift their right wheels (because of torque reaction around the final-drive pinion) when accelerating hard, allowing them to spin and impair performance. Cars with a high roll couple tend to lift their inside wheels when cornering hard, again allowing wheel-spin to intrude and severely impair the handling by interrupting the torque to the outer wheel. The LSD is intended to maintain the transmission of torque to the gripping tyre in these conditions.

Racing cars with very wide tyres still need some form of differential locking that can allow free differential action when the amount of grip exceeds the tractive torque available. Cars of really exceptional power, notably the Porsche 917 in its turbocharged Can-Am form, always have enough power to overcome the drag of tyre scrub around corners in the absence of differential action; accordingly, they have no differentials at all. Vintage sports and racing cars with narrow tyres and narrow axle tracks used to be the same, for if their power was much less, their tyre grip was too. The 'solid' axle, with both wheels fixed to the extremities of a single shaft, to which the crown wheel is bolted directly, gives better results when accelerating or lifting a wheel in a corner than any limited-slip or other differential. In ordinary driving, however, it plays havoc with steering response and wears out the tyres at an alarming rate.

ELECTRICAL & IGNITION SYSTEMS

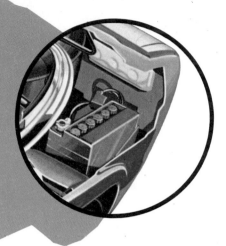

IGNITION

setting fire to the charge

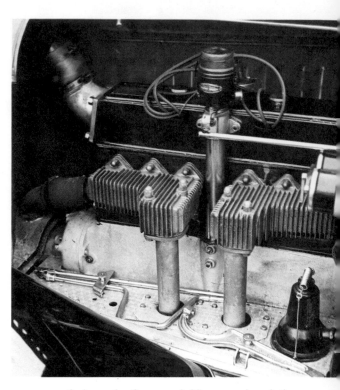

Right: In the early days of the internal-combustion engine, the fuel/air mixture was ignited by a platinum tube which passed through the cylinder wall and was heated on the outside by a petrol-burning flame; illustrated is a Daimler engine of 1887

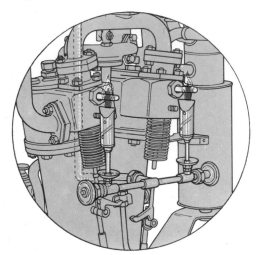

Far right: the distributor was first introduced around 1925, thus allowing one set of contact breakers to feed any number of cylinders; the Avions Voisin C11 of 1927 was one of the first cars to use this system

Below: a high-tension magneto, mounted on a Chenard Walcker of 1910; (this type of unit was popular until World War II); a glow plug used on the Fiat 621 diesel of 1937; a French sparking plug of 1902 with two sets of electrodes for connection to two different ignition systems—one with a battery and vibrator, the other with a low-tension magneto; a Champion spark plug, of the type popular until World War II—it has an 18 mm thread and can be dismantled for cleaning purposes

SETTING FIRE to the compressed charge of fuel and air, in the combustion space of a car engine, has, for a long time, been a matter of fairly simple electrical and mechanical engineering. It may not be as crude as the early hot platinum tube which kept the most primitive engines banging away so long as a spirit lamp was played upon its exposed end; nor is it as costly and mechanically intransigent as the magneto which thereafter served most cars until the late 1920s or early 1930s, and whose performance and reliability kept it supreme for aero engines and racing engines for another 30 years. Since then, the usual equipment has been what is comprised in a coil set: a battery to supply electricity, a coil to transform that low voltage supply to a much higher electrical pressure, with the assistance of a contact breaker which triggers it to provide a very high voltage pulse, which is then led, via a distributor, to the appropriate spark plug where the pulse comes across the gap between the electrodes, igniting the charge in the process. The only other essential is a condenser, wired to the contact breaker to prevent excessive arcing or sparking across the points as they open to trigger the pulse from the coil. It is a simple arrangement, cheap to make, and easy to maintain; but it may seem excessively patronising to describe it as rudimentary, considering that even in the engine of an ordinary family car, the system provides 200 sparks a second, each timed to an accuracy of 1/7000th of a second. However, in relation to the engine's needs—especially if it is to comply with the most modern requirements of environmental legislation governing exhaust emissions and the like — the conventional coil-ignition apparatus makes a rather poor job of ensuring that the spark occurs at exactly the right moment with exactly the right characteristics, particularly in view of the fact that the timing needs to be different for every combination of speed and load within the engine's operational envelope.

Even disregarding these new requirements, satisfactory ignition is often overlooked as an essential prerequisite to good engine performance. How often do we find people doing all sorts of mechanical work on their engines, raising compression ratios, altering valve timing, improving induction and exhaust breathing, revising carburation, and so on, only to find that they have not achieved the improvement they sought and reasonably expected. Sometimes, it is even worse and they have holed a piston. Almost always, the explanation proves to be that they have made no alteration to the ignition system, despite the fact that any one of these modifications to the mechanical specification of the engine is almost certain to require ignition retiming, if not a change in the shape of the advance curve or something even more fundamental. In some cases, especially when engines have very large cylinders

or are running at exceptionally high speeds, severe
variations in performance of a given cylinder from one
operating cycle to the next, may result in a much
poorer performance overall than theory or snap
measurements may suggest, and will almost certainly
produce rough running into the bargain. In such a
case, even more drastic alteration to the ignition
system may be necessary, such as the provision of
multiple spark plugs, or a change of spark-generation
system so as to produce sparks of a different character.

Basically, the study of engine ignition requirements
may be broken down into three divisions: the timing
of the spark, the qualities of the spark, and the means
of generating it. Needless to say, these three are
closely related, sometimes to the point where we have
to sacrifice a little in one direction in order to avoid
jeopardising another.

Before we consider how to get our spark and when,
we must examine the kind of spark we want to produce.
How long should it last, for example, and how long
should it take to build up to its peak voltage? For that
matter, what should that peak voltage be?

Although we are concerned at this stage with ends
rather than with means, it is worth remembering the
old basic distinction between coil and magneto
ignition; the former gave its healthiest spark at low
speeds, and grew progressively weaker as the spark
rate increased, because there was less time between
each triggered pulse for the coil to 'soak'—to build up a
magnetic field in its secondary windings as the current
from the battery flooded its primary windings.

The magneto, by contrast, gave a stronger spark as
the rate increased, the voltage in its windings increasing
as they were rotated faster in the instrument's magnetic
field. So, there is another thing to bear in mind; do we
want the best spark at high speeds in order to get
optimum power from the engine, or would we rather
have a good spark at low speed so that we can actually
get it started? Clearly, it is desirable to have both the
chicken and the egg present, and many of the most
modern ignition systems, notably those employing
electronic circuitry, achieve this by producing a
substantially constant spark voltage over the full
range of operating speeds.

Consider a typical voltage available from ignition
systems in general current use. The output characteristics of a conventional coil ignition system, under
simulated fouling conditions with a one megohm
load, gives a voltage output of perhaps 15 kilovolts
from say 1000 to 3000 rpm. Under the same conditions,
a typical transistor-controlled system will have a
voltage output somewhat less whereas, in the case of a
capacitor discharge system, even with a shunt resistance of only 50,000 ohms, the output is a good 7 or 8
kilovolts higher over this speed range. At higher
speeds, however, we notice a most important contrast:
the coil output drops steadily for reasons already
explained, the others do not, and may even increase.
Nevertheless, it must be remembered that in the
lower speed range, the contact or magnetically
triggered transistor systems under fouling conditions,
actually have less output available to fire the spark
plugs than is available from perfectly ordinary bread-
and-butter coil systems.

It is evident from this that the capacitor-discharge
system, widely used in two-stroke engines and
beginning to be applied to others, has certain very
definite advantages. It also has certain very definite
characteristics that may not be so advantageous, and
this is where the question of arc duration and rise time
intrudes. The CD (Capacitor Discharge) system
produces a spark of very short duration, as little as ten
or twelve microseconds. Often, this is grossly inadequate, for arc duration has a marked influence on the
ability of the spark plug to ignite lean mixtures.
Broadly speaking, on lean mixtures, the longer the arc
duration, the better spark advance the engine will
accept and the better will be the specific fuel consumption. Nor is it any use arguing that your engine
is not set to run on lean mixtures because, apart from
the fact that all the latest engines are (for emission
control purposes), there are certain conditions of part-
throttle or idle running in any engine when the mixture
is often anything but homogeneous, and the region
around the spark plug may very well be lean, although
elsewhere in the combustion chamber it may be
extravagantly rich. If, in these conditions, which
prevail during starting and in traffic, the spark is of

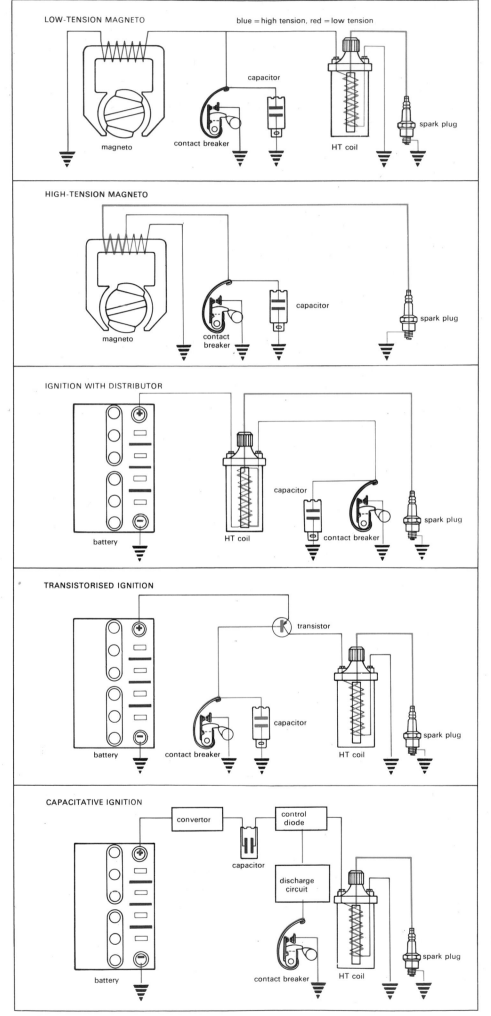

LOW-TENSION MAGNETO

blue = high tension, red = low tension

capacitor

magneto

contact breaker

HT coil

spark plug

HIGH-TENSION MAGNETO

magneto

contact breaker

capacitor

spark plug

IGNITION WITH DISTRIBUTOR

battery

HT coil

capacitor

contact breaker

spark plug

TRANSISTORISED IGNITION

battery

transistor

contact breaker

capacitor

HT coil

spark plug

CAPACITATIVE IGNITION

battery

convertor

capacitor

control diode

discharge circuit

contact breaker

HT coil

spark plug

very short duration, the probability of appropriate and optimum ignition is very poor. Lengthening the duration of the spark improves things enormously, and improves the cleanliness of the exhaust, the longer arc reducing emissions of hydrocarbons and of carbon monoxide. When the mixture is homogeneous, as is more likely to be the case at high operating speed, the arc duration does not exercise this same influence.

Only the most refined CD systems have been adapted to provide a spark of adequate duration, the most notable being the Mobelec which gives a spark of 250 microseconds, and doubles this at lower engine speeds. Such refinements are inevitably costly, but are essential if the other advantages of the CD system are to be enjoyed without handicaps. These advantages are that it produces a very rapid rise of voltage to the peak level, and this has a profound influence on spark plug tracking—what happens when the spark is dissipated and run to earth through conductive deposits on its surface (eg carbon, water, or lead salts) instead of arcing across the spark plug gap. The faster the voltage rise time—which is usually defined as the time needed for the voltage to reach 90 per cent of its maximum—the longer the plug can run without the usual tracking in fouling conditions, and the better the chance of the fouling being broken down and normal conditions resumed. An ordinary coil system might give a rise time of perhaps 80 microseconds, and most of the so-called 'electronic' ignition systems (which are basically coil systems with transistor-assisted contacts to reduce current through the contact breaker and prevent arcing there) take even longer, perhaps 125 microseconds. With the CD System, the voltage rise time is seldom more than 6 microseconds.

So we want a spark of consistently high voltage at all engine speeds (at least 30,000 kilovolts), reaching its peak very very quickly and lasting a fairly long time. Not too long, however, lest the electrode temperature at the spark plug grow too high, and erosion of the gap between the electrodes be accelerated as a result, leading to an even higher voltage requirement—for the greater the gap, the greater is the voltage needed to jump it.

In most European engines, although not in many American ones, the spark plug temperature curve over the speed range is appreciably steeper nowadays than it used to be, and smaller engines are used more extensively at the extremes of this rather steeper curve. This is why spark plug choice has become so critical today, with the danger of the fouling of too 'hard' or cool-running a plug in part-throttle or idling conditions having to be offset against the much more

Near right: a distributor, for a four-cylinder engine, with its cap screwed on

Centre right: a four-cylinder distributor with its cap fixed by elastic

Far right: a cutaway view of a four-cylinder engine's distributor with vacuum advance unit

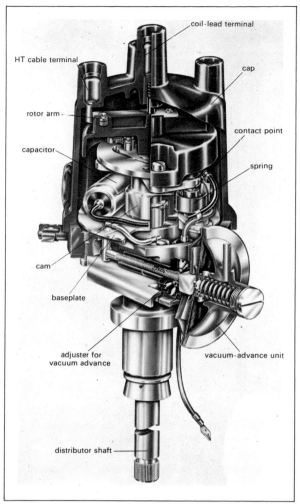

coil-lead terminal

HT cable terminal

cap

rotor arm

contact point

capacitor

spring

cam

baseplate

adjuster for vacuum advance

vacuum-advance unit

distributor shaft

Left: one type of breakerless distributor; the rotor arm is at the top, as usual, but underneath is a rotor which has as many magnetic projections on its circumference as there are cylinders in the engine; as each pole passes a coil, a current is generated in that coil and is then stepped up to cause a spark. The advantages of this system are that the timing stays exactly where it was set, as there are no points to slip out of adjustment, and the absence of points means that they cannot bounce at high speed

Far left: this series of diagrams shows the various systems which can be used to light the charge in a cylinder

serious danger of wrecking the engine through the overheating of too 'soft' or hot-running a plug when going hard or at full throttle. Of the two, the former risk is the better one to run.

Sometimes, the build-up of deposits on plug points is due to the low voltage available—perhaps just a matter of bad maintenance of the ignition system, or of its basic unsuitability. There is also the possibility that too much suppression or the wrong kind of suppression could be responsible. Radio suppression is an important thing to remember, for it is not something left to the individual's choice or conscience. It is now a matter of law, not only in Britain but in most other countries as well, although the standards do vary somewhat, being notably stringent in France.

The need for radio suppression is due to the fact that the complete ignition circuit, including the spark plug gap, resembles quite closely the circuitry of spark-gap radio transmitters such as were used in the early days of wireless transmission. In effect, the ignition system is a radio transmitter, and its broadcasts (at frequencies that may be several megacycles per second) will be detected by radio receivers in the vicinity. Picking up these signals results in spurious noise in the output of a radio receiver.

The amount of noise is related to the amount of energy that is transmitted during each train of the damped waves that the resonating element of the ignition circuit has in use, one train occurring at the time of each firing of a spark plug. The problem is a straightforward one of damping the oscillations in the circuit, sometimes by means of a resistor actually within the spark plug. Another resistor may be used in the high-voltage lead from the coil, or in the distributor rotor. Some manufacturers use instead high-tension cables with built-in suppression characteristics, but these often give trouble, for they are not consistent with temperature and they deteriorate rapidly with age, final failure usually occurring when starting in cold weather or in damp conditions.

Undoubtedly, the most difficult aspect of ignition is the timing of the spark. When the engine is running at full throttle, it is not difficult to establish the amount of spark advance at any given speed, and it is likely to be found that the ideal advance curve will rise steadily with speed and then level off as the influence of turbulence—which may be thought of as a wind fanning the flames—increases the velocity of the combustion front. However, if the throttle be closed, the weight of each incoming charge will be smaller, and the ratio of weight of residuals to fresh mixture

larger, while the compression pressure will be lower, and, because of these things, the speed of burning is a lot less rapid. Accordingly, the spark advance angle needs to be greater in part-throttle/part-load conditions; but it is very difficult to determine how much greater. On a level road at less than maximum speed, when the car is not being accelerated, the optimum spark advance could be anything up to double what it should be at full speed and full load. Running downhill it could be greater still, even at maximum speed. This is the function of the vacuum control of ignition advance built into the majority of modern distributors. The depression in the induction system is used as a measure of engine load; by operating on the aneroid capsule attached to the distributor, it can override the speed-sensitive centrifugal advance mechanism in order to increase the spark advance at part load. It is a device that cannot be relied on not to over-advance the spark in certain transient conditions, and, because of the danger of pre-ignition or detonation thus created, it is best deleted from the ignition system of a highly tuned engine. Even when the engine is idling and induction vacuum is high, the compression pressures are low, the ratio of burned residuals to fresh gases is high, turbulence is slight, and the speed of burning is low and erratic. In these circumstances, the engine runs better when the spark advance angle is reduced. Likewise, the advance must be reduced in any circumstances where detonation might occur.

While an over-advanced ignition is to be avoided at all costs, unnecessarily retarded ignition is nothing but a burden. It can cause misfiring because retarding the spark increases the voltage requirement across the plug gap for a satisfactory spark to occur. On the other

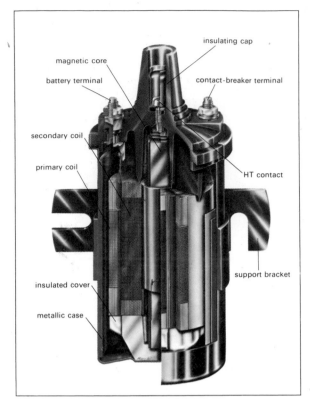

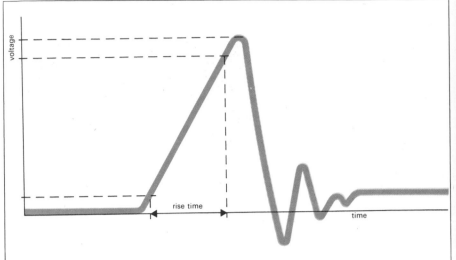

hand, retarding the ignition reduces the temperature of the plug tip, much more so at full load than at part load, and this could either save the engine from pre-ignition or encourage plug fouling, according to the heat-range suitability of the particular plug in use.

Hitherto, it has not been possible to make an ignition system so perfect that at any load level it could ensure optimum ignition performance throughout the operating speed range. Today, it is theoretically not impossible, but to achieve it would be so forbiddingly expensive that it is still practically impossible. The art of devising a suitable ignition advance curve has to stay subservient to the mechanical limitations of most advance mechanisms, which are surprisingly crude affairs of weights and springs, spinning in the nether regions of the distributor. In fact, the majority of engines already have retarded ignition settings in the lower speed ranges. If you were to examine their centrifugal advance curves you would find that they are running down at 1000 rpm at something like 5 per cent torque loss. There are so many conflicting requirements that have to be taken into account: engine starting, regular idling, and the absence of hot stalling, are some of them, and the situation is now being further complicated by legislative requirements about exhaust emissions that postulate the ability to burn leaner mixtures than used to be considered normal in such conditions.

There is little to be done about it; the average amateur and most professionals will have to be content with the curve determined by the engine manufacturer, but they still have control over the actual degree of advance. How this is set depends on a lot of things, notably on how gullible you are in believing what manufacturers tell you. Strobe lights and flywheel marks are merely a means to an approximation that takes no account of the production variations between one engine and the next off the same production line, and it is widely thought that the most reliable method is to use a vacuum gauge or revolution counter, setting the engine at a very fast idle, and then swinging the entire distributor until the maximum induction

vacuum or highest rev-counter reading is indicated at that particular throttle setting. The distributor is then clamped at that point, the timing being just about as good as you can hope to get it.

It is unlikely to remain where you put it. The distributor may not shift, but steady erosion and pitting of the contact points in the mechanical breaker of the conventional ignition system will gradually alter the timing and, incidentally, alter the coil performance as well by varying the dwell angle during which the primary windings of the coil are allowed to soak, as already described. Some engines with a large number of cylinders and a high rate of revolutions have distributors incorporating two sets of contacts, reducing the further dangers of contact float or bounce at high speeds; but, although one contact breaker can be adjusted in just a few minutes, synchronising two can take half a day. There is no doubt that the conventional simple mechanical contact breaker works amazingly well when it is new; neither is there any doubt that its performance displays severe degradation in quite a short time thereafter. Several modern electronic ignition systems substitute a contactless form of electrical trigger to replace the mechanical circuit-breaker; most commonly, it takes the form of a magnetic detector, which notes the passage of a projection or a recess on the rim of a rotor in close proximity, but there are some versions (the first was the Lumenition apparatus) which rely on a photo-electric cell responding to interruptions by a shaped rotor of a beam of light directed at it.

The most advanced electronic ignition systems now function with notable accuracy and consistency over a tremendously wide range of operating speeds, and the majority of them are immune to most troubles provided they are located in a suitably cool place. Increasingly stringent emission laws have forced many manufacturers, notably the Americans, to adopt electronic ignition for all their production engines, in place of the older breaker systems, simply in order to achieve consistent results over long periods of running. Further developments can be expected, the first probably being electronic rather than mechanical control of ignition advance (already developed by Mobelec and by a number of specialists in ignition systems for racing motor cycles), after which the next great challenge will be the evolution of a miniature computer aimed to provide the spark timing variations demanded by the approaching generation of stratified-charge engines. The whole problematic business was foreseen in Job: *Man is born unto trouble as the sparks fly. . . .*

Left: a cutaway view of a high-tension coil as used in nearly every car

Above: a graph showing how the high-tension current builds up in the ignition circuit, and how it decays after the contact points have opened to allow the plug to spark. The time taken for the voltage to rise from 10 per cent of maximum to 90 per cent of maximum is known as the 'rise time'

The first plug:
Lenoir, 1860

Bosch racing plug
with mica insulator

SAGT with three
brass electrodes

Way-Assauto of 1904
with two electrodes

RMV of 1910 with
several parts

SPARK PLUG

the heart of the fire

Champion of 1901
with several parts

Beru of 1905 with
brass segments

plug with cooling fins
and mica insulator

Champion of 1910 with
priming tap

Above: a selection of
early spark plugs of
vastly differing types and
sizes

DURING WORLD WAR II the major British spark plug manufacturers, like most other companies with names to preserve and frozen profits to disperse, continued to advertise their wares. The insulators of the sparking plugs that kept our fighters in the sky, they told us, were made of a material that would be a true ruby if suitably pigmented—but of course, they assured us, no such impurity as colouring matter would be allowed in their precious ceramics.

Precious materials were already familiar in some spark plugs, and they continue to find a place therein from time to time. Gold and silver, platinum and iridium have all found uses, admittedly in very small quantities. Those albino ruby insulators were merely chemical siblings of the ruby, just as coal is to a diamond; and while Lodge christened theirs *Corundite*, KLG called theirs *Sintox*, which was more honest and down-to-earth. The stuff was merely sintered aluminium oxide.

Very good stuff it was, and remained. Sintered alumina creates a material of surprising mechanical strength, excellent electrical insulation characteristics, astonishing heat resistance, and a heaven-sent suitability for mass production methods.

All these properties are of great importance, for the spark plug leads an extremely hard life, enjoying very little attention (indeed, if it demands a lot it is the wrong sparking plug for the job) and expected to be sold at knock-down prices. It may vary in proportions but not in principles, whether it has to do duty in such extreme services as a water-cooled four-stroke hearse or an air-cooled two-stroke racing motor cycle. In either case, or in any between these extremes, the spark plug is just a little thing that can be screwed into the wall of an engine's combustion chamber, and there

offer a gap across which a high-tension spark may be prompted to leap in order to ignite the fuel/air mixture, which has already been compressed.

Thus the construction is fundamentally simple. There is a steel body which screws into the engine and has convenient hexagon flats formed on it for spanners, and into the bore of this body is an insulating mass through the centre of which passes a metal electrode. To the outer end of this electrode a suitable high-voltage pulse is brought by the high-tension lead from the engine's distributor; at the other end, where the electrode protrudes into the combustion chamber, it is kept company at a distance of 20 or 30 thousandths of an inch by an earthing electrode protruding from the metal body of the plug.

The central electrode has an arduous task, and this is where the fancy metals often feature. Because heat resistance and electrical conductivity are necessary attributes, alloys of nickel are commonplace, sometimes sheathed in copper or fused silica for a better bond with the insulator material. This bonding and sealing is important for a number of practical reasons of which some are very simple and fundamental: a leak would be deleterious, looseness could be disastrous. In the quite recent past it was common for special-purpose plugs—notably for racing—expected to have a long life or to endure particularly severe heat, to have points made of platinum alloy in which iridium or tungsten would also be present. Platinum being very costly, these points were made of thin wire welded into position; but they have been known to loosen and fall out of the plug into the engine cylinder. The result can be a wrecked engine, and for peace of mind it is worth taking the trouble to select plugs so constructed that the electrode points cannot fall out of it.

Manufacturing techniques are better nowadays, and for the past three or four years certain racing two-stroke engines have been relying upon a new centre electrode material known as gold palladium: a fine wire of this alloy, which has a gold content of about

113

50 per cent, is fixed to a stub of the nickel alloy that is otherwise regarded as conventional nowadays in all plugs, even in racing. This special tip extends the heat range of the spark plug and makes it less susceptible to fouling.

Heat value is the most important factor determining the suitability of a plug for a given engine. The difference in operating temperatures between a mild-mannered touring engine doing a lot of idling and a highly-tuned racing engine run at high loads and speeds for protracted periods, is considerable. In the former, it is necessary for the plug to run fairly hot so that any depositions of oil or other contaminants will be burned away. If they are not, the oil will accumulate and turn to carbon, forming an encrustation over the walls of the insulator body around which the spark can track to earth without jumping its appointed gap, and therefore without igniting the compressed charge in the combustion chamber. At the other extreme, if a

Right: the plug on the left has a gold palladium central electrode, which lowers the minimum voltage required for a spark and, due to its small nature, facilitates the elimination of deposits

Far right: a diagram showing the temperature gradients present in an average spark plug

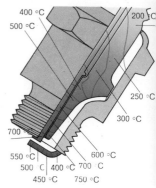

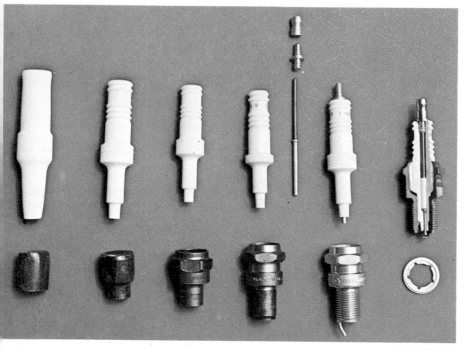

Above: the components of a spark plug at various stages of manufacture; in the top row, the insulator starts off as a raw piece of ceramic material and is turned until the shape is correct —the central electrode is inserted down the centre; in the bottom row, the metal body is formed by extrusion— the second electrode is welded on; to the right is a cutaway view of a complete plug

Above right: a transverse section through a spark plug with an internal air gap

hot-running plug were fitted in a high-performance engine driven hard, its tip would soon become incandescent, causing pre-ignition that would probably wreck the engine—starting by burning a hole in the piston crown—before the plug itself failed.

Plugs that run cool are also known as 'hard' plugs, hot-running ones as 'soft'. It does not matter which terminology is employed, so long as the correct principles are remembered: a soft plug for a soft engine, a cool plug for a hot engine, and vice versa. Clearly it is vital to use the type of plug specified by the engine manufacturer: it might be permissible to choose one grade softer when doing a lot of gentle driving (such as in urban traffic) if fouling and eventual misfiring is a problem, as it might be if the condition of the engine were such as to allow more than the usual amount of lubricating oil to get past piston rings or valve guides into the combustion chamber. If this course is adopted, care must be taken not to use full throttle for long, nor high revs at all. Conversely, if some very hard driving is anticipated, especially on motorways or tracks that allow high speeds and loads to be sustained for long periods, and most especially if the engine is suspected of running on a mixture slightly weaker than is correct, then a harder grade of plug would be recommended. Again, if the engine has

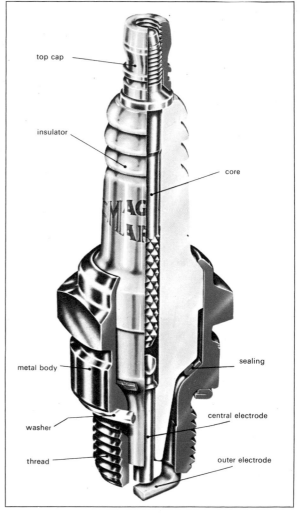

been fitted with a capacitor discharge ignition system, a harder grade could be adopted because the characteristics of these systems include a very rapid voltage rise, encouraging the spark to jump the gap regardless of fouling conditions.

Only inside the walls of the plug body can any significant difference be seen between a hard plug and a soft one. A cool hard plug has very little of its central electrode protruding from the tip of the insulator, and not much area of the insulator itself will be exposed to the heat of combustion, for the insulator will be seated in the metal body of the plug quite close to the nose. The object of this is to shorten the path whereby heat may escape from the plug tip to the body and thence, through the contact area of its threaded portion, to the material of the engine cylinder head and thus away. A soft hot-running plug provides a longer path for the

engine fault diagnosis; but the art is by no means as simple as is commonly supposed, for the various additives present in fuels and oils sometimes play tricks with the deposition processes, creating a plug

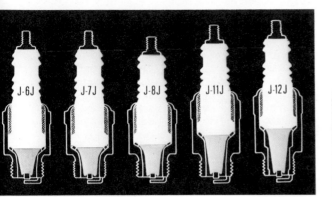

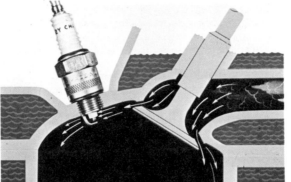

Far left: a series of spark plugs with differing heat ranges; from left to right they vary from cold to hot types, the heat having to travel further through the insulator to escape in the latter sort

Left: some modern plugs have projecting electrodes, which are cooled by the incoming charge of petrol and air

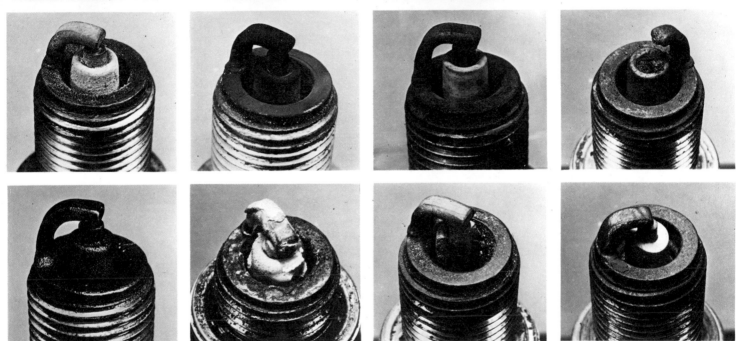

heat to travel: the insulator material leaves more of the central electrode exposed, and is seated high up in the plug body, from which it follows that it exposes more of its surface to combustion heat. This greater exposure ensures that the tip remains hot, encouraging the immediate burning off of any potential deposits: even if they do not burn immediately, they have to extend over a greater surface before eventually creating an effective short circuit, or tracking path whereby the spark might be earthed, and thus fail.

The formation of deposits on the plug tip is clearly a constant problem, for it is implicit in the nature of the internal combustion engine that it should continually produce carbon so long as it is running. The art of spark plug design and selection is to ensure that the plug runs hot enough to burn up deposits, without running too hot. It is very sensitive to carburation: if the mixture be too rich, the latent heat of evaporation of the excessive fuel will cause it to run cooler, leaving a tell-tale coating of black soot on the plug. An excessively weak mixture will conversely make it run hotter, in which case the usual signs of overheating are a bleached or pale brown colouration of the metal surfaces of the plug exposed to combustion. These and numerous other signs may be interpreted by a skilled and experienced eye to constitute a valuable means of

appearance that could be wrongly interpreted. Amongst these spurious deposits the most easily recognisable are little beads of lead salts, which form on the insulator in certain high-temperature conditions: these originate in the lead compounds added to petrol to suppress detonation or knock, and it was the introduction of these compounds (tetraethyl lead being the most famous) that forced the spark plug industry to develop its present type of insulating materials. Previously the best spark plug insulators were made of mica, which had superseded the simple porcelain of the earliest plugs; but mica could not stand the chemical attack of the lead compounds, and modern ceramics took its place.

For some years after this it remained the practice to make plug bodies in two parts that could be unscrewed for cleaning purposes. This practice has been abandoned because the seating and sealing of the insulator, upon the washers which provide its only thermal contact with the plug body, could not be reliable. Modern sealed plugs can be cleaned by careful scraping with a thin-bladed knife, though that will not get very far, or by sand blasting, which creates danger of residual abrasive particles remaining embedded inside the walls of the plug body where they can grow incandescent in the heat of combustion. In any case, if a

Above: from left to right in the top row, the pictures show a normal spark plug and ones fouled by carbon and damaged by overheating and pre-ignition; in the bottom row from left to right, the pictures show oil fouling, heavy deposits due, perhaps, to excessive use of upper-cylinder lubricant, impact damage to the insulator and abrasive erosion caused by excessive cleaning

set of plugs needs to be cleaned more than once during its useful life, which is limited by the prudent to about 10,000 miles, either the plugs are the wrong grade for the engine, or the engine itself is at fault.

There is still some useful cleaning that can be done: the outside of the plug, in particular the surface of the insulator body, must be kept clean by regular wiping (with a rag or tissue dampened with petrol or alcohol) lest accretions of dirt provide a tracking path whereby the spark can escape to earth from the top of the central electrode. The only other desirable maintenance is the checking and correct setting of the spark gap. This used to be as little as 0.018 inch in the old days of magnetos and inefficient coil ignition systems, but on modern high-compression engines the gap is commonly 0.03 inch or even more. Gauges are marketed

with which the gap can conveniently be measured, but they are not always accurate: a pitted or bent electrode will offer a bigger gap than conventional gauges will indicate. Use of a round wire of known diameter is preferable, and with some of the less common types of earthing electrode such as the once-popular multiple-point, and the racing side-electrode, the wire is often easier to use.

Variations in spark gap design are amongst the most notable, even notorious, of departures from spark plug convention. There have been numerous so-called 'fuel igniters' marketed in or by American manu-facturers, all claiming better performance, greater economy and longer life, without needing any atten-tion. Some of the claims are undoubtedly excessive, but the working principle of these igniters (which can still be called spark plugs) is valid in certain circum-stances. These exist within the combustion chambers of the flat-12 Formula One Ferrari engine, and also in the Formula Two BMW motor sometimes employed by March; and for these applications the most reputable and responsible of American plug makers, Champion, furnish what they more accurately describe as surface discharge plugs. In these the fairly large-diameter tip of the central electrode is surrounded by a constant gap, the earthing electrode being a concentric ring or annulus, and the entire nose of the plug is given a flush surface because the gap is filled by a semi-conductor material. The spark jumps across this surface from the central electrode to the annulus, usually taking the shortest route: as this causes microscopic erosion, the next spark moves to the next point on the annulus, so the effect is for the spark to travel round in circles. The erosion is barely more than theoretical, plugs of this type having an extremely long life. What is far more important is that they have a virtually infinite heat range, so fouling is emphatically not a problem. In fact the surface discharge plug does not really work properly until it is dirty! Nor does it work properly unless the spark pulse has the requisite characteristics, which again are supplied by a capacitor discharge system. Even that is not enough, for the plug annulus must be in the right position relative to the

combustion chamber, and engines that are not designed to use plugs of this type are seldom able to exploit them effectively.

The sensitivity of engines to these niceties of construction are often surprising. Some engines, but by no means all, may be well served by plugs of the extended-nose variety, in which the electrodes and the tip of the insulator protrude into the combustion chamber, relying on the high velocity draught of cool fresh mixture during each induction phase to carry away the excess of the heat absorbed during the previous combustion and exhaust phases. Otherwise most of the constructional differences in modern plugs are invisible, consisting of spark-intensifying gaps in the central electrode, resistors, and other inclusions to improve ignition performance or suppress radio-

Below, far left: a Champion surface discharge plug, as used in certain racing applications, and a double-electrode variety common in Wankel engines

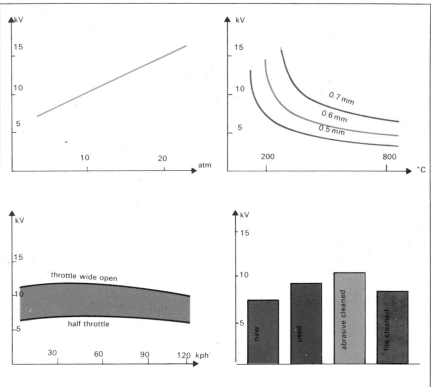

Above: a series of graphs showing the variation of spark-plug efficiency as a function of compression, temperature and gap, speed and electrode condition (the lines or blocks show the voltages required to produce a spark)

frequency interference. Elsewhere, plug construction is remarkably uniform and almost as standardised as tyre valves: there are only three standard diameters for the threaded portion of the body (10, 14 and 18 mm), the smallest being welcomed for the space it saves, and the largest being enjoyed for its greater heat range, while the 14 mm plug is standard for most road-going cars. The length of the threaded portion also varies, and is a dimension that is too easily overlooked: a short-reach plug in a medium or long-reach hole will be too shrouded to work effectively, and is likely to become fouled rapidly—although some engines are designed so that the plug tip is deliberately shrouded—while a plug that is too long may either protrude into the combustion chamber and there overheat or even cause mechanical damage by contact with the piston or valves, or alternatively if the head construction prevents this it will not be able to seat properly on its flange, in which case it will not be able to shed its heat properly nor be gas tight. This flange is usually flat, and seats on a sealing washer that should be replaced by a new one whenever the plug is removed; but some plugs, notably those employed by Vauxhall and certain other GM cars, have an angled seat which is stronger and provides a better heat path.

SPARK-PLUG CARE

the importance of cleaning and setting

DESPITE THE FACT that spark plugs carry out a straight-forward and simple task, in that they cause the fuel/air mixture in an internal combustion engine to ignite, they require regular, careful attention to keep the engine running well. It is fairly obvious that a plug fouled with oil or carbon may fail to fire, but not so obvious that there is no black-and-white division between a spark plug working and not working.

Most car manufacturers recommend that spark plugs be cleaned and adjusted every five or six thousand miles and that they be changed every ten or twelve thousand. This is probably a good rule to go by, but different engines place differing stresses on spark plugs, as do different working conditions.

If the carburettor is not adjusted properly, this will undoubtedly lead to reduced plug life: a rich mixture will cause the formation of excessive carbon deposits, while a weak mixture will cause overheating and burning off the spark-plug electrodes. Although in the former case it is possible to clean off the deposits, it is very difficult to remove all foreign matter from the space between the plug body and the insulator. In the end this build-up can lead to a short-circuit.

The solution, then, is to make sure that the carburettor is correctly set and to check the plug condition

When the plug is completely clean, the gap should be set, taking care to bend only the side electrode. This contact should be adjusted by bending it as a whole, not by bending it in the middle. Special gap-adjusting tools are available for this purpose.

The clearance between the two electrodes should be fixed, at that recommended by the car manufacturer, by using a feeler gauge of the correct size. The gap will be correct when the weight of the gauge can just be supported by the friction between it and the electrodes.

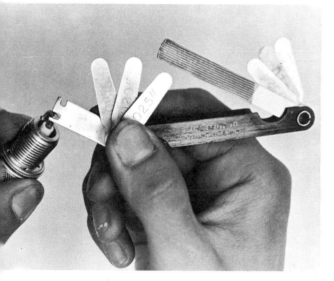 

regularly—it is annoying, to say the least, when an engine starts misfiring on one or more cylinders, no matter how intermittently.

To most people, cleaning a spark plug involves no more than a quick scrub with a wire brush and, perhaps, a rub with a piece of emery cloth. In fact, the spark-plug manufacturers will say that this is not sufficient to remove all contamination. The best way of cleaning a plug is to sand-blast it, since the sand can find its way into the gap we mentioned above. Very few people have access to a sand-blasting machine, however, so another method has to be sought. It is true that a wire brush is very useful, but it is also a help to make use of a thin, sharp object, such as a nail, to scrape out the plug-body/insulator space.

In many cases, especially where a weak mixture has existed, a hard deposit will have been formed on the electrodes. This must be scraped off, not forgetting the underside of the side electrode. Finally, the electrodes should be thoroughly cleaned with a file (special points files can be obtained for this purpose). Experiments, by one of the leading plug manufacturers, have shown that the voltage required to provide a spark in a wire-brushed plug is considerably higher than that required for one which has been filed.

Before replacing the spark plugs, the insulators, on the outside of the cylinder, should be cleaned, in order to prevent the voltage (around twenty thousand) from 'tracking' between the terminal and the nut. Although oil and grease are not very good conductors, at voltages such as the one mentioned even a poor conductor will pass a current.

With the plugs back in the engine and tightened to the recommended torque, something which is especially important with an aluminium-alloy cylinder head, the plug caps should be cleaned before replacement. As with the plug insulators, deposits of dirt can lead to 'tracking', which, in turn, will impair the efficiency of the engine.

The high-tension leads should be firmly connected to the plug caps, especially in the case of the suppressor type, which have carbon cores rather than wire ones. It is not uncommon for a gap to form in the carbon, which may eventually become too large for a spark to jump, thus rendering that particular plug inoperative.

If the leads have to be replaced, it is better to fit the wire variety, together with new plug caps containing built-in suppressors. The likelihood of a fault is greatly reduced and these leads are somewhat easier to connect.

Above left: the best tool with which to adjust a spark plug gap is a special gapping device; apart from the electrode-bending facility, these usually include feeler gauges and a file

Above: once the electrode gap has been altered, the setting should be checked by passing a feeler gauge of the correct thickness between the points

DISTRIBUTOR & TIMING

controlling the ignition system

Below: adjusting the points. The engine should first be turned until the points are wide open (*below left*) and then the gap should be checked with a feeler gauge (*below right*). If the gap is incorrect, it should be adjusted by loosening the fixing screw and moving the stationary contact to the required setting (bottom left)

Bottom right: when adjusting the timing, a light connected to the 'CB' lead of the coil will judge when the points are open

WE HAVE DEALT WITH the correct maintenance of spark plugs, showing how this is important to the running of an engine, but clean spark plugs will be no good without a distributor which is working correctly.

The exploded diagram shows how many parts go to making up a distributor, but fortunately most of these will continue indefinitely to function correctly. A small amount of regular attention will ensure that this part of the ignition system performs adequately.

The contact breaker points require the most frequent servicing, because the plastic knob, which rests on the distributor camshaft, will wear and the points themselves are inclined, slowly, to burn. If the camshaft is lightly greased every few thousand miles, the wear will be cut to a minimum, but unless transistorised ignition is fitted the burning is unavoidable.

When greasing the camshaft, it is important not to apply too much lubricant, as any excess may find its way onto the points and cause a break in the electrical circuit. A smear is really quite sufficient for a long period of running.

If the contact points were to wear evenly, the job of adjustment would be simple, but unfortunately the tend to wear with a bump on one side and a dent o the other.

Adjustment is normally carried out using a screw driver and a feeler gauge. The fixed contact should b moved until the clearance between it and its movin partner is that specified by the manufacturer (whe the gap is at its widest). The points should just nip th feeler without having to open to admit it.

If a knob is present on one of the contacts, it will b impossible to obtain a correct setting with a feele gauge. There are two courses of action: fit new poin or grind the present ones flat. Let us deal with th latter course first.

Distributor points are hardened, so it is not at a easy to file them. The correct procedure is to grin them on a flat oil stone until both bump and dent a removed. Great care should be taken to ensure that th surfaces are kept flat and parallel, so that the poin still meet properly.

There are two types of contact set: the older two piece variety and the modern one-piece 'Quickafi version. The one-piece points are easier to fit than th older sort, but they can be less reliable. Removal an refitting of both types involves the unscrewing of th screw which holds the points down and fixes th adjustment. One nut holds the wires on and with th one-piece points the wires can be removed or fitte with the points on or off.

The distributor has more functions than simpl providing the basis for a spark. It decides when th spark should occur and at what point each cylinde should receive it (this is done by the rotor arm).

Basic ignition timing is simply a matter of distr butor position rather than distributor function, b alteration of this setting with increasing engine spee is definitely a function of this complex instrumen Centrifugal weights are thrown outwards as speed rotation rises and thus move the points relative to tl camshaft (within the distributor). It is possible fc these weights to stick either 'advanced' or 'retarded Oil should be applied sparingly down the centre of tl distributor camshaft (the main spindle).

In addition to the centifugal advance mechanisn there is usually a vacuum unit which alters tl ignition timing with throttle opening (as depressic increases the ignition is advanced). With the distr butor cap removed, the tube leading to the distribut should be sucked. If the base-plate, which carries tl contact set, moves, all is well, but if it does not and a is felt to be passing through the tube, then there probably a leak, either in the diaphragm unit, or the pipe.

The final job of the distributor is that from whic the unit takes its name: distributing. The rotor ar fitted to the end of the shaft spins and passes hig tension current from a central contact in the distribut cap to several peripheral ones in turn (one for eac

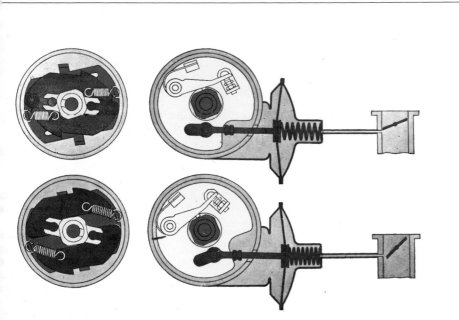

cylinder). In fact the arm should not actually touch the peripheral ones—a spark jumps from its tip to each contact.

However, the central contact is meant to touch the arm and is sprung for that purpose. Should the spring weaken or the carbon contact wear unduly, then the fault will need to be remedied. All the contacts should be cleaned regularly as should the rotor arm itself.

With all these simple procedures carried out every so often, the distributor should present no problems. There is no point in trying to adjust the ignition timing until the distributor has been correctly set up, as already detailed. For every variation of 0.001 in in the setting of the contact-breaker points, there is a possibility of a three-degree timing error. What is more, the biggest spark possible will be no good at all if it occurs at the wrong time or in the wrong cylinder.

In most modern engines, the correct time is when the piston is about to reach the top of its compression stroke. A setting in advance of this will usually lead to 'pinking' (the name given to the tinkling noise caused by the detonation of the mixture in the combustion chamber), and a retarded setting will lead simply to a loss of efficiency. The reason that the spark plug fires before the piston is ready to move down on its power stroke is that the full effect of the spark is not immediately felt—it takes a few milliseconds for the mixture of fuel and air to combust.

Before attempting to set the timing, it is necessary to ascertain the position recommended by the manufacturer and especially to check whether this is a static setting (with the engine stationary) or a setting for so many rpm, in which case the automatic advance mechanisms may have taken over.

Assuming a static figure is given, then the setting

Above: most distributors are equipped with two types of automatic advance and retard mechanism—mechanical and vacuum; in the mechanical type, centrifugal weights are interposed between the baseplate and the body, so that as the speed builds up, the weights move out and turn the baseplate, thus moving the points relative to the cam (*left*); in the vacuum type, manifold depression causes a diaphragm to move against a spring, once again altering the position of the baseplate (*right*)

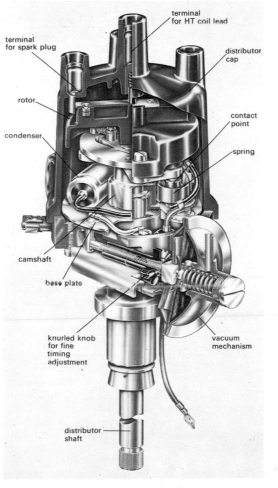

terminal for HT coil lead

terminal for spark plug

distributor cap

rotor

contact point

condenser

spring

camshaft

base plate

knurled knob for fine timing adjustment

vacuum mechanism

distributor shaft

Two types of distributor: on the left is a complete unit, while above is a cutaway of a slightly different type with a vacuum-advance unit; not only does this unit serve as an automatic advance and retard device, but it facilitates static adjustment, by means of the knurled knob in the unit's linkage

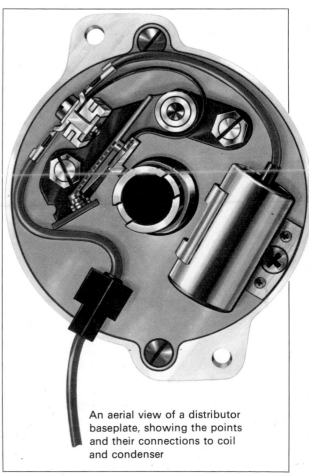

An aerial view of a distributor baseplate, showing the points and their connections to coil and condenser

119

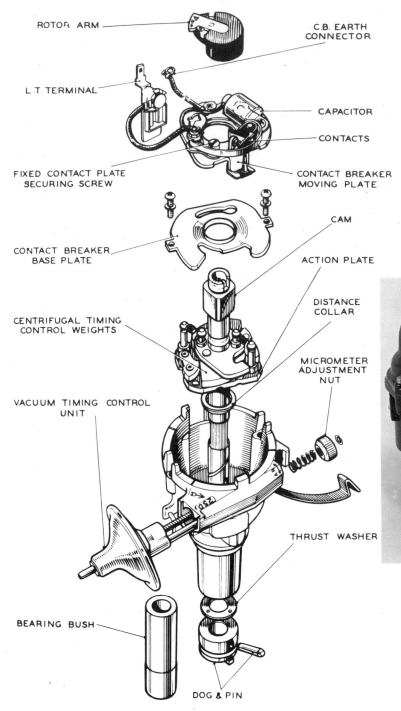

ROTOR ARM

C.B. EARTH
CONNECTOR

L.T. TERMINAL

CAPACITOR

CONTACTS

FIXED CONTACT PLATE
SECURING SCREW

CONTACT BREAKER
MOVING PLATE

CONTACT BREAKER
BASE PLATE

CAM

ACTION PLATE

CENTRIFUGAL TIMING
CONTROL WEIGHTS

DISTANCE
COLLAR

MICROMETER
ADJUSTMENT
NUT

VACUUM TIMING CONTROL
UNIT

THRUST WASHER

BEARING BUSH

DOG & PIN

Above: an exploded
diagram showing the
parts which go to make
up a Lucas distributor

Above right: two types
of distributor—on the
right an eight-cylinder
unit with double points
and facilities for two
coils, and on the left a
water-tight unit used on
four-cylinder-engined
military vehicles

limited range, but if the setting is a long way out, it will be necessary to loosen the body of the distributor and turn it in the direction of shaft rotation to retard the setting and in the opposite direction for more advance. The distributor is held into its fixing bracket by a clamp bolt (like an exhaust clamp), so it is only necessary to loosen this one bolt in order to turn the mechanism.

If an incorrect setting can be rectified by the use of the fine adjustment, all well and good (in most Lucas distributors there are eleven 'clicks' to one degree). However, should this system be unable to cope with the alteration, then the adjuster should be centred, the number of clicks from one end to the other should be counted and the nut left at a setting midway between the two.

With the clamp bolt loose, the distributor body should be turned and the setting checked in the same way as before. It it is nearly correct and a fine adjustment mechanism is fitted, then the clamp should be retightened and the final setting procedure left to this adjuster.

It should be noted that although most cars have their timing marks on the crankshaft pulley, as stated, some, notably the British Leyland Mini with its transverse engine, have them on the flywheel (a plate has to be removed from the Mini's clutch housing in order to see the marks, and even then a mirror is needed).

If the static setting is not known, or it is required to check the static setting in another way, then a stroboscopic timing light can be used. This type of light has a high-voltage 'bulb' which is connected to the spark plug lead on number one cylinder so that, every time the plug fires, the bulb lights up.

By shining this light onto the timing marks, when the engine is running, the pulley should appear stationary and it should thus be possible to ascertain the setting of the ignition for any number of revolutions per minute.

In many engines, it will be necessary to remove the cooling fan in order to avoid the loss of a hand, so great care should be taken when experimenting. Also, there is no point in checking the ignition in this way if there is no means of knowing the speed of the engine. An accurate tachometer is needed for this.

The main point to remember is that ignition timing should never be tackled without first correcting the contact-points gap.

should be checked by connecting a small bulb to the contact breaker terminal on either the distributor or the high-tension coil and to earth (something like the cylinder block). This bulb should light up when the ignition is on and the points are open—when they are shut, the bulb will be short-circuited.

With the bulb connected, the engine should be turned until number one piston is approaching the top of its compression stroke. A mark on the crankshaft pulley usually denotes 'top dead centre' as it is known when it coincides with a further mark on the timing cover. Also, there are usually degree marks on the timing cover to indicate how far before top dead centre the crankshaft is. The engine should be turned by hand with the ignition on (perhaps by pushing in top gear) when approaching the relevant one of these marks. The light should just be coming on as this mark is reached. If it comes on before, the ignition is advanced and if it comes on after, the ignition is retarded.

Most distributors have a knurled nut built in, with which it is possible to alter the ignition setting over a

DYNAMO

a popular generator

A cutaway view of a dynamo as used on a car. In this type of unit, the armature consists of a large number of coils, each connected to the commutator. The greater the number of coils, the smoother the output of the dynamo; unfortunately, however, the mass of the armature has to be great and too high an operating speed can lead to the component's explosion. Note that there is a roller bearing at the front *(left)*, where the unit is driven, and a plain bearing at the relatively unstressed rear *(right)*, where, on the unit shown in this example, tachometer drive is provided

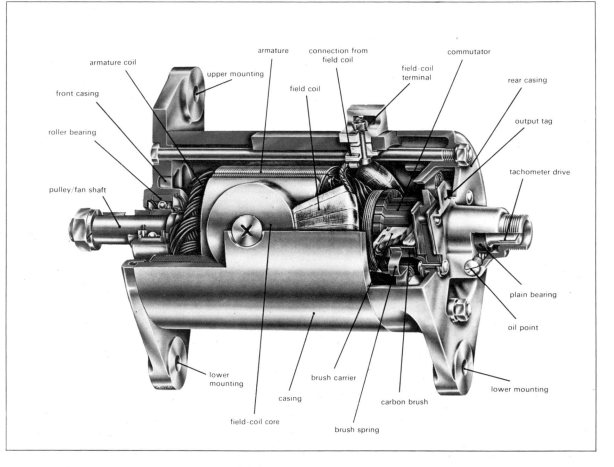

UNLESS A MOTOR VEHICLE has a diesel engine, it is bound to consume electricity, because ignition is brought about by an electrical spark. A battery can provide this current, without any trouble, but it will eventually run flat if it not recharged by a generator, be this an alternator or a dynamo.

Most cars built since the early 1970s have had alternators, because these are more reliable and more efficient than the older dynamos. Previous to this time, however, dynamos were standard items on motor cars, producing sufficient electricity to power not only the engine ignition system, but also the lights, windscreen wipers, heater fan etc.

Since the early part of the twentieth century, electric starter motors have been fitted to cars, thus dispensing with the need to 'swing the handle'. These motors demand enormous current supplies, which would soon discharge the battery if it were not for the generator.

In just about every road-going car, the dynamo is driven by a rubber belt from the end of the crankshaft. By varying the relative sizes of the crankshaft and dynamo pulleys, it is possible, too, to alter the relative speeds of the two items. Before considering this,

however, we should discuss how a dynamo works.

If a coil of wire is rotated within a magnetic field, an electric current will be generated in that coil. The size of the current will depend on the speed of rotation and the strength of the magnetic field. If the current is taken direct from each end of the coil, through two slip rings and brushes, it will alternate, changing direction twice for every revolution of the coil. The best way of avoiding this alternation, which is no good for charging a battery, is to fit a commutator, which is in the form of a single slip ring split into two parts, so that when the current changes direction it is fed into the wiring system 'the other way round'.

In practice, the dynamo has more than one coil—usually 28, in fact—with 28 segments on the commutator (there is no need for 56 segments, because two coils can share two segments between their four wires). The result of having a large number of coils is that any ripples in the current output, caused by the change in current direction, will be all but smoothed out.

The electrical output is taken from the commutator by means of two carbon brushes. These make contact with the commutator as it turns with the armature—the

121

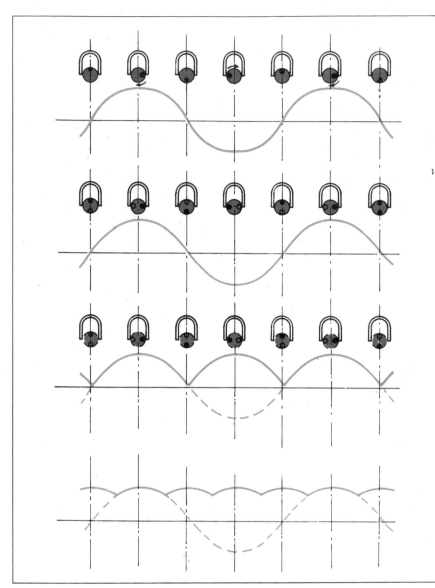

name given to the coil assembly—and transmit current to the regulator, which controls the voltage and current output, and thence to the battery.

If the dynamo were allowed to produce its full output at all times, it would use engine power unnecessarily, because the higher the output, the harder the unit is to turn. To overcome this, the permanent magnets used to produce the field, in which the armature spins, are replaced by further coils of wire, known as the field coils. When these coils are energised, an equivalent magnetic field is produced, but the beauty of the arrangement is that if the field-coil supply is cut down, the dynamo output will be reduced accordingly.

The supply to the field coil is controlled by the regulator, which is sensitive to dynamo/battery voltage and to the charging current. In other words, the dynamo should only give its full output when the battery is not fully charged or when large demands are being made.

Although the dynamo is a reliable and fairly efficient piece of equipment, it has certain drawbacks when compared with the more modern alternator. The main one is that it will not produce sufficient current to charge a battery if it is rotating at less than about 1200 rpm (or at tickover). Unfortunately, it is no use fitting a smaller dynamo pulley to overcome this, as the maximum safe speed of this type of generator is around 7000 rpm (it has been known for the armature to explode when over-revved). The alternator is safe to around 12,000 rpm, so it can be higher geared.

The maximum output available from a modern dynamo is around 22 amps, which is sufficient for most uses, but which can be too little when driving on a wet night with the heater fan on as well as the headlights and windscreen wipers. An alternator can produce up to 50 amps, although the figure is usually more like 40.

The only maintenance necessary is an occasional drop of oil, on the rear bearing. The most important point is to keep the drive belt at the correct tension—with half an inch of play in its longest section; it may take half a horsepower to drive the dynamo when the battery charge is low and a loose fan belt will start to slip under these conditions, allowing the battery to become further discharged.

Above: these diagrams illustrate the basic principle of the generator. They represent, graphically, the current produced by coils turning in the field of a horseshoe magnet. In the top two cases, an alternating current is produced by single and double coils, respectively, half being positive and half negative, with respect to zero. The third diagram shows two coils, but with the current collected by a commutator, thereby producing a pulsing direct current. The last diagram shows the output from a four-coil dynamo

Right: a dynamo on a Vauxhall 1500 cc engine

ALTERNATOR

taking over from the dynamo

IN RECENT YEARS the output demands made upon a motor car's generator have increased considerably, due both to the more powerful lighting systems now being used and to the many electrically-operated accessories now fitted as standard equipment to production vehicles. Traffic conditions also have a bearing on the situation. Because heavy traffic compels low-speed driving, the conventional DC generator, or dynamo, is not usually capable of producing sufficient current to meet the heavy demands made upon the battery. When an engine is idling at 600 rpm, the dynamo will not be charging the battery. The problem can be solved by replacing the dynamo with a unit capable of supplying a high output of current, even at low engine speeds. This is the AC generator, otherwise known as the alternator.

All electrical generators work on the same principle. If an electrical conductor passes through a magnetic field, a current will be induced in the conductor. In the dynamo, the conductor is in the form of a looped coil of wire, which rotates inside the field of an electromagnet. Any part of the coil which passes through the magnetic field in one direction will, half a rotation later, be passing through the field in the opposite direction; the current in the coil will therefore reverse its direction every half-revolution. This is overcome by the commutator, which correspondingly changes the direction of the rest of the electrical circuit every half revolution, so that the dynamo supplies a succession of quick impulses, all through the circuit in the same direction.

Current generation in the dynamo coil produces a certain amount of heat, which cannot easily escape through the surrounding electromagnet, and the quantity of heat produced increases with the speed of rotation. Mechanical shortcomings in the design of the commutator also limit the speed at which the dynamo can rotate. The upper limit to a dynamo's operation is therefore about 6000 rpm, with an output of 30 amps.

In an alternator, the magnetic field rotates inside a wound coil. Because the generating windings are stationary, there is no problem over cooling. An alternator can be geared to run twice as fast at the engine, idling at 1200 rpm and reaching a speed as high as 12,000 rpm, with an output up to 50 amps.

Construction

The principal parts of an alternator are the stator, the armature or rotor, and the diode rectifier.

The stator is composed of a cylindrical laminated soft iron ring, slotted so that the windings can be passed through the slots. There are three sets of windings on the stator, and the alternator therefore produces a three-phase current.

The rotor consists of a soft iron armature which is wound with a single continuous coil, and which is fed current from the battery by means of two small sliprings at the end of the rotor shaft. This turns the rotor into an electromagnet, with a north pole at one end and a south at the other. The two end-pieces of the armature are formed into metal fingers, so that the rotor

becomes a succession of smaller magnets, with south and north poles alternating, interlocked but not touching.

As the rotor is turned by the engine, the stationary windings on the stator are subjected to a rapid alternation of magnetic field, exactly comparable with what happens in a dynamo when the coil rotates in a stationary magnetic field. But since the alternator has no commutator, the generated current is rapidly alternating with the rotation of the magnets.

Although this three-phase alternating current could be used to power the lights and some of the accessories, the battery must be charged, and other electrical circuits operated, by direct current.

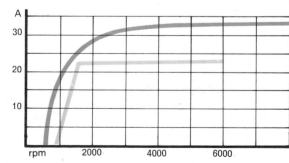

Above: a special cut-away of an alternator.

Below: output in amps against the speed in rpm for a (green) dynamo and a (brown) alternator. Note how the alternator, which weighs considerably less (3 kg) than the dynamo (7 kg), charges at lower speeds and has a higher output

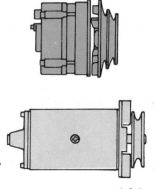

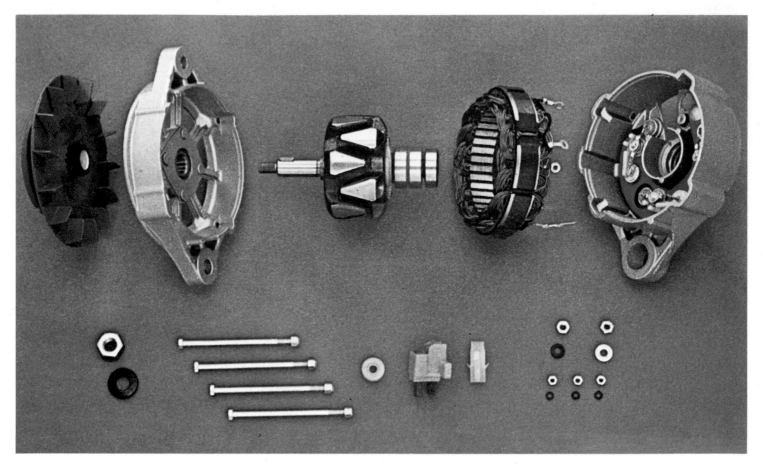

The components of an alternator, from left to right: pulley and cooling fan; front housing and bearing; rotor; stator; rear housing and bearing, including the rectifier

The 'rectification' of this alternating current into direct current is done by means of diode rectifiers. These are, in effect, one-way electrical valves which will allow the current to flow in only one direction. On modern alternators transistors are employed, and their small size enables them to be mounted inside the alternator casing. Because transistors are sensitive to temperature they are mounted in 'heat-sink' plates, which are kept as cool as possible by directing a stream of air through the casing.

An alternator will limit its own current output, and requires only voltage regulation. Since the rectifiers will not pass current in a reverse direction there is no need for a cutout, and the voltage regulator can be transistorised and mounted inside the casing.

Maintenance
The first requirement of efficient alternator operation is that the drive belt should be tight. Because of the load applied to an alternator when it is working, the belt should be tighter than the drive belt on a dynamo. Under no circumstances should any attempt be made to lubricate the alternator bearings. These are pre-lubricated when assembled and need no attention.

Nor should any part of the charging circuit – and that includes the battery – be disconnected when the engine is running. Damage to the diodes and the windings can be caused if this precaution is not taken. Also, the correct polarity must of course be followed when connecting a battery or battery charger.

A simple way to test whether an alternator is working or not is to connect a voltmeter to the battery terminals. Note the voltmeter reading before starting the engine, and then run the engine at moderate speed – about 3000 rpm. If the system is working the voltmeter reading should increase.

As far as servicing or repair goes it is advisable to have an alternator dealt with by a competent elec-

trician, or to fit a new service exchange unit if the old one fails. Special equipment is needed to check components such as the stator or rotor, but it is possible to carry out minor checks and, in some cases, replace certain parts.

In many cases, for instance, it is possible to renew the fixed brushes for the slip-rings of the rotor shaft. How these are reached varies slightly from one make of alternator to another, so it is not possible to give precise dismantling information. The points to watch, however, are that care must be taken when removing the brushes from their holders, damage to the holders must be avoided. Clean the holders thoroughly and make sure that the correct brushes are fitted. Ensure also that the brushes slide freely in the holders before fitting back in position.

Before replacing the brush holders, the condition of the slip-rings should be checked. These will usually be dirty and covered with carbon dust from the old brushes. Clean the slip-rings with methylated spirits but do not use petrol as this does not disperse quickly enough and the remaining fumes could be ignited when the alternator first starts working again.

It is possible to test the diodes in an alternator by rigging up a test lamp using the car battery, or a torch battery, with the diode in between. As this is a one-way electrical valve the test lamp will light when the current is flowing in one direction, but will not light when it is flowing in the opposite direction. If the bulb lights in one direction only then the diode is good, if it lights in both directions, or does not light in either, then the diode is faulty and needs changing.

Should any soldering be necessary, always grip the soldered wire with a pair of pliers to conduct the heat away from any vulnerable part of the unit. Heat can easily damage an alternator and what may have started as a fairly simple job could result in the need for a new unit if this precaution is not observed.

BATTERY

the car's electricity store

A CAR BATTERY consists of a number of cells, almost always either three, giving a six-volt battery, or six, for twelve volts. Each of these cells is a typical electric cell, converting the energy of a chemical reaction into electrical energy. In a car battery, unlike a torch battery, this process is reversible. The chemical reaction can be reversed by passing an electric current into the battery, thus recharging it.

Each cell in a lead-acid battery, which is the type normally used in cars, contains two lead frameworks, the plates. The positive plate is filled with lead peroxide and the negative plate with spongy lead. These plates stand in dilute sulphuric acid, and the negative plate of one cell is connected to the positive plate of the next. When the cell is in use, that is, when it is being discharged, the lead peroxide, lead, and sulphuric acid change to lead sulphate, on both plates, and water. This chemical reaction produces electricity. When the plates have a complete surface covering of lead sulphate, the battery is flat. On charging, the reaction is reversed, and the lead sulphate is turned back again into lead peroxide and lead.

Immediately after charging, each cell has a voltage of about 2.6, but this soon falls, even on standing, to about 2.15 volts. When the battery is used, the voltage of each cell quickly falls to about 2.0 and it stays at that value for a considerable time, until the battery is nearly discharged. It then falls to about 1.8 volts.

A battery must, of course, have the correct voltage for the car it is to be used in, but merely having the correct voltage is not enough. If it were, one could join torch batteries to produce the correct voltage and use them in a car. In fact, a series of torch batteries would light only one of the smaller bulbs in a car. It would be totally useless for the main headlight bulbs and windscreen wipers, let alone the enormous demands of the starter. A car battery must be able to deliver a fairly large electrical current for some time.

Electrical current is measured in ampères (usually shortened to amps) and the battery's capacity in ampère hours (Ah). A smallish battery with a capacity of 40 Ah could deliver a current of one amp for forty hours before becoming discharged, or two amps for twenty hours, and so on. The capacity of a battery is not always exactly the same. It depends on the rate at which it is being discharged, so the capacity is usually given as, for example 40 Ah at a 10-amp rate.

A car with a large engine needs more current to turn the starter, and because the amount of electricity that can be supplied depends on the quantities of each chemical available on the plates of the battery, a large car will need a large battery. A typical large-car battery will have a capacity of 75 Ah.

When a car is in use, its generator or alternator normally keeps the battery more or less fully charged. However, in winter, when the lights may be used a lot and when the starter often has to be used more to get the engine started, the battery may become discharged.

It can be recharged by removing it, or at least disconnecting it, from the car, and connecting a charger that draws its electricity from the mains and converts alternating into direct current. The positive terminal of the charger must be connected to the positive terminal of the battery so that the electricity is, so to speak, forced back into it.

There are two basic ways of telling if the battery is adequately recharged. A third way, that does not work, is simply to measure the voltage across the terminals of the battery. The stable voltage of a cell before use is

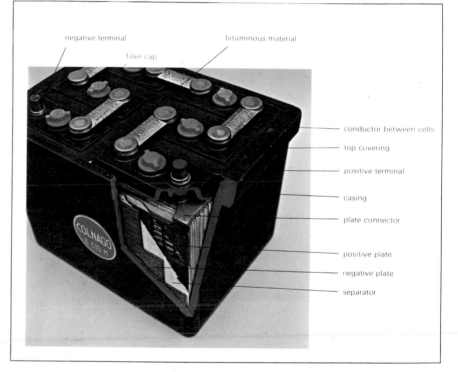

negative terminal

filler cap

bituminous material

conductor between cells

top covering

positive terminal

casing

plate connector

positive plate

negative plate

separator

COLNAGO

about 2.15 volts so it might seem that if a six-cell ('twelve-volt') battery records a voltage of 12.9 volts (6 x 2.15) or even 12 volts, then it must be fully charged or at least nearly so. Unfortunately, you need to know what voltage the battery can deliver in action, and if a battery is old or has been damaged, the twelve volts measured with a voltmeter when the battery is not in use will drop to nine or ten volts when it is. A simple test is to measure the voltage across the battery when it is in the car and connected, with the headlights switched on. If it still produces 12 volts, it is in at least reasonable condition.

A garage uses a more specialised version of this test. It has a device that consists of a voltmeter and a resistance: it is used to test each cell of the battery separately. The current from the cell flows through the resistance and the voltmeter therefore measures the voltage the cell produces when it is in action. Usually

This cutaway shows clearly how a lead-acid battery is made up of plates and separators, which are immersed in sulphuric acid. Cells are connected in series (+ to −) to give the required voltage

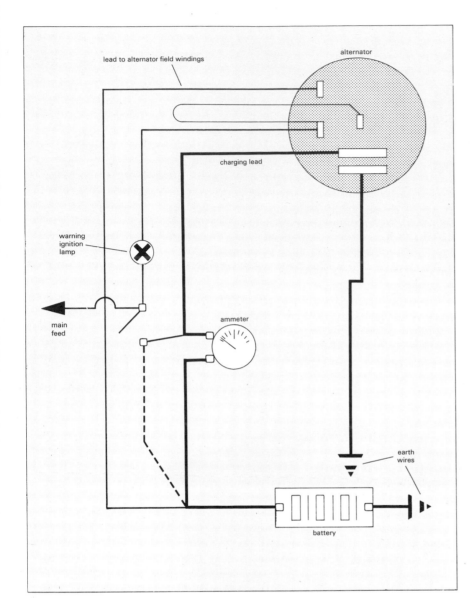

they stand in changes from sulphuric acid to water. Sulphuric acid is more dense than water, so the density of the liquid—its technical name is the 'electrolyte'—gets lower as the battery becomes discharged. The specific gravity, which is the most useful way of comparing densities, of a fully charged battery is between 1.28 and 1.30. The specific gravity of a fully discharged battery is about 1.15 (the actual values vary with different makes of battery). A hydrometer will tell you the specific gravity, so that you can tell if the battery is fully charged. Some makes of hydrometer are coded and give direct reading of the state of charge.

If some of the chemical on the plates cannot be changed back into lead and lead peroxide, the battery cannot be fully charged, and this is what happens as a battery gets older. The vibrations of the car shake material from the plates so that it falls to the bottom of the cells; sometimes the lead sulphate appears in a form that resists conversion (the cell is then said to be sulphated), sometimes a battery is so ill-treated that two of the plates get bent and touch one another, which makes that particular cell useless. Any of these faults will mean that the density of the liquid in the cell cannot rise to its proper value and, while the battery may still be adequate for summer use, it will have to be replaced for the winter.

An ill-treated battery has a short life. One that is properly looked after can last for many years. If a battery is overcharged, either in the car or on a battery

Above: a circuit diagram showing how the battery is connected

Above right: two cells from the beginning of the century. The one on the left has been dismantled to show the central lead electrode surrounded by a paste electrolyte and usually contained in a glass jar. The second electrode is not visible. The capacity was about 1Ah

Right: it is common, nowadays, to use a translucent or transparent casing for a battery, so that the fluid level can be checked without removing the caps. Most manufacturers have replaced the individual caps with a single, 'easy-fill' one

the voltmeter is colour-coded, so that the user can tell immediately whether the cell is working properly.

A simple device that anyone can use to test a battery is a hydrometer. This measures the density of the liquid in each cell. As the battery discharges, the solids on the plates change to lead sulphate, and the liquid

charger, some of the water in the dilute sulphuric acid is split up into hydrogen and oxygen and bubbles off as gas. This mixture is explosive, so naked flames should be kept away from batteries that are being charged. The lost water should be replaced with distilled water so that the plates are just covered. If tap water is used, there is a risk that chemicals in the water will contaminate the plates. A battery should not be left in a nearly-discharged state, as the plates are then likely to become sulphated so that they cannot be recharged. In addition, the liquid in a discharged battery freezes more easily than the liquid in a charged one, and a severe frost may freeze the liquid and split the battery casing. Incidentally, a cold battery delivers electricity more slowly than a warm one, and people who live in cold climates often keep their car batteries indoors overnight. The plates can become bent if the battery is badly overloaded, but this is usually an accident and difficult to avoid.

The lead-acid car battery is rather unsatisfactory. It is expensive, it has a short life, and it is heavy, because the chemicals in it are lead compounds, and if it is to store a large amount of electricity, it must contain a lot of the chemicals.

The sheer weight of a car battery is one of the reasons that no successful electric car has been built. To go quickly, or a long way, a large number of batteries are required and in the end the car is carrying more batteries than useful load.

There have been attempts to produce different batteries, that is batteries that use different chemical reactions to generate electricity. Ideally, they would be reactions involving lighter chemicals. The NiFe batteries, as they are called, have plates of nickel and iron and have some advantages—they can be even more expensive, but they have much longer lives.

Almost certainly the battery of the future, particularly for electric cars, will be of the kind known as the fuel cell. In a fuel cell, one of the substances reacting is air or oxygen: the other is carbon or some other fuel. Fuel cells using hydrogen and oxygen have been fitted to space craft, but they have been unsuccessful on earth. The problem is that they are usually very expensive and need very complicated control gear. In one demonstration, a fuel cell was fitted to a pick-up truck. The electric motor was fitted under the bonnet and the battery under the seats, but the whole of the back of the truck was filled with the control gear.

The ideal fuel cell would use a freely available fuel plus air, and would run at ordinary temperatures. If such a fuel cell could be made, it could be connected to the motor of an electric car. Fuel cells are extremely efficient—experimental models have extracted 80 per cent of the energy of their fuels, and a fuel-cell car could be silent and non-polluting. Unfortunately, no-one has yet been successful in making a fuel cell of this type.

Above left: an ebonite container for six cells, showing how each cell fits into a separate compartment. The positive terminal of one cell is connected to the negative of its neighbour, thus multiplying the voltage by the number of cells

Above right: a cell removed completely from its casing. It has four positive plates interleaved with five negative ones

Left: the components of a positive and a negative plate. The lead frames or grids (top) support the active material of the plates, which is lead peroxide (centre right) for the positive plate and spongy lead (centre left) for the negative plate. The two plates are prevented from short-circuiting by inserting porous separators (bottom), of paper or plastic, between them

Specific gravity of electrolyte	Condition of battery
1.28+	fully charged
1.25	75% charged
1.22	50% charged
1.19	25% charged
1.16	almost flat
1.15−	totally flat

The specific gravity of the electrolyte indicates the state of charge of the battery. During discharge, the acid becomes diluted as lead sulphate is formed on the plates.
The figures above are approximate and will vary from make to make.

Below left: lead sulphate and oxide form if the top is not kept clean *Centre:* a hydrometer shows a flat battery (left) or a charged one *Right:* sulphation caused by lack of electrolyte (left), bent plates by over-loading (centre) and broken plates by inactivity accelerating sulphation

LIGHTING

seeing in the dark

LIGHTING IS A FUNDAMENTAL PART of the modern car concept. It is a major consideration for the body designer because no driver would dream of using a car without lights and the legal system of any civilised country would prevent him doing so even if he wanted to. Today's motor car has built into it upwards of thirty different light sources. If any one of them goes out, it is missed very quickly by the driver or soon noticed by other road users or a policeman enforcing the legal requirements of the British Construction and Use Regulations.

However, it was not always like that. In the beginning, the motor car inherited the existing lamps from horse-drawn vehicles. Splendid devices of polished brass and copper they were; functional they were not. With a single candle as the light source they would scarcely light the way for the man walking in front with the red flag. Four hours was about as long as the candle would last and it was pushed up as it burned by a spring positioned underneath.

A better light source was furnished by lamps burning Colza oil and in some cases petrol. There were many variations of style and these lamps remained popular up to about 1910. Refinements were introduced, like a parabolic mirror to beam the light and an optical front glass, but from the turn of the century they were competing with the first of the acetylene lamps. The trouble with oil lamps was that they were dirty, smelly and always likely to blow out in a wind.

Acetylene lamps shared the dirty and smelly qualities of the oil types. They were also noisy and had an endearing trait of their own—they were inclined to explode!

The lamp's characteristic hiss is still remembered nostalgically by many people motoring over fifty years ago. In spite of the numerous snags, acetylene lamps produced a surprisingly good light—bright, white and reasonably steady. This was just as well because by about 1912, cars were travelling considerably faster.

The principle of operation of the acetylene gas lamp is a simple one. There are two containers, one mounted over the other. The lower one is half-filled with carbide in lump form and the upper one contains water. The water from the top chamber is dripped on to the carbide by means of an adjustable needle valve and chemical reaction between the two gives off acetylene gas and leaves a chalky residue. A pipe leading off is crowned with a jet and it is here that the gas is lit to burn with a bright green flame.

Generally the lamp would burn for about four hours before the carbide supply needed replenishing. The chamber also then needed cleaning before refilling.

The models in use just before electricity came on the scene had become technically advanced enough to incorporate the first dimming system—forerunner of today's dipping system. Positioned behind the flame was a hemispherical concave mirror, designed to intensify the light. In town or when approaching other vehicles, this mirror could be turned through 180 deg to obscure the flame. In this position there was enough reflected light to serve as a dimmed warning of approach. The system was designed by Zeiss and continued to be used in the first electric light systems which followed.

However, these were not efficient. They were powered by non-rechargeable batteries of limited life and the light they gave out was little improvement over the old oil or candle lamps. It was only after the introduction of the generator that electric car lighting really began to improve in efficiency and reliability. The popularity of the acetylene lamp began to wane.

In the period immediately before the start of World War I, oil lamps, acetylene lamps and electric lamps were all in use for headlights, sidelights and tail lights. Often cars of the day would have a mixture of types. To make the situation even more complicated a catalogue of S. Smith & Sons (now Smiths Industries) listed lamps to be used with adaptors. Designed

Above: two types of oil-burning lamp, as used in the early 1900s; these gave way to electric lighting

Below: in the early days of motoring, lighting was considered a luxury, lamps being offered as optional extras after about 1902; acetylene replaced oil as the fuel around 1906, the gas being produced by dripping water on calcium carbide in a tank (as shown here)

primarily for paraffin, they could also be used with acetylene and electric adaptors.

A popular installation was the separate acetylene generator, connected by means of rubber and brass pipes to the various lamps, although self-contained acetylene lamps were also available.

Several varieties of electric lighting kit were advertised. A set of side and tail lights, wired up to a 4-volt 50-amp accumulator and used in conjunction with acetylene headlamps was a fairly common arrangement at that time.

Also being marketed around this time was the S. Smith & Sons Perfect Lighting System. The components which this included were somewhat similar to those in use today. It had what was described as a 'constant current dynamo' and this was driven by means of a split pulley arrangement clamped around the propshaft, linked by a Whittle belt. A magnetic cut-out was used to disconnect the dynamo from the battery automatically when the former was running below its generating speed or at rest. This, of course, was to prevent the battery discharging itself through the dynamo. A typical battery was described as a '12-volt 40 Actual Ampere Hour Accumulator'.

There was a range of headlamps to choose from, ranging from 5 in in diameter to 13 in in diameter, and all the components were wired through a switchboard. This was usually mounted in front of the driver and incorporated a voltmeter and ammeter. Two controls only were included—a light switch and a manual on/off switch for the dynamo. Shades of things to come—available as extras were an interior roof light, cigar lighter, steering-column lamp and electric horn.

Foreshadowing another very much later development in headlamp design was the Smith Patent Electric Motor Lamp. This had a completely sealed reflector, filled with gas—today's sealed-beam unit has the same idea. Smith's lamp, however, had a glass envelope at the centre of the reflector. The bulb fitted into this from behind and shone through the glass of the envelope. The silver-plated or gold-plated reflectors were thus insulated from the atmosphere, would not become contaminated or need cleaning and would retain their light power very much longer.

With the increase in the brightness of the lights came the beginning of the problem of dazzle and the need for dipping or dimming main beams. In the twenties a great many schemes were tried. Headlamps at this time still had single-filament bulbs. Double filaments had been tried but as they relied purely on a reduced power filament which did not dip the beam, they were not regarded as successful. More in favour were mechanical means of tilting the actual reflectors up and down.

One scheme which was popular for a few years was the Barker mechanical dipping system. This one, however, tipped downwards the whole body of the light, actuation being by means of a manual lever, operated from the driving seat. Pneumatic dipping was incor-

porated on a lot of vehicles in the late twenties. This was a very simple idea where the tilting mechanism on the back of each reflector was connected by means of rubber or small-bore copper pipes to a little manual pump mounted on the dash panel. This was similar to a small bicycle pump and was inscribed *PULL SMARTLY*. Only a small movement was needed to dip the reflectors. A quick push in the other direction and back up again they came. A lot of other less successful ideas were tried, including venetian blind type slats and various hoods. Lens design was altered but nothing enjoyed any great success until around 1930 when the 'dip and switch' system was introduced.

Using this system, when the dip switch was operated, the offside headlamp went off completely. The nearside reflector had a tilting mechanism operated by a solenoid. It was a scheme in constant use until the late forties when pre-focus and twin-filament bulbs were introduced.

The changes which followed led directly to the modern lighting system we know today. At the centre of things (literally) was the bulb. The basic theory of the electric light bulb—that of maintaining a thin wire filament at white heat without burning or destroying the metal—has not changed. Filaments may be different shapes, glass envelopes vary hugely in size and shape and the system of contacts and bulb holders may appear in infinite variety—but the basic principle remains the same. An electric current is passed through a thin resistance wire conductor which glows white hot and emits light. If this were done in the open air, the oxygen present would cause the metal to oxidise and burn. To avoid this it is enclosed in a glass envelope or bulb, from which all the air has been extracted. This basic concept can be improved upon if the evacuated bulb is filled with an inert gas, like

Top left: oil lamps quickly replaced the one-candlepower variety which had been inherited from the early days of the horse-drawn coach

Top centre: some of the lamps from the first years of the car were ornate and very beautifully made and finished; it was usual to fit only a single headlamp

Top right: electric lights began to oust the acetylene variety around 1912, although the early ones were not as efficient as their gas contemporaries

Above: road surfaces have improved a great deal—in the 1930s, when this Bentley was built, it was not uncommon for stones to penetrate the headlamp glasses; in order to combat this, fine-mesh guards were fitted over the lights

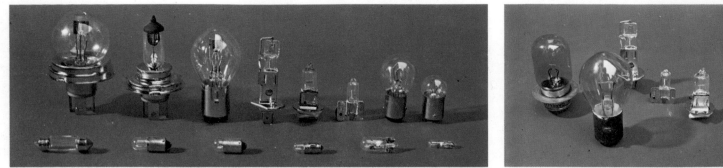

Above and right: selections of bulbs to suit every type of lamp found in the motor car of the seventies, be it a massive headlamp or a miniscule panel lamp or flasher warning lamp

Below right: an exploded diagram showing the parts of a rectangular Lucas headlamp, as fitted to many modern cars; note that this is fitted with a bulb, rather than the popular sealed-beam unit

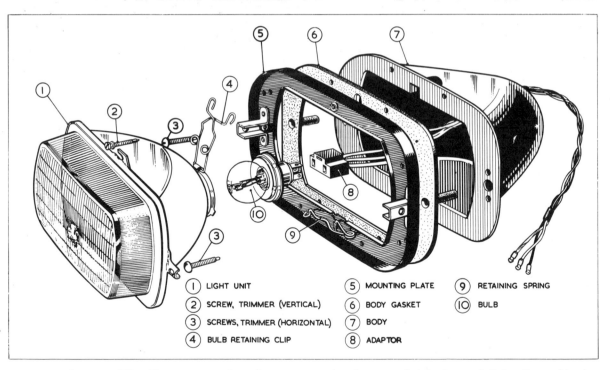

①	LIGHT UNIT	⑤	MOUNTING PLATE	⑨	RETAINING SPRING
②	SCREW, TRIMMER (VERTICAL)	⑥	BODY GASKET	⑩	BULB
③	SCREWS, TRIMMER (HORIZONTAL)	⑦	BODY		
④	BULB RETAINING CLIP	⑧	ADAPTOR		

argon or nitrogen. The filament can then be run hotter without burning or melting, producing a brighter light. But there is a disadvantage. Heat dissipation from the filament is proportionally greater than the extra power required to maintain the heat. To overcome this a coiled filament is used. This too is subject to variations. It may be in a simple straight line, shaped in an arc or a vee or a near circle, depending on the bulb's purpose. The ends of the filaments are welded to supporting wires. One is usually connected to the side of the metal cap and the other goes to a central contact point separated from the cap by insulation material. When the bulb is in use, current is carried to the central contact usually by means of a spring-loaded contact. The other side of the filament and the side of the cap are then earthed via the bulb holder and its mounting.

All bulbs provide illumination, but in the car this can be used in two ways—either as a local illumination or signal, or as a bright-beamed light. Stop, side, interior and dashpanel warning lights are examples of the former. The latter includes headlamps, spot lamps, fog lamps and reversing lights.

With stoplights and direction indicator lights, etc, there may be some sort of elementary reflector, but the purpose of this and the associated lens is usually merely to achieve the right degree of brightness and visibility. The headlamp reflector has a much more important job to do. It must collect the rays of light from the bulb which spread in all directions and concentrate them in a single bright beam. Once in the form of a beam the light is further shaped or angled by means of the front lens.

The reflector is shaped as a parabola and the bulb is positioned in the middle at the centre of focus. The reflecting surface is an aluminium coating on metal or glass. Almost all the light produced is thus projected forward, but there are some rays which pass directly

Right: a Lucas foglamp with a halogen light source which gives a higher light output than a conventional bulb, but consumes less power

Above: the famous Cibie Oscar

Right: a Cibie sealed-beam unit

Above: a light-unit on a Ford Capri Mk 1; a special headlamp unit has been fitted to this car, which has its side and flasher lamps neatly incorporated in a cluster with the headlamp

mistake. In the modern pre-focus light unit the reflector and the lens are made in one piece. The bulb aperture at the back is so shaped that the bulb with its notched locating collar can only go in one way.

Years ago, with some designs of lamp, it was possible to vary the position of the bulb in relation to the reflector. It was up to the owner often to adjust the bulb and focus the light beam—a very hit and miss affair by modern standards.

Before the present construction technique of the light unit was adopted, the lens, reflector and bulb were all available separately, so the problem of dazzle came up again. This was during the fifties and was caused by people matching up the wrong components.

A further advantage of the modern light unit is that with the lens and reflector constructed as a single unit, the vulnerable surface of the reflector is much better protected against dirt and damage. The only opening is via the bulb fitting aperture at the rear and this is virtually sealed by the bulb locating ring.

At the present time there are a great many vehicles still fitted with the pre-focus light unit and bulb, but most manufacturers now use the sealed-beam unit exclusively on their production models. The combined reflector and lens of the sealed-beam unit is made entirely of glass, the internal reflector surface being coated with aluminium and the lens design being a special block pattern. The big advance with this design, however, is that there is no separate bulb. Instead the stem supports for the filaments are precision positioned in the glass reflector shell. In effect, the whole unit is a very large bulb. The advantages are better light and longer life but set against this is the greater cost when failure does occur.

One of the reasons that better light output is achieved is that the problem of bulb ageing is considerably reduced. The outer layer of the filament of a tungsten bulb vaporises and deposits itself on the inner surface of the glass, appearing as a black shadow. The thickness of the filament is also reduced by this action, consequently lessening the temperature and power of the light.

In the sealed-beam unit there is a far greater area of glass on which the tungsten can deposit itself, giving less blackening of that glass. The filament can be made stronger, giving longer life. It can also be positioned with greater accuracy in relation to the reflector, providing a better light. Finally, the fact that the unit is completely sealed ensures that the reflector surface won't deteriorate.

There is naturally some variation in lens design, too. One manufacturer will have different ideas from another; the sealed-beam pattern is different from the light unit; four-lamp system lenses are different from two-lamp. Optically, lens design is a very complicated business, but generally the lens is constructed of flutes and prisms on the inner surface, being smooth on the outside. The flutes (concave surfaces) act as spreaders to widen the beam and the prisms control light distribution vertically.

The 7 in light unit was standardised in the 1940s and during the 1950s, as car designs changed, lamps, instead of being separate units tacked on afterwards, were included in the body and wing shapes. The latest in the design progression has been the introduction of four-headlamp systems and more recently square, or more correctly, rectangular headlamps.

Four-headlamp systems use 5 in units. The two inner ones provide the main-beam light, using single $37\frac{1}{2}$ W filaments. The outer units provide a supplementary main beam and dipped beam, using $37\frac{1}{2}$ W filaments and 50 W filaments. On main beam the four

from the bulb forward and upward and could cause dazzle. These are controlled sometimes by the use of a small metal hood shrouding the underside of the filament and sometimes by a subsidiary reflector turning the rays back into the main reflector for re-direction through the lens.

If the light filament is not positioned at the exact focal point of the reflector, the beam is distorted. If it is further back, the beam will be wide and diffused. Forward, it will be converging to a concentrated point and then spreading out again.

This principle is used to obtain the dipped beam. A twin-filament bulb is fitted. The main beam filament is at the exact centre. The dipped beam filament is higher and to one side. The result is a beam that is directed downwards and to the nearside.

From this it will be understood why it is vital that the bulb is positioned in exactly the right position. With modern lights, it is not really possible to make a

Right: most countries have a minimum-height requirement for the headlamps of a motor car; in Britain, this height is two feet, which means that manufacturers of sleek GT cars have to incorporate 'pop-up' lamps in order to avoid spoiling the lines of their dream machines

Far right: rally cars are fitted with batteries of driving lamps to give their drivers as much vision as possible at night; often, the centre pair of lamps has its beams crossed in order to light the edges of the road. In order to power all these lights, a high-output generator is necessary—usually an alternator

$37\frac{1}{2}$ W filaments are lit. On dip it is the two 50 W filaments which light. The single filaments on the inner lamps provide the long-distance lighting and the supplementary filaments on the outer units fill in the nearer section of road.

In 1974, square headlamps were the latest styling gimmick, but it was generally considered that they offered little in the way of technical advantages. Many of the earlier versions were decidedly inferior in light output. Additionally, the design's complications made the units large, difficult and expensive to produce and, logically, expensive to replace.

Also more costly, but in this case offering considerable technical advantages, is the quartz-iodine or tungsten-halogen bulb, now available incidentally in sealed-beam form. The most obvious advantage to the user of this lamp is the increase in light output. It can be increased, for a given wattage, by as much as 50 per cent—and this without an increased tendency towards blackening of the bulb.

The light source is a quartz envelope with a tungsten filament and filled with a mixture of krypton and halogen gases. The halogen trace permits an increase in filament temperature. The way it works is that, provided the walls of the bulb are kept hotter than 250 deg C, the tungsten vaporised off the filament when it is lit combines with the halogen in the relatively cooler region of the bulb wall and forms a volatile metal compound, incapable of being deposited on the inside of the bulb. In the region of the white-hot filament the tungsten and halogen part company and the tungsten is re-deposited on the filament. This is why it can work at a higher temperature without deteriorating, or alternatively, if it is run at a more normal temperature, can give greatly increased life to the expensive bulb.

The bulb used is small so it can be maintained at a high temperature and to withstand the temperature it is made of quartz. This is strong enough to cope with a greater filling pressure and the increased gas pressure further slows up filament vaporisation.

The first tungsten-halogen bulbs were single filament only and immediately found favour in long-range driving lamps and in the main beams of four-headlamp systems. For some time no one produced a twin-filament bulb, but ultimately these too became available. The bulbs were supplied as a kit together with light units and bulb adaptors and there was the unlikely situation of enthusiasts converting back from sealed-beam tungsten to bulb type tungsten halogen. Now, however, it is possible to buy and fit tungsten-halogen sealed-beam units.

Major influences on headlamp design and lighting development have been the technical advances in bulb

lighting are detailed and complicated. The full story can best be read in the Construction and Use Regulations, but briefly they are as follows.

Headlights must always work efficiently. During darkness, driving on an unlit road, they must be switched on, except in conditions of fog or falling snow, when two fog or spot lamps may be used instead. You must have at least two headlamps and they must be the same height, shape and area and colour when lit (either white or yellow).

To avoid dazzling oncoming drivers the lamps must deflect down, or down and to the left, or cut out in favour of another dipped beam, as with a four-headlamp system.

With four headlamps, if the outers have no dipping arrangement they must be dipped permanently. The inner pair must give a main beam. Dipswitch action must simultaneously extinguish all main beams. A single headlamp is forbidden so the old 'dip and switch' system is illegal.

Fog and spot lamps in pairs or one of each, may be used instead of headlamps in conditions of fog or falling snow only. They may be used any time, in pairs or singly, with headlamps. If they conform in every respect to the headlamp regulations, they can be used as a pair any time. If they are fitted lower than the minimum headlamp height of 2 ft, they can only be used in conditions of fog or falling snow.

Sidelamps must be white and there must be two of them, clean and properly lit. They must be less than 1 ft from the outer edges of the car and under 5 ft in height from the ground. They can be incorporated in the dipping pair of headlamps but must not exceed 7 watts each.

Rear lamps, two of them, red in colour and clean must be fitted together with two reflectors and all must be of regulation size. They must be of equal height on each side of the car and be of at least 5 watts.

Stop lamps have been obligatory since January 1971, except on a car first used before January 1936. Two, red in colour, clean and working, must be fitted, unless your car is older than January 1971 and in that case you need only one light.

Number-plate lamp must be fitted and working to illuminate the rear number plate during the hours of darkness, so that in the absence of fog the letters and figures are easily legible.

Flashing indicators have been obligatory since January 1971, except on a car first used before January 1936. For cars older than September 1965, many types are permitted, including semaphore arms, roof blinkers and flashing lights combined with the side and rear light system. After that date you must have four lights—two front and two rear—and they must be amber in colour. They must flash between 60 and 120 times per minute, and a visible or audible warning must be given to the driver, except where one indicator can be seen.

Reversing lamps are not compulsory. You can fit two 24 W maximum lamps, angled downwards. They must be switched automatically through the gearbox or by means of a manual switch incorporating a warning light. They must not be left lit when not reversing.

The full regulations are more complex than this and include exact dimensions, etc. These are just the main points of the law.

To stay legal with a fairly modern car, just ensure that all the lights fitted are working and have the headlamps aligned periodically so they won't dazzle oncoming drivers. Get the job done professionally on an optical alignment device and you'll know it's done properly.

Left: Citroën introduced a system whereby the inner pair of four headlamps turned with the steering on their DS range, and continued it on the new SM; this is a useful set-up for showing the way round a corner at night

Above: the French Citroën organisation also owns the famous Italian Maserati company, a link which is obvious from the headlamp layout on the 1974 Quattroporte; in addition to the swivelling light units, this model also has the height of sophistication in the form of headlamp wipers (lying along the top of each cluster)

and reflector design, the changing motoring scene, the increase in speed, the build-up of traffic, improvements in roads, the changing shape of the motor car and notably the vast improvement in battery and generator design, including the development of the alternator.

In addition to all these, changes in the law have played their part. Today, the law's requirements on

133

HORN

an audible warning device

Above: the kit of parts which goes to make air horns work; these horns give a high-pitched, piercing shriek and operate on a different principle from that of electric horns. When the horn button is pressed, a relay operates and switches on an air compressor; the compressor pumps air to the trumpet-like sound producers

Right: the finger is pointing to the compressor, fitted to a car; to its right is the relay; the horns are out of sight in front of the radiator

Top right: the old-fashioned bulb horn, which functions in a similar way to an air horn

BRITISH LAW REQUIRES that all motor vehicles be provided with an audible and sufficient warning unit and, in most cars, this law is observed by fitting an electric horn. The obvious alternatives are mostly illegal. Bells, sirens, gongs or two-tone horns are not allowed other than on emergency vehicles.

There are two types of electric horn, one nowadays much more popular than the other. The earlier type was known as a high-frequency horn, and the one most commonly used now is the windtone horn. The former uses an electro-magnet and contact breaker to vibrate a diaphragm and resonator; in the windtone, the job is done by the same parts minus the resonator.

The high frequency horn is usually a simple round shape and is easily recognised by the round resonator plate secured by a nut in the centre. The plate is joined to an armature and this is fixed where it passes through the centre of a metal diaphragm.

Underneath the armature is an electro-magnet attached to the back of the horn body. A set of contact breakers, also inside the horn, is wired into the circuit.

The way it works is simple. When the circuit is completed by pressing the horn button, the armature is drawn down onto the electro-magnet. This action opens the contact breaker points, the circuit is broken and the diaphragm attached to the armature reasserts itself, pulling the armature up with it. This allows the contact-breaker points to touch again. Current flows

once more, and the whole process is repeated over and over again. The rapid flexing of the diaphragm sets up a high-frequency vibration in the resonator plate. This is where the sound comes from. The diaphragm vibrates at about 300 to 400 times per second, but the frequency of resonator plate vibration is much higher. It is the combination of these two which produces the characteristic horn sound. It is really a low-frequency note with a high-frequency note superimposed. The powerful low-frequency note will carry long distances but can be lost under other low-frequency traffic rumbles. The high-frequency sound soars above traffic noise and can still be clearly heard. Often, two of these horns are wired together in the horn circuit.

The windtone horn is the horn mostly found on present-day cars. You can recognise it usually by the addition of a short, shaped trumpet extension. Like the HF type it has a diaphragm which vibrates but, instead of a resonator plate, a column of air is caused to vibrate inside the trumpet to produce the horn's note. The trumpet is involuted (rolled up) and longer than it looks. It is the length of the trumpet, together with diaphragm frequency, which produces the pitch of the note. It is pre-tuned and cannot be altered. There are normally two horns and two notes.

You can identify which horn is which quite easily. The low-pitched windtone has a longer trumpet than the high-pitched one. They are also marked L and H.

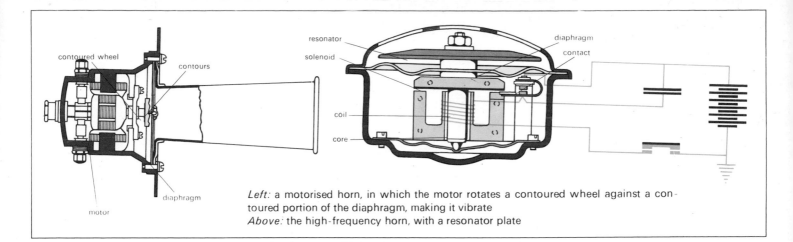

Left: a motorised horn, in which the motor rotates a contoured wheel against a contoured portion of the diaphragm, making it vibrate
Above: the high-frequency horn, with a resonator plate

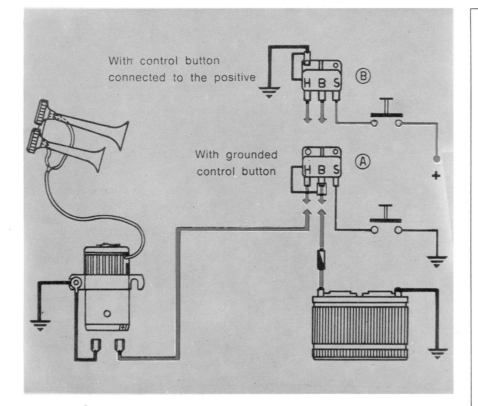

With control button connected to the positive

With grounded control button

Above: the wiring diagram for a set of air horns; a relay is used in order to reduce the load on the horn button, as the compressor will require a heavy current

If your car is fitted with one only, you can always wire a second horn in parallel.

Windtones, at one time, always included a relay in the circuit—with the idea of decreasing the voltage drop in the circuit, and because less current passes through the horn button, increasing the life of its contacts. Now, because of more efficient construction, the relay is no longer necessary.

Adjustment is possible on both HFs and windtones. On the former, it is the contact breaker that is adjusted and by this means it is possible to alter the pitch of the note. On windtones, adjustment is still to the contact breaker, but its purpose is to take up mechanical wear only, and the note will not be affected.

Air horns are more often fitted as an extra accessory than as original equipment by the manufacturer, these work on a different principle again from the previous two. They are still electrically powered and operating the horn push completes a circuit. This time, however, it drives a small compressor which supplies air under pressure to a diaphragm causing it to vibrate. The sound is pushed out through the long slim trumpets which are the most noticeable feature of air horns. These horns are usually louder and more musical in tone than other types, and sometimes a whole battery of them is used to play a tune when the horn button is operated. You might do well to take legal advice, however, before fitting these.

A klaxon, manually operated, of between 1910 and 1920

A motorised klaxon of 1914: the diaphragm is vibrated by the motor

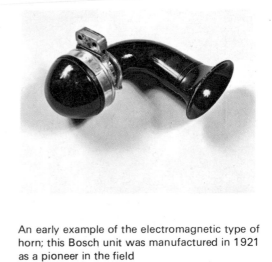

An early example of the electromagnetic type of horn; this Bosch unit was manufactured in 1921 as a pioneer in the field

STARTER

firing up the engine

THE SELF-STARTING, or cranking, motor was introduced in the 1920s when motoring began to grow in popularity and manufacturers were competing to make their cars more attractive to the would-be purchaser. Previously, turning the starting-handle or pushing the car, with the gears engaged were the only methods of starting the engine. Most motorists were only too pleased to adopt the new device, although the starting-handle was retained as a ready stand-by for another thirty years or more.

The heaviest load on a starter motor occurs when it first turns the engine from rest; this is known as the 'breakaway' torque. After this first movement, the 'resisting' torque comes into effect. For an average-sized engine, the initial current required to overcome the breakaway torque is approximately 450 amperes for a 12-volt system, falling to about 250 amperes at an engine speed of 1000 rpm. This means that, however large and powerful the starter, both the battery and its connecting cables must be adequate to supply this heavy starting current; and the starter motor must always be considered in relation to the battery and associated wiring.

The components of the breakaway torque consist of the inertia of the engine, which depends upon its size; the friction of the cylinder walls and bearings; and the viscosity of the lubricating oil, which depends partly on the grade of oil and partly on its temperature.

A cranking speed of 70 to 100 rpm is usually sufficient for a petrol engine to draw in an ignitable petrol/air mixture, to start firing and to run up on its own. Diesel engines require a higher cranking speed and a longer starter engagement period.

Starter motors are invariably series wound: that is to say, the field coils and armature are continuous, the same current flowing through each. This type of motor delivers its highest torque at low speeds, so that it is ideal for overcoming the breakaway torque at its maximum efficiency.

The transmission of the turning moment of the motor to the engine is accomplished by mounting a ring gear on the outer edge of the engine flywheel, so that it can be engaged by a small pinion on the end of the starter-motor shaft. The gear reduction ratio is large, usually between 10:1 and 15:1. The leading edges of the pinion teeth are chamfered to facilitate their engagement.

To keep the two gears permanently engaged would result in a waste of power and possible damage, so a device is incorporated that disengages the pinion when not actually performing its starting function. This device operates as follows: with the engine stationary, the starter switch is operated and the motor revolves, accelerating rapidly. The pinion, turning on helical splines (coarse screw threads) on an extension of the motor armature shaft, spins away from the motor as the result of its own inertia to engage in the flywheel at the end of its travel. When the engine fires and runs up to a speed greater than the starter speed, the pinion is

Below left: a modern starter motor of the pre-engaged type; instead of spinning into mesh, the pinion is engaged by a solenoid; this solenoid also controls the motor itself, so that it does not work until the pinion is fully engaged

Below: many early racing cars did not have built-in starter motors, so an external starter was used in much the same way as a handle might be; three Mercedes M154s are shown at Tripoli in the 1938 Grand Prix

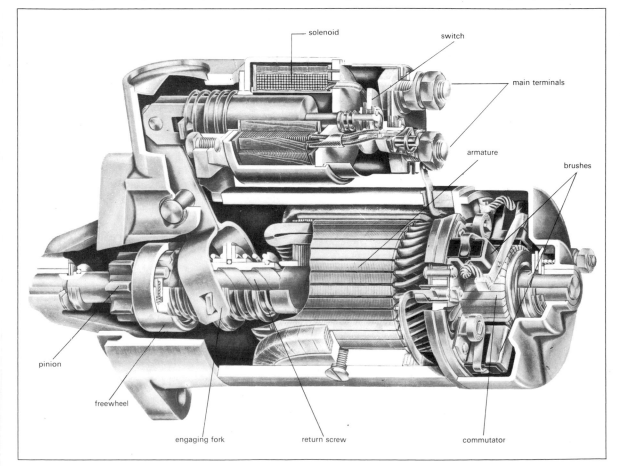

solenoid — switch — main terminals — armature — brushes — pinion — freewheel — engaging fork — return screw — commutator

COPYRIGHT DI F. ZAGARI

automatically thrown out of engagement with the flywheel ring gear and rapidly travels back along the helical splines.

As can be imagined, the shock of the first engagement of the two gears is considerable. To overcome engine speed is nevertheless greater than that of the starter motor and the pinion is thrown out of mesh. This state is known as premature ejection and is particularly troublesome with light flywheel engines. If the starter switch is immediately operated with the engine still turning, the motor can be heard whirring round while the starter pinion grates against the flywheel gear, unable to engage.

To overcome this defect, the *pre-engaged* starter was developed; in this type, the pinion remains engaged until, with the engine running evenly, the starter switch is released.

Additional components are required for the pre-engaged starter; these are a solenoid, which actuates an engagement lever, and an overrunning roller clutch assembly. A feature of the latest type of motor is the face-type commutator, which has four brushes mounted on the motor end plate. This commutator has a lower rate of brush wear, greater reliability and is cheaper to manufacture than the still more common barrel type.

When the starter switch is operated, the solenoid is energised and the engagement lever moves the starter pinion along its shaft until it is fully meshed with the flywheel ring gear. At the completion of this movement, the lever operates a switch that closes the motor/battery circuit and the motor turns the pinion. The pinion can be held in mesh until the engine has overcome any initial hesitation, so that premature ejection is prevented.

If the engine overspeeds in relation to the starter motor, the pinion is not thrown out of engagement, as with the inertia starter, but the clutch disengages, acting as a freewheel device.

To overcome the difficulty that can arise if the pinion teeth butt exactly against the teeth of the flywheel ring gear and are unable to enter into mesh, the starter-motor pinion is actually driven through the spring.

This design constitutes the original American Bendix drive and it and similar arrangements are 'outboard meshed'; that is, the pinion moves away from the motor towards the flywheel on engagement.

A British variation is 'inboard meshed'. This starter is positioned so that the flywheel ring gear lies between the starter motor and the pinion. The starter motor rotates a sleeve splined on its inner surface mating with splines on the armature shaft. The outer surface of the sleeve has helical splines, similar to the Bendix, and the pinion rides on the sleeve. On switching on, the inertia of the pinion throws it into mesh with the flywheel ring gear, but the reverse thrust so generated forces the sleeve back against a compression spring, to absorb the considerable shock of engagement.

The advantage of this inboard meshed design is that the shaft between the motor and the pinion is very much shorter and more rigid, for a given diameter, than the outboard meshed type.

Both the American and British variants are known as *inertia engaged* starters. There have been various developments from time to time, one of the most important being the Eclipse and barrel drives, in which the pinion is mounted on the closed end of a separate member. This enables the pinion size to be reduced and the starter-to-engine gear ratio increased lessening the enormous initial exertion of the starter.

Other additions include an anti-drift spring to prevent the pinion working forward along the helical

threads and into contact with the flywheel, and a spring to prevent the pinion from bouncing back when it is ejected by the flywheel.

Inertia engaged starters are still widely used today engagement lever is spring loaded. This allows the lever to over-reach and close the starter-motor contacts, thus turning the motor so that the pinion can slide into mesh.

In larger engines, a dry-plate clutch is often employed instead of the roller type.

It will be clear that 'outboard meshing' must be used with this pre-engaged type of clutch; however, the long tension spring of the Bendix type is not required and the overall shaft length is no greater than that of the inboard meshing type.

Mechanical methods of starting are occasionally employed. The *spring starter* consists of a large 'clockwork' spring, wound up by a handle and ratchet device and released by a press button. This will deliver sufficient stored energy, through a gear train, to turn the engine over for several revolutions.

In another type, a rope is used to draw a spring-return rack across a pinion attached to the engine, or a ratchet wheel is employed in a similar manner.

Cold-weather starting

There are three main causes for starting difficulties in very cold weather:

1. Increased viscosity of the lubricating oil, hence higher breakaway and resisting torques. This problem can be largely overcome by the use of multigrade oils, the viscosity of which does not markedly increase at low temperatures.

2. Reduced output from the battery, because chemical reactions within the battery are slowed down by low temperatures. This, coupled with the increased effort required to turn the engine over, means that less current is available to operate the ignition system

so only a weak spark appears at the spark points.

With a 6-volt battery, the voltage available to feed the ignition system under a heavy starting current drain diminishes almost to vanishing point; for this reason, amongst others, most manufacturers have changed to 12-volt systems, which provide a greater margin under these conditions.

3. The lower cranking speed means that less petrol/air mixture is drawn into the cylinder, and much of the petrol is not properly vaporised. The use of the carburettor choke overcomes the fuel deficiency, but not the lack of vaporisation, hence the danger that too much use of the choke will tend to wash the lubricating oil film off the cylinder walls.

Starter motors rarely give trouble: one of the most common with the inertia engaged type is the jamming of the pinion in the fully meshed position. The starter motor is unable to turn because the torque required is too great—it has no opportunity to spin up from rest, as in normal starting. The remedy is either to turn the motor shaft with a spanner (the shaft has a square end, protruding from the motor case, for this purpose), or to switch off, engage gear and push the car to and fro. Both methods release the pinion and wind it back clear of the flywheel.

Road dirt thrown up onto the sleeve is obviously undesirable; the best remedy is to fit a light gauge protective shield. Subject to manufacturer's recommendations, the only lubrication required is a little light oil on the sleeve. The motor armature shaft bearings are usually supported in sintered metal bushes and do not require lubrication.

When a roller clutch is fitted, it should not be cleaned out with solvent as this would wash away the grease with which it is prepacked.

If the battery is clearly failing, as evidenced by increasingly sluggish action on first starting up, the only remedy is to replace it.

Below: the most common type of starter used for many years was this, with a Bendix gear arrangement which spins the pinion into mesh with the flywheel ring gear as soon as the motor turns and out of mesh as soon as engine speed exceeds motor speed

BRAKES, STEERING & SUSPENSION

BRAKES & BRAKING

stopping a car efficiently

BRAKES ARE devices for retarding or stopping a vehicle, usually by checking the rotation of some or all wheels. Although there have been instances of this work being allotted to electromagnetic eddy couplings, air compressors or even retro-rockets, the friction brake has been the only wholly successful means since the beginnings of motoring. In this type of brake, the energy of motion must be translated completely into heat energy, so that the efficiency of the brake depends entirely on how quickly this translation takes place and how quickly the heat is dissipated.

Early adaptations of horse-drawn vehicle practice, with a friction block rubbing on the rim of a road wheel, were soon abandoned on early motor vehicles. Flexible bands, lined with a friction material such as leather, were wrapped around drums attached to the wheels (or to a live axle) and tightened by the action of the driver's brake lever or pedal. These external-contracting or 'band' brakes survived, notably in the USA, until the 1920s. Long before then, the internal-expanding drum brake was proved much more effective: in it, rigid metal segments or shoes faced with friction material were pressed against the interior cylindrical surface of the drum, from which dirt, moisture and other contaminants might be excluded more effectively.

Above: a set of linings, ready to be fitted to brake shoes. The asbestos used is the best friction material and the fibres are moulded or woven into a resin matrix

Right: the massive drum brake at the front of Ferrari's 1953 GP car. The edge of the drum was finned for extra cooling. It was not long before discs had ousted drums on Formula One cars (Jaguar had used them in the 1952 Mille Miglia)

It was soon recognised that the best friction material was asbestos; and so it remains to this day, the fibres being moulded or woven densely in a resin matrix, sometimes with inclusions of copper, zinc or aluminium to ensure high-temperature stability. Other design features, intended to help dissipate the heat built up during braking, included the use of high-conductivity alloys for the shoes and drums, as well as finning and ventilation of the latter. If the brake becomes too hot, the friction material is likely to lose its efficiency, and hydraulic brake fluid may boil.

Drum brakes remain in use today, and only in the details of their construction do they differ from the earliest examples. Such alterations have been made to improve power, stability of performance or behaviour at high temperatures—but to some extent, the requirements of these factors are mutually exclusive. Thus a large-diameter brake is more powerful than a smaller one, but more affected by thermal expansion which causes the drum and shoes to adopt different radii and thus to lose contact over most of the friction area. More power was therefore sought from a drum brake of a given size, and this was found by exploiting the self-operating tendency of a shoe pivoted about its trailing end. Originally, the usual two shoes were forced apart and into contact with the drum by a single wedge or cam: the relative motion of the drum was accordingly from leading end to pivot for one shoe, and opposite for the other. By placing the shoe pivots diametrically opposite each other and using two cams, both shoes can be given the same action; and the twin-leading-shoe brake, in which both shoes do equal shares of work and tend to fit themselves more firmly against the drum surface, when applied, has proved more powerful. It is also more fierce and more sensitive to heat, but only in cars employing strong servo assistance (a servo derives power from the engine to boost the effort of the driver's leg) could the more stable but less powerful alternative of two trailing shoes be used for all four wheels. To give adequate braking response when the car is travelling in reverse, the rear brakes usually remain of the one-leading/one-trailing variety. Because of weight transfer onto the front wheels during deceleration, the front brakes bear the brunt of the work when the car is braked from high speeds, and this compromise is fairly satisfactory, but a very few cars (notably in racing, where stability and freedom from grab are most important) have had parallel-action shoes which are moved strictly radially against the drum surface.

The degradation of braking performance at high temperatures remains an insoluble problem of the drum brake. The shoes and linings are difficult to cool, heat distorts the drums, differential thermal expansion impairs good contact between drum and linings, and the resulting local high pressures and temperatures can cause temporary loss of friction in the linings, producing a form of failure known as fade. In the 1950s, the disc brake was adopted: it was an adaptation of the type already developed in aviation, where the same problems had beset heavy bombers twenty years earlier.

The principle of the disc brake was not new, occasional examples being tried in motor cycles in the 1920s and in machine tools even earlier. It substituted a flat disc for the drum, and the faces of this disc were nipped between fairly small pads of friction material, carried by a suitably robust 'caliper'. In such a brake, there is no danger from expansion of the heated disc, which remains flat; the pads are flat and small, avoiding risks of distortion there. All surfaces subjected to frictional heat are exposed to the air, the greater part of the

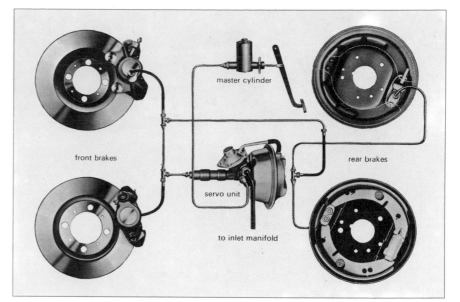

Above: a typical hydraulic-brake layout. The servo is vacuum operated, the vacuum being created in the inlet manifold

Left: there are two basic types of drum brake: single-leading shoe (above), where one cylinder operates both shoes, and twin-leading shoe (below), where there is a separate hydraulic cylinder for each shoe, so that the movable end of each faces against drum rotation

disc surface being free to shed its heat even during braking when only a small portion of it is being masked and heated by the pads. The disc may even be 'ventilated'. In this case it's two faces are separated by radial passages, open to the air at the outer edge, thus promoting an internal flow of cooling air.

A disc brake possesses no self-wrapping or unwrapping tendencies. In other words, it has no self-servo effect. Because of this and of the relatively small size of the friction pads, considerable force is needed to

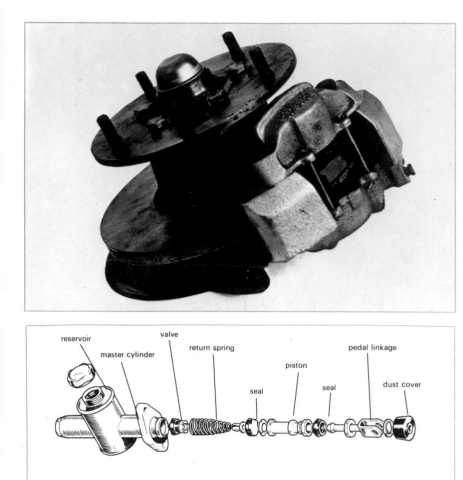

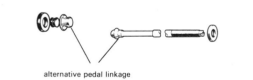

reservoir   valve
master cylinder   return spring   pedal linkage
piston
seal   seal   dust cover

alternative pedal linkage

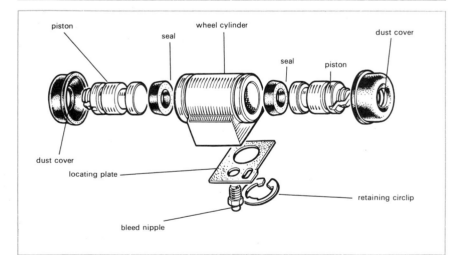

piston   wheel cylinder   dust cover
seal
seal   piston
dust cover
locating plate
retaining circlip
bleed nipple

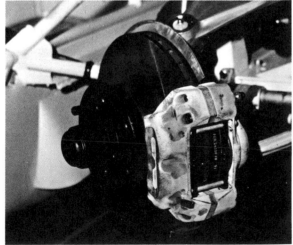

depressed, it moves the piston in the master cylinder and sends special fluid down a pipe to the 'slave cylinders' fitted to each brake. Their pistons move a corresponding amount (the liquid is incompressible) and movement is communicated to the shoes or pads.

This type of brake had been used earlier by some makers; some were even literally hydraulic, employing water as the fluid, as in the Grand Prix Duesenberg and Bugatti of 1921 and 1922 respectively. Nowadays, the fluids used are made just for that job, having a boiling point considerably higher than that of water. If the fluid boils, it forms vapour locks in the system and the compressible nature of these leads, at best, to a 'spongy' pedal and, at worst, to a complete loss of braking action.

The disc brake brought, in its turn, a widespread adoption of servo aids, usually energised by engine inlet manifold depression—although this form of so-called vacuum servo was displaced, as early as 1955, by an engine-pumped, high-pressure, 'powered hydraulic' system in the then new Citroën DS and, in a slightly simpler form, in racing Jaguars two years earlier.

Considerable development work has refined the disc brake in every detail since its introduction, but the principles have remained intact. More change has been apparent in the operating system, as always throughout the history of motoring. In the pioneer days, brakes were applied to the rear wheels only, through linkages worked by hand or foot. Four-wheel brakes appeared in 1909, to become general by 1930—by which time mechanical servo motors, driven off the gearbox, had become a popular feature of heavy luxury cars and most Grand Prix racers. By this time, too, it was a general practical or legal requirement that a car should have primary and secondary braking systems, the former applying all four brakes in response to the pedal, the latter applying two (usually checking the rear wheels) via a hand lever and being used for parking or to supplement a weak pedal system. This division of primary and secondary systems has been obscured by more recent legislative requirements for

squeeze them against the disc and an operating system of great efficiency and minimal lost motion or backlash is essential if slight wear of the pads is not to be translated into unacceptable travel of the driver's pedal. It was the widespread adoption of hydraulics for brake operation that made the use of disc brakes feasible in the 1950s, when it would have been beyond the capabilities of the mechanical systems generally favoured earlier. These hydraulic brakes have a 'master cylinder' connected to the brake pedal. When the pedal is

two separate circuits, designed to retain balanced and safely distributed braking action in response to the pedal, even if one circuit should, for some reason, fail.

Other recent developments include mechanical, hydraulic, pneumatic or electronic sensors to detect incipient wheel-lock during braking and inhibit it automatically, so as to reduce the risk of skidding on slippery surfaces; and the more general adoption of powered hydraulics is being energetically propounded by some manufacturers.

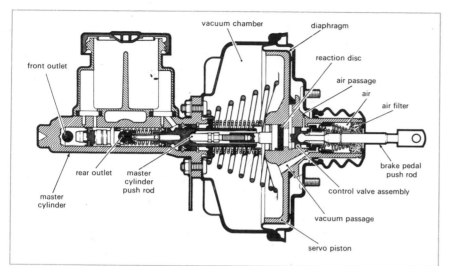

Above: a sectional drawing showing the important components of a Lockheed vacuum servo. The hydraulic systems in this unit are split so that either the front or rear brakes will continue to work should the other pair fail

Right: a pair of disc-brake pads; the linings are similar to those for shoes, but they are always bonded to the backing material. Changing disc pads is far simpler than changing shoes, as there is no brake drum to be removed the pads being slid into the caliper

Top far left: the disc brake was widely adopted for car use in the '50s, although the idea had been tried, on motor cycles, in the '20s

Centre and bottom far left: exploded diagrams of typical master and wheel cylinders used in a hydraulic system

Left: in recent years, racing and high-performance cars have become so fast that solid discs cannot dissipate heat quickly enough. The solution has been found in separating the two friction surfaces of the disc, thereby adding ventilation

THE ART OF STOPPING

DECELERATION IS a state of affairs, but phenomena associated with the design of the vehicle or the state of the road may transform it into an event. The steady-state condition is rather rare and the occasions when a constant rate of deceleration is achieved by a constant pressure on the brake pedal occur very seldom on the road, though most drivers are unconscious of their instinctive modulations of braking effort and steering to correct losses of equilibrium.

For a start—for a stop?—do not kick the brake pedal hard, even for an emergency. Squeeze it gradually from the slightest pressure to as much as it will take without the wheels locking. This precaution need occupy only a fraction of a second, but if omitted the result will probably be a skid—straight ahead if the front wheels lock together, sideways if the rear wheels or only one wheel should lock. More sensitive treatment of the pedal allows all wheels to be held just short of locking point, which yields optimum braking: one of the many peculiarities of the tyre is that it gives maximum retardation when slipping by about 11%, so that at 50 mph the brakes should be holding the wheels back to a rate of rotation equivalent to 44 mph. Overstep this mark and the rate of retardation falls

dramatically and dangerously: what tyre technicians call the 'peak-to-locked ratio' varies from about 1.5 at 30 mph to as much as 8 at 80 mph, which means that the stopping distance is multiplied correspondingly when the car is sliding on locked wheels. Sensitive gradation of pedal pressure allows the driver to feel just how much braking the road surface will allow—and it is worth remembering that roads have many different characteristics, especially when wet: some offer only a twentieth as much grip as others.

If the wheels on one side of the car are on a wet surface and those on the other side are on a dry one, then strong braking will cause the tyres on the more slippery side to lock prematurely and the car will, if unchecked, go into a spin. Once again it is necessary to ease the brakes as the wheels begin to lock, and then apply them firmly again, repeating the sequence as often and as rapidly as required; and in this particular case some steering correction will be wanted as well.

Supposing that the road surface is good and the tyres and brakes are in perfect condition, what can be achieved? The classical laws of physics show that it is impossible to achieve a deceleration greater than the acceleration due to gravity, which is approximately 32 feet per second per second and equivalent to stopping in 30 feet from 30 mph. The classical laws of physics are fortunately wrong—or rather, inadequate, since they do not take such phenomena as tyre hysteresis (or energy absorption) into account. Current racing cars are capable of braking 1.7 times harder—we express this as 1.7g—and figures as high as 2.2g have been recorded. Nevertheless 1g is about the limit for most ordinary roadgoing cars in current production.

Fade is a condition that affects brakes when they are overheated by excessive use. It is a loss of braking power that may build up progressively or manifest itself quite suddenly—depending *inter alia* on the nature of the friction material used for brake linings or pads. Frequent heavy use of the brakes, as when driving hard down a twisting hill, is the most likely cause; but it can also be brought about by continuous gentle use of the brakes (as when checking the car's speed down a long, steep hill) because if they are worked without relief they have no opportunity to shed the heat that builds up in them.

Drum brakes are more sensitive than discs to heat, and give a more tangible warning of their loss of effectiveness by increased pedal travel. The feel of such a system has its antithesis in a powered-hydraulic disc system (such as that of the larger Citroëns) in which there is no pedal movement at all, the control responding purely to pressure. Brake response is something that has to be learnt empirically in each car: in one, the rate of retardation may increase progressively (that is, 50 lb force at the pedal will achieve deceleration twice as rapid as 25 lb force), but in another the increase may be disproportional. With practice, the driver's foot learns sensitivity to these things.

Another technique that needs practised acquisition before employment on the public highway is heel-and-toe braking. Here, the heel (or side) of the braking foot is applied to the accelerator at the appropriate time to accelerate the engine for a downward gear-change while braking is maintained. The object is not to supplement the brakes by engine braking, but to ensure that braking may continue uninterrupted by the necessity for effecting a downward change of gear for whatever reason. Engine braking can certainly be useful—it is a valuable adjunct to smooth driving—but it is not a particularly economical or efficient method of slowing down. With some forms of automatic

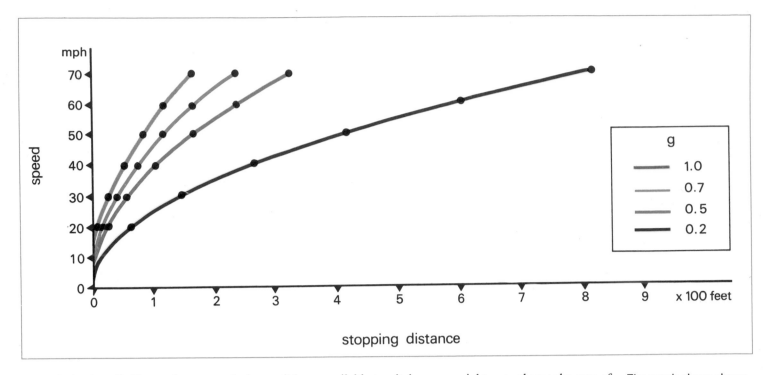

stopping distance

transmission installed it may, in any case, be impossible.

Many of the finer points of braking technique are bound up with the behaviour of the car on its suspension (including the tyres) when the brakes are in use. The most obvious effect is that of forward weight transfer: because the centre of gravity of the car is above the level of the road (where the braking force is applied in the contact area between road and tyres), there is a tendency for the car to tip forwards when decelerating. The higher the centre of gravity, or the shorter the distance between it and the front wheels, the greater this nose-down pitch will be. Its effect is to increase the load on the front tyres and commensurately to decrease that on the rear tyres; and from this it may be deduced that the harder the braking, the more of it the front brakes and tyres have to do and the less those at the rear can do, until the limit is reached where the rear tyres are off the road and the front wheels are doing all the braking.

This is why front brakes are commonly larger and more powerful than back brakes. Some cars enjoy the refinement of a pressure-limiting device which reduces the braking effort applied to the rear brakes in proportion to the load carried by the rear tyres: this is mechanically operated by a linkage which measures the extension of the rear suspension. An inferior substitute for such a mechanism is the process known as 'cadence braking', in which the driver is recommended to increase his braking effort to the wheel-locking maximum as the nose of the car pitches downward, and then to release the brakes and allow it to recover its equilibrium before repeating the cycle. The process is self-defeating: if the pitch frequency is low, too much time will be lost in the non-braking portion of the cycle, and if the pitch frequency is high enough to overcome this objection it will be too rapid for the driver to match it effectively.

A more complex aspect of weight transfer is introduced by the tyres. The more heavily they are laden, the more braking effort they can transmit—but only up to a certain point, beyond which further increases of load effect no further improvement. A car designed to exploit forward weight transfer in braking may not be able to achieve it in slippery conditions, when the front tyres skid before a high enough braking force is available to pitch more weight onto them: the rate of deceleration is then limited to what the front tyres can achieve in this lightly-laden state. This used to be a common failing of tail-heavy cars.

Weight transfer effected by braking will alter the cornering ability of all four tyres, and lateral weight transfer to the tyres on the outside of a corner will alter the braking ability. Depending on the generosity of the tyre size in relation to the load they carry, and also on the state of the road surface, a car's cornering ability may be increased or decreased by braking while cornering—and it will also depend on the severity of the braking. Skilled competition drivers may use the brakes to reduce or increase understeer right up to the apex of a corner, or indeed to produce any desired effect from a stright-forwards slide to a full spin. The latter is in fact a very effective way of stopping a car in the shortest possible distance, but it is emphatically not a technique for the road car, which may easily overturn in the attempt. The ordinary driver is better advised to stick to the time-honoured advice to get all his braking done while travelling in a straight line before the corner, and to leave the brakes alone while going round it. He would also do well to remember that when the front wheels have been locked by heavy braking, they can do no steering.

What if the brakes fail? At times like these, it pays to be one of the specially skilled fraternity. Changing down to as low a gear as can be reached and relying on engine braking is all very well if there is plenty of room to slow down, but there seldom is enough for such gentle deceleration and it might be necessary to take to the hedgerows or scrape the side of the car against a wall or (best of all) a snowdrift. Such facilities are not always available, alas, and that is when the skilled driver scores: using the handbrake hard enough to lock the rear wheels may not achieve much retardation (handbrakes seldom achieve better than 0.25g) but in conjunction with nicely timed steering he may be able to slew the car sideways or spin it, exploiting the lateral scrubbing of the tyres to slow the car while the gyration itself dissipates some kinetic energy. You see, advanced driving skills are worth acquiring; but the only safe place to do so is on the skid pan of an advanced driving school.

The graph above shows how stopping distances, at different speeds, vary with the retarding force. 'g' represents the acceleration due to gravity, which is approximately 32 feet per second per second. 1.0 g is the theoretical maximum which can be obtained, but in practice as much as 2.2 g has been recorded

EVERY CAR MADE TODAY, no matter where, is fitted with hydraulic brakes in which movement of the brake pedal is transmitted to each brake by means of a liquid. Liquids are incompressible, so that there is no 'play' between pedal and brake. However, gases can be compressed, so that any air that finds its way into the system takes up some of the pedal movement and leads to a spongy feel. The greater the amount of air, the greater the loss of efficiency.

Bleeding the brakes

All the hydraulic-brake manufacturers allow for the removal of air by building bleed nipples into each wheel cylinder. By unscrewing these about half a turn, the air can be pumped out. The procedure for carrying out bleeding is fairly standard for all makes of car, although a servo will have to be bled separately.

If any of the brakes are drums, the adjusters should be tightened as far as possible before starting the air removal process. Starting with the brake farthest from the master cylinder, the car should be jacked up and the wheel removed. Having made sure that the master cylinder is topped up with the recommended fluid, the bleed nipple should be loosened using a special spanner.

A rubber tube should be placed over the nipple, with its lower end in a jar of clean fluid so that air cannot be sucked in.

Depressing the pedal firmly and releasing it slowly will pump fluid and air out of the nipple. When air bubbles cease to appear at the end of the tube, the pedal should be held down and the nipple tightened.

This procedure should be repeated at each wheel, topping up the master cylinder each time, working towards the cylinder. Finally the brakes should be correctly adjusted (free the adjusters until the wheels turn easily).

It is obvious from the above description that this job requires two people. However, it is possible to obtain a set of special bleed nipples with valves which obviate the need for a tube and a jar of fluid. The only snag is that it becomes a matter of trial and error to remove all traces of air.

Any fluid into which air has been passed should be allowed to stand for some days before it is re-used,

BRAKE REPAIR

maintaining stopping power

because some of the air will have been absorbed.

Renewing hydraulic brake seals

There must be a reason for air in the hydraulic system. Unless there is a loose connection somewhere, the chances are that the air is leaking in round the seals in the wheel cylinders.

Usually, this leakage will be accompanied by a loss of fluid, indicated by dampness round the offending unit or components.

Once the faulty cylinder has been traced, it should be removed. For drum brakes this means taking the brake drum off and removing the shoes before starting on the cylinder itself. Drum-brake cylinders are usually held on by a circlip or by a nut, and the hydraulic pipe should be unscrewed before the fixings are tackled. Discs are easier, since the wheel is usually all that need be removed before attention is turned to the cylinder(s) which are situated within the caliper. In most cases, the caliper is attached by two bolts, although, once again, the hydraulic pipe should be removed before the fixings are undone.

Disc-brake pads can be left in when removing the caliper, but it is best to remove them before reassembly, as they may catch on the edge of the disc.

Drum and disc-brake cylinders have a fundamental difference in that the fluid seals for a drum are fitted to the piston while that or those for a disc are fitted to the cylinder. However, servicing procedures are similar.

Repair kits can be purchased for a small amount of

Below: when bleeding the air from the hydraulic-brake system, the bleed nipple should be loosened and the pedal depressed while a tube affixed to the nipple is led into a jar of clean brake fluid; once bubbles cease to appear, the pedal should be held down and the nipple tightened

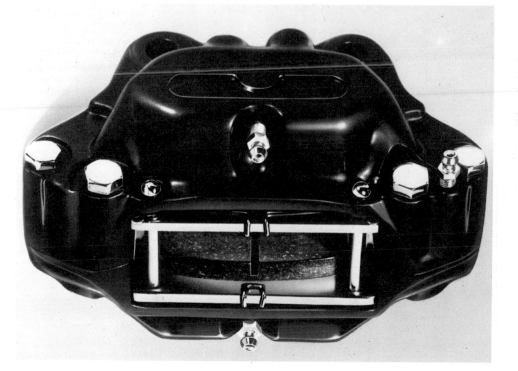

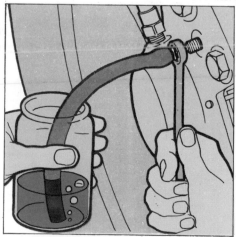

Left: a disc-brake caliper assembly of the modern type; the pads can be seen in their slots, retained by two pins (the disc would normally be between them) and three bleed nipples are provided, in order to rid the system of as much air as possible

money from most accessory shops. These comprise new fluid seals, new dust covers and any circlips or retainers necessary. There is often a tube of rubber grease supplied with the kit as well as a cover for the bleed nipple.

With drum-brake wheel cylinders, the piston or pistons (depending on whether the brake is twin or single-leading shoe) can be pulled from the cylinder. If there is any resistance, then the hydraulic pipe can be re-connected and the offending parts freed by pumping the brake pedal.

The cylinder and its pistons should be cleaned with a clean, dry cloth; any corrosion in the cylinder can be smoothed down by using fine abrasive such as metal polish. If the cylinder is scored, then new seals will not cure any fluid leak, the only answer being to replace the whole cylinder assembly. Having fitted the new seals, assuming the old cylinder is being retained, the parts should be liberally coated in new brake fluid of the correct type before they are reassembled. Don't forget to replace the dust covers which prevent dirt and moisture creeping between piston and cylinder

and causing corrosion.

When fitting seals, be very careful not to overstretch them or break them; be especially careful not to cut them while using an implement to prise them out of their grooves.

Discs can be slightly more complicated. The manufacturers are firm in their recommendation that the calipers are not dismantled, so that there is not much space in which to remove the pistons. Once again, should they stick, hydraulic pressure should free them, but perseverance is often the order of the day for this task as with many others.

The cleaning procedure is the same as for drum brakes, although seal-fitting is easier, because it or they fit in a groove or grooves in the cylinder wall. Pistons are usually chrome plated, so if they are corroded they should really be replaced. They can be bought as separate items and are not expensive.

Once the braking system has been reassembled and reconnected, the air will have to be removed, using the process already described. By the way, don't spill fluid on the paint, it is highly corrosive.

Left: a single-leading-shoe set-up in use on the rear of a Sunbeam Rapier

Below left: disc brakes are self-adjusting, as are some drums, but most drum brakes are adjusted by turning the square knob with a spanner

Below centre: disc brakes have between one and six pistons per caliper unit, but the principle is always the same, there being four important sections in each unit

Below: the components of a typical hydraulic wheel cylinder, as used on many drum-brake set-ups

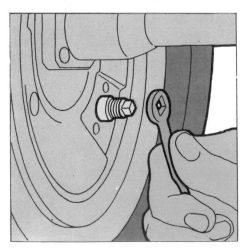

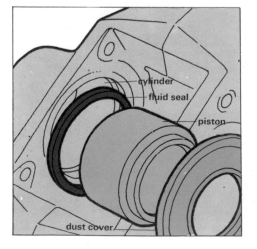

STEERING

a matter of course

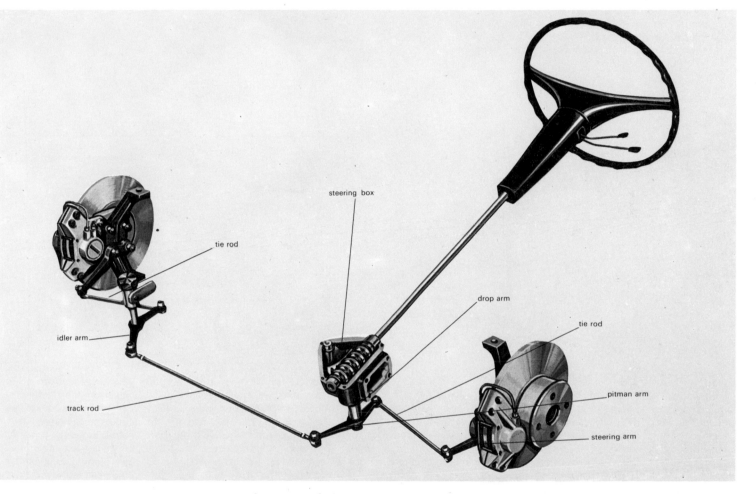

steering box

tie rod

idler arm

track rod

drop arm

tie rod

pitman arm

steering arm

PROVIDING MEANS FOR TURNING the front wheels of a car to right or left in order to steer it would not be at all difficult were it not also necessary to make provision for their movement up and down with the suspension system. When those front wheels were mounted at the extremities of a rigid beam axle, as was general practice until the late 1930s, the independence of the two systems—steering and suspension—remained fairly easily ensured. When the front wheels were independently sprung, it followed that the distance between them could vary with different degrees and divisions of front suspension deflection, as for example in unilateral bump or in roll; and steering gear then took on a complexity that was for a while the ruination of many cars and remains the bane of some.

Given a beam front axle, not much more is required: a couple of steering arms rigidly attached to the hubs, a track rod to connect them through flexible joints at its extremities, and a three-bar linkage connecting one hub to the steering gearbox, was all that was necessary apart from the conventional steering column and wheel, though in very early days the wheel was not

entirely conventional, and some designers, such as Lanchester, preferred the tiller.

Even with this simple arrangement, mistakes could be made. The middle portion of the three-bar linkage, called the drag link, caused most trouble, because it swung about the tip of the drop arm from the steering box in an arc that did not correspond with the path of the axle moving up and down on its springs, so there could be some fight between the steering and the wheels. Making the drag link long was a palliative that sometimes worked, but at others caused problems due to flexure of this long unsupported bar; shifting the steering box right forward close to the axle, and having a transverse drag link, often caused more wheel fight than it cured, though it sometimes saved space. Either way, the fight could be seen and felt by the driver: the wheel would twitch and judder in his hands, which could become bruised or blistered if he held on too tightly.

It was clearly necessary to give the steering gear a partially irreversible characteristic, so that it was reasonably efficient in transmitting effort from his hands to the front wheels, but much less efficient when

A diagram showing the steering connections from the worm-and-sector steering box to the wheels of an independent-suspension system

147

transmitting shocks from them back to the driver. This was usually achieved in the steering gearbox which was popularly based upon the principle of worm and wheel gearing: a little friction in this would provide the uni-directional characteristics desired. Moreover, the greater the numerical ratio of the gears, the more naturally irreversible did such a mechanism become, and within limits the effects of such gearing could be offset by adjustments to the geometry of the three-bar linkage, usually by lengthening the drop arm—which, on sparsely bodied sports cars, was visible from outside and became a styling feature.

In any case, some reduction gearing was necessary between the handwheel and the steered wheels, to give the former a suitable mechanical advantage by reducing the forces necessary to steer the car (especially at low speeds) and to prevent the steering being too

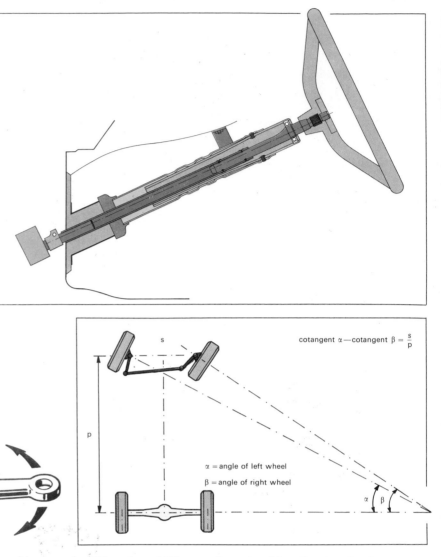

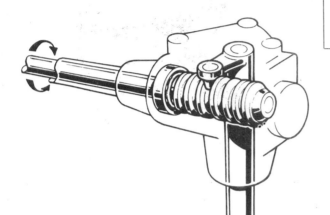

sensitive when the car was going quickly.

When cars were light and tyres slender, not very much reduction gearing was necessary. Racing cars and sports cars of the early days had quite high geared steering, only about one and a half turns of the handwheel being necessary to go from one extreme of lock to the other. Big heavy cars needed lower geared steering, but even they managed to get along with perhaps three turns from lock to lock, and if the steering was still heavy it was assumed that one would hire a chauffeur strong enough to manage it. The expression of the steering ratio in terms of handwheel turns from lock to lock was not, incidentally, universal practice, for it did not tell the whole story: steering needing three turns lock-to-lock was obviously higher geared in a car with a 35 ft turning circle than in one with a 40 ft turning circle, for example. Many people preferred to quote a steering ratio that explained how many degrees of movement were necessary at the handwheel to one degree of movement by the front wheels: if one and a half turns of the former turned the latter through 45 degrees, the steering ratio would be expressed as 12:1. This ought to be high geared by modern standards, when something between 16 and 24:1 is more normal; but the ratio still does not tell the whole story, for the degree to which the front wheels are turned has to be related to the length of the wheelbase to determine the radius of the curve that the car would describe.

Everything took a turn for the worse when independent front suspension was introduced. With a few

notable exceptions (Lancia and Morgan, for example) the old simple track rod could no longer be used because it would foul the suspension linkages as they moved. Instead, the steering linkage had to be divided into three parts, the outer ones involving tie rods that ideally (but very seldom) were the same effective length as the suspension arms and would pivot in similar arcs, while the arms to which they were connected were linked through the steering gearbox and an idler bearing to a track rod across the width of the chassis frame. The result was a hideous proliferation of bearings and ball joints that wore and grew sloppy with amazing speed, while the steering geometry was debased in nearly all suspension systems that did not employ equal parallel wishbones, because the tie rods moved in arcs that did not correspond with those of the wheel as the springs flexed. Only if the tie rods were directly in front of or behind one of the wishbones in any other system would the steering geometry remain accurate throughout the suspension travel, and somehow it was seldom possible to arrange this. The same problem beset the relatively simple linkage associated with the trailing-link independent front suspension devised by Ferdinand Porsche for the Auto-Union GP car and the Volkswagen: in this layout, as in others, it became common practice for an hydraulic damper to be attached to the steering mechanism to take out road shocks before they could reach the steering column.

For obvious reasons a greater degree of irreversibility was now desirable in the steering gear, and for

Top: in a head-on collision, the steering wheel can cause serious injury to the driver; in order to reduce this risk, many steering columns are manufactured so that they can telescope (the plastic plugs—red for the outer column and black for the inner—will shear and allow the two parts to collapse)

Above left: a see-through drawing of a cam-and-peg steering box, with the column on the left

Above: according to Lankensperger, the inner wheel should follow a tighter circle than the outer one for perfect steering; ideally, lines drawn perpendicular to each front wheel should converge on a line extended from the back axle

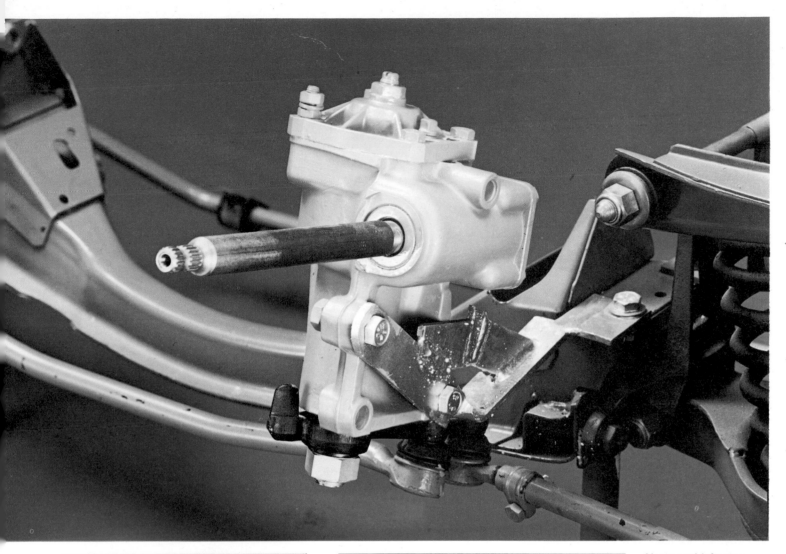

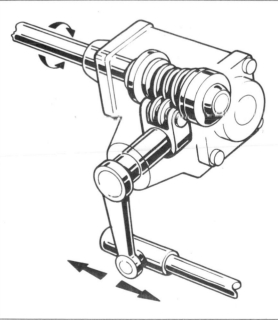

Above and left: two views of the worm-and-roller steering set-up, the photograph being of a unit as fitted to a Fiat-Abarth 124 Rally

Far left: the most convenient type of swivel joint to use on steering linkage is the ball and socket; a typical track-rod end is seen cutaway to show the spring-loaded ball in its socket

the same reason as before a lowering of the steering ratio (to a higher numerical ratio) was a palliative to which many designers resorted. It was often desirable for another reason, this being that the adoption of independent front suspension encouraged the location of the engine much further forward in the chassis now that room could be liberated for it by the elimination of the old transverse beam axle. As a result there was now more weight over the front wheels, and steering became heavier, so that a greater reduction in gearing was the only way to keep the handwheel manageable.

In surprisingly few years the quality of steering had been greatly debased. Where it had once been possible to direct a car through a corner with mere wrist movement, it was now necessary to twirl the handwheel wildly, with a great deal of shuffling of the hands on its rim, and a corresponding loss of that elusive quality described as 'feel' by which the driver could sense through the handwheel the loads to which the tyres were being submitted on the road in each manoeuvre. Worse still, the multiplicity of joints in the steering system aggravated the inaccuracies caused by wear at each point, and the whole additive mess of sloppage in the linkage was magnified by the reaction gearbox to become apparent at the handwheel as an extraordinary amount of backlash, that might in extreme cases allow half a turn of the handwheel before anything happened to the front wheels. Experienced drivers were appalled; but the new generation, who had known no better, found it comforting that their unskilled manipulation of the wheel could be cushioned by the system's insensibility, and especially in America—where mass produced cars were growing grotesquely heavy and were being sold in increasing numbers to women who were blindly assumed to be incapable of exercising

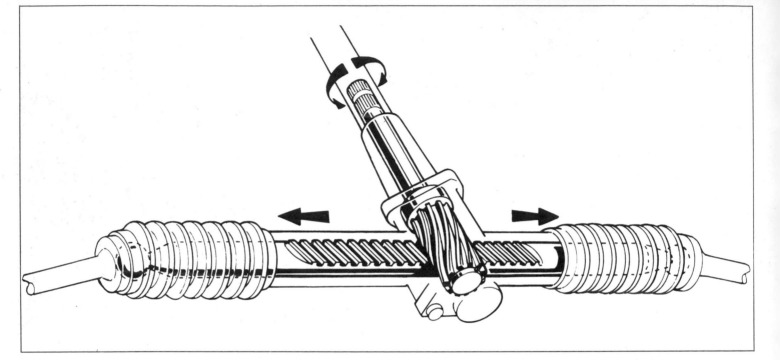

either strength or discrimination—the quality of steering reached a nadir of inexpressible squalor and deplorably international influence.

Gradually things began to improve as work went on in the development of bushings and bearings that would be more wear-resistant. Steering gears were further developed too, the worms being geometrically refined to emerge as a kind of cam engaging either a peg or a roller rather than another gear wheel. Generally, however, little work was done on the reconciliation of steering and suspension geometries.

A very small number of manufacturers were properly solicitous about geometry, and they were able as a result of their efforts to eliminate most of the friction that had been thought necessary in the steering mechanism to damp out road shock. A fine example was offered by BMW who in the 1930s succeeded in making practical the essentially very simple and sturdy rack-and-pinion steering mechanism. In this, a small cog or pinion at the end of the steering column engages with teeth on a rack or transverse bar, sliding in a guide fixed to the chassis, with its ends carrying the inboard joints of the steering tie rods. Such a system was theoretically completely reversible, though the effect could be modified slightly by cutting the gear in helical form rather than straight; but where the rack was installed at the correct height in relation to the suspension linkages, very little damping of the system might be required and this was usually contrived by a simple spring-loaded pressure pad rubbing against the rack to produce some frictional damping. Apart from the accuracy implicit in the use of the system, the other virtues of rack-and-pinion steering were its modest spatial demands and the reduced number of flexible

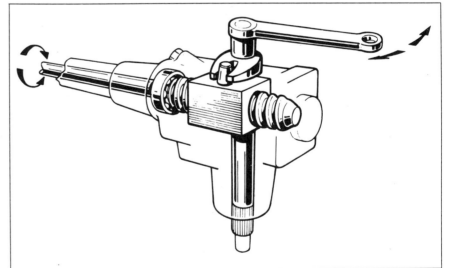

joints susceptible to wear: in a well engineered system such as that of the 2-litre Bristols, the backlash at the steering wheel rim would be only one eighth of an inch or 45 minutes of angle—a degree of accuracy once the prerogative of Bugatti steering—and it would be just the same whether the car was new or twenty years old. Of course most manufacturers found the cost of installing a centralised chassis-mounted lubrication system for all the moving parts altogether too daunting, and, recognising that owners could not be relied upon to have servicing done frequently and properly, developed low-friction bearing materials such as nylon which, if used properly, did not introduce too

Top and centre: a complete rack-and-pinion unit and a cutaway drawing showing how the teeth are helically cut in order to minimise kick-back

Above: a worm-and-nut steering box

much elasticity to the system. In Europe, if not in America or Japan, the quality of steering improved enormously during the 1960s.

The other important steering development during that period was the popularisation of servo assistance. With cars growing heavier and tyres much broader, while parking in ever more congested cities grew more and more tiresome, some kind of power assistance was necessary. Naturally it first became common in the American behemoths; inevitably it was done with no thought for anything but to make the steering lighter. No thought was given for the feel of the steering, since it had already been virtually lost in the domestic American car, nor was the opportunity taken to raise the steering ratio now that the driver's muscles did not have to do all the work. A simple hydraulic ram was attached to one of the steering arms and energised by an engine-driven pump which supplemented the driver's efforts, now no greater than was necessary to open and close valves which controlled the admission of high-pressure fluid to either side of the piston in the hydraulic cylinder.

The more fastidious manufacturers found this intolerable, and turned for guidance to the aviation industry, which had had to develop fully-powered controls for the transonic jet aircraft of the 1950s, and had encountered the same problems of control feel or feedback. The difficulties were exacerbated by the need for the steering to remain operable in the event of an hydraulic system failure. In other words the steering had to be power assisted, not fully powered— and the degree of assistance had to be related to the force applied to the steering wheel, rather than to the extent of its movement.

A lot of development work had to be done on the design of the valves which controlled the fluid, and on the design of the load-sensitive linkage which relayed handwheel forces to the valves. The preferred link is a slender torsion-bar spring on the end of the steering column, the twisting of which would be proportional to the steering force being applied. In their very advanced SM model, Citroën exploited the centralised high-pressure hydraulic system developed since the introduction of their DS in 1955 (perhaps the first car to have power steering of acceptable quality) to provide fully powered steering with entirely artificial feel. This was provided by a secondary pump driven by the transmission, so that its output was proportional to the road speed of the vehicle: the delivery of this pump opposed the operation of the steering in such a way that at parking speeds it offered virtually no resistance, but as the car went faster the steering grew correspondingly heavier so as to inhibit any dangerously excessive steering input when the car was travelling quickly.

This idea was a sophisticated extension of a simple mechanical cam-and-spring system of introducing self-centering artificial feel to the steering of small French front-wheel-drive cars years earlier, when the dynamic peculiarities of front-wheel-drive steering had been causing problems. These peculiarities were due to the elastic characteristics of the pneumatic tyre, which imposed their own dictates on the car's steering in a way that only began to be appreciated in the late 1930s and was generally ignored until much later. The flexibility of the tyre complicates the issue because instead of rolling in exactly the direction in which they are aligned, the tyres drift slightly sideways under cornering forces—and the degree of drift varies according to numerous other variables including the tyre load, pressure, construction, and condition, as well as extraneous factors including camber imposed by the suspension geometry and tractive or braking

loads to which it would be subjected from time to time.

All these variables have to be taken into account in designing the geometries of the steering and suspension systems, which must be considered inseparable. Suspension movement introduces variations in camber and in directional alignment (toe-in or toe-out) to complicate basic steering geometry which is compounded of castor angle, camber angle, king-pin inclination, and offset or scrub radius. All these things are fixed by the position of the king-pin in relation to

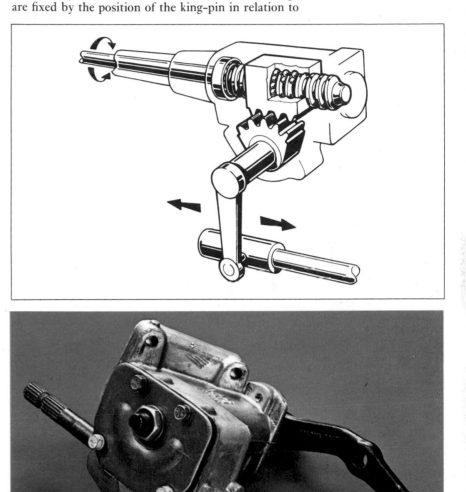

the wheel—and the implications are enormous.

The king-pin is simulated by a couple of ball joints at top and bottom of a hub bearer or 'king-post'—the king-pin is that piece of metal about which a front wheel pivots to steer the car. Each front wheel has one, so a car has two king-pins. This sounds implausible, not to say revolutionary, but the simple explanation is that the term is a relic of the horse-drawn carriage, when the horse trotted between shafts ahead of a front axle that was pivoted at its centre on a vertical bolt, or pin driven into the front cross-member of the carriage. This was the king-pin, or more popularly kingbolt, but with very few early exceptions, car designers have eschewed this singularity of steering pivot because of the dangerous instability in roll when the axle was turned to steer the car.

The modern king-pin, or king-post (which, in the case of MacPherson suspension, embodies the entire front strut), is not the simple upright of the horse-

Below: a sophisticated version of the worm-and-nut system, known as the recirculating-ball unit

Above: the recirculating-ball steering box from a Fiat 130; this type. as many others, has gradually been ousted in favour of the simple rack-and-pinion unit

drawn days. It is tilted sideways so that its axis intersects with the road surface somewhere near the centre of the tyre contact area—usually a little inside, sometimes (as in certain Citroën and Saab models) coinciding with, and sometimes (as in the Audi 80 and VW Passat designs) a little outside the tyre centre line. The tilt responsible for this is known as king-pin inclination, and is not to be confused with the fore-and-aft rake given to the king-pin, so that its axis intersects the road ahead of the centre of the tyre contact patch. This longitudinal inclination is called the castor angle, recalling the practice in some early cars of setting the king-pin upright ahead of the wheel centre (instead of being angled forwards), so as to create what is called steering trail, just as in an ordinary furniture castor. The idea was not popular and was found to aggravate the steering shimmy that too many cars of the time suffered from anyway, and castor angle was substituted by a natural inference from bicycle geometry.

These two deviations—king-pin inclination and castor—result in some very peculiar motions of the wheel as it is steered. Consider what happens when the steering is turned hard left, for example: the two front wheels are tilted to fairly steep camber angles so that

the tops of both wheels are tilted over to the left. The castor angle alone is sufficient to do this, and in principle it ought to increase the cornering power of the tyres by setting them at an advantageous angle to the road, but the king-pin inclination in the transverse plane can aggravate the effect and add further peculiarities: the right wheel will have its camber reduced, and the left-wheel camber will be increased. More peculiar still, the effects of normal steering offset—the distance between the tyre centre line and the slightly inboard intersection of the king-pin axis with the road —will be to reduce the trail of the right wheel and increase that of the left. These variations in steering trail will cause an increase in the self-aligning torque of the left tyre, and a decrease in that of the right which, when turning left, does most of the work. The variations in wheel camber cause corresponding variations in cornering force, which may be positive or negative according to the actual amount of camber, the load and inflation pressure of the tyres, and numerous other factors. When driving at high speed and cornering hard, and particularly in the event of a skid, these peculiarities of steering geometry can create alarming variations in the handling characteristics of the car, and in particular are largely responsible for the vicious counter-skid that sometimes follows over-correction of an initial rear-wheel slide.

At the other extreme, king-pin inclination and castor angle create some most peculiar effects at low speed, and noticeably when the car is at a standstill. What then, when you turn the steering hard left? Here the

operative word is 'hard'. You may find it very hard work indeed on some cars, because the combination of steering offset and king-pin inclination forces the nose of the car up as the steering is turned away from the straight ahead position. This is why steering is sometimes found inexplicably low-geared; as you wind away at the wheel, you are literally jacking up the front of the car. Opposing this jacking action is the effect of castor angle. The greater this angle, the more does the nose of the car drop towards the ground over the outside wheel as the steering is turned. It is thus possible to specify a combination of castor angle and king-pin inclination for these two effects to be balanced out, with the unexpected result that low-speed steering may

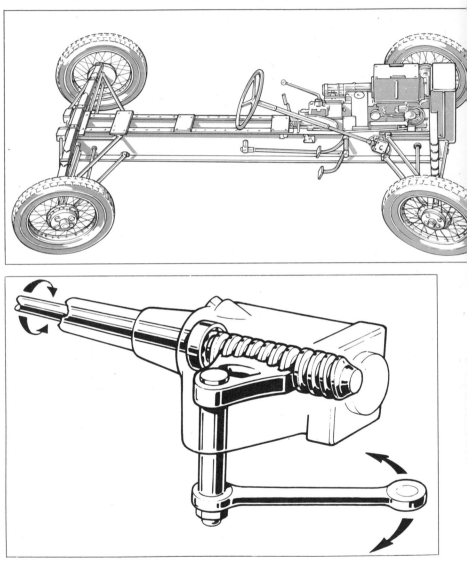

actually be made lighter by an increase in castor angle, contrary to what one would normally expect.

If instead of conventional steering offset we have geometry like that of the Audi 80 and its related Volkswagens, where the centre of the tyre contact patch lies inboard of the steering axis, we shall observe the same variations in the front-wheel camber as before when steering, but the variations in trail will be quite opposite. The trail of the outside wheel will now be increased, and that of the inside wheel decreased, so that the more heavily laden tyre on the outside of the corner will generate greater self-aligning torque, and the less effective one on the inside will generate less. The effect of castor angle remains unchanged, being to lower the outside of the car as the steering is turned

Below: a prototype chassis constructed by Pietro Amati in 1925; it had not only four-wheel drive, but also four-wheel steering, which gave it good manoeuvrability

Below left: the tiller-steered Lacroix de Laville of 1898

Above: another variation of the worm unit, this time the worm-and-sector steering box

towards full lock. Now, though, instead of this being balanced by the jacking effect of king-pin inclination, the nose is lowered still further. In other words, turning the steering away from the straight ahead position makes the nose droop; the weight of the car tends to do the steering for you. To straighten the steering again will be harder work, but the increased self-aligning torque of the significant outer tyre may counterbalance this load when the car is travelling fast.

With centre-point steering, where the king-pin axis and the tyre equator and the road all meet, there are no changes in trail at all, as the wheels are swung to left or right, nor are there any changes in ride height imposed by king-pin inclination. However, the force necessary at the steering wheel to turn it when the car is stationary is relatively high in this case, because the tyre contact patch has to be scrubbed around the steering axis against the frictional resistance of the road surface. When steering offset is considerable, this scrubbing action is greatly reduced, and the tyre can simply roll along an arc whose radius is equal to the amount of steering offset at road level. Thus, considerable offset can make low-speed steering appreciably lighter, although at higher speeds it will probably grow heavier and certainly more sensitive to kick-back. It might be thought that perfect centre-point steering, with the king-pin vertical in the centre of the wheel without any inclination or castor angle, might be the most desirable, but the car would then be difficult to steer especially at high speeds. It is true that there would still be some effective trail, because it is a characteristic of the pneumatic tyre that the effective centre of the contact patch lies somewhat behind its geometrical centre, the distance between them being known as pneumatic trail, which may be relied upon to provide the essential minimum of self-aligning torque. In a car with fully powered irreversible steering, such as the Citroën SM, there are no reasons for retaining either form of king-pin tilt, and many good reasons for eliminating them.

Long before it was realised that the steered wheels did not travel in exactly the direction they were pointed, it was accepted that they should not always point in the same direction. It was a purely mechanical consideration that encouraged designers to set the front wheels with a fractional toe-in to prevent any flexibility in the steering linkage from allowing them to become splayed apart when the brakes were applied, and it was a strictly rational extension of this argument that prompted a toe-out setting of the front wheels on cars where they transmitted the drive. Nowadays, when radial-ply tyres are used, it is frequent practice to set the front wheels parallel; but as long ago as 1820, long before the petrol-engined car was on the roads, it had been accepted that the steering wheels of a vehicle with two or more axles should only be parallel when pointing straight ahead. When the vehicle was steered around a corner, it was argued, the inner wheel should be turned through a greater angle than the outer, so as to eliminate lateral scrub of the tyres on the road surface. The trouble was that in 1820 tyres were made of iron.

The principle was patented by Rudolph Ackermann, a German of good repute as a fine arts publisher, bookseller, and humanitarian; but he also dabbled in contemporary technology, and somehow contrived to establish as the 'Ackermann principle' a geometrical notion that had in fact been conceived by another man called Lankensperger. For iron-shod horsedrawn carriages it was a valid notion, though it only gave a perfect correspondence of steering angles and radii at one particular angle of steering deflection. Alas, it was invalid when applied to the rubber-tyred motor car

which, when cornering, develops a greater slip angle on its outer, more heavily laden, tyre than on the inner one, as weight transfer is effected by the cornering forces involved. Obviously in this case the outer wheel should be turned through a greater angle than the inner one—but the extent of the difference would vary according to the speed and severity of the corner. As the knowledge of these insuperable imperfections sank

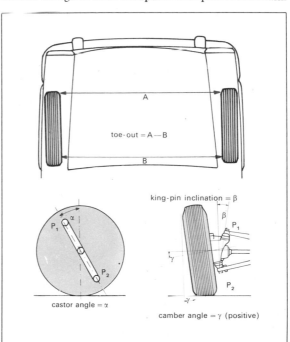

Left: diagrams showing toe-out, castor angle, camber angle and king-pin inclination for a front-wheel-drive car

toe-out $= A - B$

king-pin inclination $= \beta$

castor angle $= \alpha$

camber angle $= \gamma$ (positive)

Above: a partly dismantled worm-and-sector steering box from a Fiat 500

in, some designers compromised by arranging the front wheels to remain parallel at all times, while others set them to toe-in with increasing steering deflection, this being known as anti-Ackermann steering. A car set up in the latter manner might steer beautifully when cornered hard and fast, the steering remaining reasonably light in defiance of traditions that had been accepted for decades; but when being manoeuvred gently at low speeds, the anti-Ackermann geometry would aggravate the tyre scrub that Lankensperger had sought to prevent. There is at least one recorded instance of a car's anti-Ackermann geometry coming under stringent review because, although it behaved beautifully at high speeds, it made a dreadful mess of the gravel in the directors' car park!

ALIGNMENT

correct angles for the wheels

THE TWO common meanings of 'alignment', as applied to the car, describe the positioning of the two front road wheels, and the angle of the headlamp beams. The wheels must be accurately set if the car is to run a true course and to handle properly. The headlamp beams, of course, must be positioned at the correct angles, to comply with the strict legal requirements laid down by the laws of different countries.

Front wheel alignment
Basically, wheel alignment involves all the mechanical components responsible for the proper adjustment and running of the wheels. If these are not correctly set-up, the vehicle's steering may be heavy, or the vehicle uncontrollable at speed. At best, maladjustment will cause the tyres to wear out quickly.

Wheel alignment is not only, as is commonly supposed, a question of setting up the track of the two front wheels. Both the 'castor' and 'camber' angles of the wheels and suspension must be considered.

The castor angle can best be illustrated by the normal castor fitted to household furniture. If the furniture is pushed, the castors turn in their pivots until the wheels are facing the direction of travel with the wheels trailing behind the pivot point of the castors. The same principle is applied to the wheels of a car. If the king-pin, or the swivel-joint, on the hub is tilted backwards at the top, then the centre line through the pivot strikes the road ahead of the point of tyre contact.

This castor angle plays an important part in maintaining the directional stability of the car. It is this angle which provides the self-centring action, ensuring that the front wheels return to the straight-ahead position after the vehicle has made a turn.

Camber angle is the tilt of the wheel, either inwards or outwards at the top, when viewed from the front of the car. If the wheel leans inwards at the top this is called 'negative' camber, if it leans outwards at the top it is called 'positive' camber. If the wheels are vertical to the road the condition is referred to as 'zero' camber.

The need for camber was forced upon car designers because they could not relieve stress on the steering linkages by placing the pivot point directly over the wheels. With many independent suspension systems the camber angle changes from positive to negative under normal running conditions, and when a load is applied to the car. The benefits of properly set camber angles are easier steering, especially when parking, and less feed-back and juddering when the car is travelling at speed.

Incorrect camber angle soon shows up. Excessive tyre wear is the most common sign, but it also has a markedly adverse effect on the handling characteristics of a car.

Camber and castor angle, together with king-pin inclination, can only be checked using specialised equipment. If a fault in these settings is suspected, the vehicle should be taken to a garage to be thoroughly checked out.

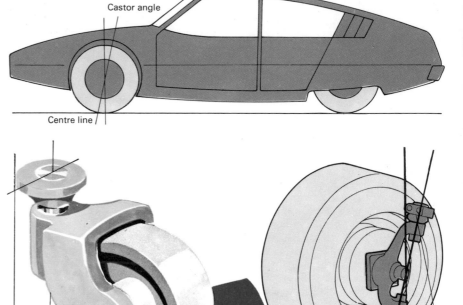

Castor angle
Centre line
Steering swivels or 'k pin'

The other factor that affects alignment of the wheels, and the most common, is tracking. Ideally the wheels should be parallel to each other. In practice, because of the opposing forces applied to the wheels, this is not practicable. The best steering characteristic is therefore achieved by setting the wheels slightly out of parallel to each other when pointing in the straight-ahead position. This is called 'toe-in' or 'toe-out', depending on the steering characteristic of the suspension system.

Toe-in or toe-out is the difference in distance

Above: If the centre line through the wheel pivot strikes the road ahead of the point of tyre contact, the wheel will tend to return to its straight-ahead position

Below: negative and positive camber with an independent suspension

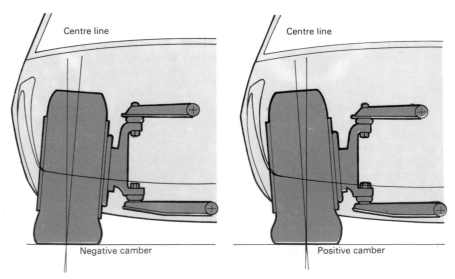

Centre line — Negative camber

Centre line — Positive camber

between the extreme front and extreme rear of the tims on the front wheels measured at axle height. To obtain maximum tyre mileage both front wheels should run parallel to each other, and to obtain this under running conditions it is generally necessary to set the wheels with a very slight toe-in, usually between 1/16 and 3/16 inch. As the wheels are moved along the road the fronts tend to splay out, until they are running parallel to each other. If insufficient toe-in is given the front wheels can, under running conditions, adopt a toe-out attitude, which could lead to vibration and wheel wobble.

There is an exception to this instance, and that is with front-wheel-drive cars. In most cases, because the drive power is applied through the same wheels that are used to steer the car, the opposite happens: the wheels tend to be drawn in under running conditions, so they have to be pre-set with a certain amount of toe-out. To 'track' the front wheels a special machine is used to align both front wheels together. Adjust-

ment is provided on all cars, either on the track-rod, which is attached to the steering, or on the ball-joint ends of the steering arms on a rack and pinion steering assembly. Unless you possess an alignment gauge it is a job better left to a garage that has the proper equipment.

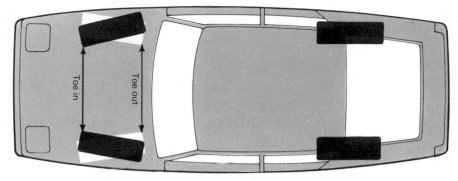

The diagram above shows where toe-in and toe-out measurements are taken on the front wheels when tracking is adjusted

Left: tracking is adjusted by means of the threaded track-rod ends. Undoing the lock-nut shown allows the track rod to be turned (as arrowed) thus altering its overall length. When the setting is correct, the lock-nut should be retightened. If a large adjustment is necessary, then it should be divided between the two sides of the car

Below: in racing cars built for oval circuits like Indianapolis, the track is offset; the diagram shows the set-up used on an Indy car of the type pictured, built for left-hand corners; the offset is greater at the rear than at the front, as shown by a and b

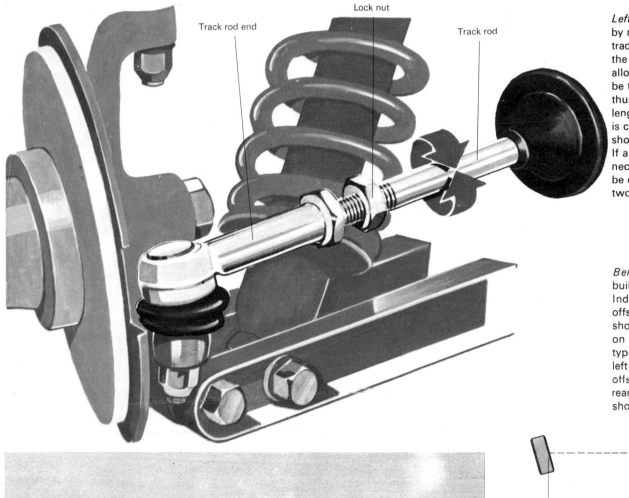

Track rod end

Lock nut

Track rod

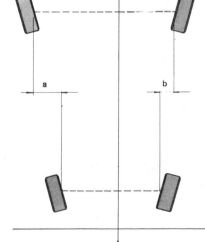

SUSPENSION

smoothing out the bumps

HANG A WEIGHT from a tension spring and it can be described as suspended. Rest it on top of a compression spring and the weight's poise or equilibrium may be identical—so the physicist and applied mathematician still describe it as suspended. Likewise, that is just what we mean when we describe a car as being suspended on springs of some sort or other. That really is all that suspension entails; the rest of it, the kinematic linkages by which the motions of the wheels are controlled in relation to the suspended mass, ought really to be called something else. However, we motorists are masters of misapplied jargon, and because in the first half of motoring history the springs were the linkages, we have continued to lump the two together ever since.

The primary purpose of the suspension system was to minimise the transmission of road shocks to the car's occupants. Pioneer designer Frederick Lanchester took elaborate pains to perfect a spring system of such periodicity that his car moved gently up and down on its suspension at the same rate as a man's body moves up and down when he walks—a natural function that was emulated in the hope of avoiding any disturbance of the body's mechanism. In fact it is not enough to calculate spring rates for this purpose, for the tyres and the seat cushion also have a suspensory or bottom-cossetting action: not many years ago a new small car had a hilariously bouncy ride because the seat springs resonated in sympathy with the road springs.

Were the insulation of the car's occupants from the road the only justification for suspension, the art would never have prospered. Hard men might still be buying unsprung cars, and the rest might make do with marshmallow upholstery. In fact the suspension plays just as important a part in protecting the car itself from the asperities of the road surface, and an even more important role in maintaining contact between the tyres and the road so that control can be exercised in braking, accelerating, cornering and so on. The problem is one that can be understood readily enough with two absurd examples: if the wheels weighed a ton each and the rest of the car were insubstantial, the wheels would bounce wildly and uncontrollably upon encountering each bump, and the springs would be powerless to control them; at the other extreme, if the wheels weighed but ounces and the car weighed a ton, then the softest springing could be employed to keep the car on an even keel while the wheels faithfully followed every contour of the road's surface. It is clearly a matter of proportion, not of quantity: what matters is the *ratio* of sprung to unsprung weight—and that is why the nature of the linkages or other mechanisms whereby the wheels are located and supported has to be considered along with the characteristics of the springs themselves.

In the earliest cars, the suspension systems used were generally derived from those of horse-drawn vehicles. Even in those days it was usual for the springing to be interposed between the axles and the chassis of the car. Some horse-drawn carriages had the chassis frame unsprung—mounted directly on the axles—and only the body was carried (or suspended) on springs. However, the pioneer designers appreciated that such a layout was not practicable for the motor car: control was to be effected not through flexible reins but through various mechanisms for which the relative movement of a sprung body would have been at least inconvenient.

Leaf springs of tempered steel strip soon became the most common suspension media, but quite soon examples appeared of helical (commonly miscalled 'coil') springs. The final form of steel spring was the torsion bar, its application to the motor car being patented by Ferdinand Porsche and widely used after 1950 when the patents expired. The torsion bar is a steel rod which is clamped to the chassis at one end and has a lever at the other end connected to the wheel; movement of the wheel causes the bar to be twisted, and its resistance to this twisting (or torsion) provides the springing. The helical spring is in fact merely a helical torsion bar.

Where leaf springs were employed, the longitudinal semi-elliptic configuration—still quite common today—was the most favoured. Such springs have a curved leaf or leaves and normally one end is pivot-mounted to the chassis, the other being connected by means of a link—called a 'shackle'—to accommodate the change of length as the spring's curvatures alter with varying loads. The axle is clamped to the spring at or about the middle of its length. An alternative arrangement favoured by designers of luxury cars in the Edwardian and Vintage era, was to pivot the middle of the springs on the chassis, clamp the axle to one pair of ends and have the shackles at the other ends. This was known as cantilever springing.

Other variations tried on the leaf-spring theme were the quarter-elliptic, three-quarter-elliptic and fully elliptic forms. The first of these is (as its name indicates) half a semi-elliptic, carrying the axle at one end and chassis-mounted at the other. As one would expect, the

Below: a graph showing how a metal helical spring compares, under compression, with a rubber spring; after only a small change in length, the rubber becomes almost incompressible

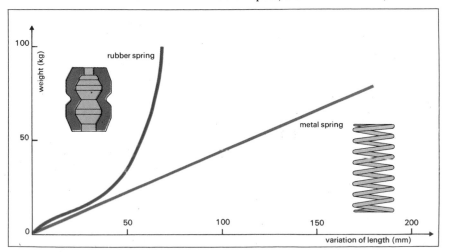

Left: the legendary Model T Ford, known affectionately as the 'Tin Lizzie' and available in any colour so long as it was black. At the time of the Model T's announcement in 1908, its transverse-leaf suspension at front and rear was quite unusual, because most manufacturers were using longitudinally mounted springs; this arrangement was relatively simple, the springs being connected to the chassis at their centres and to the axles at their ends, but the single mounting offered very low resistance to twisting and to lateral roll

Below right: examples of the various types of spring used in the motor car

Below: the front suspension of a single-seater racing car; wishbones are used at top and bottom, together with an anti-roll bar and a helical-spring surrounding a telescopic hydraulic damper

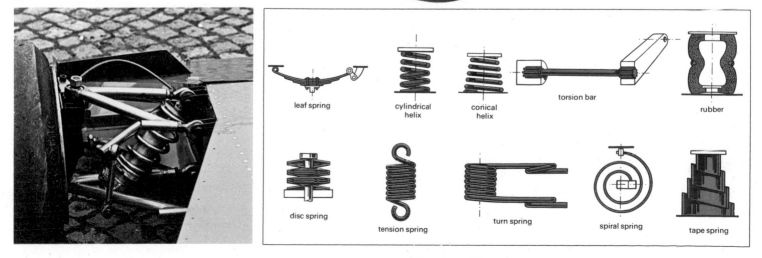

leaf spring   cylindrical helix   conical helix   torsion bar   rubber

disc spring   tension spring   turn spring   spiral spring   tape spring

three-quarter-elliptic spring is a combination of quarter and semi, while the fully elliptic is two opposed semis connected at the ends.

These last two—hangovers from the horse era—had the disadvantage of providing poor lateral location between body and axle, and hence a rather 'swaying' ride. Quarter and semi-elliptics are reasonable in respect of lateral location (though far from perfect, as we shall consider later) but the former are the less easy of the two to endow with adequate flexibility unless the metal is relatively highly stressed. Either the springing had to be jolly firm, as was that of the beam-axled Frazer Nash sports cars of blessed memory and GN

Right: early motor cars inherited their suspension systems from horse-drawn carriages, although designers soon realised that the springs would have to be placed between wheels and chassis, rather than between chassis and body, as shown here

Far right: the leaf spring can take many different forms; this series of diagrams shows, from top to bottom, the evolution of this popular and useful component

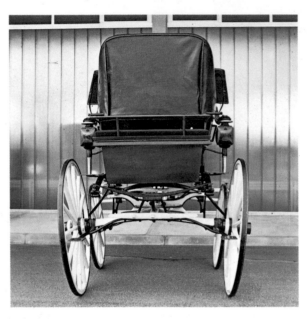

inspiration, or the springs had to be very long.

On most leaf-sprung cars, as already explained, the suspension system amounted to little more than a pair of longitudinally disposed semi-elliptic springs, one each side of the chassis, with the axle bridging them. However, one or two manufacturers in search of even greater economies preferred to employ a single transverse semi-elliptic in place of longitudinal springs.

Among these firms was Ford, using transverse leaf springs from the original Model T of 1908 until well after the end of World War II. Such springs were attached in the middle to the chassis structure and at the ends, through shackles, to the axle.

On the face of it, the single medially mounted transverse spring had quite a lot to commend it, in that it was mechanically simple and economical of materials. All was not sweetness and light, though, since the central anchorage imparted only limited resistance to swivelling in the horizontal plane. It followed that some additional means of axle location was necessary: it usually took the form of a V-shaped member attached at its apex to the chassis, by a universal joint, and to the axle at its extremities. A secondary disadvantage was the low resistance to lateral roll of the body on the springs. This was not a serious snag in the days when the cornering abilities of cars were considerably restricted by limited tyre adhesion and lack of understanding of handling phenomena. It might never have done for a Bugatti or an Alfa Romeo, but the buyers of economy cars such as the Fords probably knew no better and certainly seemed to desire nothing better.

For the first decade or two of existence of the automobile, when performance was low and inter-leaf friction high, the springs were left to function in a fairly uninhibited manner. In those rare instances when

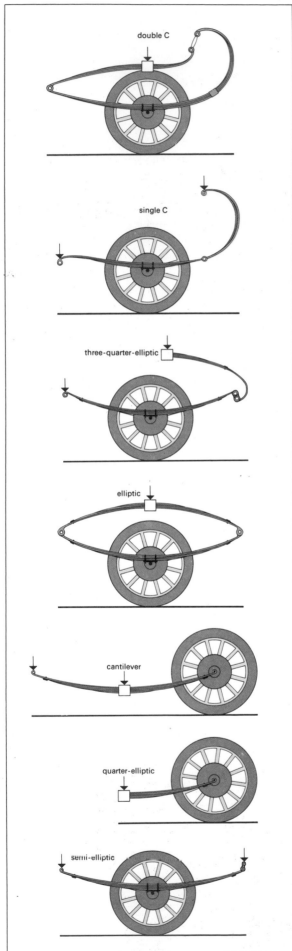

performance was high, it was even rarer to find any dampers to modulate their elasticity, though there were pot-type dampers as early as 1902 on the big racing Mors. However, it is a physical fact that any mass mounted on a spring (or suspended from it) has a tendency to continue oscillating once it has been disturbed from its position of rest and then released—as happens when a wheel passes over a bump or a pothole.

The resulting bouncing tendency of the body became increasingly noticeable as speeds rose and occupants became more comfort-conscious. As an indication of what unrestrained springing could achieve, there is a fascinating story from racing history in

maximum when it should have been minimal for the best ride; conversely, bigger impacts received a relatively smaller damping effect.

Since car performance was continuing to rise, underlining the friction damper's deficiencies, something better had to be found—something that was more 'velocity-conscious'. The answer lay in the hydraulic damper which, from relatively humble origins in the 1930s (it was, of course, invented much earlier) soon became the general wear that it has remained to this day. Early hydraulic dampers were of the part-rotary type, consisting of a chassis-mounted housing and an external lever arm that was connected to the axle by

Below left: a cantilever rear spring in use on a type 20 Diatto of 1926; the advantage of this type over the semi-elliptic unit is its reduced unsprung weight

Below: a rear view of a 1909 Model T Ford, showing clearly the transverse leaf

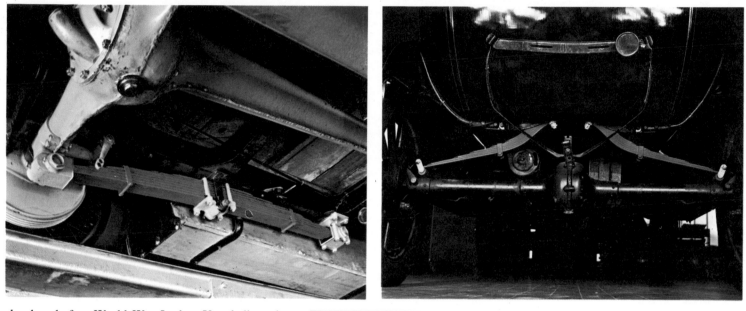

the days before World War I when Vauxhall used to participate. One of their cars is reputed to have met an undulating bit of road surface at such a speed that the bump spacing coincided with the natural frequency of bouncing of the body on its springs. The resulting 'resonance' caused the amplitude of the oscillation to build up to such an extent that the car bounded off the road, over a hedge and into a field!

To prevent such untoward occurrences, most car makers had begun by 1920 to employ some sort of inhibiting devices for the springs. Often they were content to fit the so-called 'snubbers' which served merely to limit the rebound travel of the springs after deflection, and thus prevent any resonance from building up to unmanagable proportions.

Next on the scene came the friction damper. In its simplest form this comprised a pair of jointed links, one attached to the chassis and the other to the axle; sandwiched between them at the joint was a disc of friction material, and the connecting bolt could be tightened or slackened to increase or reduce the amount of resistance exerted by the joint. This additional friction in the system damped the natural tendency of the springs to continue oscillating after deflection.

Friction dampers of this type were improved during the succeeding years, to the extent that by the early 1930s some cars had versions that were adjustable by the driver, while seated at the wheel, to achieve the best setting for any particular combination of vehicle loading and road conditions. Even such sophistication was unable to mask the fundamental inadequacy of this method of damping. This was that the 'stiction' or static friction between the two components was always greater than the sliding friction. Consequently, the resistance of the system to initial movement was at a

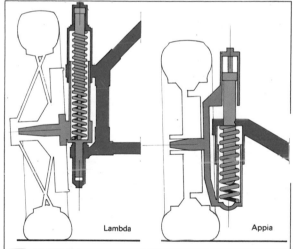

Lambda   Appia

Left: sliding-pillar front suspension has been used on several types of car and was long favoured by Lancia, who first used it in the Lambda of 1922 and persevered with it right up to the Appia of the fifties

means of a link. Inside the body was either a part-circular space containing a paddle vane operated by the arm, or a cylindrical chamber containing a similarly actuated piston. In each case, movement of the arm caused the fluid in the chamber to be forced through a valve from one side of the vane or piston to the other. The resistance of the fluid to the forced flow absorbs energy and provides the required damping effect on the spring movement; it is controlled primarily by the size of the valve orifice and by the viscosity of the fluid. However, these dampers have the great operational advantage of being speed-sensitive in that the fluid flows readily in response to leisurely wheel movements but meets with increasing resistance—because of the limited orifice size—as the rate of wheel travel rises.

Although the piston-type lever-arm damper is still fitted to a number of cars today, it has been supplanted in popularity by the telescopic variety. This was just beginning to establish itself immediately before World War II and made rapid strides thereafter. In some applications the telescopic damper has installational advantages, and it can carry a coaxial helical spring (thus simplifying the system), but it cannot form part of the linkage as readily as a lever-arm unit.

It was not unknown for the arm of an old-fashioned friction damper to double as a suspension linkage in helping to locate a beam axle, as examination of an old Frazer Nash would confirm. However, by the 1930s performance increases and the demand for matching standards of comfort and handling had begun to highlight the weaknesses of the beam axle and 'cart' springs. Independent suspension had been on the scene for ages before: even the sliding-pillar frontal systems of Morgan and Sizaire-Naudin were not the first, and when Lancia adopted something similar for his 1922 Lambda it was only after considering it with a whole host of other independent front suspension (IFS) systems drawn up by his gifted engineer Falchetto.

Why the sudden interest in IFS? Because front brakes were getting common and big, and because tyres and wheels were getting fat and heavy. It was not just a matter of keeping down the ratio of unsprung to sprung

Right: the steered swinging arm arrangement of the Dubonnet suspension, shown here on an Alfa Romeo P3 of 1935; one of the main advantages of this was that the unsprung weight was low due to the spring and steering linkage being chassis mounted

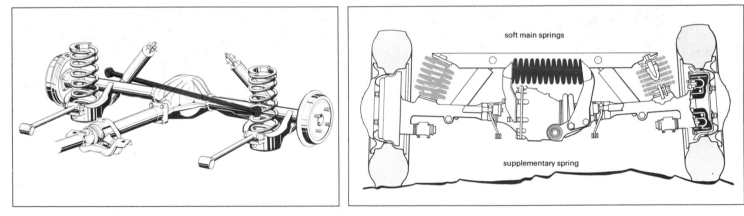

soft main springs

supplementary spring

Above: a Panhard rod (shown red) is an excellent way of providing lateral location of a beam axle; the rod is made as long as possible in order to minimise the arc created by suspension movement

Above right: Mercedes-Benz improved on the standard swing-axle suspension layout, when they fitted low-pivoted arms on their 1937 GP car; this was further enhanced in later cars by the addition of a compensating spring to control the ride height of the car and the overall stiffness of the suspension

weight, although independence was a marvellous way of halving it at a stroke: it was a matter of keeping gyroscopic precessions at bay. A hefty tyre on a large-diameter wheel acts as a flywheel and a gyroscope. If tilted in one plane while spinning it will react by tilting in opposition in a plane perpendicular to that one. Lateral tilt of a beam axle makes both wheels try to precess: if the left wheel rises over a bump, both wheels will steer left. On a rigid rear axle they cannot, but the extra degree of freedom they enjoy on their swivels at the front allows them to fight back.

So long as the front springs were stiff, the axle could not tilt much, so the precessional effect was kept within reasonable bounds. Any serious attempt to improve the ride by softening the springs, though, led to unacceptable steering characteristics. This *impasse* caused car designers to begin a complete rethink on front suspension layouts. Their answer lay in independent suspension, in which the behaviour of one wheel would not markedly affect that of the other. If the geometry of the independent front suspension (or IFS) were designed so that each wheel could travel up or down quite a long distance without tilting much, then the ride comfort could be considerably improved without sufficent precessional tendency to affect the steering adversely.

In several of the earlier IFS designs, use was made of a transversely mounted leaf spring which served the secondary purpose of forming part of the wheel-

locating linkage; the latter was usually completed by a transverse pivoted arm, usually of the triangulated form (hence the term 'wishbone') to resist the longitudinal forces imposed by braking. This was a reasonably economical layout in respect of material usage but had the geometrical disadvantage that the length of one of the links was not fixed, since that of a leaf spring of course varies with its curvature which in turn changes with the loadings.

The result was some variation in camber angle, which could not only reduce the cornering power of the tyre but also introduce a precession. A further objection to the transverse spring was its claim to space: IFS encouraged a forward mounting of the engine if cross members could be shifted out of the way, and by using two wishbones the move could be accomplished.

This double-wishbone arrangement, with the outboard ends of the wishbones jointed to an upright carrying the hub, is kinematically described as a four-bar linkage, and it has been the most popular form of IFS. Designers soon learned that the wishbones need to be neither equal in length nor parallel, and that all manner of motional subtleties (affecting camber, roll-centre height, steering, ride quality and even spring rates) could be introduced by modifying the geometry of the linkage. This made it popular, though other systems (the Porsche system of twin trailing links and the Dubonnet system of a steered swinging arm, for instance) enjoyed some popularity among designers with objections to tyre scrub and unsprung weight.

The softer springing made practicable by the adoption of IFS brought its own problems, one of which was excessive body roll in cornering. This tendency was countered on some cars by the addition of an anti-roll torsion bar—an innovation that was first seen in normal production just before World War II.

An anti-roll bar consists of a steel rod with angled ends. The straight portion is freely mounted trans-

Below: an interesting adaptation of the swing-axle system used in the Fiat 128 coupé; the transverse leaf spring forms the major link

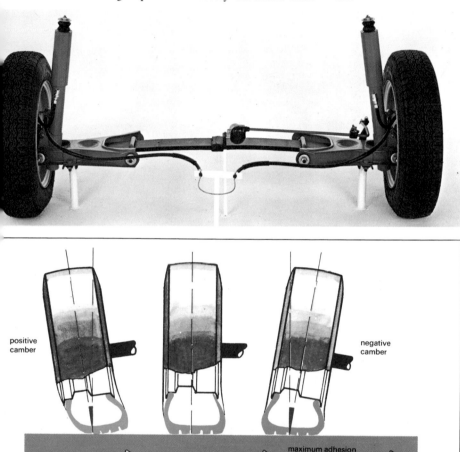

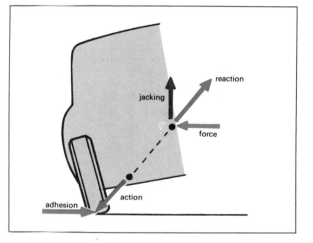

troduced the MacPherson strut front suspension. This contained no completely new ingredients, its novelty lying in the combination employed. In essence the MacPherson system comprises a telescopic strut (with the stub axle at the bottom), a transverse pivoted arm for location and an anti-roll bar. The strut is flexibly anchored at its top to the body structure, encloses an hydraulic damper, and usually carries an external coaxial helical spring. The special feature that distinguishes the McPherson from other strut-type suspensions before or after is the use of the anti-roll bar to triangulate the transverse arms so as to cope with longitudinal loads. This is done by mounting the bar ahead of the arms, inclining its ends obliquely rearward and attaching these to the outboard ends of the arms.

Because of its mechanical simplicity and the reasonable geometry that it provides, the basic strut/arm layout has since been adopted by several other manufacturers (although these designs are often referred to as 'MacPherson strut', this designation is inaccurate since they cannot incorporate the essential, patented MacPherson integrated anti-roll bar). However, there are two potential disadvantages of strut suspension: because of its offset line of action, the strut itself is subjected to bending, which can interfere with its

positive camber

negative camber

maximum adhesion

freedom of telescoping, and—in the case of front suspension—the body structure has to be reinforced at the upper front corners to take the loads.

While independent layouts were coming into use at the front, little progress was being made in rear suspension. The combination of a 'live' beam-type rear axle, semi-elliptic leaf springs and hydraulic dampers worked well enough in most instances though it had obvious deficiencies. Since it was also economic to manufacture, and provided quite good insulation of the body from transmission and road noise, there was little real incentive to improve it. The main drawbacks of this rather primitive system are only two: leaf springs do not provide very positive location of the axle beam, and the ratio of unsprung to sprung weight is high.

During the past decade or so there has been a growing tendency—particularly for the higher-performance type of car—to improve the behaviour of the live rear axle by endowing it with some form of positive location. The simplest type of locating device is the Panhard rod. This very old invention is a long transverse bar attached to the axle at one end and the body/chassis at the other; its purpose, clearly, is to limit lateral movement of the axle relative to the body; but because the rod swings in an arc there is still some lateral movement of the axle.

Some manufacturers adopted the alternative or additional procedure of restricting slewing of the axle

versely on the body, and the ends are connected to the axle or suspension arms, either directly or through links. If both wheels rise or fall equally, the bar merely rotates in its mountings without twisting. In cornering, though, lateral weight transfer causes the outboard wheel to rise and the inboard one to fall. The ends of the bar therefore move in opposite directions to apply torsion to the bar, the reaction of which resists the roll of the body relative to the wheels.

This sounds such a good idea that the layman must be forgiven for asking why anti-roll bars are not in general use. The answer, briefly, is that they reduce the sensitivity of the springing in some circumstances (single-wheel bump, for example) and, unless the front and rear stiffnesses are correctly balanced, the addition can adversely affect the car's handling characteristics. Moreover, an anti-roll bar can be caused to oscillate in torsion at its natural frequency, since it is an undamped spring; if it is a stiff bar, this oscillation gives rise to an unpleasant transverse motion known as 'roll-rock'.

The double-wishbone layout became very well established world wide in the first few years following World War II. Then Ford put the cat among the pigeons with their 1951 British models, which in-

Above: these diagrams show how negative camber allows the maximum amount of radial-tyre tread to stay on the road surface during cornering; the green arrows indicate the amount of cornering power

Above right: in cornering, centrifugal force is applied through the centre of gravity to the contact patch of the tyre; the reaction results in the car being lifted and, with swing-axle suspension, the wheel tucking under and losing adhesion

by means of longitudinal links. These served the useful secondary purpose of preventing 'wind-up' of the axle on the springs during heavy braking or acceleration, which forces a flexible leaf spring to adopt a reflex or S shape. The combination of Panhard rod and longitudinal links certainly locates the axle positively and so can significantly improve handling characteristics.

Any system of trailing links must introduce some rear-axle steer because their arcuate motions draw each axle end forward in roll or unilateral bump. A better method was devised by Dr Fiedler who went from Horch to BMW in the 1930s and created a torsion-bar rear suspension with transverse links connecting the ends of the axle to the ends of the longitudinal torsion bars, retaining the A-frame for lateral location and axle torque reaction at some expense in roll-centre height, which had to be above or below the big final-drive housing in the middle of the axle. The final refinement was introduced by Bristol in 1958, with a Watt linkage to locate the axle laterally and a simple link to replace the A-frame for torque reaction. The result was complete elimination of rear-axle steer, the axle moving only in a vertical plane perpendicular to the direction of travel of the car, while the roll centre could be at any chosen height.

The last mentioned layout probably represents the ultimate for a conventional front-engine/rear-drive car with a live rear axle. Nevertheless, it still suffers from the previously mentioned unfavourable ratio of unsprung to sprung weight. In theory, therefore, it cannot provide the optimum riding qualities, although it (and other live-axle layouts) can be made to work surprisingly well for quite modest production costs.

Those who sought independent rear suspension did so with a variety of motives, but accurate steering and good handling seemed not to be among them. The swinging half-axle, which Rumpler and Ledwinka propounded in the early 1920s, enjoyed far more popularity than it deserved, mainly due to its adoption by Ferdinand Porsche for everything from the Volkswagen to the GP Auto Union: it was a particularly convenient and cheap way of integrating the transmission with a rear engine. Front-engined cars with rear-drive and IRS were doomed to the same imperfect

Below: the Fiat 500, introduced in 1957, made use of a transverse leaf spring at the front, complemented by upper wishbones, and semi-trailing arms at the rear, transmitting the loads through helical springs

system until, in the 1950s, some makers of higher-class cars (particularly, but not exclusively) sought improvement with a modified swing-axle geometry or with a suspension that (as inspired by the 1937 GP Mercedes-Benz) gave independence of tractive torque reaction (resisting which demands stiff springs) and final-drive weight without real independence of the wheels. Where rear-wheel drive is employed, either solution enables the heavy final-drive unit to be mounted on the main structure instead of flapping up and down on the springs; the resulting reduction of the unsprung weight is considerable, but the isolation of transmission and road noises and vibration, now given an easier and more direct path to the passenger compartment, becomes much more difficult.

Only one semi-independent layout has achieved lasting success and is in fact an excellent 'halfway

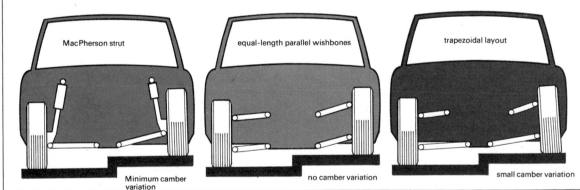

MacPherson strut

Minimum camber variation

equal-length parallel wishbones

no camber variation

trapezoidal layout

small camber variation

Left: diagrams showing how camber changes as a wheel traverses a bump with various types of suspension layout

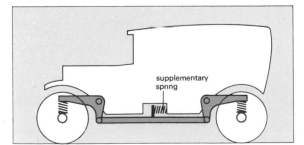

supplementary spring

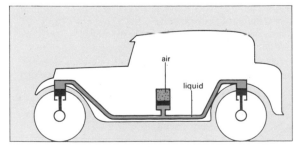

air

liquid

Below far left: the type of mechanically linked suspension used by Citroën

Below near left: an alternative form of interconnected suspension using liquid transmission to a single air spring

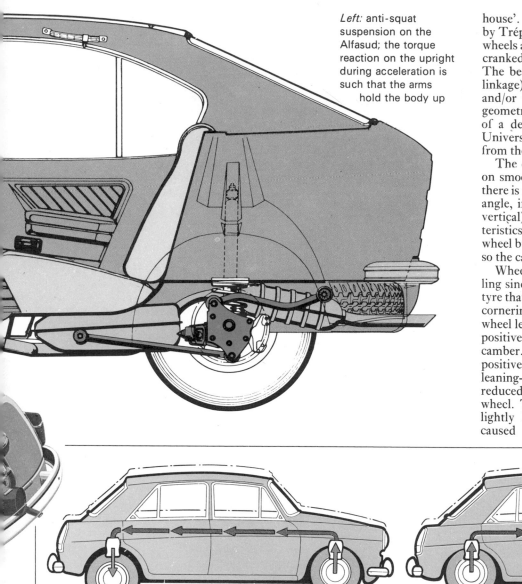

Left: anti-squat suspension on the Alfasud; the torque reaction on the upright during acceleration is such that the arms hold the body up

house'. It is the de Dion system (invented for de Dion by Trépardoux in the nineteenth century) in which the wheels are connected by a relatively light tubular beam, cranked amidships to clear the fixed final-drive casing. The beam is ideally located (usually by some sort of linkage) so that it can only move bodily up and down and/or tilt laterally; but the ideal is rarely achieved, geometrical solecisms being as common in the location of a dead beam axle as in that of the live variety. Universally jointed half-shafts transmit tractive torque from the differential to the wheels.

The de Dion layout has the advantage in cornering on smooth roads or traversing two-wheel bumps that there is no change in the camber angle of the wheels (the angle, if any, between the plane of the wheel and the vertical). This gives more consistant handling characteristics than when camber variations occur. Over one-wheel bumps, on the other hand, the axle obviously tilts so the camber is effectively changed.

Wheel camber has an important influence on handling since it affects the cornering power of the tyres: a tyre that is leaning in the direction of a turn exerts more cornering force than one leaning outward. When a wheel leans outward relative to the car it is said to have positive camber, a leaning-in wheel having negative camber. One might think that, if both wheels have a positive camber, the extra cornering power of the leaning-in inside wheel on a bend would offset the reduced cornering power of the leaning-out outside wheel. This is not true: the inside tyre is also more lightly loaded owing to the lateral weight transfer caused by centrifugal force, and cannot contribute

much to the total cornering power of the pair of tyres. It follows that a pair of negatively cambered wheels generate a higher *total* cornering force than do their positively cambered equivalents.

Even on a de Dion axle this can be arranged with advantage. The 1957 GP Vanwall had its rear wheels set at a negative camber angle on the ends of its dead beam axle; so did the Gordon-Keeble of the mid 1960s, although the angle was only 30 minutes. In general, though, IRS has been a post-war development, and the rapid rise to popularity of front-wheel drive on lower-priced cars (inspired by the Issigonis Mini of 1959) has been largely responsible. When there is no final-drive unit to contend with, IRS becomes much simpler and cheaper—though VW and Alfa-Romeo have shown that good ride and wheel control can then be achieved with a light beam axle.

When front-wheel drive came in, swinging rear half-axles went out: there was no need to pivot them on a final-drive casing that was no longer there. Only a few (mostly rear-engined) small cars survived to illustrate the dynamic terrors of a system that looked frightening even when static.

Because of the swing-axle system's inherently poor

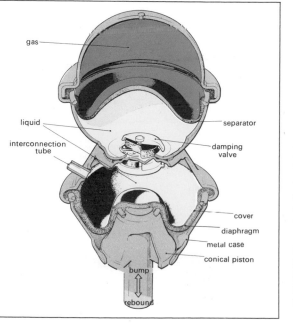

Above: British Leyland's Hydrolastic suspension was introduced with the 1100; a rubber spring takes the load, but as the spring of one wheel is compressed, so fluid is transmitted to the other wheel on that side in order to keep the car level

Right: in the later Hydragas arrangement, the rubber springs are replaced by gas-filled balls, but the liquid interconnection is retained

gas

liquid

separator

interconnection tube

damping valve

cover

diaphragm

metal case

conical piston

bump

rebound

geometry, satisfactory handling qualities in cornering can be attained only with difficulty. Unless the system is set up with appreciable negative camber in the static-laden condition (one object of which is to lower the roll centre), the outside wheel tends to 'tuck under' when the car is cornered hard, raising the back of the car (and the roll centre) and causing a marked loss in cornering power. The resulting oversteer can occur quite violently, easily leading to loss of control by the driver.

More satisfactory geometry is obtained by mounting each wheel carrier on a 'semi-trailing' arm or wishbone member pivoting about a horizontally skewed axis; the two pivot axes converge towards the rear of the car. This arrangement requires half-shafts with a universal joint at each end, usually with a splined sliding coupling or other means of accommodating any changes of length that occur with wheel travel. Since the wheel is at an angle to the pivot axis it follows a conical path in moving up and down. Hence there are variations in both the camber angle and the direction the wheel is pointing, leading to some rear-end steering effects. The layout is therefore a compromise; but it liberates so much space that it is widely used on medium and high-priced cars.

Fully trailing arms, with transverse pivot axes, are rarely used for IRS on rear-wheel-drive vehicles. One reason for their unpopularity is that the geometry results in greater length variations in the half-shafts, as the suspension operates, than occur with semi-trailing arms. This phenomenon does not apply, of course, to front-drive cars which consequently often feature trailing-arm systems at the rear.

Strut-type IRS has been used in one or two instances, most elegantly in the Fiat 130. While it has the mainly good characteristics already discussed in connection with IFS, a strut system is less easy to install at the rear since the upper ends of the struts encroach undesirably into the body space. The same objection applies to double-wishbone suspension, use of which is therefore virtually confined to racing cars where the point is of no significance. In its racing-car form, the double-wishbone layout can give the minimum camber and directional changes that are essential.

So far we have been considering car suspension in general terms, covering aspects that are applicable to the majority of vehicles. However, there are several systems which are markedly unorthodox for various reasons and so are worthy of special mention. The first of these unconventional layouts is known as interconnected suspension, in which there is some sort of link between the front and rear wheels on each side. As a result, the natural *frequency* in 'pitch' (longitudinal rocking) is made very low, with benefit to the riding comfort, without adverse effect on the suspension except that pitch *amplitude* may be increased.

The two major users of interconnected suspension are Citroën and British Leyland; the former employ it

Below: by using leading and trailing arms, the suspension can be arranged to prevent dive or lift during acceleration and braking; in braking, the wheels are forced backwards relative to the body and this tends to lift the front and lower the rear; in acceleration, the opposite is true

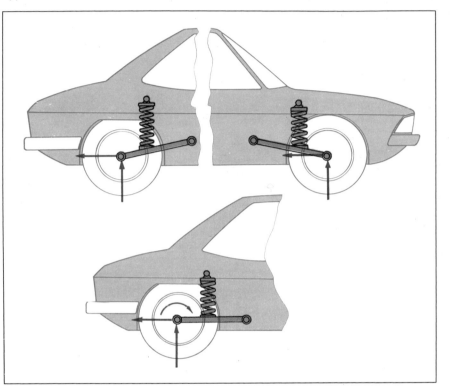

Below: unsprung weight must be kept as low as possible in order to make the wheels follow the contours of the road as closely as they can; these diagrams show the unsprung components in red and demonstrate clearly the importance of using independent suspension on the modern motor car

on their small cars and the latter on most of their front-wheel-drive models. Since the Citroën design is the simpler of the two, it is convenient to discuss it first. The front wheels are mounted on leading (forward-pointing) arms and the rear ones on trailing arms. Each arm is cranked at its pivot end, to incorporate a downward-projecting lever, and the two levers on each side of the car are connected by rods and a horizontal tension spring unit incorporating hydraulic damping.

If a front wheel rises over a bump, it tends to lift that corner of the body. It also applies a force to the spring which in turn reacts on the lever of the rear-wheel arm. This causes the latter to be rotated in the same direction as the front-wheel arm, thus causing the rear end of the body to be lifted also and so keeping it level instead of pitching. If both wheels on one side encounter a bump simultaneously, or if they are deflected upward by body roll in cornering, the resistance of the spring is greater than in the single-wheel bump situation since it is being stretched in both directions. Consequently, the spring can be made very flexible in its response to individual bumps without unduly low roll stiffness.

British Leyland have adopted two more complex systems of this type, both designed by Dr Alex Moulton. The first, the Hydrolastic system, appeared in 1962 on the Austin 1100 and was subsequently adopted

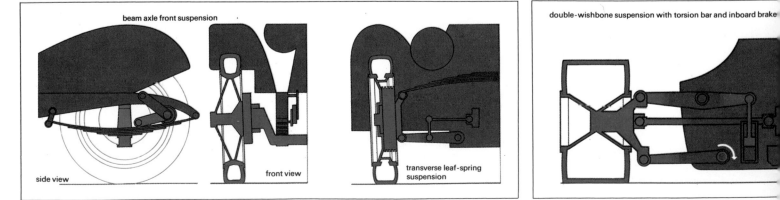

beam axle front suspension

side view

front view

transverse leaf-spring suspension

double-wishbone suspension with torsion bar and inboard brake

for a number of other models. In the Hydrolastic arrangement, each wheel has its own suspension unit comprising a rubber springing element and a fluid chamber with integral damping valves; the interconnection between the front and rear chambers on each side is by means of a fluid-filled pipe. The upward movement of one wheel displaces fluid through one damping valve and along the pipe to the other unit, which is thereby extended to compensate for the compression of the first one. This principle has been refined in the more recent Hydragas system introduced in 1973 on the Austin Allegro and later fitted to the Corporation's 18/22 cars. The rubber side of the

reduction of wheel loading moves the valve the other way and releases fluid from the suspension unit.

The Citroën and the Hydragas systems (and the related system on the Mercedes-Benz 450 SEL 6.9) rely on a constant mass of compressed gas—actually nitrogen—to act as a spring. Another form of pneumatic suspension uses a constant volume of gas, and this gives a different character to the ride: constant mass gives a rising spring rate (it gets stiffer as it is deflected) allowing soft springing in normal conditions without excessive wheel travel under heavy loads, whereas the other type gives a virtually constant rate and is no longer employed by any manufacturer.

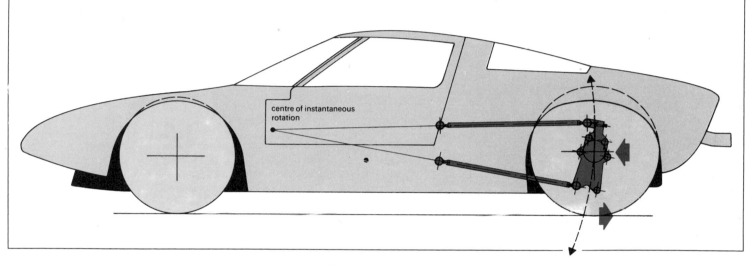

suspension units has been replaced by gas under compression, to enhance the spring response, and the damping and other details have been improved also. The effect is to make possible independent provision for soft ride and good handling stability.

For many years the bigger Citroën cars have featured an outstanding hydro-pneumatic suspension system in which the individual spring units consist of chambers containing gas which is compressed (through a diaphragm) by fluid displaced by upward movement of the wheels. The arrangement also incorporates a self-levelling facility to maintain the 'ride height' regardless of the load carried by the car, thus ensuring that full spring travel is available even when the car is fully laden. The self-levelling is effected by means of an engine-driven hydraulic pump which supplies a valve adjacent to each suspension unit. These valves are actuated by links from the wheel-carrying arms. An increase in the load on a wheel causes upward movement of its arm relative to the body; that movement operates the valve and causes fluid to flow into the unit to restore the original position of the arm. Conversely, a

Finally, there is perhaps the most advanced system of all—Automotive Products' Active Ride Control which is still in the prototype stage. In effect this is derived from Citroëns hydro-pneumatic design but taken several stages further so that, in addition to self-levelling, it also virtually eliminates roll, dive and squat, thus giving the occupants a level ride at all times. Apart from the 'amenity value', the system also makes for improved cornering ability and tyre life by obviating the usual camber changes resulting from roll.

Like Citroën's, this suspension requires an engine-driven hydraulic pump and so is relatively costly to produce. It achieves its success through a highly ingenious control arrangement for the hydraulic valves. This device distinguishes between the normal road-induced wheel travel and angular movement of the body relative to the road. It opposes the latter, by varying the amount of fluid in the suspension units, without interfering with spring response over road irregularities. Consequently the springing can be soft enough for real comfort without introducing the usual accompanying deficiences in road behaviour.

Above: anti-squat can be obtained by arranging twin trailing arms so that imaginary forward extensions of them would converge at a point, above the road surface, known as the centre of instantaneous rotation; in order for the back of the car to sink during acceleration, the wheel must move relatively backwards and this means opposing the accelerative force

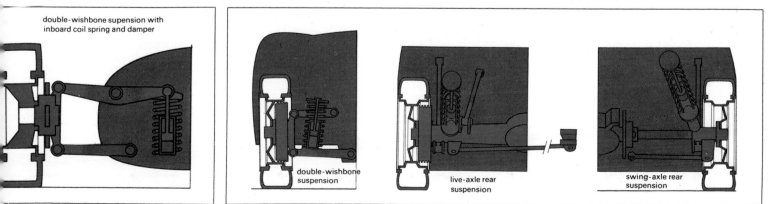

double-wishbone supension with inboard coil spring and damper

double-wishbone suspension

live-axle rear suspension

swing-axle rear suspension

DAMPERS

controlling the springs

Above: a coil-spring/ telescopic-damper unit in use on a Formula Atlantic racing car. This type of assembly is popular on road cars as well as on the vast majority of racing machinery

Right: four types of damper which have been used over the years. The ribbon damper consisted of a ribbon wrapped round and fixed at one end to a sprung pulley (rather like a tape measure) which was stiff to turn. The other end of the ribbon was connected to the suspension, thus giving damping on bump or rebound, depending on the point of connection. The friction damper was slightly later and gave two-way damping, but was not reliable or efficient. The rotary-vane damper was an early type of hydraulic unit, incorporating a two-vaned rotor which turned and moved fluid from one side of a partition to the other. The only difference between this and the lever damper is that the latter uses a normal piston

DEFLECT A SPRING and then release it; it will spring back past its original position and go on oscillating for some time, each swing being of smaller amplitude than the one before yet taking the same amount of time. The only thing that stops the oscillation from continuing undisturbed is hysteresis: the loss of energy internally through a kind of molecular friction in the structure of the spring material. A well made steel spring has low hysteresis so, when a car bounces on its springs on riding a bump, the bouncing will continue for some time afterwards. This could be dangerous and is at least disconcerting, so some means of ensuring the necessary hysteresis, or energy loss, in the system must be provided. The quality of the spring material must not be debased, so the means must be external to the spring: the damper does the work, checking the free oscillation of the spring by converting the energy stored in the spring into heat.

The damper is not a shock absorber, despite the common misuse of the term. The spring absorbs the shock, converting the force applied in deflecting it into energy stored in its mass; the damper dissipates that energy, converting it into readily dissipated heat. A good one will virtually stop the oscillation of a suspension spring in $1\frac{1}{2}$ cycles of flexure, while the torsional damper on a crankshaft should check any torsional flutter within half a degree of twist. The damper does not have to be anywhere near as strong as the spring, for surprisingly little effort may be needed to alter the frequency of oscillation from what is natural to the spring in question.

Although damping is applied to many car components having natural spring characteristics (such as crankshafts, valve springs, seat upholstery, steering, body panels, fan blades, and dozens more), the best known dampers in a car are those controlling the suspension. Nearly always, but not invariably, they are to be found near each wheel and are hydraulic. Their working principle is based on the observation that if you try to pump a lot of liquid through a tiny hole in a short time you will find it very hard work indeed: the hydraulic damper is essentially a pump in which the working fluid (oil) is forced through a small hole, or holes. The resistance of the fluid to passage through a hole becomes greater as the rate of pumping is increased, so the sharp and profound spring deflection caused by the wheel hitting a big bump at high speed will require, and get, more damping action than the gentle flexure of the spring when the wheel is rolling slowly on a smooth road.

This convenient property was not shared by the friction dampers which were in general use until the late 1930s (though the racing Mors had hydraulic dampers in 1902). These offered more resistance to spring motion when the spring was still than when it was oscillating. Various methods of varying the pressure between their friction plates were tried in attempts to improve their behaviour by reducing the

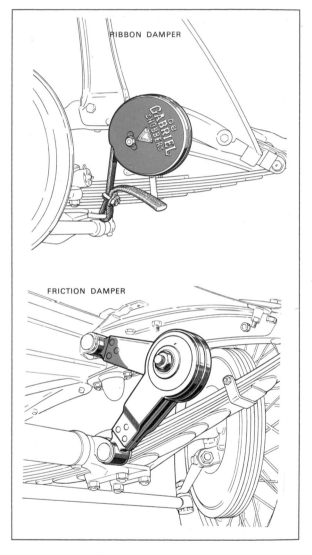

RIBBON DAMPER

FRICTION DAMPER

'stiction' or binding of the stationary plates: this culminated in the very costly, complicated and sensitive de Ram dampers most notably to be seen on some late Bugattis. Most of these methods relied on hydraulic control, so it was natural to rely on hydraulics entirely, and this became universal practice in the '50s.

Most early hydraulic dampers were linked by levers to the axle or hub carrier, the lever imparting a rotary motion to a spindle carrying a vane which pumped the fluid from one side of an internal partition to the other. Gradually, this rotary vane type (and the intermediate lever type which contained pistons in hydraulic cylinders) gave way to the telescopic damper, which is most popular today. The telescopic damper has two advantages: one is that its linear action accurately reproduces the amplitude and velocity of wheel movement (provided, as is not always the case, that it is appropriately located), the other is that it has a high ratio of surface area to volume and can therefore shed its heat more easily. Both these factors make the telescopic type more consistent and less sensitive to extraneous influences, while internally more sensitive to adjustment.

The heyday of development for this type of damper was the 1960s. Special formulations were then developed for the working fluid, based on silicone anti-foaming agents invented in the 1940s. Foaming or aeration is inimical to damping efficiency, for the bubbles of entrained air reduce the apparent viscosity of the fluid so that it can more readily be squirted

action: the pressurised gas merely controls the working fluid and replaces the old recuperation chamber which used to contain air.

There are three kinds of valve or hole through which the oil may be forced when the damper operates. One is the orifice, a plain hole of modest diameter, another is the bleed, a small hole, or holes, often arranged to act as a by-pass for certain working conditions and, thirdly, there is the blow-off valve, spring-loaded to remain closed until the pressure and rate of flow overcome the spring. Most telescopic dampers embody all three types, some only two. They are located in the piston of the moving member and at the foot of the

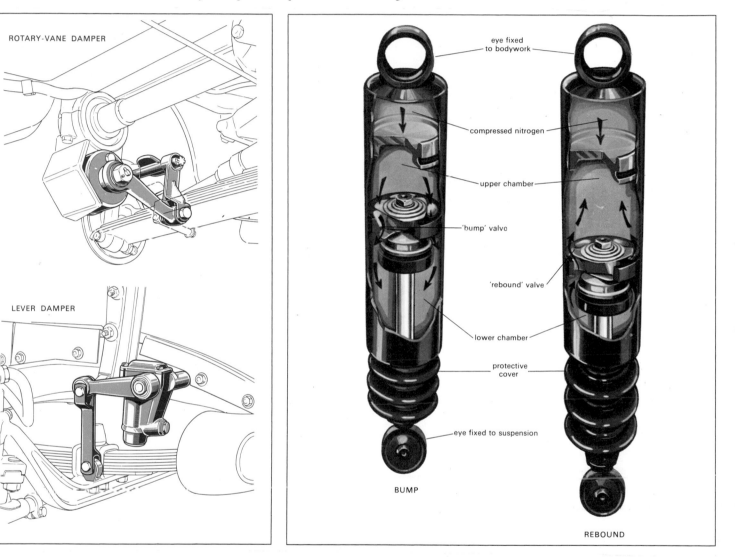

ROTARY-VANE DAMPER

LEVER DAMPER

eye fixed
to bodywork

compressed nitrogen

upper chamber

'bump' valve

'rebound' valve

lower chamber

protective
cover

eye fixed to suspension

BUMP

REBOUND

through the orifices which control its rate of flow. For similar reasons, the oil must have a high viscosity index (that is, a low rate of change of viscosity with temperature) or it will be too sensitive to heat. Damper fade, caused by heat and aeration, was a frequent problem in high-performance cars of the early 1950s.

A variety of means are adopted to combat these effects. In some dampers, the fluid is always circulated in one direction, returning by a parallel route and being cooled on the way. In others, the vacant space necessarily left inside the damper, when the correct amount of fluid has been inserted, is filled by a closed-cell plastics sacs which expand to take up space. Another innovation is the use of an inert gas in a pressure chamber separated from the oil by a free piston or an elastic diaphragm. The gas-filled damper does not in any way rely on the gas for its damping

static member, so as to control flow in either direction at any point of the piston stroke. Each type has different characteristics of response to speed and load and, by adjusting the diameter of a hole, multiplying or decreasing the number of holes, and altering the strength of the springs controlling valves, it is possible to achieve hundreds of different settings.

Some types of damper, especially those used in racing, are adjustable by external means. Adjustment may be confined to the rebound stroke only, or extend to the bump stroke as well, and may only affect the damping at high speeds (by altering the blow-off valve setting, for example) or at low, or overall. Dampers electrically controlled by the driver, while the car is in motion, have been produced in the past, but have encountered little welcome other than from Aston Martin, Bristol and Rolls-Royce.

Above: two cutaway views of a telescopic damper, showing the movement of the piston through the fluid on bump and rebound. Note how different valves open and close on each stroke, so that the damping factor can be adjusted

167

TYRES

the shoes of the motor car

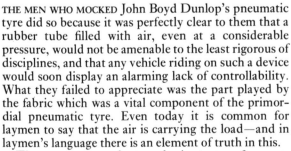

THE MEN WHO MOCKED John Boyd Dunlop's pneumatic tyre did so because it was perfectly clear to them that a rubber tube filled with air, even at a considerable pressure, would not be amenable to the least rigorous of disciplines, and that any vehicle riding on such a device would soon display an alarming lack of controllability. What they failed to appreciate was the part played by the fabric which was a vital component of the primordial pneumatic tyre. Even today it is common for laymen to say that the air is carrying the load—and in laymen's language there is an element of truth in this.

There are currently two basic types of carcass construction: one is commonly known as radial-ply, the other as cross-ply—although bias-ply or diagonal-ply would be more accurate descriptions of the latter. Combinations of the two types are also possible and have been tried from time to time.

The bias-ply is the oldest established version. In this the carcass consists of two or more layers of virtually unwoven fabric—ie all warp and no weft. The cords or threads in these layers run at an angle from one rim bead to the other. Each bead consists of a fairly stiff hoop of strong wire embedded in rubber which serves to prevent the tyre from stretching and so leaving the wheel rim, and also as an anchorage for the layers of carcass cords. This anchorage may be reinforced by additional layers of cord in more or less narrow strips

wrapped around the bead and extending for a short distance up the lower sidewall to help in bearing the severe stresses to which this clinch area around the bead is subjected. There are several variations in the arrangement of these bead wrappers, but our primary concern must be with the basic and indispensable layers or plies of carcass cords.

These layers are superimposed so that their diagonal cords lie in opposite directions, crossing to form a biased or latticed pattern. Actual inter-weaving of the cords, as in woven fabric, cannot be permitted because of the considerable friction that would occur between the cords as the carcass is flexed.

Because the pneumatic tyre must not only cushion the ride of the vehicle, but also provide its means of direction, some sort of compromise must be reached in establishing the angle at which the cords run across the tread from bead to bead. This is because the requirements of comfort and directional stability are mutually opposed. When the cords are at an angle approaching the circumferential direction of the tread, the tyre will give good stability and steering response but a harsh ride and, as speed and inflation pressure increase, the cross-sectional shape of the tyre will show considerable distortion. If on the other hand the cords could be turned until they were at right angles to the tread circumference, the ride would be the softest obtainable but the lateral stability of the tyre would disappear almost completely. For many years the obvious compromise was adopted where the cords ran at an angle of 45 degrees across the tyre, the angle between the cord

Below left: the main problem with pneumatic tyres has always been the possibility of a blow-out; this 1906 picture shows the difficulty of repairing such a puncture in the early days of motoring

Below: a Michelin 'town and country' type of tyre

explained, such a construction gives great pliability but little or no directional or dimensional stability, and this defect is rectified by the interior belt of cords running circumferentially around the carcass.

The belt has not only to prevent the radial growth of the tyre but also to provide directional stability and steering response. This is possible because, although flexible in one plane, it resists deformation in the other, behaving like a slender beam or girder. To assist in maintaining this lateral stiffness the belt is made of at least two layers of cords, which are not quite truly circumferential, but slightly diagonal, the angles usually being in the region of 18 to 22 degrees. The number of layers varies according to the material of which the cords are made and the amount of lateral stiffness desired. When the cords are spun from fine steel wire there are almost invariably (in car tyres) only two layers or plies of breaker cords; when the cords are made of rayon or polyester, the number of plies may be four, five or even six. It is very rare to find seven.

Until World War II practically all tyres had carcasses

and the equatorial or centre line of the tread being known as the crown angle. Later this angle was reduced to about 40 degrees, and 30 degrees or even less for tyres built for very high speeds.

The idea behind the radial-ply tyre was to eliminate this compromise in cord angles and to divide the carcass into two parts, one to provide the desired ride qualities and the other the necessary directional qualities. By motoring standards the idea is of great antiquity. It can be traced back to a British patent granted prior to World War I to Messrs Gray and Sloper. Their claim was sufficiently detailed in 1913 to establish all the basic principles of the radial-ply tyre from which all subsequent patterns have evolved.

In 1913 it was thought that the girder belt should be on the inside of the casing, beneath the tyre tread; but today the manufacturers of radial-ply tyres universally put the belt on the outside of the casing. This belt consists of a relatively stiff band of cords that have adequate flexibility but great resistance to stretching: being inextensible, they are relied upon entirely to restrict the radial growth of the inflated tube. Paradoxically, this inability of the belted tyre's circumference to expand serves to prevent it from contracting in the same way as does the part of a cross-ply tyre's circumference in the region of the contact area, but this is something into which we will go later. At any rate the inextensible nature of this broad belt makes it behave like a girder in its own plane, preventing it from distorting or flexing appreciably in any plane but that at right-angles to its surface.

This being so, it is possible to introduce the other essential feature of the construction, tyre cords running radially from bead to bead—that is, crossing the crown of the tyre at right angles, not diagonally. As already

Right: a selection of automobile tyres chosen from various motoring periods—from left to right and top to bottom they are Pirelli Cord (1900–10), Dunlop (1900–10), Michelin (1910), Martin (1910), Goodrich Balloon (1915), Goodrich Souple Cord (1918–25), Pirelli Super Flex (1918–25), Dunlop (1920), Dunlop (1930), Michelin (1930), Pirelli White Star (1935) and Metzeler asymmetrical (1952–3)

made of long staple cotton; but then rayon was introduced, not as a means of making a stronger carcass but as a means of saving rubber. A rayon tyre could be made thinner than a cotton one of equivalent strength, and therefore needed less rubber to separate the plies and cords from each other to prevent chafing. Cotton rapidly disappeared, and rayon is the staple material in the majority of tyres today.

More recently nylon was introduced, originally in aircraft tyres. It is stronger, more elastic, more flexible and consequently cooler running than rayon, and is therefore used principally in tyres built for high speeds or heavy loads. Its elasticity makes it unsuitable for use in radial-ply tyres on its own, although it is sometimes used in ultra-high-speed radial-ply tyres in combination with other materials. Even in bias-ply tyres, however, it has certain disadvantages, the most evident being a tendency towards what is called flat spotting or cold flatting: the nylon cords tend to lose their flexibility when cold, and if a tyre is left to stand for

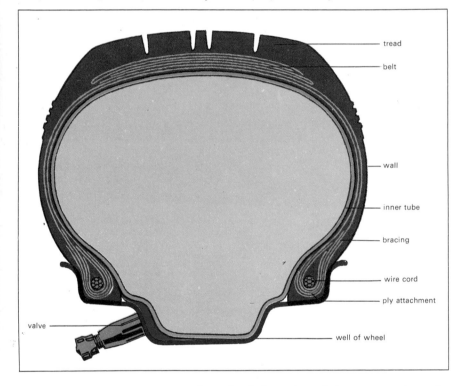

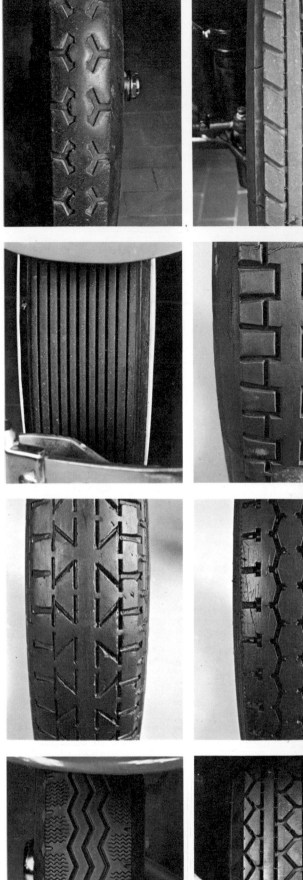

Above: a section through a tubed radial tyre

Far right: as cars have become faster, so tyre design has had to change; not only have materials improved, but the shape of the tyre has altered considerably

some time, the deformation of the carcass where the tyre is resting on the road takes on a semi-permanent nature, so that when the car is driven again the ride is harsh and bumpy until the tyre casing has warmed up sufficiently to recover its flexibility.

For many years, efforts have been made to substitute Terylene (or polyester) as a carcass material, the principal difficulty having been the achieving of a satisfactory bond between this and the rubber. The material is tough and durable, but its principal attraction to the tyre manufacturer is a lower cost of production.

We may note briefly the recent development of glass fibre as a material for the cords of rigid breakers. Glass is exceptionally strong and surprisingly elastic, but special techniques have to be used to prevent chafing of the glass filaments that must be wound or spun into cords, and further expertise is necessary to achieve a satisfactory bonding of the glass to the rubber. Subject to the few exceptions already noted, the breaker plies of radial-ply tyres are made exclusively of steel or rayon; and although the trend of the 1960s was towards a more general adoption of rayon, there are now signs of a

Tread labels on diagram: tread, belt, wall, inner tube, bracing, wire cord, ply attachment, well of wheel, valve

reversal of this trend. Recently, manufacturers have increasingly returned to the use of steel.

This reversal is due to the important part played by breaker construction in determining the tread-wear resistance of the radial-ply tyre. The resistance of the breaker band to edgewise bending is responsible for the dimensional stability of the tread in the contact patch; and in fact the greatest possible rigidity is achieved by the use of steel breaker cords at a low crown angle.

The greater beam stiffness of the steel belt is not the only attraction of steel; its greater strength allows the use of fewer plies and thus encourages a thinning of the tyre. The situation is analogous to the reasons for replacing cotton with rayon in bias-ply tyres: less rubber is required, and therefore the tyre can flex more easily, the build-up of heat is less rapid, and the dissipation of the heat accumulated occurs more readily due to the reduced ratio of mass to surface area.

Rayon is preferred in the carcass because it forms an exceptionally strong bond with the rubber to which it is

permits lateral displacement of the tread with respect to its relationship with the rim.

Thus these differences in basic construction give the radial-ply tyre lower rolling resistance than the bias-ply alternative, longer tread life, higher cornering power at smaller slip angles, better tractive and braking grip, a better high-speed ride, and comparative freedom from centrifugal growth, from wander induced by longitudinal ridges in the road surface, and from side loadings induced by wheel camber. Together with these advantages, there are disadvantages: a harsher low-speed ride, heavier steering at low speeds and when parking, a tendency to break away more suddenly at the ultimate limit of adhesion, an occasional instability in S-bends, and a certain vulnerability of the sidewalls.

Rubber is a marvellous material, but a weird one. It is very non-linear in its behaviour, which offends engineers; but it is also remarkably accommodating, which delights them.

Vulcanization makes the natural *plastic* material (that

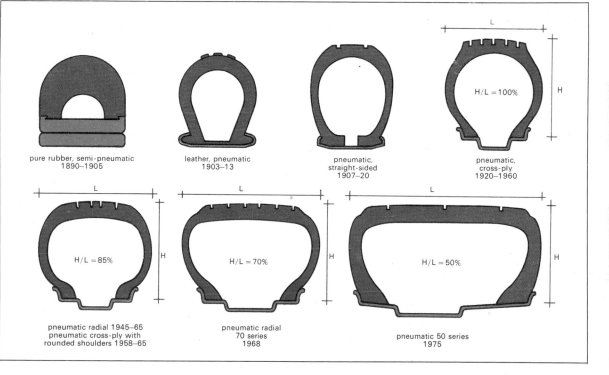

pure rubber, semi-pneumatic
1890–1905

leather, pneumatic
1903–13

pneumatic,
straight-sided
1907–20

pneumatic,
cross-ply
1920–1960
H/L = 100%

H/L = 85%
pneumatic radial 1945–65
pneumatic cross-ply with
rounded shoulders 1958–65

H/L = 70%
pneumatic radial
70 series
1968

H/L = 50%
pneumatic 50 series
1975

mated, and because satisfactory flexibility is combined with a good resistance to endwise stretch.

This whole problem of sidewall stiffness has been the subject of concentrated study in the past few years, in the effort to improve the handling characteristics of radial-ply tyres in the more violent type of manoeuvres. It was some time before designers learned the importance of controlling the flexibility of the sidewalls in radial-ply tyres, as this flexibility permits an appreciable delay in response between tyre tread and wheel rim. Furthermore, radial-ply sidewalls are especially sensitive to the transmission of tractive or braking torques which (according to circumstances) may degrade or heighten their lateral response.

Work on this problem has led to the evolution of what might be called the 'second generation' of radial-ply tyres, in which the real or apparent stiffness of the sidewalls has been increased in order to improve lateral response. This capacity for lateral distortion is called side-wall compliance. The flexural ability of the sidewalls should not be reduced, as this accommodates variations in the distance between the tread and the wheel rim; but it is advisable to avoid the distortion that

is, one which flows under the effect of heat or pressure) into an *elastic* one which, after stretching, returns to its original shape. This is the critical property in engineering, the key to the term 'elastomer' that we use to describe all materials, natural or otherwise, that have this particular rubbery property.

A further property of elastomers is unique: when stretched they become warm, and when contracted they become cool. Conversely they can display what is known as the Joule effect, contracting when heated and elongating when cool. Today there are fifteen families of elastomers many of them suitable for incorporation in tyre compounds.

Now that such a large variety of polymers and compounding ingredients for tyre rubber is available, the tyre designer has much more scope in the selection of a compound for a particular job. Tyres perform in a great variety of conditions, each one calling for a tread compound or a combination of compounds in the tyre, each with its own particular behaviour and characteristics. As in most kinds of design, success depends on achieving the best possible compromise, and one physical property in rubber is often obtainable only at the expense of others that are equally desirable.

To appreciate what the tyre chemist has to face, let us briefly consider the various enemies of rubber in one form or another. Probably the greatest of these enemies is heat which, if allowed to build up unchecked, will eventually cause chemical and physical degradation of the vulcanized rubber and a disastrous loss of strength. The heat may be put into a tyre by radiation or conduction from its surroundings, but most of it is the product of internal friction resulting from the inevitable flexure of the tyre as it rolls along the road. The tyre being an elastic body, its entire structure is subject to one flexure in the course of one complete rotation of the tyre. Fifteen years ago an average car tyre would suffer 750 flexures in the course of a mile, suffering them at the rate of about 20 flexures per second when the car was doing 100 mph. The corresponding figure today is more likely to approach 980 flexures per mile or 27 flexures per second at 100 mph. Every flexure involves a displacement of material and therefore the generation of internal friction in the tyre material, which inevitably engenders heat. Furthermore, friction heat attributable to the transmission of tractive, cornering or braking efforts on the road surface, and any of the other things that may cause abrasion or distortion, must be considered.

Rubbers are also generally susceptible to chemical attack, being unsaturated organic compounds which

wet cobblestones, but if it excels in any one of these things it will probably have little capacity to deal with the others.

The term *hysteresis* should be explained before proceeding further. 'High hysteresis' is a comparative term, and for the sake of definition it is applied to compounds having a rebound resilience of appreciably

Left: a cutaway view of a tubeless-tyre valve; the rubber base is vulcanised into the tyre carcass and the valve core is screwed into the housing

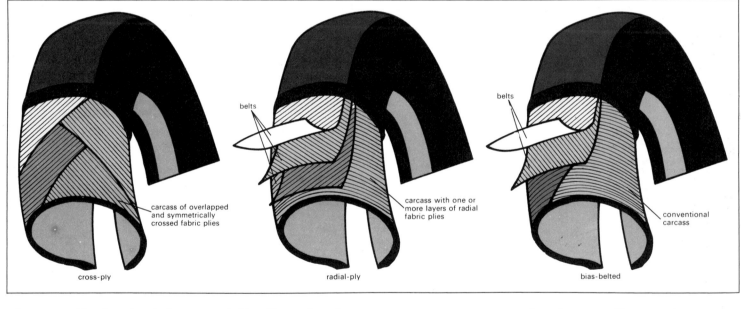

carcass of overlapped and symmetrically crossed fabric plies

cross-ply

belts

carcass with one or more layers of radial fabric plies

radial-ply

belts

conventional carcass

bias-belted

often react with other chemical reagents. Acids, chlorine, hydrogen, sulphur, oxides of nitrogen, and many other everyday commodities may be severely degrading. Even atmospheric oxygen attacks rubber, slowly causing it to become hard and brittle. Ozone attacks it more rapidly and is often present in greater concentrations than might be thought. Many liquids act as solvents of rubber; water, alcohol and acetone do not but petrol, benzine, turpentine, carbon tetrachloride and several other things will cause rubber to swell and disperse. This is a convenient way of making viscous cements, but very damaging to tyres. Even ultra-violet light can damage rubber.

There are other problems that must be dealt with by the tread rubber. Abrasion resistance is an obvious one, as are resistance to tearing and cutting (which are not related). Furthermore the tread must be compounded so as to behave in the desired way on wet roads, cold roads, hot roads or even where there are no roads at all. It may be expected to grip best on snow, melting ice, or

less than 50 per cent at a temperature of 50 degrees centigrade. In other words, it only gives back half the energy that is put into deforming it. The other half is absorbed, which is what hysteresis means. A high-hysteresis rubber is less springy, less resilient, than a natural rubber: it does not have the characteristic lively rebound, but is sluggish. Because of this it has a greater tendency to stay in intimate contact with the road surface, to envelop any projections of surface texture, and thus to provide very good grip, especially when the surface is wet. This last feature is quite remarkable, for water is a natural lubricant not only of natural rubber but also of many synthetic varieties; this will be discussed later. However, there is relatively high internal friction in such a rubber, and an obvious corollary of this is a considerable power absorption, therefore a car fitted with tyres of extra-high-grip rubber may be slightly slower and have a slightly heavier fuel consumption than one running on tyres of more resilient rubber.

Above: the three types of tyre reinforcement in common use in the 1970s; the bias belted tyre is a combination of cross-ply and radial-ply constructions

The perplexing situation is made yet more confusing by the effect of temperature on the performance of these various types of rubbers. For any particular one, the coefficient of friction that it can manifest on a given road surface rises to a peak as its temperature is increased to a certain point, and then as the temperature rises further the coefficient of friction becomes reduced.

violent acceleration and braking increase the tyre temperature markedly. Further one must remember that the essence of the high hysteresis, lazy, or 'cling' rubber is a high level of internal friction which tends to make the tyre run hot, in contrast to the cooler and more friction-free tyre treaded with highly resilient or low-hysteresis polymers.

excessive pressure   normal pressure   insufficient pressure

Above left: the Pirelli BS3 tyre, characterised by its interchangeable tread bands

Above: diagrams showing how tyre-pressure settings affect the amount of tread which rests on the road

Left: radial covers are used in racing as well as on the road; these are tyres which were available for use at Mugello in 1975 by the victorious Alpine team

An important thing to bear in mind here is that the critical temperature is that of the rubber, not that of the road nor that of the surrounding air. Climate certainly makes a difference, but not as much as the duties to which the tyre is subjected. The bigger the tyre's load-bearing capacity, the higher its inflation pressure, or the greater its diameter, the cooler it will run; and of course the additional frictional heat built up by the trellising motion of the carcass cords in a bias-ply tyre is absent from the radial-ply tyre, which therefore runs cooler still. The high-speed tyre (deliberately designed with relatively thin treads and shallow shoulders to avoid heat build-up) can dissipate its heat more readily than tyres of more conventional proportions, profiting more from air cooling amongst other things. On the other hand high speeds, heavy loads, rough road surfaces,

Several practical conclusions can be drawn from this. First, it is not strictly possible to state flatly that a particular tyre provides particularly good grip either on the roads in general, or on wet or snowy roads in particular: judgement must be related to the temperature. This has been a particular problem in racing: tread compounds for Formula One Grand Prix tyres are often designed to function at temperatures exceeding 100 degrees C, but if the track be wet they may not even reach 100 degrees F. The problems of producing a satisfactory all-weather racing tyre are therefore enormous. Even for ordinary road-going vehicles the all-weather tyre is little more than an illusion.

The detailed differences in carcass construction are usually concealed within the tyre. The secrets locked within the rubber are for all practical purposes un-

173

fathomable. Unlike these, the tread pattern is there to be seen and judged. There are (for once) some sound and simple criteria to support one's judgement, making it possible to evaluate by eye the tyre's probable behaviour in terms of noise, grip, and wear.

Noise may be generated by a tyre in three different ways. First there is the squeal that is caused by friction between rubber and road surface and varies according to the nature of the rubber compound. There are also various types of vibration caused either by the roughness of the road surface or by the distortion of the tyre carcass as it revolves. Noise is also generated by the tread pattern itself. This is overcome by introducing deliberate irregularities into the tyre pattern, slightly varying the size of tread blocks or the zig-zag pattern of grooves so as to dampen the sound rather than to amplify it.

The matter of grip is more complicated. On a clean dry road surface the maximum grip is given by a completely smooth tyre, since this will put the greatest possible area of rubber in contact with the road. But the slightest presence of moisture on the road transforms it into something lethally dangerous.

It must be recognised that the retention of tyre grip on the road is a matter which is dependent as much on the nature of the tread pattern as on the chemistry of the tread compound. Where the road surface is smooth, the nature of the rubber is far less important than the ability of the tread pattern to push the surface water out of the way so that the tyre rubber can at least grip the road metal in some places. Where the road surface is open-textured and thus to some extent self-draining, the tread pattern cannot and need not function so effectively in sweeping aside water; the important factor is the degree of friction that can be realised between the rubber and the road where they make contact at the pinnacle of every irregularity. It is a useless over-simplification to talk about a given tyre being good or bad in the wet.

The tread pattern has two basic functions: it must provide drainage and bite. These two ideals are to some extent conflicting. Bite is the easier function to understand: the tread needs a quantity of reasonably sharp

well-defined edges that will engage with the road surface to provide some mechanical rather than merely frictional transmission of load; these edges need to be transverse for good traction and braking and longitudinal for steering and cornering. Most car manoeuvres involve both, and their needs can be met by resolving these forces into diagonal biting edges in the tread pattern.

However, the tyre may never come sufficiently close to the road surface for these edges to engage with it, if there is much water on the road. On streaming wet surfaces the water may build up in front of the tyre as a wedge, which at speed will be driven underneath to raise the tyre clear of the road and make it completely waterborne. This is termed aquaplaning.

If water is not to build up ahead of the tyre on a wet road, it must either be swept aside or be channelled away. Sweeping aside is clearly difficult at high speeds, especially with the wider tyres that are gradually and on the whole sensibly becoming fashionable. The same trend makes nonsense of some manufacturers' theories about lateral drainage of water through tread channels leading to the shoulders: this works well for the outermost portions of the tread, but satisfactory drainage of the middle portion can only be achieved by the provision of longitudinal passages. For effective drainage these must be as straight as possible and unimpeded. The removal of obstructions is comparatively easy in the case of a radial-ply tyre, whose tread is relatively free from distortion so that its grooves need not be closed by buttresses put there to support the ribs. Ensuring that the groove is absolutely straight, however, removes the necessary transverse biting elements from the tread pattern and so lessens performance in acceleration and braking.

When a car stands on its tyres they will, whatever their kind, suffer a certain amount of deflection and distortion. When the car moves, further distortions are superimposed on this basic one.

The effectiveness with which a tyre transmits tractive, braking or cornering forces to the road surface is affected by the variations in size and loading of the contact area. Because the contact area or 'footprint' of a radial-ply tyre is greater than that of an equivalent bias-ply tyre performing the same duties, such a tyre gives a better flotation effect. Its action is analogous to that of a track laid by a crawler vehicle: the ground pressure is relatively low and very evenly distributed. The same applies to any tyre that is run at a relatively low inflation

Below: the construction of a radial tyre. The synthetic rubber is mixed with lamp black and squeezed into a continuous strip (**1**), while the fabric weave is impregnated with rubber and cut into strips (**2**). This fabric is rolled onto a drum to form a cylinder and narrow strips are added each side to form the sidewalls (**3**). The cylinder is transferred to another machine where it is inflated and squeezed into shape (**4**); at this stage the bracing belts are added (**5**). The tread bands are next glued, cut and applied to the belts (**6**). The final process is to vulcanise the tyre to make the parts stick together and to give them elasticity; it is heated and squeezed in a press, which also adds the tread pattern and the writing (**7 & 8**)

1

2

3

4

pressure, and the effect is to give better grip on mud, sand and other loose surfaces.

On the other hand there are occasions when penetration rather than flotation is required. The small-section high-pressure tyre can often produce better results in snow (which has no shear strength) or on very thin ice (on frosted roads for example) than the large low-pressure tyre.

It must be remembered that load transfer during braking, acceleration, cornering, or combinations of braking or acceleration with cornering, will similarly vary the size of the contact patch.

The reason for the change for tyre and pressures having dropped considerably, especially markedly in the last ten years, is simply that lower profiles offer the possibilities of improvement in most performance parameters except ride comfort, which is sensibly decreased. All these changes, whether improvements or otherwise, are derived from the generally greater vertical and lateral stiffness of the low profile tyre. There must be accepted as its characteristics, although it is perfectly possible to build a low-profile tyre that is less stiff in both directions than a given tyre of higher profile.

The greater vertical stiffness is responsible for the less comfortable ride of such a tyre and for its greater load-carrying capacity. A more important effect of the increased vertical stiffness is the change it makes in the shape of the contact patch, which becomes shorter and wider. Many performance parameters are changed by this simple readjustment of proportions. It will run cooler and last longer and may even demand a different type of rubber compound in order to suit these different temperatures or to exploit the better wear potential. Finally there are the changes in tyre behaviour brought about by the increased lateral stiffness of a low profile, these involving increased sensitivity to camber variations and a more prompt response to steering inputs.

There are greater complications issuing from the interdependence of load, inflation pressure and cornering power. The cornering force that the tyre is capable of sustaining may increase up to a certain point with an increase in the load that it is carrying, and beyond that point it will decrease again. If, instead of altering the load, the inflation pressure is altered, the same thing may or may not happen: up to a certain point the cornering ability increases, but beyond that point it may or may not increase, again according to the type and size of the tyre and the load it is carrying. Thus armed with one or two basic principles it can be seen that there are circumstances in which the car on fat tyres may in fact corner no faster than a car on thin tyres, although it generally has better handling characteristics.

An increase in rim width may have the effect of reducing sidewall compliance in even the most flexible of conventional radial-ply tyres. Within reasonable limits the idea is a good one, but the limits beyond which it becomes dangerous are strict. the mode of flexure may be very different from what the sidewalls were originally intended to suffer, and the flexure may in particular be concentrated in an area not designed to submit to it. Fatigue failures of sidewall, clinch or bead areas may be shockingly premature where these limits are transgressed.

Below: four pieces of tyre from various eras; *top left,* 1906, *top right,* 1917, *bottom left,* 1927, *bottom right,* 1947

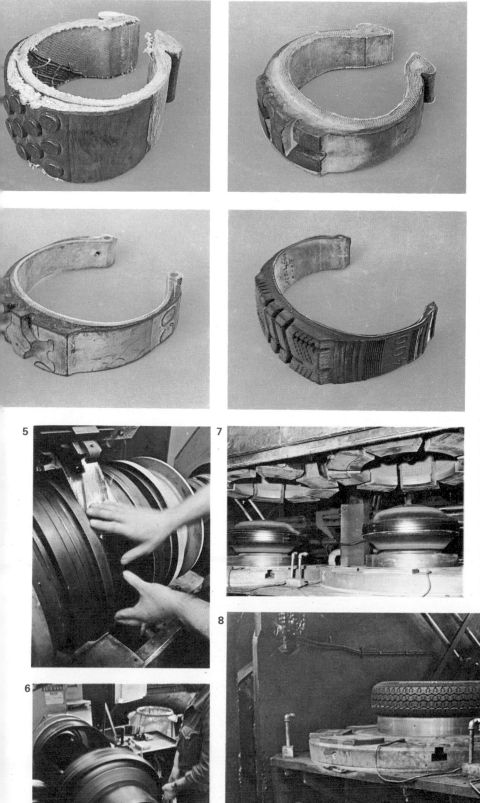

5

6

7

8

The relationship between rim width and tyre width is not immutable, but there are some sound general rules by which to abide. First note that the actual cross-sectional width of a tyre often differs from its nominal width: a 6.00V16 tyre, for example, is actually 7.2 inches wide when set on a 4½ inch rim. Next, note that an increase of half an inch in rim width will add a fifth of an inch to the tyre width. Now, allowing for all this, the rim should normally be at least 60 per cent as wide as the tyre, and preferably 70 per cent. Especially in the case of radial-ply tyres, it is better to err on the wide side, but 85 per cent should not normally be exceeded. Special tyres may demand different fittings: racing tyres sometimes have rims as wide as themselves, while most of the recent generation of 'safety' or 'run-flat' tyres are designed to fit narrow rims.

Best known of these is the Dunlop Denovo, a belted radial of low profile, designed so that when deflated it will allow itself to be distorted radially but not laterally. Thus the deliberately narrow rim specified for the special wheel falls closer to the ground until the bead area of the tyre makes contact with the inside of the tread area, cushioning the rim against the road; the friction likely to be generated there is abated by lubrication with a fluid secreted in capsules lodged within the tyre cavity and broken when the tyre goes down. The fluid contains a volatile component that then generates a vapour pressure of about four pounds per square inch which is enough to partly repressurize the tyre. With these aids the Denovo can be run in the post-deflation state for about one hundred miles at speeds of up to fifty miles an hour.

Capable of running without any internal pressurisation at all, without relaying on internal liquids and *without any carcass cords*, the prototype Pirelli triangular tyre is a signpost to a future in which tyres promise to be very different. Its sidewalls are a pair of incurved arches in compression, springing from a very narrow rim which firmly clasps their unwired bead ends, whilst the outer ends are connected and restrained by transverse tension in the tread belt which is the only reinforcement within the tyre. External applied loads, horizontal and vertical, are transmitted by the sidewalls acting as solid rubber compression springs; static load and inflation pressure both tend to pre-stress the sidewall arch so that it is always in compression, even when cornering. Furthermore, the shaping of the sidewalls and the characteristics of the rubber (much more accurately predictable in the absence of carcass cords) produce a non-linear response to loading, so the capacity of the tyre actually increases to meet any extra demands on it. For example in cornering, the lateral load compresses, thickens, and stiffens the opposing sidewall 'spring' in a progressive way that positively assists prompt and accurate steering.

The result is a tyre that gives an astonishingly soft ride and beautifully damped kick-free steering but yet combines outstanding adhesion and steering response with high cornering power—all without any material sensitivity to inflation pressure, camber, load or speed. It is a very squat tyre, being made initially as a 50 per cent aspect ratio tyre (that is, the distance from rim to road is half the width of the tyre) but capable of being made even lower in profile, down to about 10 per cent: this brings attractions of space saving, not only because the spare tyre is otiose, but because either wheel arches can be made smaller, or else the brakes and steering or suspension mechanisms can occupy more space inside the wheel.

More extraordinary facts continue to emerge. Perforating the sidewall has no effect: the compressive state closes the holes—so the conventional valve can be eliminated, inflation being done through a hypodermic needle! Because there is no carcass to be hand-lasted as in a conventional tyre (in the manufacture of which there is a great deal of manual work), the thing can be processed almost entirely automatically, to the benefit of uniformity and therefore of ride—though, in any case, the tyre will itself absorb and damp any vibrations entering or engendered in it. Suspension can therefore be simpler because compliance (which isolates belt-induced vibrations from conventional tyres) will be unnecessary. The lack of camber sensitivity allows suspensions to be even simpler, to be much less expensive to manufacture and to require much less space. The conventional tyre has come an amazingly long way in about ninety years; inside another ten years what now appears to be a most unconventional tyre may be expected to supplant today's version.

Top left: Pirelli across the world

Top right: one of the earliest types of tyre, made in leather, which is primitive compared with the Pirelli run-flat tyre of 1974 (centre); the triangular-section tyre requires a special wheel, as shown

Above: studs are fitted to many tyres used in snowy conditions for extra traction

BODY & CHASSIS

BODYWORK REPAIRS

keeping the body beautiful

Any rust holes must be thoroughly cleaned up before filling. If the back of the panel cannot be reached, the edges of the holes must be hammered in to allow glassfibre and resin to be used. Brush the edges with resin and hardener, then apply a glassfibre patch just larger than each hole. Push the patch gently into the hole, using a stippling brush, dipped in resin and hardener, to impregnate the fibre

When the resin is dry, filler paste should be used to fill any remaining indentations. Allow the filler to stand slightly proud, then it can be rubbed down, using a file or wet-or-dry paper, until it matches the body contours. Any minor imperfections will have to be refilled

Left: the filler should now be rubbed down with progressively finer grades of wet-or-dry paper, finally leaving a perfectly smooth surface for painting

Right: the area to be sprayed should be masked from the rest of the car, using paper and tape. Primer should be applied before turning attention to the top coat

OWING TO A NUMBER of factors, including the soaring cost of skilled labour and constant increases in the price of spare body parts, perhaps the most expensive repairs carried out on the average motor car are those concerned with bodywork damage. These high costs and, in some cases, a low standard of finished work, are encouraging more and more private motorists to attempt to repair minor body damage themselves. This can, in many cases, be carried out quite successfully by a reasonably competent do-it-yourself man but it must be borne in mind that a modicum of skill, a lot of patience and considerable time must be spent on carrying out such work if a high standard of finish is to be achieved.

Furthermore, no attempt at rectifying body damage should be made unless a thorough study of the cause and effect of the incident responsible for the damage is carried out. Although body damage may appear to be only superficial to the untrained eye, a creased panel or a slightly buckled wing may hide a much more serious condition which is inherently dangerous to the performance and safety of the vehicle.

If a car has received what appears to be superficial damage to the front or front wing areas, a careful inspection should be made to ensure that the radiator has not been punctured or moved. Following this a careful check should be made on the water level at every opportunity to ensure that water is not leaking away through a badly fitting or stretched hose or from a damaged coupling. If the vehicle in question is fitted with a water temperature gauge this too should be checked; first of all to make sure that it is still in working order and then a watch should be kept on it to ascertain whether the cooling system is still functioning at the same level of efficiency as before the incident causing the damage.

Yet another check may be instituted by inspecting the headlamp settings. If it proves impossible, or even

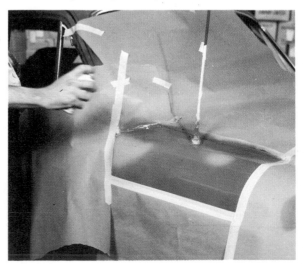

When using resin, only a small amount should be mixed with hardener at a time, otherwise it may dry before it is needed. A plastic cup is ideal for mixing the two components, which should be stirred thoroughly. To fill a split in a metal panel, resin should be applied to the back of the split, after the surface has been thoroughly cleaned and derusted. Plastic tape should be stuck to the front of the split, to prevent the resin running through

A suitable grade and size of glassfibre matting should be chosen—the patch should generously cover the split. It pays to wear plastic or rubber gloves when dealing with glassfibre, as it tends to stick in the skin. The matting should be laid on the resin, then more resin should be worked into the matting, using a stippling brush, until the glassfibre is totally impregnated. This should then be allowed to dry

It is advisable to lay up a second piece of matting on the first, after it has dried, to give it added strength. The same procedure should be followed. When this is dry, the tape can be removed from the front of the split and the indentation filled using a paste mix worked carefully into the damaged area. When mixing filler, do so by 'layering' as stirring tends to introduce air bubbles which need refilling after rubbing down

just very difficult to set these correctly following what appears to have been a minor accident, this could indicate something quite serious, such as a twisted subframe or a deformed side rail in the vehicle's unitary body.

A careful study should also be made of the steering performance of the vehicle following minor shunts. If the steering should develop a distinct pull to one side, or be unable to hold a straight line when the driver removes his hands from the steering wheel, this usually indicates that some damage has been caused to the steering linkage or that the steering geometry of the car has been affected. Furthermore, the braking action of the car should still ensure that it pulls up in a straight line when the brakes are applied. Another check should be made for uneven tyre wear on one or both front wheels. If the steering geometry has been affected in any way, uneven wear should quickly manifest itself and the services of a proper garage be used to return the whole steering system to peak efficiency.

Other indicators that serious though hidden damage has occurred, include a badly fitting bonnet lid or passenger doors that do not shut without extra effort being applied or which, suddenly, do not match up with the door striker plates on the door pillars.

A similar check should be carried out following damage to the rear section of the car. The boot lid should be checked for ease of action and tight fit. Uneven tyre wear should be watched for on the rear wheels also. A simple method of testing the rear-wheel geometry and brakes is to use only the handbrake to pull up the vehicle on a deserted stretch of road. As the modern car's handbrake usually works only on the rear wheels, any pulling to one side by the vehicle would indicate that a more thorough check should be made on the whole rear suspension and braking system.

Rust is another factor that should be considered when discussing body damage. Any rust appearing on the surface of a motor car's bodywork should be dealt with immediately by sanding away and then repainting with primer and a matching proprietary paint.

Body damage is not dealt with quite so easily, even though repairs are within the capability of most people, provided sufficient time and care is taken at each stage of the repair procedure. The equipment needed consists, usually, of an electric power hand tool, a body file, some sheets of rubbing down paper of various grades, a rubbing block, a screwdriver and a proprietary body filler kit which contains both the filler compound and a catalytic agent. For finishing the repair the usual method is to use aerosol cans of primer and paint, readily available from most accessory shops.

It can be deduced from the above, that amateur body repairs do not involve the body straightening or panel beating techniques used by the professional. The main method for the amateur is to use the body filler to restore the original contour of the damaged panel and to repaint it, rather than to attempt to restore the damaged metal to its original condition.

The first step in a repair of this nature is to fit a coarse sanding disc to the power tool and use this to sand away paint, primer, dirt and rust from the damaged area until bare metal is showing. Care should be taken to sand right to the edges of the area under repair and just slightly into the surrounding, undamaged paintwork. After power sanding a medium grade of rubbing paper should be fitted to the rubbing block and used on the metal to give a high degree of smoothness to the affected area. Touching the sanded area with the fingertips should be avoided as grease from the skin will prevent the filler compound from

179

'keying' properly to the prepared area and could result in an unsatisfactory standard of finish.

The next stage is to prepare the filler compound. A quantity of paste (perhaps half a small can, but dependent on the size of the area to be repaired) should be scooped out of the can and placed on a clean, smooth working surface which is free from pitting or ridging—a piece of Formica is ideal. The paste should be spread out and the catalytic agent—which converts the paste into a hard setting, very tough and durable compound—is added to the paste. The usual proportion is a half tube of the catalyst to a half can of paste.

Using the paste applicator, usually a piece of stiff plastic which is included in the filler kit, mix the paste and the catalyst with a smooth forwards and backwards action of the wrist. This should be done in such a manner as to ensure that not only are the two parts of the compound mixed thoroughly, but also that any air bubbles trapped in the filler are eliminated.

Again using the applicator, apply the filler to the damaged area of the car, just a little at a time and spread in layers. Pushing the filler hard down onto the area, layers should be applied until the filler stands a little proud of the remainder of the body panel under

repair. The filler should then be allowed to harden. Time taken for this varies and heat can be used to accelerate the process, but the longer a car can be left in a clean, dry atmosphere the better. Even so, two or three days is more than sufficient.

Once the filler has set, the high spots of it should be rubbed away. The first step in this process is undertaken with the special, but inexpensive body file which can be adjusted to conform to the curvature of the vehicle's contours. Following this, a medium grade of rubbing paper fitted to the rubbing block should be used to smooth the repaired area and to feather the repair into the surrounding, undamaged areas of the vehicle's bodywork.

Once a smooth finish has been achieved—and in order to effect a really first class job—the repair should be left for at least a week, preferably two. After this, a final skim coat of the body filler is applied to the area after sanding down once more with a fine grade of wet or dry paper and then drying off thoroughly. The skim coat should be so thin as to allow the original filler to be seen through it and the purpose of this final coat is to fill in any small and in some cases invisible holes which might have appeared on the original surface.

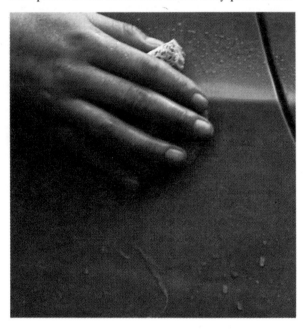

Left: before repairing a scratch, clean the surrounding area with a cloth dipped in white spirit. This will remove any grease or wax which might prevent filler from 'keying' into the damaged part

Right: mix a small quantity of filler paste and rub it across the scratch so that it completely fills the depression. Leave the filler standing slightly proud so that it can be rubbed smooth when dry. Use only a very fine grade of wet-or-dry paper and keep it wet

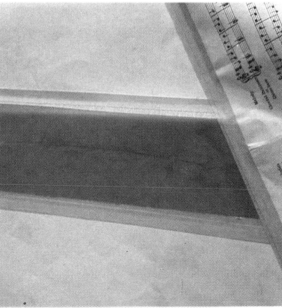

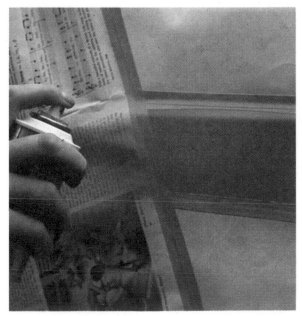

Left: once the surface of the filler is flush with the existing paint, mask the area surrounding the damage from the rest of the body, using newspaper and masking tape. Make sure the surface is dry before painting

Right: apply two coats of primer before turning to the top coat. Once again, use wet-or-dry paper to smooth the paint between coats. Keep spraying top coats until the area is completely covered and shows no patches

Following this, and having allowed time for the skim to harden, the whole area should be rubbed down once more with a very fine grade of rubbing paper, used dry, and then finally finished off with an even finer grade of wet or dry paper, used wet and without the rubbing block, using light hand pressure only.

After allowing this final skim coat to harden thoroughly, perhaps for another week, the repair is then ready for painting. To do this, the area to be painted should be washed thoroughly with clean, cold water and then dried. Brown paper and adhesive tape should then be used to mask around the repaired area in order to prevent overspray affecting undamaged paintwork. If working in the wing area of the car the wheels and tyres should also be masked off; and if working near glass this too should be covered over.

Aerosol primer is then applied, the aerosol being held about 12 inches from the area to be sprayed and a forward and backward action is used, taking care to spray in a straight line and not with an arcing action. Allow the primer to dry and then rub down with a very fine grade of wet or dry paper, used wet. Wash the primed area and then allow to dry thoroughly. Paint should be applied in the same way as the primer but with the button of the aerosol being released at the end of each stroke in order to minimise paint build up.

A further coat of paint should be applied once the original layer has been allowed to dry thoroughly, the method being the same as before. Once the final coat has been applied, it should be allowed to dry for around three to four weeks. After this period, the surface of the repaired area should be rubbed down with a special compounding paste, again freely available from most good accessory shops. By taking care at this stage, the paint will be gradually polished to an acceptable level and, if all the steps taken have been performed correctly, the repaired area of the bodywork should be undistinguishable from other areas of the car.

Right: because steel wheels are subject to rust it may become necessary to repaint them. They should first be rubbed down with a suitable wet-or-dry paper, depending upon the amount of rust, before applying a primer. It is advisable to check wheels every so often as rust and neglect can lead to weakened and damaged wheel nuts and rims

Right: after rubbing the wheels down, an aerosol primer should be applied and left to dry. The primer aerosol should be held about twelve inches from the area to be sprayed and moved in a forwards and backwards motion. Following this, the primed surface should again be rubbed down before a final coat of paint is applied

THE CHASSIS IS A STRUCTURE constituting the foundation upon which all the other parts of a car are assembled. A more modern view, reflecting the changes in design philosophy with the passing of time, defines the chassis as that structure which connects the parts in their proper spatial relationships and accepts the loads they create. In either definition, 'structure' is the important word. However, the later definition more clearly implies the requirements of that word, which are that the chassis should retain its dimensional integrity, despite the stresses imposed on it by the suspension, the drive train, or other loads. It must neither sag (which would indicate a lack of beam stiffness) nor

CHASSIS

the strength of the body

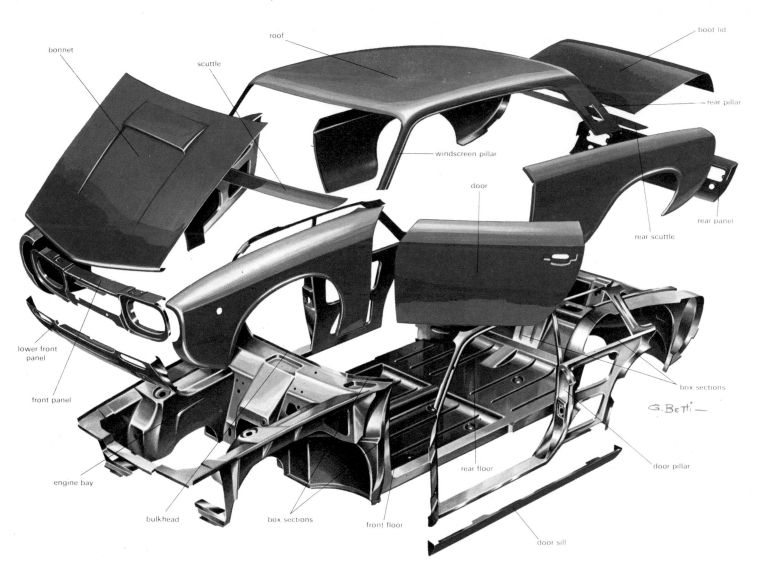

bonnet
scuttle
roof
boot lid
rear pillar
windscreen pillar
door
rear panel
rear scuttle
lower front panel
front panel
box sections
G. Betti
engine bay
door pillar
bulkhead
box sections
rear floor
front floor
door sill

twist (which reveals a want of torsional stiffness), from which it follows that it must be more than merely strong enough for its duties: it must also be stiff enough.

This need for stiffness was generally ignored by car designers during the first 50 years of motoring. In the days when front and rear wheels were mounted on rigid beam axles, it was commonly and erroneously supposed that they would be immune from the effects of chassis distortion; and the simple frames on which most cars were based were designed according to rudimentary mechanical principles that had something in common with bridge building, but little connection with any disciplines more closely related to automobile engineering. The basis of the conventional chassis

frame was two longitudinal girders, made of channel-section pressed steel and set parallel to each other; and these were spaced, rather than braced, by transverse members of similar construction. The whole was fastened together by bolts or rivets and was torsionally very weak, though its beam strength was often due to the generosity of material. The only significant contribution to the stiffness of this structure was made by the engine, which was commonly mounted rigidly between the main frame longerons; but when, in the 1920s, designers of luxury cars sought to isolate them from engine vibrations by mounting the engine on flexible bearers, the final degradation of the chassis as a structure seemed assured.

The knowledge was available at the time to counteract this decay. In the aviation industry, distinguished engineers, such as Wagner, Northrop and de Bruyne, created, between 1925 and 1931, some extremely advanced forms of stressed-sheet construction, extending ideas that had been embodied in a monocoque airframe as early as the Deperdussin monoplane of 1913. However, the majority of car designers were of inferior quality and those few who recognised these advances were tempted to dismiss them as irrelevant. There were one or two isolated examples of cars exploiting stressed sheet metal to create the beginnings of a kind of primitive unitary structure, such as the Lancia Lambda and 11.9 hp Lagonda of the 1920s. In general, though, the old girder chassis held literal sway, and only Bugatti provided a frame that did more than offer a convenient datum about which to construct a car. The others often relied upon the superimposed bodywork to contribute to the overall stiffness of the vehicle, and they were rewarded for their indolence with splits, cracks and tears in the bodies. Weymann contrived a body structure which deliberately allowed itself to flex with the chassis and yet be free from creaks and rattles; the rest sought the palliative of flexible body mounting, or simply made their chassis of stouter metal.

Car design emerged from this sorry situation by two divergent routes which were explored more or less contemporaneously. One, the revolutionary and, in the long term, more important approach, was the pressed steel body, rigidly attached to the chassis so as to become unified with it; and the other, evolutionary, the introduction of the ladder-like chassis frame built up from tubes. This coincided with the convincing application of independent suspension for the first time: although designers had not been adequately aware of the importance of maintaining the proper geometrical relationship between the front and rear axles, they were very conscious of the relationship of the two wheels linked by a beam axle, and recognised that where no such axle existed the car itself must act as the intermediary. It is clear that if the wheels are not then to adopt some rather wayward attitudes, to the detriment of performance and controllability alike, then the car must possess sufficient intrinsic stiffness to constrain the wheels to move only in the desired paths and to resist distortion from the forces transmitted to it by those wheels. The softer the springs, the greater the amplitude of wheel movement, the more diverse the variations of camber, toe-in and castor angle that the suspension designer may introduce, the more important does it become that the frame of the car be torsionally stiff, the better to resist deformation of itself and deviation of the whole.

Although round section tubes are by no means ideal in resisting bending loads, the mere use of such tubes in place of channel sections for the chassis frame was sufficient to multiply considerably the stiffness of the traditional chassis. The factor of multiplication depended on the diameter of the tubes and the extent and nature of the cross-bracing between them, which might be by simple straight transverse members, by diagonal bracing, or by cruciform (cross-shaped) bracing, this last means being superior, but surprisingly little used. On the other hand, the manufacturers of the more elaborate conventional chassis, who were gradually learning to box in parts of the channel sections so as to give them much of the stiffness of tubular sections, often took great pains to introduce cruciform bracing between the two main members. The cruciform has, when its metal is properly distributed, ample beam stiffness and commendable torsional stiffness, and has sometimes been used as a chassis in itself. Probably the most perfect example was the chassis of the 2.6 (later 3)-litre Lagonda of 1949 to 1956, but more recent and very inferior approximations to the true cruciform may be found in the Triumph Herald and Lotus Elan.

The antithesis of the ideal cruciform, in which suspension and other loads may properly be fed towards the centre of the structure, is the perimeter frame which has enjoyed long use by American manufacturers. Here the mass of metal serving as a chassis is distributed around the edge of the floor area of the car, in which position it allows the floor to be much lower (impossible with the cruciform of the Lagonda, though feasible in the two-seater Lotus where the passengers sat on either side of the central portion of the chassis) and so permits the whole car to be lower, lighter and, in mass-production terms, significantly cheaper.

The Americans deliberately made their perimeter frames flexible, mounting their bodies on resilient bearers and accepting that in return for a soft ride they would have to sacrifice cornering, handling, controllability and steering qualities. In the meantime, the tubular ladder frame was developing into a multi-tubular frame, a light tubular superstructure gradually becoming more massive and the base rails slightly less so, until there evolved from this the basis for many successful racing cars of the 1950s, a multi-tubular, four-rail frame. This did not make the most effective use of the material employed and therefore had to be made unnecessarily robust and heavy, but, at the same time, Lotus and Daimler-Benz (Mercedes) both introduced competition cars with multi-tubular space frames, a type of construction representing the ultimate in the notion of a framework.

A space frame is not just a collection of tubes assembled end to end at random so as to enclose a space and provide some sort of foundation for brackets whereon such things as engines, suspension, fuel tanks and pedals might be mounted. There have been many such chassis frames constructed and too often dignified with the space-frame description. In fact, the true space frame is much more subtle and usually much more efficient when it is properly done. To qualify for the appelation, the tubular structure must be so complete (by triangulation, for example) that it would lose none of its shape or stiffness, even if all joints were pin-jointed so as to be flexible instead of being welded. From this it may be inferred that none of the tubular members may be anything but straight and none may be subjected to any bending loads. All joints and tubes must be loaded in compression or in tension.

There are no theoretical obstacles to this degree of completeness being attained, but practical difficulties are almost insuperable. Every bay of the structure must be a complete structure in itself, the weakest being the one that determines the performance of the whole. Thus, every rectangular frame should be braced against lozenging by having a diagonal member added. Theoretically this is simple; in practice it is often impossible. The diagonal may impede the introduction or extraction of the engine or some other equally vital component—not to mention the access of the driver and passengers.

Thus, in almost all examples of space-frame construction applied either to single-seat racing cars or to multi-seat road cars, the central bay has been incomplete and has borrowed torsional stiffness from the bays immediately before and behind. The most refined examples mitigated this weakening of the cockpit area by the addition of external beams on either side of the inevitable opening, each beam being a space frame structure itself.

Left: an exploded view of a typical unitary construction car showing the main floor pan and the bolt or weld-on body panels. Note the front and rear pillars are the main body bracing points. The pillars are the key to whether the structure will have the desired amount of torsional and longitudinal stiffness— they complete the 'box'

Acceptable in a competition car, this is far from satisfactory for a more practical road vehicle and, in any case, the amount of time and skilled labour involved in the fabrication of such a complex assembly is quite beyond countenance by production engineers. Only a very few relatively expensive and therefore small-production cars were built around welded multi-tubular chassis in this way, principally in the early 1950s: the Aston Martin DB1 and DB2, the Pegaso and the Mercedes-Benz 300SL are the most outstanding examples, and only the last of these had a true space frame—of which the lateral bays around the passenger compartment enforced the use of shallow gull-wing doors. More recently the E-type Jaguar has continued

the monocoque loses much of its strength if it is not a completely closed structure. In a car, apertures for the passengers and engine and the like to be inserted and extracted are unavoidable. Any such aperture must be reinforced around its edge to maintain the necessary stiffness. By the time this has been done to all the door-ways, hatches, wheel arches, air passages, window frames etc, the average car has lost all resemblance to

the compromise, previously effected in the competition D-type, where a simple triangulated tubular structure around the engine and front suspension feeds its loads at widely distributed points into a stressed-skin centre section.

Whereas the extensive hand welding of a multi-tubular frame is unsuitable for quantity production, the automated welding of pressed steel sub-assemblies to form a monocoque shell or tub is perfectly adapted to production in very large quantities and is the usual method involved in the manufacture of ordinary modern cars. Actually the true monocoque is rare: by definition it is a single skin or shell, structurally analogous to an eggshell, with everything being attached to it, at a variety of points, by brackets so designed as to spread loads into the shell over a sufficiently wide area for local concentrations to be taken without the shell bending or breaking. Like the eggshell of the analogy,

This superb cutaway of the exclusive Rolls-Royce Silver Shadow shows all the car's major components. The body/chassis is an integral unit, but the engine and suspension are mounted on separate front and rear frames. By fixing these frames to the body via specially designed resilient rubber mountings, the transmission of noise to the car's interior can be cut to a minimum. A unitary-construction body/chassis unit tends to be much stiffer than a unit comprising a body bolted to a separate chassis

a monocoque and must be considered instead as a series of steel boxes (each of which may be considered a small monocoque in its own right) fastened together, with large areas closed in by panels which may be stiffened by curvature or appropriate ribbing. 'Monocoque' would be a misnomer; 'stressed skin' construction is a perfectly adequate description.

It is one that is not limited to pressed-steel con-

Above: the tubular chassis from a McLaren sports-racing car. Nowadays, these types of car use monocoques, which are somewhat stiffer than their predecessors

185

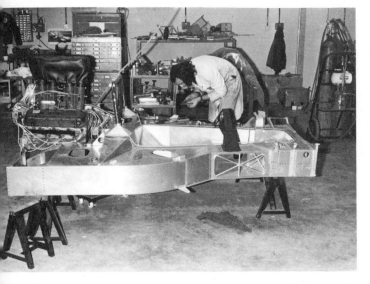

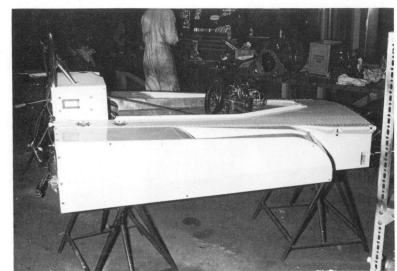

Above: various forms of monocoque racing chassis.

Top left: a Can-Am Shadow; *top right:* a Surtees TS14 Formula One; and *above,* a Shadow Formula One car. The usage of this form of chassis is now almost universal in top-flight racing

structions, the tooling for which (comprising large presses and elaborate electric welding installations) is extremely expensive and inappropriate to anything but very large production runs. A stressed-skin structure may be produced economically for smaller quantities by rivetting and/or gluing, as is the practice in most racing cars built of aluminium and other light alloys that are more difficult to weld than steel. More commonly, it may be achieved by the use of reinforced plastics (the usual reinforcement being glassfibre) as in the case of many sporting cars of which the outstanding examples are the Lotus Elite, the Chaparral, and the Clan Crusader. Plywood can also be used very effectively to build up a series of stressed-skin boxes to form a very stiff and light chassis. The outstanding exponent of this is the designer Frank Costin, who was responsible for the wooden Marcos and Amigo cars and, incidentally, for much of the Lotus Elite already mentioned.

In quantity production, where economy in labour and material must be studied with scrupulous care, the most common technique, outside America, is to build up stressed-skin boxes, bulkheads and panels into the type of construction already distinguished from the

true monocoque and commonly described as unitary. This forms a completely self-supporting structure in which the chassis and body are one and the same thing. Its resistance to bending is largely owed to box-section sills along the outside edges of the floor pressings, passing from front to rear wheel arches under the door apertures, and from similar rails extending upwards past the windscreen and along the edges of the roof. Extra strength is often derived from a longitudinal tunnel along the floor, necessary in many cars to accommodate the transmission, but present in some front-wheel-drive or rear-engined designs simply because of its structural value. Resistance to twisting is derived mainly from bulkheads and boxed structures (notably in the wings) and partitions between passenger compartment and the luggage boot and engine bay.

The influence of diaphragms is very great—out of all proportion to the quantity of material they embody—which is why, for example, a luggage boot may have a small hatch and a high sill (making loading and unloading difficult) in order to increase the torsional stiffness. Similarly, bonding in the front and rear windows to spread stresses through them may increase the torsional stiffness by 20 per cent or even more.

A variation on the ordinary unitary construction has been described as endo-skeletal: the door posts, roof rails, sills and floor are made particularly robust and with joints that ensure ample rigidity and load resolution, so that vulnerable external body panels (doors, wings, etc) may be left unstressed and quickly detachable to facilitate repair. More common is the platform chassis, in which all the structural strength and stiffness required by suspension and body designers is supplied by a sturdy floor composed of pressings, to which the body may or may not be flexibly attached. If it is not, then the attachment of the body negates the individuality of the chassis, for the two become one; and it is the impossibility of separating them in any kind of unitary construction which makes a study of body engineering inseparable from one of chassis engineering.

The meaning of the word 'chassis' is allowed less breadth than in former years, when it was often the practice of a manufacturer to sell a rolling chassis for some coachbuilder to turn it into a finished car. Then, the 'chassis' would not only include the suspension, engine, steering, and all mechanical adjuncts, but also even the wings. In casual usage the word 'chassis' may still include, by implication, many of these elements, particularly the suspension.

FAULT FINDING

The previous sections of this book explain clearly how the various systems of the car work and how they have been developed; in certain instances, methods of repair and maintenance are detailed. In this section, however, the most common symptoms which afflict the motor car are listed, together with the faults which they indicate. The different parts of the car are under separate headings, which are *Engine, Brakes, Suspension, Transmission* and *Steering*, so that if, for instance, the brakes fail, you should look for that heading and then look for the particular symptom in the left-hand column.
Once the likely fault has been located, the next section, on page 189, should be consulted in order to find the cause of and suggested remedy for that fault. Some tasks are not within the scope of the average handyman with a 'standard' set of tools and where this is the case the details of the job are not given, as a manufacturer's workshop manual would be needed in any case.

ENGINE

Symptom	Fault
Starter will not turn engine (headlights dim when trying)	Battery flat Corroded or loose connections Starter jammed Seized engine
Starter will not turn engine (headlights unaffected)	Defective starter solenoid, switch or motor Starter gear not engaging (motor will be spinning fast)
Engine turns too slowly to start	Battery flat Corroded or loose connections Defective starter motor Oil in sump too thick Partial seizure of engine
Engine turns normally but will not fire	Defective ignition system: spark plugs, contact breaker points, condenser, high-tension coil, rotor arm, distributor cap, leads and connections Defective fuel system: fuel pump, carburettor, fuel lines, fuel tank (check fuel level and make sure air can enter at the top)
Engine backfires through exhaust pipe or carburettor, or kicks back	Spark-plug leads transposed Ignition timing faulty Valve timing faulty
Engine fires but will not run	Defective fuel system, as above Inconsistent spark (sporadic fault in ignition system)
Engine will not idle when cold	Choke operation incorrect
Engine will not idle when hot	Incorrect carburettor slow-running or mixture adjustment, blocked slow-running jet, choke stuck on, float chamber flooding, carburettor piston sticking (SU or Stromberg) or intake air leak
Engine idles roughly	Carburettor mixture incorrectly adjusted, incorrect contact-breaker points gap, dirty or incorrectly set spark plugs, ignition timing faulty or intake air leak
Engine will not accelerate cleanly	Carburettor faulty: accelerator pump, choke, mixture setting or, in SU or Stromberg, seized piston or lack of damper oil Insufficient fuel supply Dirty air cleaner Short circuit inside distributor Intake air leak
Engine loses power	Accelerator adjustment incorrect Insufficient compression Ignition timing incorrect Valve timing incorrect Contact-breaker or spark plug points gap incorrect Valve clearances incorrect Intake air leak Partial seizure
Engine misfires or pulls back	Ignition system faulty: check as for 'Engine turns normally but will not fire' Dirty air cleaner Contaminated fuel or low level
Engine runs on after switching off or 'pinks' (light tinkling noise during acceleration)	Excessive carbon deposits in combustion chambers Incorrect fuel grade Incorrect spark plug type Overheating
Engine overheats	Lack of coolant Faulty hose Loose fan belt Defective thermostat Coolant passages blocked Air passages through radiator blocked Faulty cooling fan Ignition timing incorrect Carburettor mixture setting incorrect Faulty cylinder-head gasket Faulty water pump
Excessive fuel consumption	Incorrect carburettor mixture setting Choke stuck on
Excessive oil consumption	Worn piston rings, cylinders or valve guides Oil leak
Oil warning light comes on at low speeds, or stays on all the time (also applies to low gauge readings)	Low oil level Faulty switch Faulty gauge Worn crankshaft bearings (usually accompanied by knocking noise) Faulty oil pick-up pipe Faulty oil pump
Oil warning light comes on during cornering or braking (also applies to low gauge reading)	Low oil level Faulty oil pick-up pipe
Ignition warning light stays on above tick-over, or ammeter shows discharge	Broken or loose fan belt Faulty generator Faulty control box Faulty wiring

BRAKES

Symptom	Fault
Brakes judder	Brake component at wheel not firmly mounted Faulty disc or drum Worn or damaged linings
Excess pedal travel	Brake shoes maladjusted Air in hydraulic system Maladjustment between pedal and master cylinder
Pedal not firm (spongy) or needs pumping	Air in hydraulic system Fault in master cylinder Slight hydraulic fluid leak
Car pulls to one side under braking	Damaged or worn brake linings on one side Seized piston in wheel cylinder on one side Maladjustment of brakes on one side Under-inflated tyre on one side
Greater force than usual needed to operate brakes	Damaged, worn or incorrect linings Seized wheel-cylinder piston Faulty servo (if fitted) Overheated linings
Brakes stick on when pedal released	Seized wheel-cylinder piston Maladjustment of shoes Broken or weak return springs Handbrake linkage seized
Brakes fierce	Damaged discs or drums Rust on discs or drums Worn or damaged linings
Complete and sudden brake failure	Broken hydraulic pipe Failed hydraulic cylinder Low fluid level Broken pedal linkage

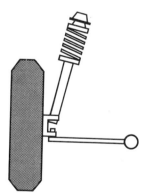

SUSPENSION

Symptom	Fault
Soft and bouncy ride	Failed dampers Broken spring Broken damper mounting Tyre pressure too low
Hard ride	Seized suspension joint Stiff or seized damper Broken spring (causing suspension to hit stops) Tyre pressure too high
Car handles badly	Failed dampers Failed wheel bearing Flat tyre Failed suspension component: wishbone, radius arm, trailing arm, spring, anti-roll bar etc Loose wheel
Car rolls excessively	Failed damper Broken damper mounting Weak or broken spring Broken or disconnected anti-roll bar

Symptom	Fault
Nose drops excessively under braking	Failed front dampers Broken damper mountings Weak or broken front springs
Rear drops excessively under acceleration	Failed rear dampers Broken damper mountings Weak or broken rear springs
Knocking felt through steering or body, especially when passing over bumps	Worn suspension bushes Weak springs allowing bottoming Failed dampers Loose wheel Loose suspension component Failed wheel bearing

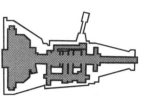

TRANSMISSION

Symptom	Fault
Car does not move when in gear with engine running	Slipping clutch (if prop shaft not turning) Gear not engaged properly or gearbox faulty (also if prop shaft not turning) Broken prop shaft Broken drive (half) shaft Faulty final-drive unit Hub slipping on drive shaft
Gears difficult to engage	Clutch out of adjustment or faulty Clutch hydraulic system faulty Faulty gearbox Lack of gearbox oil
Clutch slips	Out of adjustment Worn out Greasy linings
Clutch judders	Clutch internals off centre Spring(s) broken (inside clutch) Worn engine or transmission mountings
Steering or whole car vibrates when travelling (with engine on or off)	Wheel(s) out of balance (usually felt through steering) Wheel(s) buckled or loosely fitted Tyre(s) damaged or of incorrect type Universal joint(s) on prop shaft or drive shaft(s) worn out Prop shaft or drive shaft(s) bent Wheel bearing failed (especially front)
Gears grate when changed	Incorrect clutch adjustment Faulty clutch Worn synchromesh in gearbox
Slips out of gear **Gearbox noisy**	Worn internal gearbox linkage Low oil level Wear
Clutch noisy when depressed	Worn release bearing

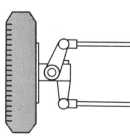

STEERING

Symptom	Fault
Car handles badly or wanders	Loose wheel Flat tyre Incorrect steering alignment Play between two steering or suspension components Failed steering or suspension component
Car pulls to one side	Incorrect tyre pressure one side Unmatched tyres Incorrect steering alignment Brakes binding Broken or weak spring

MAINTENANCE & REPAIR

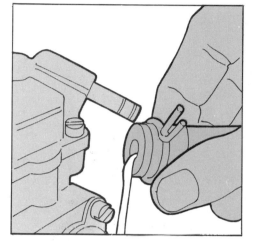

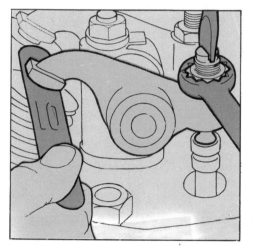

ENGINE

Flat battery Push or tow-start the car, but check that there is no discharge when everything is turned off, either with an ammeter or by looking for sparks on disconnecting or reconnecting the main battery lead. If, after charging, the battery soon runs down, even though it is correctly topped-up, it must be renewed.

Starter jammed Engage third gear and remove the handbrake, rock the car backwards and forwards until the starter disengages. If this fails, turn the squared end of the starter shaft with a spanner. If this is a persistent fault, the starter motor should be removed and the Bendix gear unit cleaned, as detailed below.

Seized or partially seized engine The unit should be stripped to find the cause; this is a skilled job and is best left to a trained mechanic.

Defective starter solenoid or switch These items should be replaced if the starter works when either is bypassed.

Starter gear not engaging If the starter is of the older inertia type, then it must be removed and the bendix gear freed by cleaning with petrol; if it is of the newer pre-engaging type, then the solenoid must be checked and, if necessary, replaced.

Defective ignition system Remove a spark-plug lead from its plug, hold its end close to the cylinder head and look for a spark when the engine is turned with the ignition on. If there is a spark, then the spark plugs must be cleaned or replaced. If there is no spark, the distributor points should be cleaned and adjusted, but if this does no good and the leads and connectors are okay, then there may be a fault in the distributor cap (check that the central carbon brush is protruding far enough to touch the rotor arm) or rotor arm (it may have twisted on its shaft). It is very rare for the condenser to break down, but it can be disconnected temporarily. If all else fails, the high-tension coil must be checked or changed.

Defective fuel system First check that fuel is reaching the carburettor, by removing the pipe from the float chamber and turning the ignition on (electric pump) or turning the engine over (mechanical pump). If no fuel pours out of the pipe, then the fuel pump is probably faulty, although there may be a blockage in the pipe or the fuel-tank vent. *Make sure there is fuel in the tank.* The diaphragm of a mechanical pump can be replaced quite easily and cheaply, but spares for electric pumps are not so easy to come by, so it is common to fit a replacement unit. If everything is working here, and fuel is coming out, then the fault probably lies in the carburettor itself. Make sure fuel is entering the float chamber and is filling it to the correct level; also clean all the jets, without disturbing settings.

Ignition timing or valve timing faulty These should be checked and adjusted as shown in the maker's literature; procedures vary from make to make.

Inconsistent spark This can be caused by any of the faults listed under 'Defective ignition system'.

Incorrect carburettor adjustment The settings should be checked, following the makers instructions.

Float chamber flooding The fuel level should be altered by adjusting the float valve.

Carburettor piston sticking This only applies to SU or Stromberg instruments and could be due to two faults. The first is a decentralised main jet, which can be cured by adjustment; the second is corrosion on the piston or cylinder, which can be rectified by cleaning both surfaces.

Intake air leak This is usually caused by a faulty gasket or a loose mounting. All nuts and bolts should be checked and any faulty gaskets replaced.

Valve clearances incorrect With a pushrod-and-rocker set-up, the clearances can be adjusted by means of a spanner, a screwdriver and a feeler gauge, or a special tappet-adjusting tool. The rocker cover should be removed so that the clearances between rocker and valve stem can be checked. If they are incorrect, the locknuts must be loosened and the screw-adjusters turned until the correct setting is obtained. The

Above: far left: any blockage in the fuel line will be apparent when the pipe to the carburettor is removed with the pump in operation

Above left: if the starter is jammed in mesh and rocking the car fails to free it, a spanner should be applied to its square shaft-end in order to turn it

Above: the most common type of valve-clearance adjuster, with a pushrod-and-rocker set-up, is a lock-nutted screw; with the gap as wide as it can be, the setting should be checked with a feeler gauge and adjusted if necessary, by means of a spanner and screwdriver

locknut must then be tightened. Overhead camshafts usually require the use of shims (spacers) to give the required clearance, and the maker's literature should be consulted.

Carbon deposits in combustion chambers The cylinder head should be removed and the deposits scraped from the chambers and piston crowns, using a blunt instrument. At the same time the valves should be ground on to their seats, using a special tool and grinding paste—remember to readjust the valve clearances.

Loose fan belt This is usually adjusted by loosening the generator mounting bolts and moving that component until the play in the belt, on its longest run, is half an inch.

Defective thermostat This item can be checked by removing it and placing it in boiling water. If it opens and closes, when hot and cold respectively, then it is functioning correctly.

Defective water pump The unit must be replaced, if it is defective, as it is not practicable to repair the pump.

Worn piston rings etc The whole engine must be dismantled and overhauled: a job for skilled labour.

Defective oil switch or gauge Switches are fairly cheap, but gauges should be repaired by their manufacturers.

Worn crankshaft bearings In most cases, if the crankshaft bearings are worn, the shaft itself will be damaged and will have to be reground by a specialist before new bearings are fitted.

Defective oil pick-up pipe Unfortunately, major dismantling is required to reach this pipe—probably a job for a garage.

Defective generator Alternators are best left to a specialist, but dynamos need new brushes every so often. These are cheap and can be fitted by removing the end cover from the dynamo.

Defective control box It is best to fit a new or exchange unit, if this goes wrong, as it is very delicate, although some manufacturer's workshop manuals do describe the details of maintenance.

BRAKES

Brake component at wheel not firmly mounted In the case of drums, this may be the back plate, the cylinder(s), the shoes themselves or the pivot opposite the cylinder. Discs are simpler and the chances are that either the caliper or the disc has come loose.

Faulty disc or drum The most common fault in this area is that of scoring: if worn linings have been left in, metal will have touched metal, this cutting grooves in the disc or drum. Sometimes, however, overheating may cause distortion of either of these parts, so that the braking will be very jerky. In both cases, if the damage is not too severe, skimming can be the cure.

Worn or damaged linings It is possible to buy brake-shoe linings to fit at home, but this is not worthwhile: it is far better to buy exchange shoes. Disc pads must be replaced as a whole: it is not feasible to reline them. They are not sold on an exchange basis, since there is so little metal involved.

Brake shoes maladjusted Check whether the brakes on your car are of the adjustable type, then jack up each wheel in turn, tightening the adjuster(s) until the brakes are just binding.

Air in hydraulic system This usually leads to a spongy feel at the pedal. Each brake should be bled individually, starting with the one farthest from the master cylinder and ending with the nearest.

Maladjustment between pedal and master cylinder It is very rare for this kind of adjustment to be

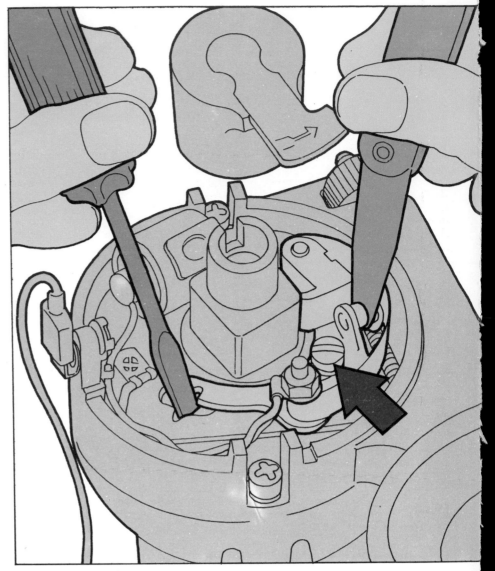

provided, so, unless anything is worn or broken, the fault is unlikely to be in this area.

Fault in master cylinder The most common fault in a master cylinder is wear in the rubber piston seals. These can be replaced cheaply by removing the cylinder and stripping it down (usually by undoing a circlip).

Faulty servo Unless the fault is in the pipe which links the servo to the inlet manifold, in which case this can be replaced, it is wise to have the servo checked by an expert.

Overheated linings This phenomenon is known as fade and is very rare in disc brakes, although even in modern types, drums can be affected. Fade is caused by unequal expansion of drum and shoes giving rise to reduced contact areas. The only cure is to stop and let the brakes cool down for a few minutes.

Seized wheel-cylinder piston Wheel cylinders should have covers to prevent dust and moisture creeping between the piston and cylinder. However, these covers perish with age and this can lead to rust forming on both piston and cylinder. If enough rust builds up, the piston may stick (usually in the on position). The remedy is to remove the offending piston(s) and remove all traces of rust, using metal polish if necessary. If you do use metal polish, make sure that all traces of it are removed before reassembly, as any which remains will contaminate the fluid and may lead to further seizure or to complete brake failure.

Above: when the distributor points are to be adjusted, the gap should be at its widest (the heel of the points should be resting on one of the cam lobes); if the clearance, when measured with a feeler gauge, is found to be incorrect, the screw, arrowed, should be loosened and the fixed contact moved by means of a screwdriver

Broken or weak return springs This only applies to drum brakes. Both faults are extremely rare; a broken spring is obvious, but a weak one can only be spotted by comparing its length with that of a new spring.

Seized handbrake linkage If all pivots are lubricated regularly, this problem should not arise. However, if seizure does occur, the answer is to 'work' the pivots until they are completely free. Penetrating oil is a help here, but once the joints are released, ordinary lubricating oil or grease should be applied.

Rust on discs or drums This builds up very quickly, especially in damp weather, and it is easily dealt with by applying the brake several times, fairly gently.

Broken hydraulic pipe This is an easy fault to find, as there will be a pool of fluid under the car, near the broken pipe. Replace the offending part and then bleed the brakes. It is worth checking all the flexible pipes, from time to time, to make sure that they are not rubbing against anything and are not perished. Brake pipes, especially non-flexible ones, usually have to be made up to order; good accessory shops can usually do this on the spot at a reasonable price.

Failed suspension component Whichever part has gone wrong, the remedy is replacement, unless welding can be carried out.

TRANSMISSION

Gears not engaging properly This may mean that the gearbox itself is worn (this will require a major overhaul—it is often cheaper to fit a replacement box). Some cars, however, have adjustment provided in the linkage between the gear lever and the box itself. Even if there is no adjustment here the fault may lie in these parts—perhaps a bush is worn or a rod is bent.

Faulty final-drive unit If the drive has completely disengaged, the chances are that a gear has stripped its teeth. It is possible to overhaul the unit, but it is easier to fit a replacement unit.

Hub slipping on drive shaft This is a very unusual fault and can only happen if the Woodruff key, which is supposed to prevent this, has broken. The remedy is to remove the hub (a special extractor may be needed), get rid of any traces of the broken key and, assuming no further damage has been done, fit a new part. On some cars, splines are used instead of a key

Below, far left: if the engine is decarbonised, the valves should be ground on to their seats, in order to provide a gas-tight seal; the method used is shown (grinding paste is first placed under the valve)

Below left: dynamo brushes can be changed quite simply after removing the end cover and the screws which fix the wires on; brushes are available very cheaply at most accessory shops

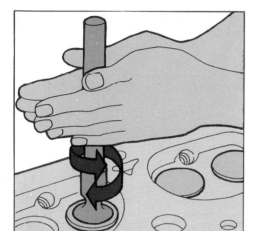
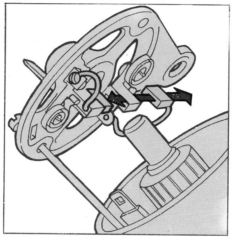
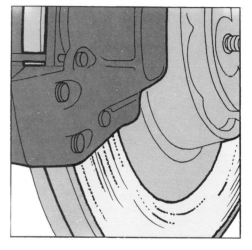

Failed wheel cylinder Once again, fluid will be evident, either on the ground, or around the faulty cylinder, should one of these have failed. As with the master cylinder, the cure is to remove the cylinder, take out the piston(s) and replace the rubber seals. In disc-brake cylinders, the seal is often found in the cylinder rather than on the piston.

SUSPENSION

Failed dampers It is not possible to dismantle telescopic dampers, but lever-arm dampers come apart and can be repaired. In fact the fault may simply be a lack of hydraulic fluid (this is special damper fluid and can be obtained from most accessory shops). If your car has MacPherson struts or Chapman struts (found only in Lotus models), you should be able to buy a damper insert kit.

Seized suspension joint This is a rare fault, but it may occur, usually being caused by lack of lubrication and consequent rust. Brute force and penetrating oil provide the answer here. Make sure plenty of grease is applied, once the joint is free.

Stiff or seized damper Again, a very unusual fault, which normally requires replacement of a telescopic damper or repair of a lever-arm one.

Failed wheel bearing Specialist tools may be required, in order to replace a wheel bearing. First the hub must be removed, then the bearing extracted—in some cases, the drive shaft must also be removed.

and if these have stopped functioning, the shaft or hub must be replaced.

Clutch out of adjustment The manufacturer's literature should be consulted to find out whether or not your car has any clutch adjustment provided and, if so, what the correct setting should be.

Clutch faulty If the gears are difficult to engage, then the clutch release bearing may be worn or broken. Alternatively, mechanical linkage from the hydraulic cylinder or cable may be damaged.

Clutch hydraulic system faulty If hydraulic fluid is not leaking out, then the fault is likely to be in the master cylinder, operated by the clutch pedal. The seals will probably be worn, so these should be replaced, making sure that the cylinder itself is not damaged. Kits of seals can be bought for a small amount of money.

If fluid is leaking out, then either the pipe is damaged or loose, or the slave cylinder, which actually operates the clutch, is faulty. The procedure here is as for the master cylinder—in fact, if one cylinder is being overhauled, then it is advisable to do the other.

Clutch worn out Any part of the clutch can become useless through wear, but the most common is the driven plate (this is the friction disc which sticks the engine to the gearbox). If a car has done many thousands of miles, then the springs which make the clutch work may well be weakened, so if the driven plate is being replaced the cover assembly, which incorporates the springs, is worth attention.

Above: scoring of a disc is caused by worn pads; the rough surface will lead to shortened life for any new pads used, unless the disc is first skimmed to renew the smooth surface

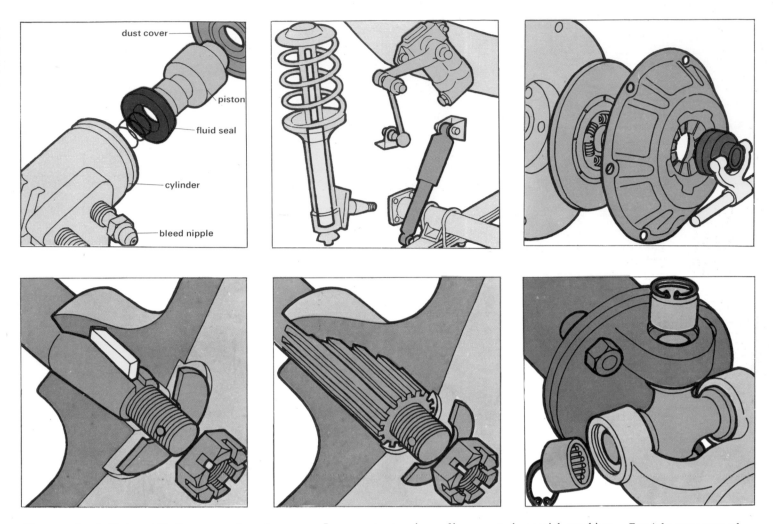

Top left: every type of
wheel cylinder has seals
which can be replaced;
this is a drum-brake
example

Top centre: the three
types of damper—
telescopic (right), lever
and MacPherson strut (a
telescopic type)

Top right: an exploded
view of a clutch
assembly showing
flywheel (left), driven
plate (centre left)
pressure-plate assembly
(centre right) and the
thrust bearing (right)

Above left and centre:
Woodruff-key and spline
drive, respectively

Above right: the most
common type of
universal joint, known as
the Hooke joint

Greasy clutch linings If oil or grease have impregnated the linings, then the only real solution is to fit a new driven plate. The main thing, however, is to ascertain where the oil has come from—the chances are that either the crankshaft rear oil seal or the gearbox mainshaft front oil seal have failed.

Clutch internals off centre This usually means that the clutch cover assembly, and probably the driven plate too, will have to be replaced.

Worn engine or gearbox mountings The engine and gearbox are mounted on rubber, which stretches and perishes with age. Usually, wear will be obvious because the mountings will sag, but this is not always so and it may be worth renewing the mountings anyway.

Worn universal joints These can be replaced fairly easily, but the relevant shaft must be removed in order to carry out the job.

Worn synchromesh New synchromesh parts can be fitted, but this requires a major strip-down and the workshop manual for the car should be consulted.

General gearbox wear It is probably easiest and quickest to replace the whole gearbox, once it reaches this stage, since new gears, shafts, bearings etc will be expensive and fitting them will require a great deal of labour.

STEERING

Loose wheel Obviously it is important to make sure that the wheels are not falling off, but be careful not to overtighten them; this may lead to the threads stripping or the studs shearing. Knock-off (centre-lock) wheels should be tightened with a soft hammer until the nuts will not turn any more.

Incorrect steering alignment A special tracking gauge is needed to rectify this fault, but a sure sign of maladjusted steering is a feathering of one side of every tread block on the front tyres. If a tracking gauge is available, the most usual method of adjustment is by loosening the locknut on one of the track-rod ends and screwing the rod in or out of the end, until the correct setting is achieved.

Play in steering or suspension It is sometimes possible to take up any play by adjustment, but it is more usual to replace the offending parts (with older steering boxes adjustment is provided, but removal of play in the straight-ahead position can lead to stiffness on lock). Suspension play is usually cured by the fitting of new rubber or metal brushes, whereas play in a track-rod end will require replacement of that part—and subsequent re-alignment of the steering.

Unmatched tyres It is illegal to mix radial tyres on the front with cross-ply tyres on the rear, but it is not advisable to mix different makes of tyre on the same axle (sizes are sometimes slightly different, bracing materials vary and rubber mixes—not to mention tread patterns—are far from standard).

Brakes binding Most drum brakes require occasional adjustment, although the latest types are self adjusting. If your brakes are the type that do require attention in this way, then they should be tightened up, with the wheel off the ground and the handbrake off (for the relevant end of the car), until they are just beginning to bind. Noticeable binding, when the car is in use, may be caused by over-enthusiastic adjustment or by either the mechanical or hydraulic parts sticking. In the case of disc brakes, any binding can only be caused by this sticking, as all discs are self adjusting.